"We have no idea what happened to her.
She left no trace."
Chief Bruce Reed
Mount Holly, New Jersey

DEAD MEN DO TELL TALES SERIES

"I Want to Come Home Tonight" (2017)
Blood, Guns & Valentines (2023)
Bloody Chicago (2006)
Bloody Hollywood (2008)
Bloody Illinois (2008)
Dead Men Do Tell Tales (2008)
Fallen Angel (2013)
Horribly Mutilated (2021)
Blood, Bullets & Booze (2023)
Murder by Gaslight (2013)
Murdered in Their Beds (2016)
One August Morning (2015)
One Midnight in Texas (2024)
One Night at the Biograph (2016)
Suffer the Children (2018)
Two Lost Girls (2016)
Until Death Do Us Part (2024)
Victims of the Ax Fiend (2020)
Without a Trace (2020)
Without a Trace 2 (2024)

DEAD MEN DO TELL TALES

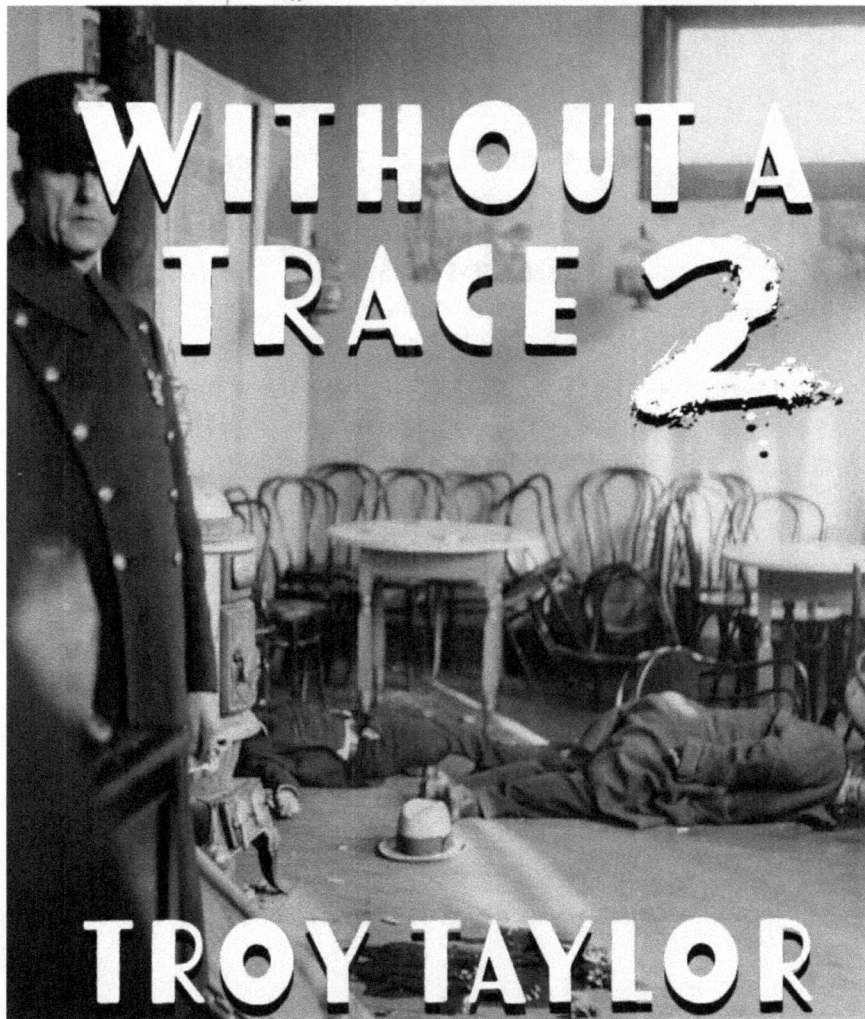

WITHOUT A TRACE 2

TROY TAYLOR

AN AMERICAN HAUNTINGS INK BOOK

WITHOUT A TRACE 2

MORE UNSOLVED ACCOUNTS OF THE MISSING AND THE LOST

© Copyright 2024 by Troy Taylor

Published by American Hauntings Ink
P.O. Box 249 - Jacksonville IL - 62651
www.americanhauntingsink.com

Cover Design by April Slaughter
Interior Design by Troy Taylor

Printed in the United States of America

TABLE OF CONTENTS

INTRODUCTION -- PAGE 7

THE 1930S – PAGE 11
- WALTER ROBINSON
- JOSEPH HALPERN
- HARRY "BUDDY" BROWE
- MARJORIE WEST

THE 1950S – PAGE 48
- CONNIE SMITH

THE 1960S – PAGE 58
- JOAN RISCH
- MARY SHOTWELL LITTLE
- THE LOST BOYS OF HANNIBAL

THE 1970S – PAGE 116
- ROBIN GRAHAM
- JANICE POCKETT
- MITCHEL WEISER AND BONNIE BICKWIT
- SHARON PRETORIUS
- JOSEPH SPISAK
- THREE LOST GIRLS: RACHEL, RENEE & JULIE ANN?
- KURT NEWTON
- LOY EVITTS
- EVA DEBRUHL
- SIMONE RIDINGER
- JUDY MARTINS
- LORRAINE HERBSTER

THE 1980S – PAGE 212

- ROGER ELLISON
- SHERRY EYERLY
- KELLIE BROWNLEE
- CHARLIE HOPE
- EUGENE MARTIN
- JENNIFER SCHMIDT
- JEREMY BRIGHT
- PATRICIA MEEHAN

THE 1990S – PAGE 273

- ANGELA HAMMOND
- MISTY COPSEY
- ANGELA FREEMAN
- AMY LYNN BRADLEY
- LAURIA BIBLE AND ASHLEY FREEMAN

THE 2000S AND BEYOND – PAGE 319

- LEAH ROBERTS
- ZACHARY BERNHARDT
- PATRICIA ANN ADKINS
- BRANDY WILSON
- MAURA MURRAY
- BRIANNA MAITLAND
- ROBERT HOURIHAN
- JASON LANDRY

2008: THE LAST RIDE HOME (REVISITED)
STILL SEARCHING FOR BRANDON SWANSON

INTRODUCTION

I NEVER PLANNED TO WRITE THIS BOOK.

I had no intention of ever doing a sequel to *Without A Trace*. It just sort of happened. Don't misunderstand; my interest in missing and vanishing people has never waned. I've been fascinated with the idea that someone could simply disappear one day without explanation for as long as I can remember.

It's all about that mystery that just can't be solved, I guess. We want to solve it – especially when it comes to a mystery that is so tragic and heartbreaking that you can't imagine how the family of the missing goes on – but being able to do so feels impossible.

So, why return to telling stories that seem hopeless?

I wouldn't have done so without the listeners to the *American Hauntings Podcast*, which I started hosting about eight years ago with my friend, Cody Beck. We've been devoting entire seasons to murderous and macabre topics for about eight years by the time you read this, and they've included New Orleans, Hollywood, St. Louis, the Villisca Ax Murders, American Folk Horror, and more. But in 2023, we launched a year-long season on unexplained disappearances. Many episodes featured stories in the 2020 edition of *Without A Trace*, which covered historical mysteries like Roanoke Island, the *Mary Celeste*, Charlie Ross, Dorothy Arnold, Ambrose Bierce, Glen and Bessie Hyde, and Everett Ruess. We also tackled more modern stories like the disappearances of William and Margaret Patterson, Helen Brach, the "Springfield Three," missing news anchor Jodie Huisentruit, and others.

But it turned out that the stories that we didn't cover got the most attention.

As with the first volume of my book about the missing, we covered all the famous cases of strange disappearances on the podcast, but then our listeners started sending me stories I didn't know about. The more I researched the stories they sent me, the more I realized how important it was to me to get those stories out there, too.

And so came the idea for a second volume, which you now hold.

In this book, I'm taking you off the beaten path and to places in search of people that – in many cases – you've never heard of before. Some you might know, of course, but with others, unless you were the person who contacted me and suggested the story, you will likely be exposed to people you've never heard of before.

And once you know about them, I don't think you'll ever forget them.

THE FACT THAT I COULD EASILY PUT TOGETHER STORIES for a second book about missing people – and could easily do a third, fourth, or fifth – should tell you a lot about how many people still vanish without a trace and are never found.

Current numbers say that as many as 600,000 people go missing and are never found each year in America. These are not the people who show up hours or days after going missing – these are the people who are never found. It seems hard to believe this can still happen, with cameras, cell phones, and social media seemingly following our every move, but it can and does. These stories never really end – I have to stop writing and hope that someday, the lost will be found, and the story will have a real conclusion.

However, there are no conclusions to the stories in this book, even though every case collected here occurred in the last century, most of them within the last 50 years. Some of them are even uncomfortably close to the present day and are stories that should have an ending, yet they don't.

The oldest case dates back only to 1933. It was a time when it was still politically correct to use a word like "gypsy" to describe what his family believed had happened to him and when the use of a Ouija board to look for clues to his location was widely reported in newspapers without a touch of sarcasm.

There are stories ahead of:

* The Rocky Mountain vanishing of a young man who had his whole life ahead of him yet walked into oblivion.

* A stolen baby who never had the chance to grow up with his family.

* A little girl who was picking flowers one day in a state park – steps away from her family – who was never seen again.

* The Massachusetts housewife who mysteriously disappeared, leaving nothing behind but some empty beer bottles, a ransacked house, and bloodstains on her kitchen floor.

* The happy newlywed who vanished from a shopping center parking lot.

* The "Lost Boys" of Hannibal, Missouri, who launched one of the first cave rescue operations in modern history.

* A young couple who attended a rock festival in 1973 but never came home.

* A handful of paper boys and girls, pizza delivery drivers, and others who disappeared right from their own neighborhoods, never to be found.

* The blond in the yellow sports car who went to lunch one day and never returned to her office.

* The girl who was taken from her kitchen and was never seen alive again – leaving only a pitcher of iced tea and an empty glass behind.

* The Florida real estate developer who became a legend by disappearing.

* The boy who only wanted to enjoy the county fair with his sister but somehow disappeared without a trace. And the girl who did the same thing a decade later at a very different fair in another part of the country.

* Two young pregnant women – one vanished from a pay phone and the other from a pizza place – disappeared with their unborn children, leaving no clue about what happened to them.

* The two best friends from Oklahoma whose disappearance became tangled in stories of meth, madness, and a modern-day ghost town.

* And literally dozens of other stories of vanishing hitchhikers, college students, young job seekers, high school athletes, abusive husbands, missing mistresses, wandering truth-seekers, dishonest spouses, and more.

But always remember that these accounts – and many more you'll find in the pages – still only scratch the surface of the vanished. Hundreds of stories still have yet to be told, but I think the ones I have chosen here are enough to make you baffled, confused, intrigued, and often terrified.

It doesn't have to be "possible" for a person to go missing. Many vanishings in the pages ahead seem like they couldn't have happened, yet they did.

So, let that serve as a warning. At the heart of all these stories is one simple fact that we must remember: if all these people vanished so easily off the face of the earth, the same thing could happen to anyone – perhaps even you and me.

Troy Taylor
Spring 2024

1933: "DID GYPSIES STEAL A MISSING IOWA BOY?"
THE VANISHING OF WALTER ROBINSON

THE STORY OF WALTER ROBINSON MAY be one of the strangest disappearances ever to take place in the state of Iowa. It's been largely forgotten today, but there's no reason to feel guilty if you've never heard of it. The story vanished from the pages of newspapers within a week of Walter's vanishing.

The police had given up after only a few days. It was the height of the Great Depression. There was no money available to launch much of a search. Walter was just another farm boy who probably hopped on a freight train for California, ran away with the circus, or decided to try his luck in the big city.

Never mind the fact that he was only ten years old.

Walter's family, though, insisted that the boy had been taken by "gypsies," although the police refused to take this seriously. Even if they did, they'd never catch up with them. Gypsies packed up, moved on and disappeared with no forwarding address.

The Robinson family was dismayed, but there was little they could do. They didn't have the money to hire detectives to search for the boy, not when nine other children needed food, clothing, and care at home.

But then, in October 1933 – two months after Walter disappeared – the Robinsons decided to try something the police certainly wouldn't have approved of. As the newspaper said, they "ventured without fear into the realms of what is commonly thought of as the supernatural."

Soon, a Ouija board brought them the first tangible clue in the case.

WALTER GREW UP AN ORDINARY BOY OF THE early 1930s. He was raised with his brothers and sisters in the small town of Newton, Iowa, in the middle of nowhere, about 30 miles east of Des Moines. Loving parents had raised him, and he loved baseball, Cracker Jacks, and going to the movies whenever his parents could afford it or when he managed to scrounge up 25 cents or so when he helped a neighbor with some chores.

His mother cared for the house and the brood of Robinson children, and his father, Leonard, worked at the Newton Welding and Machine Shop. He didn't make much – only $18-a-week -- but knew he was lucky to have a job when so many across the country were flat broke and busted.

In mid-August 1933, everyone in Newton and the surrounding Jasper County was excited by the arrival of a traveling carnival. During the dark days of the Depression, a carnival coming to town was seen as the highlight of the summer. Adults and children saved their coins for ride tickets, popcorn, hot dogs, games of chance, hootchie-cootchie shows, and everything else the carnival might bring.

The local authorities, though, were usually not so excited. The carnival usually brought trouble. Young men often drank too much – especially now that Prohibition was over – and got into fights, usually over women. One of the girls in the grind show was sure to show a little too much. Someone would complain that the games were rigged.

Worst of all, though, were the gypsies, who followed alongside the carnival, telling fortunes, playing music, and, well, just being no-good, dirty gypsies.

The police and the public alike distrusted the Romani people, an itinerant ethnic group who began migrating to America in the late nineteenth century. Likely because they traveled from place to place, never putting down roots, they were given a reputation for lawlessness and theft. These prejudices led to them being widely known by the term "gypsies," which comes from the word "gyp," which meant to steal or cheat.

This was a common term in 1933, used by the public, police, and newspapers, and while most townspeople would claim to fear and despise them, it didn't stop them from going to Romani camps for card readings, fortune-telling, or other things offered. The "gypsies" could always be found on the edge of town, away from the carnival, and usually on the land of a farmer who'd been paid off to let them stay for a few days. This kept the comings and goings of the camp relatively quiet since the Romani knew that "proper folks" wouldn't want to be seen setting foot there.

Did Gypsies Steal Missing Iowa Boy?

Thus far a ouija board has given the only clew to whereabouts of Newton lad, believed a captive of wandering band.

By Milton Lomask.

Ten-year-old Walter Robinson ... believed in the hands of gypsies.

Gypsies have been known to kidnap young white children, train them to do house hopping, and help around the camp.

Mrs. Leonard Robinson at the ouija board which sent three of her sons on a 3,000 mile hunt for their missing brother

Leonard Robinson ... he has aged.

The county fair wrapped up on August 23, and the roustabouts spent the night tearing down the rides, closing the shows, and packing up the tents. By the following morning, they were on the road again, heading for their next destination.

The "gypsy" camp was packed up, too, and on the way out of town, the Romani made one last stop – at the Newton Welding and Machine Shop so they could have some hooks made for one of their cars, a 1927 Buick. The owner took their order and referred them to Leonard Robinson, who heated the forge and began hammering away on the hooks. He'd later recall that the "gypsies" were in a hurry, and the shop's owner was eager to get them out of his place and on down the road.

While Leonard was working, his son, Walter, came into the shop to ask his father who had the family car. His mother needed it for a shopping trip. Leonard told his son he didn't know but thought Melvin had it. Melvin was one of the Robinsons' older sons, and he worked in a garage down the street.

Walter said goodbye to his father and started to leave. Leonard watched him walk out the shop door. He assumed Walter was going down the street to see Melvin and tell him that his mother needed the car.

That was the last time he ever saw his son alive.

A few minutes later, Leonard finished the hooks. "Pretty soon, the gypsies took their hooks and went off," he later recalled. "I didn't pay no attention to 'em after they left the shop. It was noon and I thought I'd get Walter and go home."

Leonard went down the street to the garage where Melvin worked, but the older boy told him that his little brother hadn't arrived. The two of them checked the street between the welding shop and the garage, but there was no sign of Walter.

And that was when Leonard called the sheriff.

THE LOCAL POLICE AND THE COUNTY Sheriff's department began an immediate search for Walter, but there was no sign of him in town. Word quickly spread through the small community, and neighbors were immediately on the lookout for the boy, but he was nowhere to be found.

Eventually, the authorities would contact the Bureau of Investigation – soon to be the F.B.I. – once it was determined that Walter was really missing. However, they could not agree on whether Walter was taken or had run away. Since the kidnapping of the son of famed aviator Charles Lindbergh the previous year, the federal authorities had started taking missing children more seriously than ever before. But the trail of Walter Robinson soon went cold.

The Robinsons – and the local police – were convinced that Walter had been taken by the Romani who had entered the welding shop that day. Everyone knew that "gypsies" loved to snatch little white children and carry them off. Walter had become the next victim of their "thieving ways," and the sheriff agreed to do everything he could to find the boy.

At first, the search had been intense. Leonard thought he remembered the Romani saying something about going to the "big fair in Des Moines," but a search around the city turned up no signs of the "gypsies" who had been in Newton.

The police ran down sightings that came in from all over the state. From Elkhorn came reports of a Romani camp with a "young white boy" in their custody. The encampment was raided, but there was no sign of Walter or any other boy who didn't belong.

Word spread throughout the Midwest, and more sightings of Romani with a boy who might be Walter came in from all over Iowa, Illinois, and even Black River Falls and Elva, Wisconsin. Every sighting turned out to be a mistaken identity, and the authorities soon accepted the idea that Walter would never be found.

And by early September, the official search came to an end.

BUT THE ROBINSONS WEREN'T READY TO give up. By October, it seemed that everything they had tried had failed. The family didn't have much money, but they'd spent what they could placing classified ads and spreading the word about the Romani they were convinced had taken their son. But, so far, no helpful clues had turned up – Walter had now been missing for over two months.

But then help came from a very unlikely source – a newcomer to Newton who didn't know the Robinsons but heard about the missing boy.

Mrs. W.G. Kramer – her first name was never revealed – was the wife of a Newton grocery store owner. They had recently moved to town and took over a failing business, hoping to bring it back to life. Mrs. Kramer was a mother herself and wanted to do something to help the Robinsons, so she turned to her Ouija board to try to shed some light on the local mystery.

According to Mrs. Kramer, her board had never failed her. "I know it sounds foolish," she later said, "but the board has always done me so much good that I always take a chance on it."

In the Robinson case, the first question she put to the Ouija board was: "Who stole Walter Robinson?"

She stated that the planchette on the board began to deliberately move across the board, pointing to various letters –

"G, Y, P..." Of course, the finished word was "gypsies." But, according to Mrs. Kramer, at that time she wasn't aware of the presence of the Romani at the shop on the day Walter disappeared.

Mrs. Kramer focused on the Ouija board and asked, "Are they along a river?" The planchette slid over to the "YES" icon on the board. She pushed for more details and claimed that the board spelled out the words "VANDERVEER PARK DAVENPORT" for her.

Now that she seemed to have some answers from the spirit world, she wasn't sure what to do with them. She said, "I felt that it was my duty to somehow tell the Robinsons about it, and at the time, I didn't want them to feel like I was butting in. I didn't know them, you see. We're new to Newton – came from Illinois. I went downtown and was in such distress about the whole thing. There was a cop on one of the corners and for a few seconds, I thought of going right up and telling him all about it, but I didn't."

Eventually, as the information continued to wear on Mrs. Kramer, she started having trouble sleeping and taking care of household chores without thinking about the missing boy. Finally, she went to see the Robinsons and told them the entire story. She was surprised to find them receptive to the source of her information.

The Robinsons had never expressed any interest in Ouija boards, fortune-telling, or Spiritualism before – although they'd read all about it in recent years, thanks to its popularity – but they were willing to try anything to find Walter.

They quickly obtained a Ouija board of their own. It wouldn't work for Mrs. Robinson, but the planchette did, however, move around the board for two of her three daughters. They questioned the board, asking for Walter's location. The planchette spelled out "YELLOW HILL MOLINE."

Was Walter all right? "YES"

Should they search for him? "YES"

Should his father, Leonard, go on the search? "NO"

Should his brothers – Melvin, Harold, and Leonard, Jr. – look for him? "YES"

Who else? "RED MCCULLIS," the board replied, referring to a family friend who lived in Newton.

The Robinsons decided to follow the board's instructions to the letter. The three brothers and "Red" McCullis drove immediately to Moline, Illinois. After asking around town, they discovered that an encampment of Romani had recently been at a place called Willow Hill. From the description they were given of the automobiles the Romani were driving, the four men became convinced they were the same ones that had been at the Jasper County Fair.

Was Walter with them? No one could say.

Following their trail, the men next went to Coalville in north central Illinois. Once again, they had just missed a group of Romani. The search took them to Indiana and then back to Galesburg, Illinois. Then, to Monmouth, Kirkwood, and finally, Alpha, Illinois, a small community about 30 miles north. According to Melvin, they met a woman there who told them she had given food to some "gypsies" a few days before. She told them they had sent a "little white boy" to the door to ask for something to eat.

Excited, the Robinsons asked for the boy's description.

She told them he was "well-mannered and shy-like. I would say he was about four feet seven. Quite thin – 80 or 90 pounds, I should judge. He was quite fair, and he had blue eyes." She added that his clothes seemed worn out, but he wore overalls, a blue shirt, and no shoes. Melvin was convinced that the description matched Walter's.

But Alpha turned out to be the end of the trail for the brothers and their friend.

"There are hundreds of little roads running there," Melvin later said. "They stretch out all about like the fingers on your hand – and nobody knew which one the gypsies had taken."

The four men did their best over the next few days, driving up and down dirt roads, stopping at farms and small towns, asking questions, but it seemed the "gypsies" had just vanished.

And they'd taken Walter Robinson with them.

The little Iowa boy was never seen again.

1933: STARS OVER THE MOUNTAINS
THE DISAPPEARANCE OF JOSEPH HALPERN

IN THE SUMMER OF 1933, JOSEPH "J.O.E." HALPERN, his parents, and a college friend went camping in the Rocky Mountain National Park, just outside the town of Estes Park, Colorado. On

August 15, the third day of the trip, Joe and his friend left camp to go on a hike. It was why they'd come, after all – to explore the woods and mountains and seek out the beauty of the natural landscape.

Joe's real passion, though, was the night sky. He attended college in Chicago, and he'd been longing to be free from the lights of the city.

Joe's passion for the stars caused his friend, Sam Garrick, not to think anything out of the ordinary when he wanted to go back to camp late in the day, but Joe wanted to keep going up the steep path. He gave Joe a wave and headed back down the trail. Sam knew that Joe would find a place where he could lie on his back and stare into the night sky, forgetting everything else.

Joe, a graduate student at the University of Chicago, was working on his doctoral thesis in astronomy, and he anticipated the annual Perseid meteor shower, which peaked in the northern hemisphere every mid-August. He'd seen the shooting stars from his family's campsite, but Sam knew he wanted a better view.

Sam glanced over his shoulder as he started down the path and saw Joe stop another hiker and ask for some directions. The hiker pointed up the trail, and Joe smiled and thanked him. Then, he trudged up the rocky hill.

Sam Garrick returned alone to camp that day. Joe's parents – Fanny and Solomon – were initially as unconcerned as Sam was about their son's whereabouts.

However, when Joe didn't return by the next day and their efforts to find him failed, they began to panic. As time passed, they clung hopefully to every possible lead, but no trace of Joe Halpern has ever been found.

JOSEPH LAURENCE HALPERN WAS 22 YEARS OLD in August 1933 when he, his parents, and his school friend, Sam, packed their camping equipment into Joe's Ford and left Chicago heading west. Joe's father, Solomon, a Russian immigrant, was on vacation from his job at the Western Electric Company. Joe's older brother, Bernard, stayed home, but his mother sent him frequent postcards from the road. When they first saw the rugged mountains, Fanny wrote on one postcard: "They are beyond description." The family had taken other vacation trips to the East Coast and the Midwest, but this was their first time in the West.

Joe did all the driving. He steered his new Ford sedan through the Badlands of South Dakota and made what was becoming a traditional tourist stop at Wall Drug, which had opened two years before. A Nebraska pharmacist named Ted Hustead had bought the store in the 231-person town in the "middle of nowhere" and tried to make a living. Business was very slow until his wife, Dorothy, thought of advertising free ice water to thirsty travelers heading to the newly opened Mount Rushmore monument 60 miles to the west. From that time on, business was brisk.

Joe Halpern in a photo taken during the trip where he vanished.

After visiting the Black Hills and Mount Rushmore, the family continued through Wyoming cattle country to Yellowstone National Park. According to a ranger's report that was later filed, Joe's first experience with hiking was at Yellowstone.

A week later, they drove southeast through Wyoming to Colorado and the 400-square-mile Rocky Mountain National Park. It had been popular since it opened in 1915, and five years later, the National Park Service opened Fall River Road for tourist automobiles. By 1929, the Trail Ridge Road took them even higher into the mountains. The eastern portion of this road opened to motorists in 1932, and the western section continued to the town of Grand Lake, Colorado, beginning in 1933 – the same summer the Halperns visited the area.

Publicity about this new road undoubtedly attracted the family and other summer vacationers. The National Park Service stated, "As one looks at the mighty array of peaks, it is hard to believe that in two hours, one can easily drive to a snowbank on a mountain crest." That would have been pretty appealing on a hot August day – even with a speed limit of 25 miles per hour on open stretches and 12 miles per hour on grades and curves. These roads, campgrounds, hiking trails, and other improvements made the park a favorite destination for travelers – including the Halperns -- in 1933.

THAT TUESDAY, AUGUST 15, SEEMED LIKE ANY OTHER vacation day to the Halperns and their friend, Sam Garrick. They'd pitched their tents at the Glacier Basin Campground, one of five free public campgrounds in the park, just off Bear Lake Road. Fanny had brought paints and brushes on the trip and set up an easel to try and capture the spectacular views of the looming peaks.

While Joe's parents relaxed at the campground, he and Sam started a hike up the Flattop Mountain Trail. The weather was sunny and clear. Joe wore a white shirt with thin blue stripes, khaki trousers, and heavy shoes. He packed several sandwiches, an orange, two bananas, and a *1933 Rocky Mountain National Park Motorists Guide Map* into a gray knapsack – no mention whether Joe brought a canteen, but he didn't take a jacket. The day was warm, and he didn't think he'd need it, even if he decided to stay and watch the meteor shower.

Joe and Sam drove to the Bear Lake trailhead from Glacier Basin and started hiking. The roundtrip distance from the trailhead to the summit of Flattop Mountain was about nine miles, and it was estimated that most hikers could make it in about six hours.

According to the Park Service, Flattop Mountain was directly between the towns of Estes Park and Grand Lake. The trail was described as "Zigzagging up the eastern slope" of the mountain. It "passed under and over enormous boulders," at one turn, "the traveler looks perpendicularly down 1,000 feet into Dream Lake."

As they neared the summit of the mountain, Joe and Sam found themselves above the tree line, with a breathtaking view of the surrounding area. Around 2:30 P.M., a tired Sam decided he was ready to return to camp. An unnamed hiker reported that Joe and Sam had a "friendly argument as to whether to turn around or go on." The hiker later told rangers that Joe had asked him for directions to Taylor Peak before he continued up the trail.

Sam arrived back at Bear Lake around 6:30 P.M. Even though he assumes Joe plans to stay and look at the stars, he decides to wait for him by car. Sam found a place to sit down and relax, ate a sandwich, and kept an eye out for his friend. As the sun began to set, he felt a pang of concern. Joe was not an experienced hiker; the trail was steep and rugged. Would Joe be able to make it down in the dark?

Finally, after waiting as long as he could, he decided to seek out officers at the Bear Lake Ranger Station just after 9:30 P.M. His friend was missing, he said.

Meanwhile, Joe's father, Solomon, had also started to worry. He began walking – then hitched a ride – from the campground to the trailhead at Bear Lake. When he arrived, he found Sam had already alerted the rangers about Joe's absence.

By 11:00 P.M., two park rangers with electric headlamps had started back up the trail, flashing their lights, yelling, and listening. They continued climbing until around 3:00 A.M. and then resumed the search in the morning.

Around the same time, another ranger, accompanied by Sam and the unnamed hiker Joe had met on the trail, hiked up the Flattop Mountain Trail to where Sam had last seen his friend. Only then did the ranger realize the hiker had given Joe the wrong directions to Taylor Peak. Instead, he'd sent him to Chief's Head Peak, which was higher and farther away.

The ranger later wrote in a report that "it should have been apparent to the most inexperienced that it would have been impossible to reach Chief's Head by nightfall."

But this didn't take into consideration that Joe may have purposely stayed on the mountain to look at the stars. After looking at the map, Sam mentioned this and suggested that Joe might have taken an alternate route that also descended the Flattop Mountain Trail.

But no one knew which way Joe had gone – or if he was still on the mountain.

WAS JOE LOST? INJURED? OR WORSE, HAD HE FALLEN to his death from one of the many cliffs along the trail? The Halperns were in a near panic by this time, but park rangers and at least 150 volunteers, including many Civilian Conservation Corps members working in the park, scoured the mountain on foot and horseback.

Three days into the search, the rangers set up a high-elevation "fly camp," where they brought food and supplies by horseback. The camp was much higher and closer to the search area than the ranger station below at Bear Lake.

Meanwhile, Solomon, Sam, and one of the rangers carefully searched the area on the mountain's west side by horseback. Another fly camp had been set up there. By the end of the week, Solomon wrote to his other son, Bernard, "Four days of helpless agony and no end to it. There is slight hope that he is only lost and cannot find his way out. Let us hope so."

Park rangers and volunteers tramped through rugged gorges, down steep trails, and across windswept slopes for the next five days. They scaled every surrounding peak and followed every possible trail between the Glacier Basin Campground, east of the trailhead, all the way to the town of Grand Lake. The searchers also picked up every piece of clothing, every scrap of paper, and every man-made item they found on every trail. Each was taken to Fanny to see if anything belonged to her son. None of them did.

On August 18, the park's newsletter became the first to break the news of Joe's disappearance. The story was titled "University Student Lost on Snowy Ridge." On that day and the next, the story was printed in the Estes Park newspaper and sent out by wire across the country. More reports followed, including one that claimed footprints – believed to be Joe's – were found on Andrews Glacier. Another story, however, stated that park officials "were certain Halpern was either seriously injured or had been killed in a fall from a cliff." Neither story turned out to be accurate.

But one news report was accurate – and filled with gloom. "So carefully has the region been hunted," an unnamed reporter wrote, "in spite of heavy fog and rainstorms Saturday, that if Halpern was still walking about, he was almost certain to have encountered one of the searchers."

On August 20, five days after Joe and Sam had climbed Flattop Mountain, the park superintendent was forced to announce that the rescue part of the search for Joe was over. He stated there was "virtually no hope" that Joe was alive but that his searchers would make every effort to find his body.

THE HALPERNS NOW HAD TO FACE THE FACT THAT Joe wouldn't be found alive – or so park officials believed. Solomon and Fanny refused to give up hope and turned one of Joe's shoes over to the rangers in case bloodhounds could be used in the search.

Unfortunately, neither the Halperns nor Sam knew how to drive Joe's sedan, so they had to depend on other people to get them back to Chicago. On Monday, they repacked their camping gear into the Ford, and a fellow camper drove them to Denver. The next day, they secured another driver to get them home.

Before they left the park, Fanny sent one last letter home to her son. "Take good care of yourself, my dear Bernard," she wrote. "You are all we have."

The return trip to Illinois was undoubtedly a somber journey.

While overnighting in Denver, Sam mailed a letter to his family. It read, in part:

I've got some tragic news. Joe Halpern disappeared in the mountains last Tuesday and nothing has been heard of him since. Everyone had lost hope of ever finding him alive. The last four days Mr. Halpern and I have averaged fifteen miles of mountain climbing in our search. Yesterday, we walked and climbed twenty miles, then a terrific wind, rain, and snowstorm with no results. It is almost impossible for anyone to remain alive for five nights, without shelter and food, in a climate so cold and stormy...

The past couple of days have been miserable out here, with a deadly gloom prevailing. Mrs. Halpern cries all night long. It is my belief that Joe is not lost in the mountains but must have seriously disabled himself. It's pitiful, but --- Well, I'll be seeing you. So long.
Sam

A reporter from the Estes Park newspaper tried to add some optimism to the grim situation, hoping that at least Joe's remains would someday be found. He wrote that, during the previous year, a trail crew had stumbled upon the bones of a Texas man who had been missing for 17 years.

This was not encouraging to the Halperns, nor was the letter they received from Park Superintendent Edmund B. Rogers a month after Joe vanished. Rogers theorized that Joe had tried to descend from the mountain using one of the stone chimneys – narrow, vertical passages in a cliff – and had fallen. Few of these passages were passable for inexperienced climbers, he explained, and Joe was likely killed in a fall. Park rangers and volunteers had been searching in the chimneys along Joe's probable trail but hadn't found anything.

And they wouldn't.

Four months passed, and Solomon wrote to the superintendent to say that he had filed a missing person report with the local police in Colorado in case Joe had "wandered away due to some injury having affected his reason or memory, or for some other reason." In other words – in case he had amnesia.

Although genuine amnesia – a psychological disorder that causes people to lose their memory -- is very rare, it was popular in Hollywood films of the era. There were at least 60 movies that had amnesia plotlines in the early days of silent films, more than 40 in the 1920s, and another 40 by the time Joe disappeared in 1933. Amnesia may be rare in real life but common in movies – and books, pulp magazines, and comic books. The suggestion that Joe had amnesia – a plot twist right out of a melodrama – did nothing more than offer the Halperns one more shred of hope.

Or maybe Joe had disappeared on purpose. There were hints in some letters that Joe had written to a friend in 1930, his family discovered, that suggested he might have become disillusioned with work and his university studies. He wrote, "And so I stare face out at a cruel, harsh, economically depressed world and am waiting for the day when I'll be a hobo."

But was this a threat to disappear and leave his life behind? It seems more like a tired, stressed-out graduate student wondering what life will be like when he finishes school during a crippling national economic depression.

A year after Joe disappeared, the Halperns moved to a farm in LaPorte, Indiana, and they sent letters to the park superintendent so they would have their new address in case there was information about Joe.

They also sent a letter to the F.B.I., asking for the bureau's help finding their son. Joe's information and photograph were officially added to their missing persons file. The F.B.I. explained that if Joe was an amnesia victim – even F.B.I. agents went to the movies – and was arrested for "vagrancy or some other crime," his fingerprints would be on file if his father wanted to send them. Solomon managed to obtain fingerprints from Joe's right index, middle, and ring fingers, which were on file at the post office in Chicago. F.B.I. director J. Edgar Hoover himself wrote to Solomon and told him that the agency was unable to initiate an investigation, though, since Joe's disappearance had not been a kidnapping or any other violation of federal law.

And then huge news arrived – Joe was alive!

Solomon wrote about this news to the director of the Yerkes Observatory in Chicago, where Joe had been working. He wrote, "We just found out that it is highly probable that our son, Joseph L. Halpern, is alive." He explained that a friend of Joe's claimed to have seen him begging for a meal at a restaurant in Phoenix, Arizona. Police later confirmed that the man in question, using a different name, had spent three weeks in a transient camp and then left. Solomon added in his letter, "We are sure our son is a victim of amnesia and is helplessly wandering somewhere in the U.S.A. His mother is heartbroken, but the ray of hope we just received helped her a great deal."

But it wouldn't last. If the man had been Joe – which is doubtful – he was never seen again.

Later that same year, Solomon established a reward for information about Joe's whereabouts. He had mimeograph copies made of a neat, hand-lettered poster with all capital letters and a photograph of Joe in the center. Solomon stated that the University of Chicago graduate was "proficient in French, German, mathematics, astronomy, and chemistry" and that he "is a good chess player, does not smoke, usually goes without a hat, and may travel under an assumed name."

Copies of the poster were mailed out nationwide, but there were no replies.

In 1936, the F.B.I. received a letter from a California man named Samuel Greenfield. The reason for writing and how he found out Joe was missing remain unknown. However, he claimed to have spent his childhood days with Joe and claimed that their parents "have been rather close friends for the past twenty-five years." The man also wrote that after Joe was "seen" in Phoenix in 1934, he went to Nebraska with the Civilian Conservation Corps and then worked in Michigan for the Lewis Brothers Circus. The letter didn't lead anywhere, and Solomon never mentioned the Greenfield family – or his connection to a "friend" in Phoenix who originally reported seeing Joe there.

In 1942, another unusual letter to the F.B.I. came from an Iowa man named Ted Wilson, who claimed that Joe "was known to be with a rather rough crowd in 1935."

During World War II, Solomon wrote to the War Department to see if anyone named Joseph Laurence Halpern was serving in the military. When he was told there was no one with that name in the service, Solomon contacted J. Edgar Hoover and asked for help to match Joe's fingerprints with military men in case he used an assumed name.

"All we want to know is that he is alive," Solomon wrote in 1944. "For the sake of his mother, who is ill with constant worry, we appeal to you to help us in locating our son."

Over the last decade, it had become easier to believe that Joe had cut off contact with his parents for some reason than to accept the fact that he was probably dead.

But there was no match to Joe's fingerprints, again dashing the Halperns' hopes.

FIVE YEARS LATER, THE HALPERNS SOLD THE INDIANA farm and moved to Florida. In 1950, they appeared in Dade County probate court, where Solomon and Fanny established a "legal presumption of death" for the "estate of Joseph Halpern, allegedly deceased." This would allow Joe's property to be distributed – although he owned little more than his Ford and a savings account – but the Halperns must have felt a need to have some sort of resolution in the case.

They'd finally come to grips with the fact that their son wasn't coming home.

But the story wasn't over yet. In 1960, Bernard Halpern, Joe's brother, wrote to J. Edgar Hoover, with whom his father had continued to correspond. In part of the letter, he wrote:

When I visited my parents recently, my father mentioned for the first time a circumstance that could possibly lead to some information concerning the disappearance of my brother. He stated that forest rangers were of the opinion that my brother's companion knew more about the disappearance than he would admit at the time. Since he was a friend of my brother's, my father asked the rangers to cease questioning him as he was obviously in an agitated state of mind.

The Halperns had run out of other options, so their minds had taken them to some darker places than an accident or Joe disappearing on his own. Honestly, I'm surprised it took them so long to start questioning Sam Garrick's motives.

Both Solomon and Fanny went to their graves not knowing what happened to Joe. Fanny died in 1963 at the age of 82, and Solomon died two years later. He was 88.

Bernard was left in charge of the family mystery, and he continued to wonder about what Sam had known about Joe's vanishing.

Sam continued his studies after returning to Chicago, graduating from the University of Chicago and Rush Medical School. In 1937, he'd earned his license as a physician and surgeon. He married Bernice Daniels, had three children, and served in the military during World War II. He died in 1976 at the age of 64. Although he and the Halpern family apparently didn't remain in touch, there was never any discovery that he'd had anything to do with Joe's disappearance. The authorities never questioned him again about his tragic last hike with Joe.

Sam did, however, have an older brother, Isadore Garrick. He was also a good friend of Joe's. In 1965, Bernard wrote to him about what Sam knew about Joe's disappearance, and he received a reply from Isadore that read, in part:

I was sorry and grieved to hear of your parents' death. They were wonderful people. In 1933 and 1934, I wrote them when they wanted the one-hundred-odd letters of correspondence that I had with Joe to see if there were any leads – and, apparently, there were none. I had not written to them since that time, as I knew the loss of Joe left a wound that would never heal, and my writing would only hurt.

I am sure my brother has told the whole story – a case of bad judgment on both his and particularly Joe's part. You state he was visibly agitated. Under the circumstances, how could this be otherwise? Joe persisted in wanting to take a different – and a very treacherous – path down the mountain than they had taken up. Sam persisted on the same path since he was bushed. They didn't agree and went their separate ways. That, unfortunately, is the simple and whole story. I need not tell you that Joe was my closest and dearest friend, and that I think of him often.

Whatever had happened to Joe, Sam Garrick had nothing to do with it. So, who did? Probably no one. I think it's likely that the disappearance of Joe Halpern was nothing more than a combination of bad luck, weather, and an inexperienced hiker who never imagined that the region's natural wonders would turn against him.

Joe was a man who was fascinated with the stars and the night sky. Perhaps he was gazing into the heavens on that August night when he made a fatal misstep that led to his death.

Perhaps. Although we'll probably never know for sure. Unless some hiker or work crew comes across some old bones in the park someday, the fate of Joseph Halpern will always remain a mystery.

1936: BABY BOY LOST

THE MYSTERY OF HARRY "BUDDY" BROWE

IT WAS SATURDAY, SEPTEMBER 5, 1936, A warm and blustery early fall afternoon in Detroit, Michigan. Two little boys pushed a baby stroller along 17th Street. Their little brother was inside, a grin on his face as the other boys laughed and teased him as they walked.

The two older boys – Charles Browe, age 9, and Edward Browe, age 7 – had permission from their mother to take their 19-month-old little brother, Harry, whom everyone called "Buddy," to Clark Park, which was about 14 blocks from home.

In those days, no one thought there was anything wrong with sending their children out to play, especially in the Browes' safe Detroit neighborhood. It was like a little town all its own – a small one where everyone knew each other and watched out for their neighbor's kids.

But that feeling of safety was about to change.

Around 6:30 P.M., a woman, accompanied by two young girls, approached Charlie and Eddie while they were playing on a swing set with a small group of other children. According to the boys, the woman immediately began fawning over little Buddy, whose stroller was sitting next to the swings, watching his brothers play. After a brief conversation, the woman offered to pay for ice cream for all three Browe children and keep an eye on Harry while the other two boys went to get it.

With money clutched in their hands, Charlie and Eddie walked to a nearby confectionary to purchase the ice cream cones. After they returned and finished their ice cream, the woman offered to

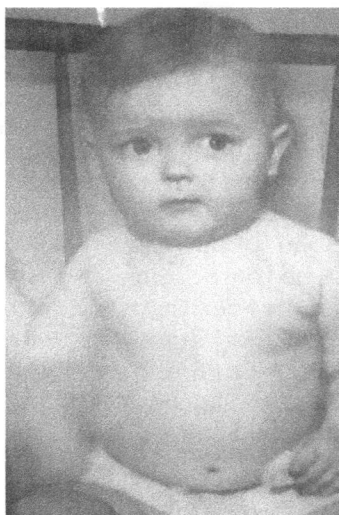

Harry "Buddy" Browe

buy them some candy, too. She handed the money to Charlie and sent Eddie with him to make sure he safely crossed the street. He went along but didn't go into the store. He stood outside, trusting his brother to get something they'd both enjoy.

As Charlie was browsing the selection, he suddenly looked up and saw that Eddie was also in the candy store. Eddie opened his hand and showed him three pennies. When Charlie asked where he'd gotten the coins, Eddie explained that a man had walked up and given them to him for candy.

Something about this bothered Charlie, and he told his brother they were leaving. They didn't buy any treats but walked back to the park instead.

As they approached the swings where they had left their baby brother, they found the stroller was there – but Buddy was missing. Panicked, they looked around the playground but soon realized that both the woman and Buddy were gone.

They never saw their baby brother again.

AFTER ANOTHER QUICK SEARCH OF THE PARK, Charlie and Eddie sprinted toward home, pushing the empty stroller. Red-faced and crying, they burst through the house's front door, startling their mother, Alice, and father, Robert, who'd come home from work at the local Dodge factory while the boys were at the park. When the boys breathlessly told their parents what had happened, the Browes immediately called the police.

Charlie and Eddie described the woman to investigators as being in her 30s, slightly heavyset, with blond hair and glasses. She was wearing a blue and white dress and black shoes. They guessed the two girls with her were probably 7 and 11 years old. Both wore dresses – one brown, the other blue – matching black shoes and yellow stockings. Eddie said that the man who gave him the three

Robert and Alice Browe

pennies was wearing a gray hat and a dark suit and had a cleft palate.

The Browes could think of no reason anyone would want to abduct Buddy. The family wasn't rich. They lived in a modest home, and while Robert made steady money at the automobile plant, Alice was a housewife who cared for their six children, who, besides Charlie, Eddie, and Buddy, included Robert, Jr., who was 4, Marion, 3, and Irene, who was three months old. She certainly had her hands full, and the police never questioned her decision to allow the boys to play in the park.

The investigators thoroughly questioned Charlie and Eddie about the events at the park. Initially, they surmised that Buddy had been injured, and the boys lied about what happened to stay out of trouble. It seemed unlikely that anyone would have kidnapped the boy for ransom since the family had little money, so they feared the worst.

But both boys insisted that Buddy was fine. They even admitted that he had fallen out of his stroller on the way to the park but wasn't hurt. Buddy was a rambunctious baby and loved to climb. He'd gotten out before Charlie could stop him and tumbled into the grass. The boys both said he'd been laughing when they picked him up.

After several rounds of interrogation, detectives were confident the boys were telling the truth.

That belief was backed up a few minutes later when two children the boys had been playing with at the park arrived at the Browe home with their mother. Dolores and Joan Gallagher – ages 4 and 11 – told the same story about the woman in the blue dress who took Buddy. Later, the police found a woman who was also at the park. She said she had seen a man carrying Buddy in his arms shortly after he had vanished. Her description of the man was almost identical to the one Eddie said gave him the money for candy.

An extensive search began. Police officers combed the park and the surrounding neighborhood. They were joined by hundreds of volunteers and Boy Scouts, who scoured the area for any sign of the missing boy.

But they found nothing.

More than 10,000 posters were printed and distributed across several states. They offered a $650 reward for Buddy's safe return and included a description of him: "Age: 19 months. Height: 2 feet, 4 inches. Weight: 26 pounds. Blue eyes, light brown/dark blond hair. Wearing: white romper, no stockings, black shoes."

The poster also noted that Buddy was missing a fingernail from his left ring finger. He also had a pair of unique, prominent scars behind each of his ears. Only three months earlier, he had undergone a mastoidectomy, a surgery that removed diseased cells from the air-filled spaces in the mastoid bone. The surgery had left behind the scars.

The police were starting to consider the idea that Buddy had been taken by a childless woman, or couple, who saw their chance to take the little boy and raise him as their own. I suppose this was a naïve idea, but not out of the question.

More likely, if someone like this had taken Buddy, it was probably so he could be sold as part of a bootleg adoption ring. Five years later, in 1941, Detroit police exposed an operation that bought and sold babies born to unwed mothers. The "adoption" ring was run by Agnes Yarrow, who sold babies to childless couples for as much as $1,000 each. They discovered records of at least 25 babies who had been sold, including one from Canada who had been kidnapped from his family.

Could this have been what happened to Buddy?

This was, unfortunately, the best-case scenario. The police had ruled out kidnapping for ransom, and while they held out hope for a couple who wanted a baby so badly they'd steal one, they knew the alternative could be much worse. No one wanted to say it, but there was every chance that Buddy had been taken by a child kidnapper – some kind of pervert – who might have killed him.

This possibility wasn't mentioned to the Browes at that point. The cops knew the family was hoping that Buddy would be returned.

AS THE DAYS PASSED, HUNDREDS OF TIPS came in from people who claimed to have seen Buddy. Some came from as close as Indiana and as far away as Canada.

A motorcyclist named Joseph Hayden told police he'd seen a boy resembling Buddy when he stopped for gas in Goshen, Indiana. He said a car with Michigan license plates pulled into the service station with a man, a woman, and a crying baby in the car. "I didn't know about the Browe kidnapping," Hayden said. "I asked the woman what was the matter with him and she answered, 'Oh, he's not standing the trip very well.' After I got back to Detroit and saw the Browe baby's picture, I was positive it was the same child."

A description of the car, the couple, and the license plate number were given to Indiana State Police, but the car was never found.

Two more Indiana calls came in. They placed Buddy in Evansville and Indianapolis, but the police found nothing.

Detectives traveled to Toronto, Canada, after a tip came in about what was called the "Great Stork Derby," a contest held between 1926 and 1936 where women competed to produce the most babies in 10 years. The winner was supposed to qualify for a bequest in the will of the millionaire who hosted the strange event.

Unfortunately, this lead was like all the rest – false clues, prank calls, and mistaken identities.

Robert and Alice Browe refused to stop hoping their baby would be returned to them. Robert had appealed to the kidnappers to leave the baby with any clergyman because he knew the kidnappers might not bring Buddy to their house because of the constant presence of curiosity-seekers and police officers. Alice even traveled as far away as New York City to appeal for Buddy's return on a national radio show.

After two weeks of searching, the couple resigned themselves to waiting, hoping, and praying. Alice told a reporter from the *Detroit Free Press*, "I can't help feeling that Buddy is alive somewhere, and that he will be brought back to us. I pray for him every time I can, and if prayers do any good, he will be returned."

In their desperation, Alice and Robert turned to a spirit medium for help. The woman, who claimed to be an "automatic writer," visited their home to try and help. Alice said, "She just held her pencil on a piece of paper, and pretty soon, it began to move.

It wrote that the child was safe and that he would be returned on Sunday."

But Sunday came and went, and so did many other days. As promising leads finally started to dwindle, a hopeful clue finally presented itself in the form of a postcard. It had been postmarked in Detroit on September 11, and it read, in part:

Mrs. Browe,

Please forgive me for taking your baby. You cannot understand how it is to be without one. You have so many, surely you can spare this one. He is beginning to like us, we want you to know....

The writing on the postcard was determined to be "feminine," and one corner of it had been purposely torn. According to F.B.I. agents, who played a brief role in the case, this was something that kidnappers sometimes used as a way of proving the identity of a baby later if their appearance changed. However, this method was used in ransom cases, and the Browes were never asked for money. Investigators believed the postcard was legitimate, but the person who wrote it was never found.

And soon, the case of Harry "Buddy" Browe went cold.

TRAGEDY CONTINUED TO HAUNT THE BROWE family in the years to come. In 1950, Alice and Robert were involved in a traffic accident. A truck came out of nowhere and struck their car in an intersection. Alice died at the scene, and Robert suffered severe injuries, including a broken pelvis and internal bleeding.

Alice's death left Robert to care for their children alone – Buddy now had 11 brothers and sisters – but the debilitating injuries from the accident didn't allow his father to keep working. Soon after leaving the hospital, Robert and the children went to live with Alice's mother, Marion Burgett.

In 1952, Charlie – now 25 – took a job driving a gasoline truck, using the money he earned to help his family as much as possible. One day, while he was working, Charlie's truck collided with another vehicle, and he was instantly killed.

In December of that same year, Marion, Robert's mother-in-law, also passed away. That same month, a devastating fire destroyed part of the family's home and left them without heat.

After a lengthy battle with the life insurance company, Robert was appointed the administrator of Marion's estate, which saved the family from further hardship.

Even after all that tragedy, though, the Browes never forgot about Buddy. Robert still spoke about him often, and the older children always remembered his smiling face and good nature. In time, Robert accepted that he'd never see his son again. He hoped that Buddy had been taken by someone to raise as their own and that he'd had a happy life.

Then, in 1962, a new and promising lead came from a young man who believed he might be Buddy. He had telephoned a reporter named Neal Shine, who, as a child, had been close friends with Charlie and Eddie Browe. Neal had written several articles about his friends and their brother's disappearance and was surprised when he received the call one evening.

The man on the other end of the line said he'd seen Neal's stories about Buddy and was concerned he might be the missing boy. He was the right age and had blue eyes, light hair, and scars behind each of his ears. Most compelling of all was the deathbed confession that he'd heard from the woman he believed was his mother. He said that before she died, she told him, "You are some other woman's baby. I took you. I have never been sorry except for breaking that poor woman's heart."

The young man called Neal several more times but finally told him he'd decided he didn't want to complicate his life if the confession was true. Neal couldn't let it go – he decided to look for the man. He knew from their conversations that he lived in Detroit and worked in a hotel kitchen. For the next six months, he visited every hotel in the city, looking for the young man with the scars behind his ears, but he never found him.

Was the young man Buddy? We may never know.

ROBERT BROWE, WHO NEVER REALLY RECOVERED from the accident, passed away in 1964. In time, his children followed him to the grave. None of them ever found out what happened to their brother.

The search continues today. Later generations of the family still ponder the mystery. If Harry "Buddy" Browe survived his abduction, he could still be alive at the time of this writing, although he'd be in his 90s. He could have his own children, grandchildren, and great-grandchildren, never knowing they have family members somewhere.

Perhaps one day – in this era of online D.N.A. tracking – someone will be surprised to discover they have relatives who once lived in Detroit, haunted by the disappearance of a grinning little boy in 1936.

1938: THE GIRL WHO WAS PICKING FLOWERS
THE DISAPPEARANCE OF MARJORIE WEST

ON MOTHER'S DAY, MAY 8, 1938, THE WEST FAMILY left their home in Bradford, Pennsylvania, for an outing in the Allegheny National Forest, about 18 miles north of the town of Kane.

It was a warm, sunny day, and Celia West had been promised a picnic after church services with her husband, Shirley – who went by his initials of "S.M." – her son, Allan, who was 7, and her daughters, Dorothea, 11, and Marjorie, who would be turning 5 in just a few weeks. Everyone was excited and looking forward to the day.

The Wests drove to White Gravel Creek in McKean County, where S.M. planned to do a little fishing after lunch. Once the family finished eating, he disappeared with his fishing rod and tackle box while Celia sat down in the front seat of the car with a book. She had the windows down and her feet propped up on the dash. She glanced at the children occasionally, squinting in the sun, and saw Allan playing with toys in the grass.

Marjorie and Dorothea were busy picking wildflowers near a boulder their father had already checked for snakes. The girls, looking for more flowers, wandered to the other side of the rocks. Celia couldn't see them, but she could hear them laughing and talking to each other, so she turned her attention back to her book.

"Mom?" Celia heard a voice calling out to her. She looked up and saw Dorothea walking toward her.

Later, Celia wouldn't remember what Dorothea wanted to talk to her about or how long she left her little sister alone, but it couldn't have been more than a few moments.

But those few moments would change the lives of the West family forever.

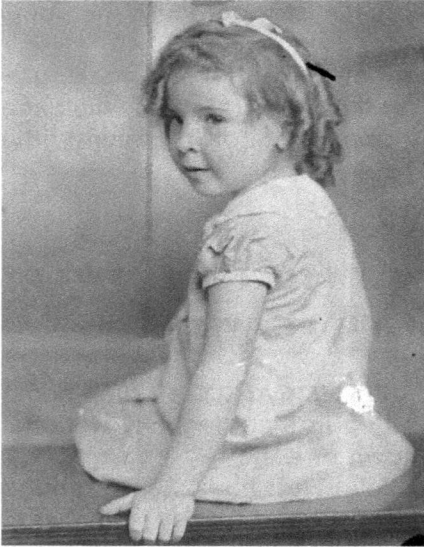

THERE ISN'T MUCH WE CAN SAY ABOUT MAJORIE'S life. She was only four years old when she disappeared. She had been born on June 2, 1933, and spent her entire existence living with her family in Bradford, Pennsylvania. She was the youngest of the West children.

Around 3:00 P.M. on that Mother's Day afternoon, Dorothea left her sister alone, picking flowers, when she went to talk to her mother. By the time Dorothea returned to the other side of the rocks that were between the family car and the nearby creek, Marjorie was gone.

Marjorie West in a photo taken the same year she disappeared.

Dorothea burst into tears and called to her mother, who came to see what was wrong. Between sobs, Dorothea explained that her little sister was missing. Celia ran toward the creek, afraid the four-year-old might have fallen into the water, but there was no sign of her. She yelled loudly for Marjorie, but there was no response.

Alerted by his wife's cries, S.M. grabbed his tackle box and ran toward the car. He saw his wife and children scattered around the area where they'd had the earlier picnic, looking around the rocks along the river and edging into the nearby woods. They were searching frantically for something – but what?

And that's when he realized one of his children was missing. Where was Marjorie?

After searching and calling out for Majorie for nearly an hour, S.M. finally sent his wife to find the closest telephone. They needed to call the police.

When officers arrived on the scene, they also searched the surrounding area but discovered they needed more help. Word spread throughout the area, and about 200 Civilian Conservation Corps workers showed up in a dozen trucks and joined the hunt for the little girl. A score of volunteers from the American Legions in nearby Kane and Bradford soon joined them.

The search wasn't in full swing until late in the afternoon, so volunteers and police officials only had a few hours to scour the nearby areas of the park. Once it began to get dark, the search was temporarily called off until the surprise arrival of a group of oil lease workers from Klondike, who used the lights on miner's helmets to keep searching the dark woods.

S.M. West was one of them – an oil field worker – and when they'd heard his daughter was missing, the men had scrambled to get to the park.

While the oil field workers continued the hunt, the authorities began planning the best way to continue looking for Marjorie. There were several theories tossed into the mix.

One group believed that the little girl might have fallen into the stream and drowned. Many of the volunteers had searched the part of the creek that was close to the scene, but plans were made to search downstream at first light.

It was also suggested that perhaps Marjorie had fallen into one of the park's many crevices and small caves. Some of the oil workers were directed to look for openings with their headlamps, but there was no sign of the girl.

The final theory was based on the fact that the flowers that Marjorie had been picking were found along the edge of the Morrison-Marshburg Road, where the family had parked their car. It was suggested that perhaps she had wandered down the road and was found by a sympathetic driver who believed she was lost. That person would likely take her to the closest town, so a bulletin was sent across the region, hoping the little girl would be dropped off at a police station.

Unfortunately, Marjorie being picked up by a passing motorist might not be the best outcome. The cops knew it was possible that if some motorist picked up the little girl, that person might not have her best intentions in mind. Well aware of the danger, police officers began stopping cars and looking in backseats for little girls – just in case.

WITH THE RETURN OF DAYLIGHT, AN ARMY OF at least 500 men – including police officers, oil workers, and C.C.C. men -- resumed the search for Marjorie. They tramped up and down hills, pushed through brush and trees, and searched the deepest parts of the creek. The water, they found, was mostly shallow, and it so began to seem unlikely that Marjorie had fallen into the water and drowned.

Later in the morning on May 9, Pennsylvania State Troopers joined the search, along with the National Guard company from Bradford. Clyde C. Porter, the forest supervisor for the C.C.C., directed the men to spread out in a mile-long line with about 25 feet between them. This way, they could cover an entire square mile at a time. They managed to beat a 15-mile swath through the thicketed national forest that day.

In addition, two private airplanes, piloted by Lewis Mallory and Joseph Fields, flew over the area in the hope that the girl might be spotted from the air. They flew over the forest several times on May 9 but failed to turn up any clues to Majorie's whereabouts.

The search continued the next day, with even more men turning up to help search the heavily wooded park. Hunters and outdoorsmen, who were most familiar with the area, led portions of the search, checking out lonely hunting and fishing cabins hidden in the trees.

Up and down the creek, rangers questioned trout fishermen, hoping they might have seen something, but they also turned up no clues.

A group of C.C.C. workers cut their way through thick brush to reach a wooded area that locals appropriately called the "Bear's Den." The area was infested with snakes and dotted with small caves where bears often hibernated for the winter. Thankfully, no trace of Marjorie was found there.

Local police officers searched culverts and bridges throughout the area, announcing that they were now discarding a recently proposed theory that Marjorie might have been hit by an automobile and her body thrown into a ditch.

On May 10, bloodhounds arrived with a Westboro deputy sheriff, and the dogs led searchers a half-mile up the side of a mountain, where they reportedly found a crumpled bouquet of violets and the small footprints of a child. From there, the bloodhounds took them to a ramshackle cabin, and volunteers were excited and convinced that Marjorie had taken shelter inside.

But they quickly found the cabin door had been nailed shut. There was no way she could have gotten inside. They checked the interior anyway, but there was no sign that anyone had been in it in years.

The dogs continued slobbering their way through the woods and thickets but always managed to return to the place where Marjorie was last seen.

MEANWHILE, DOZENS OF WELL-MEANING TIPS AND leads were coming in from people across the state. The American Legion had announced a $200 reward for information leading to the discovery of the girl – "dead or alive."

Calls poured in. Several people who were also in the park on May 8 recalled seeing two different cars that drove past the spot where the Wests had their picnic that day. The cars were quickly found, and the drivers were identified – they had nothing to do with Marjorie's disappearance.

Another promising lead came from a taxi driver in Thomas, West Virginia. He stated that he had seen a child fitting Marjorie's description in a green sedan with Pennsylvania plates driven by a man in his 30s. The driver had asked for directions to the nearest motel, and the witness sent him across the street. According to the taxi driver, the little girl was crying in the back seat, but the man assured the witness that she was his daughter and was fine.

The witness likely wouldn't have remembered the interaction if he hadn't run into the man and little girl in the green sedan again later that night. He told him that all the rooms at the motel were booked and, this time, asked for the closest liquor store. He sent him to one down the street. They drove off and the witness didn't see them again.

$2,000 REWARD!

$2,000 will be paid by the Bradford, Pa., Citizens' Reward Committee for information resulting in the safe return of MARJORY WEST, who disappeared at White Gravel, Pa., May 8, 1938.

ONE HALF THE REWARD MONEY will be paid for information resulting in the recovery of her body.

This reward expires December 15, 1938.

Description of MARJORY WEST

Age 4 (Four) Years.   Blue Eyes.   Long, Curley, Red Hair.   Freckled Face.   Wearing Red Shirley Temple Hat, Blue Coat, Blue Dress and Patent Leather Shoes. Talks with a Southern Accent.

Two days later, though, he saw the newspaper coverage about the missing girl and became convinced Majorie had been the girl in the back seat of the green sedan. He called the police.

If that little girl wasn't Marjorie, she looked a lot like her. Another witness saw the same man, the same girl, and the same green sedan a day later at a filling station, and she also believed the girl was Marjorie.

The taxi driver's sighting occurred around 11:30 P.M. on the same day that Marjorie went missing. If Marjorie was taken at 3:00 P.M., it would be possible for her to be in Thomas, West Virginia, later that night.

Was it her in the car? By the time the sighting was reported, two days had passed, and the driver of the green sedan had also vanished. This led many to wonder if help for Marjorie came too late,

Unfortunately, this turned out to be a false lead. Bradford Chief of Police Edward Edmonds identified Conrad Fridley as the man in the green sedan. He had been traveling from Parsons, West Virginia, with his five-year-old daughter, Lois. They had to stop because of the fog and decided to stay at the motel overnight. Lois became frustrated at the unexpected stop and was crying when they encountered the cab driver. The little girl in the car wasn't Marjorie; he'd had nothing to do with her disappearance.

Edmonds announced this development on May 11, and after clearing Lee Jones of any involvement in the case, he ended his time with reporters on an ominous note: "I expect the crime angle to develop six to eight months from today if anything has happened to the kid. If she is still in the woods, she's dead by now."

REGARDLESS, BACK IN THE ALLEGHENY National Forest, the ground search for Marjorie continued. The mayor of Bradford, Hugh J. Ryan, put out a call for 1,000 volunteers to join in a last "elbow-to-elbow" 10-mile search through a wild and heavily overgrown valley. They planned to start at dawn on May 12, along Marshburg Road, near where "the red-haired child wandered away from her parents while on a picnic."

Ryan, who had been part of the search since the beginning, added to reporters: "We want men who are physically fit to hike through heavy brush for 10 miles. We want them to bring their own lunches and be prepared to follow orders."

The search was planned to start at the place where the family picnic had taken place on May 8. While S.M. was out with the search parties, Celia West had remained at that spot in a tent the family had set up, waiting for any word about her daughter.

She spoke with reporters on May 11 and expressed the opinion that Marjorie had been kidnapped. She promised that "no questions will be asked" if the girl was returned. She told the reporters, "I want notice given that anyone who has her should return her to any American Legion post anywhere or bring her home. No questions will be asked."

The final search began on May 12 with double the number of men Hugh Ryan had asked to volunteer. The 2,000 men worked in a long, "shoulder-to-shoulder" line for one last push to try and determine Majorie's fate.

Their efforts were directed by the State Police, who sent the searchers to the White Gravel area in the dense forest, one of the only spots that had not been already searched. At the end of the long day, the weary men trudged back to the Marshburg road campsite, saddened by their continued failure to find the little girl.

Hope for the little girl to be found alive was now gone. It seemed unlikely that the 4-year-old could survive another night of frost and freezing temperatures in the park's elevations.

The search continued – and would for a few months – but there were few results. Rumors were spread about a man who had recently been discharged from the forest service because he had threatened another ranger and his family. Acting on this tip, the police obtained a warrant to search his home, but when they arrived, they found the house was empty, and the man was gone.

Three pieces of a blue bandana handkerchief were found seven miles apart in the forest, but whether this had anything to do with Marjorie was unknown.

Another rumor claimed that a motorist had been forced off the road by a speeding car on a narrow dirt road in the park about the time of Marjorie's disappearance. This revived the theory that the girl might have been hit by a car but with a twist – she was badly hurt, picked up, and rushed toward a hospital but died on the way, and the car's occupants disposed of the body. That "speeding car," though, was never found.

At one point, fear arose when what appeared to be a freshly dug grave was discovered in the woods. However, only an empty crate of wine bottles was found in the hole.

The search finally came to an end that summer. There were no more oil workers, volunteers, or C.C.C. men walking the trails and roaming through the trees and brush of the national forest.

Even the Wests had finally gone home. Their forlorn tent had been taken down and locked in the trunk of the car, and the place along the riverbank where Marjorie had last been seen picking flowers vanished from their rearview mirror as they drove away.

OVER THE YEARS, THEORIES THAT DIFFER FROM those of the police in 1938 have been offered to explain what happened to Marjorie West.

One of the earlier suggestions was that she had fallen into one of the hidden oil wells in the White Gravel area, one of the last places searched by the volunteers.

Majorie's parents came to believe that their daughter had been kidnapped, and this remains the most plausible theory today. Whether she was taken by some childless couple – like in the "Buddy Browe" case – or by someone with nefarious intentions is still debated.

During the Great Depression, there were several illegal adoption rings operating in the United States, where children were stolen away from their families and then sold off for a price. It was a way for people to make some quick cash.

One such ring – which many feel may be linked to Marjorie's disappearance – was revealed in 1951 during the Tennessee Children's Home Society scandal. The ring was operated by Georgia Tann, a child trafficker who was involved in the kidnapping of thousands of children and their illegal adoptions.

The children were often taken from low-income families, usually through illegal methods, and then the babies were sold for huge profits to rich couples looking to adopt. Some of the kids were kidnapped right off the street, others stole newborns out of hospitals, and other children were stolen from daycares and church basements.

Other kids – usually white, blond-haired, and blue-eyed – came from orphanages like the Tennessee Children's Home in Memphis.

Georgia Tann, a social worker, had been hired as the Executive Secretary of the Memphis orphanage in the 1920s. Well-known in local society and with political connections, she had a strong network of supporters, including legislators, prominent families, and Judge Camile Kelley, who finalized most of the adoptions of children from the orphanage.

Little did anyone know, but Tann was using the orphanage as a front for her black-market baby adoption scheme that started as soon as she began working there and lasted until her death from cancer in 1950. Young children were kidnapped and then sold to wealthy families, abused, or – in some instances – murdered. A state investigation into numerous cases of adoption fraud led to the exposure of the scheme soon after Tann died.

Even though Tann had routinely destroyed the home's records, state investigators found secret bank accounts that revealed that Tann was skimming between 80 and 90 percent of the adoption fees when children were placed outside of Tennessee.

As details of what was happening at the Memphis Children's Home were revealed, adoptive parents soon discovered that the biographies and child histories supplied by Tann were false. In some cases, Tann obtained babies from state mental hospital patients and hid the information from adoptive parents. She also conspired with some local area doctors who delivered babies at a home of unwed mothers. Tann would take the newborns under the pretext of providing them with hospital care and would later tell the mothers that the children had died and that their bodies had been buried immediately in the name of compassion.

The investigators also found that Judge Kelley had railroaded through hundreds of adoptions without following state laws. Though they could not find direct evidence that Kelley received payments from Tann for her assistance, investigators noted that her yearly income could not have otherwise supported her lifestyle. After learning that investigators had recorded an incriminating phone call – during which Kelley attempted to bribe a potential witness against her – she suddenly announced that she was retiring after 30 years on the bench. She was never prosecuted for her part in the scandal and died in 1955.

The scandal forced the reform of adoption laws in Tennessee in 1951. However, those changes came too late for hundreds –

possibly thousands – of children who were abducted, taken from their parents, or adopted illegally.

It's been theorized that Majorie West might have been one of those children. Investigators believed that children were taken from all over the Midwest and many eastern states, including Pennsylvania. It's possible that Marjorie vanished into Tann's operation or another, smaller one that was just like it.

In 2000, the tantalizing possibility that Marjorie was still alive became part of the unsolved case. There was a claim that a woman named Sylvia Waldrop London was actually Marjorie West.

MARJORIE'S FAMILY STRUGGLED WITH THE LOSS of the little girl for decades. It was a generational trauma passed on from parent to child that seemed to affect the entire family. Even relatives born well after Marjorie vanished still felt the loss.

The disappearance also affected the community in 1938. After Marjorie vanished, those who were children at the time later recalled how much more protective their parents became. They were repeatedly told never to go into the woods alone or talk to strangers. In the 1930s, it was common for children to play in the woods, go to friends' houses, or go to the park without supervision. But in communities like Bradford, parents feared their own kids might disappear one day, just like little Marjorie.

After Marjorie vanished, S.M. West had spent the entire week in the woods, searching desperately for his daughter. On May 16, Celia finally convinced him to return home with her and the other two children. He reluctantly did so but often returned to the woods, still searching for Marjorie. Celia took another approach that was no less obsessive. She refused to leave the house, staying by the telephone in case someone might call and reveal where her daughter could be found.

The West family never found any answers about their missing child. S.M. and Celia split up in 1953, their marriage destroyed by the mystery. S.M. died in July 1965, and his family said that he'd gone to his grave holding on to a sliver of hope that Marjorie was still out there, alive and well.

There's no question that Marjorie's parents blamed themselves for the disappearance, but they weren't the only ones who felt that way. In 2009, Dorothea's granddaughter, Angel, wrote, "I remember listening to my grandmother tell me stories about Marjorie and the sadness she felt for leaving her sister alone for those few moments. My grandmother held on to her feeling of responsibility until her passing two years ago."

In 2010, the West family convinced the Pennsylvania State Polie to open a new case file for Marjorie – the old records had been lost – and in 2012, D.N.A. samples were taken from two of Marjorie's cousins who lived in Bradford The family hoped the D.N.A. tests would produce some results but were disappointed. There was no match with anyone in any database.

In 2014, the police received a tip from someone who worked at a Rochester, New York hospital. They'd read about the disappearance and reported there was a patient at the hospital named "Marjorie," who never received visitors. When the police investigated, they discovered that the woman had been born in 1922, making her too old to be Marjorie West.

There were also many who believed the woman in New York couldn't be the missing child because Marjorie West had already been found.

Harold Thomas Beck, a college professor with a PhD in linguistics, had also been the editor of the Mountain Laurel Review. He'd taken an interest in Marjorie's story and wrote two articles about the case in 1995 and 1996. Two years later, he posted an online article that announced he would pay $10,000 for information leading to Marjorie's discovery.

Around this time, Beck was contacted by Dorothea West. She wanted to offer him more information and correct some errors and inconsistencies that had appeared in newspapers when her sister vanished. She also sent him some family photos, including one of herself when she was 65 years old. Dorothea hoped that the image could be used to determine approximately what her sister might look like in the present day.

Beck continued to post about the case online. Then, in 2000, he was contacted by a woman who told him that her co-worker at a company in Florida not only resembled what Marjorie would look like in the present day, but she was also the same age as the missing girl.

Beck was excited enough by the woman's story that he traveled down to meet the co-worker, whose name was Sylvia Waldrop London. She did, in fact, resemble Marjorie, but when Beck told her that he suspected she might be the missing girl, Sylvia denied it. She wanted nothing to do with the Marjorie West story, so Beck reluctantly returned home.

But Beck couldn't let it go. He contacted Sylvia again, and letters were sent back and forth between them over the next few years. By then, she'd left Florida and moved to her family farm in North Carolina. Eventually, she told Beck that she also believed she might be Marjorie West, and she said she was willing to share some private information with him but only on two conditions – that Beck wouldn't reveal her identity to anyone but Dorothea and that he wouldn't publish anything else about her until after her death.

Beck agreed, and he kept the promise. Sylvia told him that when her mother was dying, she admitted to her that her husband had stolen Sylvia from a park when she was a little girl.

In 1938, the family moved to a North Carolina farm, and Sylvia's father decided to drive up north and look for work during the winter. He got a job at one of the oil refineries near Bradford and stayed until spring. Then, on Mother's Day, as he was leaving town, he passed by the Allegheny National Forest and accidentally hit a small girl with his car. He stopped and looked around but didn't see anyone nearby, so he put the girl in his car with plans to take her to the Kane Hospital. He was terrified the girl might be dead, but she was only unconscious. She woke up and was mostly unharmed.

But now he faced a moral dilemma. The man and his wife had lost their daughter in childbirth that winter. It had been a difficult delivery, and it was unlikely his wife would be able to have any more children. The right thing to do was to take the little girl to the hospital, but he also wanted very badly to be a father, and this was his chance.

So, he chose to take the little girl with him back to North Carolina. As a young child, Sylvia often told her parents that she remembered having a different family and recalled a place that "had snow way over her head." But her parents convinced her she'd just dreamed those things whenever she mentioned it. Sylvia also admitted that the names "Dorothea" and "Allan" were familiar, but she never knew why. She didn't remember her siblings, but she soon had others – the couple managed to have four more children after World War II.

If this woman really was Marjorie, she never got to see Dorothea again. When Beck heard her story, Dorothea was in poor health and unable to travel. She passed away on April 10, 2007.

It was a convincing story – but not everyone believed it. Beck's claims of finding the missing girl have been debated for years.

As mentioned earlier, there were reports of two cars that drove past the picnic site on the day Marjorie went missing. However, the drivers were both identified as locals who had nothing to do with the case.

Also, Sylvia claimed that she had been the young girl encountered by the taxi driver in Thomas, West Virginia. But the police had tracked down the man and the little girl – Conrad Fridley and his daughter, Lois.

Despite these inconsistencies, Beck continued to say Sylvia's story was true. He dismissed all other accounts and claims, which angered locals, police officers, and Marjorie's relatives. In 2012, a West family member stated that state police officers she had spoken with didn't believe Beck was credible.

There are definitely problems with Sylvia's story. Her account offered very little information that couldn't be found in the details from newspaper articles that covered the disappearance -- such as the cars that sped past the picnic area, the little girl encountered in West Virginia, the names of Marjorie's siblings, and that she was from a state that had snow in the winter.

Had she just used those details to create a story about being Marjorie, or was part of her account true, and she really was the missing girl?

Unfortunately, with cases of missing persons – especially ones with a lot of news coverage and a reward – there are also false leads, bogus tips, prank calls, and people who claim to be the missing person. That's not to say Sylvia was lying – it's just as likely that someone lied to her and made up a story about what happened when she was a child. Perhaps Sylvia was taken from her family by the man she grew up with as her father, but at some point, the story becomes mixed up with that of Marjorie West.

We'll probably never know. Marjorie is still a missing person, even after all these years. It's possible she died in 1938, or it's just as possible that she was adopted into a new family and never knew the truth about her past. Whatever happened to Marjorie remains a mystery that the passing years have made even more difficult to solve.

1952: THE GIRL WHO LEFT SUMMER CAMP
THE VANISHING OF CONNIE SMITH

THE PERFECT CHILDHOOD MAY HAVE NEVER existed, but if it did, then Connie Smith had one that was as close to perfect as I've ever heard. She was born in northeastern Wyoming on July 11, 1942, and she and her 3-year-old brother, Nels, grew up on a cattle ranch with their parents, Peter and Helen.

The children's grandfather, Nels H. Smith, was the governor of Wyoming at the time and was described in the press as a "farmer, stockman, and businessman with western ideas as to conservation and development."

Connie and her brother did their chores, which included gathering eggs, feeding the chickens, and milking the cows. The children were raised with horses, which was Connie's most important chore. She loved to ride.

The ranch itself was a slice of paradise. To the east is Wyoming's Black Hills. To the west is the Powder River Basin, dominated by a lone mountain called Inyan Kara, which was rich in history and considered sacred by the native people.

A decade later, in 1952, Connie, her brother, Nels, and her mother, Helen, set out on a road trip to the East Coast. They traveled across the Midwest, north into Canada, and then south to New England to visit relatives in Greenwich, Connecticut.

They planned to stay for the summer, so Helen enrolled Connie for a month at Camp Sloane, located in the foothills of the Berkshire Mountains in the state's northwestern corner. Nestled in the rolling hills, the dense woods, and open fields near Lakeville, the camp was made up of wooden buildings and tents on the shore of Wononpakook Lake.

It was Connie's first experience with anything like this, but she thrived at the summer camp – or at least she seemed to at first.

On Sunday, July 13 – two days after Connie's 10th birthday -- Nels, her mother, Helen, and her grandmother came to the camp for a Family Day visit.

Connie seemed to be enjoying all the usual camp activities – swimming, canoeing, square dancing, and horseback riding – and Helen later said that her daughter had even asked her to extend her stay because she was having so much fun.

The family stayed for the afternoon, then left, making the two-hour drive back to Greenwich. On the return trip, Helen and her mother chatted about how happy Connie had seemed and were glad she was enjoying the summer.

But Connie may have fooled everyone.

Five days later, she walked away from Camp Sloane and vanished. Despite extensive searches, no trace of Connie Smith has ever been found.

ON WEDNESDAY, JULY 16, CAMP SLOANE'S gatekeeper was on duty at 8:00 A.M. when a young girl with light brown hair walked past him to Indian Mountain Road and turned north, walking toward Lakeville. The man later told police that he didn't pay much attention to her because she was so tall that he assumed she was one of the counselors. "I think she stopped to pick some flowers," he added.

Along the road, a man and a woman who were out for a morning walk later recalled seeing a girl

Connie Smith in 1952

identified as Connie. A half-mile farther from the camp, a woman answered a knock on her door to find a girl who asked her for directions to Lakeville. The woman directed her up the nearby hill and told her to go right. Later, when the police interviewed her, the woman said she thought the girl had been crying but didn't ask about it – it was none of her business. "If only I had said something," she regretted when she found out that Connie had vanished.

Two more women spotted Connie a little farther along the road, and when she was on Route 44 – the main road into Lakeville – a motorist and his wife passed her as she attempted to thumb a ride to get her the last mile or so to town. Hitchhiking wasn't uncommon in the 1950s and was considered safe at the time – especially to a young girl used to the wide-open spaces of Wyoming. It's possible that she got a ride, but where the driver took her may never be known.

Something was obviously bothering Connie. When family and friends were interviewed in the days to come, some thought she might have been homesick, which was a common occurrence for a lot of campers after a family visit. But Helen said this wasn't the case with Connie – she'd asked to stay at camp longer, but her mother said she couldn't.

Some wondered if she'd had an altercation with one of the other campers. Most of the other children at the camp were from affluent New England families. Maybe Connie, who grew up on a ranch out west, didn't fit in with the others.

It was discovered that on the night before Connie went missing, she had "fallen down" the steps of the wooden platform of her eight-person tent, bruising her hip. That morning, a tentmate whose legs were hanging off a top bunk "accidentally" kicked Connie in the face, breaking her glasses and giving her a bloody nose.

Maybe Connie had just had enough. She was an independent young girl, mature for her age, and perhaps she was ready to leave. It's possible, even likely, that Connie lied to her mother about how much fun she was having so Helen wouldn't worry. The camp's telephone was off-limits to the campers, but maybe Connie knew she could make a collect call to her mother or her father back in Wyoming if she found a pay phone. The closest one would be in Lakeville, so walking away from the camp probably seemed like her best option.

Whether they liked her or not, the girls in Connie's tent were the last people at Camp Sloane to see her. They were all questioned, and none could offer a reason why Connie might have left. But if they had been picking on her, they certainly wouldn't have admitted it. They simply said that while they were making their beds before breakfast, Connie left the tent and returned with an ice pack from the infirmary for her face. When they returned from the mess hall later, the ice pack was on Connie's bunk, but she was nowhere to be found.

When the gatekeeper was finally informed that Connie was missing, he realized the girl he'd seen that morning hadn't been a staff member. He raced to his car and drove to Lakeville and back but didn't see her along the road.

Then, at 11:30 A.M., the camp director called the Connecticut State Police and then called Helen Smith at her parents' home in Greenwich. When Helen got the news, she immediately called her husband, Peter, back in Wyoming.

Peter Smith later theorized that maybe Connie had suffered amnesia after her fall. Yes, there's that pesky amnesia again. Although, in fairness, I grew up believing that I was in danger of being hit in the head and forgetting who I was at any time. I assumed amnesia would be a constant threat when I was an adult – like quicksand.

Instead of amnesia, it's more likely that Connie accepted a ride from someone who did her harm, even though her family maintained that it was out of character for her to get into a car with a stranger. They added that it also seemed unlike Connie to stop and ask for directions several times as she walked toward town, but we know she did.

What happened to Connie that made her leave the camp and start walking to a town she'd never been to and along roads she didn't know?

FORTUNATELY, THERE WAS A STATE POLICE BARRACKS in the town of Canaan, just 10 miles from the camp. Officers immediately searched the woods around Camp Sloane and alerted newspapers and radio stations in the region. They also sent bulletins to local railroad stations, taxi services, and bus companies. They also printed a missing-person flyer with Connie's photograph on it. It was distributed to law enforcement agencies in surrounding states.

On the flyer, Connie was described as five feet, five inches tall, 85 pounds, and suntanned. When she was last seen, she wore a bright red windbreaker, blue shorts with plaid cuffs, a halter top, and tan shoes. She also had a red ribbon tied into her brown hair. Investigators believed she had no money, food, or extra clothing with her.

A paragraph was added to her physical description that described her personality. This bit of writing is particularly heartbreaking in light of the fact that Connie had never been found:

She loves all animals, especially horses; likes to swim and is a fair swimmer; likes to color with crayons and read funny books; makes friends very easily with youngsters; can handle a baton but is not very good at it; and has a vivid imagination, especially about her animal friends – some of her creations are about a rattlesnake pet and her horse "Toni" (a white mare) that can twirl a baton.

Within hours of Connie's disappearance, the state police were stopping cars along the stretch of Route 44 between Lakeville and the New York state line. The two-lane highway was a major road that connected Plymouth, Massachusetts, with several New York counties west of the Hudson River. They stopped hundreds of motorists but found no trace of Connie.

On Thursday, July 17, the Associated Press picked up the story from a local newspaper, and it was soon published in papers across the country, including in Wyoming.

But Peter Smith didn't see the story in the *Casper Star-Tribune* because he was already in Connecticut to help with the search. He'd flown in on the evening Connie disappeared and joined up with police officers to lend whatever assistance he could. He was an imposing figure at six feet, seven inches, wearing a large cowboy hat and "dungarees" a few years before blue jeans were considered fashionable.

The newspapers emphasized that Connie's grandfather was a former governor of Wyoming and that the search for the missing girl would be thorough and well-financed. The Smith family had money – but no ransom demand was ever made. They did offer a $3,000 reward for information leading to Connie's whereabouts, but it was never claimed.

The police began rounding up the "usual suspects" in the area, but all were quickly cleared. State police planes and helicopters took to the skies, flying over roads, woods, rivers, and lakes. The Connecticut wing of the Civil Air Patrol soon joined the official aircraft. There were also flyovers from Westover Field in Massachusetts, which was then the largest military air facility in the northeastern United States.

At the same time, searchers with dogs were on the ground, making their way through the heavy woods and underbrush. Some speculated that Connie could have fallen into an abandoned quarry or iron mine, so volunteers put on hip boots and waded through marshes. The teams on the ground stayed in touch using portable two-way radios.

By July 20, Peter Smith had chartered a plane of his own to assist with the search. But after two days, he called off his aerial search because the thick summer foliage made it impossible to see the ground below. But he wasn't giving up. He rented a horse and began searching the forest that way.

Overhead, planes still buzzed across the sky, in any case. Five state police planes covered a 20-square-mile area, including parts of northwestern Connecticut, southwestern Massachusetts, and eastern New York.

When Sergeant Richard Chapman, one of the first investigators on the scene, spoke with reporters, he said, "We just turned the place upside-down looking for her."

AS THE SEARCH CONTINUED, THE CONNECTICUT State Police sent out a "nationwide alarm" using a teletype, a recent addition to communication tools used by law enforcement. They also prepared over 1,000 missing posters, distributed locally in stores, service stations, barber shops, and other frequently visited locations. They were also mailed to police and sheriff's offices across the United States and Canada.

But none of their efforts seemed to be getting results.

Connecticut State Police Commissioner Edward J. Hickey was quoted in newspapers as he urged his men to work harder. "I am not satisfied," he said, "that this girl or any young girl can disappear from the face of the earth for any long period. Remain alive and forsake all friendships long. Dig a bit deeper in this case. Go into the woods again and go deeper. Search the waterways again, and don't take anything for granted."

As always seems to happen with these kinds of cases, sightings of the missing girl began pouring into the authorities. One caller was sure he had seen Connie's face in the crowd at an Alabama football game. Another claimed she was spotted in New York with a band of "gypsies" who were working as itinerant painters and farm workers.

A runaway from an Indian reservation in Massachusetts – mistakenly identified as Connie – hitchhiked all the way to Texas before the police caught up with her.

No matter how strange, all leads were taken seriously and checked, unfortunately, without success. One anonymous tipster claimed Connie was dead and told the police her body was hidden in a freshly dug grave. She wasn't.

On a grim note, Connie's dental chart was published in the *Journal of the American Dental Association* in case any of the members were called on to identify her remains.

The police continued to search as summer turned to fall, and the leaves began falling from the trees. They undertook more aerial searches now that the ground could be seen. In addition, groups of horseback riders from the Connecticut Trail Riders Association covered dozens of miles of woodland near the camp. State game wardens, who patrolled the woods during hunting season, were given the missing flyers and told to be on the lookout for Connie's remains.

Helen made a heartfelt appeal in the *Hartford Courant*, asking local hunters to search for any clothing that could be her daughter's. "Each day is a little harder to face," she said. "We all know we might lose our children. But not to know what happened to her isn't human. Please do all you can."

And then Connie's case took a paranormal turn – in the form of a horse with psychic abilities.

The Smiths learned about Lady Wonder, an allegedly "clairvoyant" horse in Richmond, Virginia. For $1, the horse's owner allowed people to ask three questions, and the horse would reply to them by pecking her nose on a crude, oversized typewriter. Supposedly, she had helped in the case of a missing boy from Massachusetts, leading to the discovery of his remains.

When Peter asked Lady Wonder about Connie, the horse indicated that he should look for her in Los Angeles – so he did.

While there, Peter spoke with police officers and reporters and even appeared with host Art Linkletter on his daytime television variety show, *House Party*. The show was a mix of quizzes, musical groups, celebrity interviews, and his well-known "Kids Say the Darndest Things" segment, in which he interviewed young children. While on the show, assured he had a sympathetic audience, Peter made a plea for help in finding his daughter.

Viewers listened and one of them even responded – a man who sent the investigation completely off the rails.

HIS NAME WAS FREDERICK WALKER POPE, and on April 8, 1953, he staggered drunkenly into the police station in Washington Court House, Ohio. Soon, the 27-year-old itinerant jewelry salesman was shocking detectives with a tale of murder.

One of his victims, he said, was Connie Smith.

Pope said that on July 16, 1952, he and a friend, Jack Walker, had picked up the girl along a highway in Connecticut and offered to drive her home to Wyoming. But they never got there, he said. Instead, he pointed the car toward Arizona, and while there, his friend Walker had choked Connie to death.

Pope helped bury her, but then he claimed he killed Walker, sold the car, and ended up in a mental hospital in Waco, Texas. But after traveling to Ohio, he'd finally gotten his head straight and wanted to confess. "I'm ready to go back to Arizona and point out the graves," he told the cops.

Ohio and Arizona police were anxious to take him up on his offer. However, the Connecticut police wanted more details and then became skeptical when Pope couldn't remember any of the places where the trio had stayed during their cross-country jaunt. One detail that seemed convincing, though, was Pope recalling that Connie often talked about how tall her father was. He stressed this to the investigators, saying, "She told me he was a real big man."

A Connecticut detective flew to Ohio and interrogated Pope for eight hours. He also looked through the belongings that Pope had with him when he walked into the station and found a card from the Indiana Security Employment Division dated the day that Connie went missing. He couldn't have been in Connecticut when he said he'd been.

His story was a fraud – and a cry for help.

Pope admitted that he had made up the confession in hopes he'd been sent to a hospital to help him overcome his alcoholism. He also said that he'd gotten the information about Connie from a flyer he saw hanging in the post office and knew how tall Peter was because he'd seen him on Art Linkletter's television show. "That was my inspiration," he shrugged.

He also received information from another source – "Jack Walker." The name of his imaginary friend came from his two favorite drinks, Jack Daniels and Johnnie Walker.

This wouldn't be the last confession in Connie's case.

Six years later, in 1959, the police received another "confession" from a Connecticut garage mechanic named George J. Davies. He had been a person of interest since 1952 when he used a screwdriver to stab two young girls to death in Waterbury. Both had refused his sexual advances, and he killed them. Initially, when Davis was questioned about Connie, he said he hadn't seen her. In April 1959, though, while he was awaiting execution at the Connecticut State Penitentiary in Wethersfield, he claimed he'd killed Connie.

No one could be sure if Davis was seeking attention or if he had actually committed the crime, but again, the Connecticut State Police were skeptical. However, Davis did lead them to a sandy bank along a river near Litchfield, where he claimed to have buried the girl in a shallow grave. A crew spent an entire day excavating the place with shovels and a bulldozer, but they failed to find any trace of human remains. A coroner told a reporter that if anyone had been buried at that location, it was likely that floods could have washed the body away.

Had Davis – the so-called "Screwdriver Killer" – murdered Connie?

Nope, it was another lie. On his way to the electric chair, he asked to speak to state police lieutenant Wilbur Caulkins. "It was all a lie about Connie," Davis told him. "I raised the hopes of the girl's parents, and I don't want to go with this lie on my conscience."

ALTHOUGH FREDERICK POPE'S STORY ABOUT Connie being picked up, driven across the country, and murdered in Arizona was a hoax, it did force the police and her family to realize that Connie could have been kidnapped and taken anywhere – including Arizona.

In 1958, six years after Connie vanished, the body of a teenage girl – estimated to be between 13 and 17 years old – was found north of Flagstaff. She was believed to have been murdered and, when found, had been dead for approximately one year.

Called "Little Miss X," the girl's remains were buried in the county's potters' field, where the bodies of the unknown dead were laid to rest.

In 1962, after a tipster suggested that perhaps "Little Miss X" was Connie, the Connecticut police closely examined the Arizona case. At the time, some of the unidentified girl's remains were exhumed so that a pathologist and dentist could compare her teeth with Connie's dental records. Coconino County Undersheriff Clark Cole drove from Arizona to Wyoming with the unknown girl's skull and mandible in his car to meet with Connie's father, Peter, who took the lawman to their family dentist in Spearfish, South Dakota.

The dentist determined that four out of five points of identification between the skull and Connie's records matched. However, the skull had a filling that Connie did not. It's possible that an additional cavity could have been filled after Connie went missing and before the death of "Little Miss X," but that seems unlikely. There were some similarities, the dentist finally said, but they were not enough to make a positive identification.

The pathologist said the same thing – there were things that matched, but he couldn't say for certain that the dead girl was Connie.

THE SMITH FAMILY NEVER STOPPED THINKING ABOUT their lost daughter.

Connie's mother, Helen, died of a heart attack in 1961. Her grandfather, the former Wyoming governor, died in 1976. At the time of his death, Connie's brother, Nels, was speaker pro temp of the Wyoming House of Representatives. He had followed in his grandfather's footsteps.

In 1984, her father, Peter, was interviewed again about the search for Connie. He always believed that she may have hit her head when she fell off the platform of her tent and ended up with amnesia. He kept open the possibility that she was still alive. He told a reporter, "I think of her when I see a tall woman walk by who would be about her age. It's a perpetual hope that something will turn up."

Peter died in 2012, undoubtedly still hoping to see his daughter one last time.

The Connecticut State Police never really gave up on the case either. In March 1988, it was reopened after the arrest and conviction of a former carnival worker who had killed an eight-year-old girl back in 1951. After that cold case was solved, Nels was interviewed about the renewed interest in Connie's case. He told a reporter, "The uncertainty of the disappearance is the worst agony that the family could go through. If this would resolve the case, it would be a relief."

But there was no relief. The case soon cooled off again.

In 2004, Nels gave his DNA to the FBI, and the agency entered it into their national database, making it available for comparison with any remains thought to be Connie's, then and in the future.

So far, though, there have been no matches, and the many mysteries surrounding the disappearance of Connie Smith remain unsolved. Why did she leave the camp that day? Where did she go? And who took her?

Perhaps someday, we'll have those answers.

1961: BLOOD ON THE KITCHEN FLOOR
THE DISAPPEARANCE OF JOAN RISCH

WHEN A WOMAN NAMED JOAN RISCH VANISHED FROM her home in Lincoln, Massachusetts, on October 24, 1961, it wasn't supposed to happen.

The 31-year-old mother of two young children disappeared from one of the most affluent residential communities north of Boston, where serious crimes just didn't occur.

No one heard or saw an attack, even though neighbors were home in the houses around Joan's residence. Two male neighbors were working in a garage less than 100 feet from the Risch house, but like everyone else, they didn't see or hear a thing. Joan's neighbor across the street was watching Joan's daughter when it happened. Joan's son was in the house with her when she disappeared.

It shouldn't have happened – not in that town, not in that neighborhood. And yet it did. Joan Risch vanished, leaving a grieving husband, two children, and a kitchen streaked with blood behind.

And she was never seen again.

SHE WAS BORN JOAN BARD ON MAY 12, 1930, the only child of Harold and Josephine Bard of Brooklyn, New York. The family later moved to the Chicago area because of Harold's job, but later, they returned east and settled in New Jersey.

Joan was a studious child and a little introverted. She loved to read and didn't date much as a teenager, but she developed warm and lasting friendships as she got older. She grew up in a happy, upper-middle-class family, but her formative years were not without trauma. In 1939, her parents died in a

Joan Risch in a formal portrait on the left, but the snapshot on the right was likely more how'd she want to be remembered – as a happy wife and mother.

house fire while Joan was away visiting her maternal grandmother in Brooklyn, leaving the eight-year-old an orphan.

Heartbroken after the fire, Joan was living with her grandmother when her mother's sister, Alice, and Alice's husband, Frank Nattrass, entered the little girl's life. They invited Joan to come and live with them in New Rochelle, New York, and she accepted. They subsequently adopted her, changing her last name from Bard to Nattrass.

In 1940, Joan was the oldest of the four children in the Nattrass home. She turned 10 in May of that year, and the couple's three biological sons were Peter, age 7, James, 6, and David, 4. In 1946, Alice gave birth to a daughter, Evelyn.

Joan continued to live with the family until she left for college in 1948, and later, there would be accusations made against Frank Nattrass that he had molested Joan at some point during that time. But these allegations were never proven. Joan only hinted at them when she told her husband, Martin, her adopted brother, Peter, and some of her friends. She told Alice in 1961, and at least one relative, her maternal uncle, James, witnessed indications of possible abuse. However, Frank denied the accusations and was never prosecuted for such offenses.

Whatever happened, it didn't interfere with Joan's schoolwork. She was always regarded as a good student and graduated with honors from high school. After graduation, she enrolled at Wilson College in Chambersburg, Pennsylvania. She majored in English literature and graduated in 1952. While attending the private liberal arts women's college, she wrote poetry for the student literary review and became the assistant editor of her class yearbook. Although still slow to make new friendships, she was elected vice president of her class and vice president of the International Relations Club.

Later in life, she remained deeply interested in reading literature and stayed knowledgeable about foreign affairs and other subjects to which she was likely first introduced at Wilson College.

After graduation, Joan moved to New York City and began working in the publishing business. She started as a secretary at Harcourt Brace & World, Inc., but soon moved into a secretarial management position. She remained at Harcourt for the next four years and became an executive secretary with management responsibilities for Jack Gallagher, the executive in charge of the college book division. When Gallagher moved over to Thomas Y. Crowell Co., another New York publisher, in 1956, he asked Joan to go with him, and she did.

As many young working women did in the 1950s, Joan shared her Manhattan apartment with several other girls. The small group became close and shared two different apartments over the next two years, but then, in 1954, Joan made a very strange choice – she moved back to the Nattrass home in New Rochelle.

Apparently, she moved back at Alice's request, hoping to reconcile with her adopted parents. No one other than her roommates knew about the allegations of abuse at that time, and Joan didn't talk about it. She loved Alice, so she agreed to move back, even though she later said she was "unhappy" during the year she lived there.

It was not a happy time for Joan, but in late 1955, she married Martin Risch, and they moved to an apartment in Brooklyn. If she disliked the Natrass home as much as she said she did, getting away from there must have been a relief.

Joan had been introduced to Martin by one of her roommates, Anne Ellsworth. In the fall of 1953, Anne attended a Harvard football game with her boyfriend and invited Jane to come along as a blind date for Martin, who was then attending Harvard Business School.

The two young women spent a long weekend in Cambridge, and a friend later recalled that when they returned, Joan told her, "I'd like to get back to Harvard again soon. I have met the man I'd like to marry."

Joan and Martin soon became a couple, and they managed a long-distance relationship over the next two years while Martin completed his studies at the business school. Joan was still working in New York, but Martin's parents lived on Long Island, so he was in the city frequently. At some point, they became engaged.

On the day after Christmas – December 26, 1955 – Joan and Martin were married in Huntington, Long Island. Friends and relatives described both as "deliriously happy."

A few days after the wedding, the newlyweds moved to an apartment in Brooklyn Heights. They lived there for the next two-and-a-half years, and it became the first home for their daughter Lillian, who was born in May 1957.

While living in Brooklyn Heights, Martin worked for the Riegel Paper Company. By then, Joan had moved to Thomas Y. Crowell with her boss, Jack Gallagher, but she only worked with him for a few more months. After Lillian was born, she stayed home full-time to take care of the baby.

By the middle of 1958, Joan and Martin started looking for a house in the suburbs that would still allow Martin a reasonable commute to work. In September, they moved to a small house in Ridgefield, Connecticut. It had a rural feel, which the Rischs liked, and it was only a 45-minute trip for Martin into the city.

Joan, perhaps shedding some of the shyness she'd had since she was a child, made many new friends in Ridgefield. Joan's neighbors all seemed to love her. Olga Madden was one of her best friends at the time. She later said, "Everyone here who knew her loved her. She was the most thoughtful person I have ever known. She was the kind of person who'd go out of her way to do things for people."

Joan seemed to love her life in Ridgefield. Her life was centered around her home. Her neighbor across the street, Alice Wesley, described her as a "very happy person."

Joan had two children to care for after the birth of her son, David, in September 1959. She was thrilled with the new addition.

One of her neighbors said, "That girl lived for nothing but her home, husband, and children."

And her books. And the outdoors. She often walked with her children to the library or along a wooded path or country road. She loved to get outside and wanted to instill a passion for the outdoors in her kids. Joan often walked with Lillian and pushed David in his carriage.

Joan also got involved with local politics. She joined the League of Women Voters soon after moving to Ridgefield and was active in the organization.

In 1960, Martin left Riegel for a position with a veteran New England operation, the Fitchburg Paper Company. Since his new employer had a sales office in New York, the family wasn't required to move – until Martin received a promotion to the company's headquarters in Fitchburg, Massachusetts, in 1961.

Moving from Ridgefield to Lincoln, Massachusetts, in 1961 couldn't have been easy for Joan. She'd finally made many friends, and she'd be leaving them all behind. Not to mention, she'd be moving even farther away from the relatives she was close with.

Like Ridgefield, though, Lincoln was more country than town and promised peace and safety for the family while offering easy access to books, shopping, entertainment, restaurants, and good schools. It also allowed Joan to renew her friendship with an old college classmate named Sabra Morton, who lived in Bedford, one town away from Lincoln.

The Rischs moved into their new home in Lincoln on April 13, 1961. After the move, Martin began commuting by car or train to his new job at Fitchburg Paper, and Lillian and David began making new friends in the Old Bedford Road neighborhood. Joan started making the new house into a home the family could love.

As she'd always been, Joan was slow to make new friends. Martin wasn't much better. For example, George Robichaud and his wife lived next door but didn't meet the Rischs until mid-July, three months after the family had moved in. The Robichauds were sitting in their backyard one evening when Joan came over with the children and introduced herself. Even by October, however, they still hadn't met Martin.

Another woman who lived two houses away would later say she never met the Rischs at all. This implied that perhaps it wasn't

The Risch home in Lincoln, Massachusetts, from which Joan disappeared, leaving a strange crime scene behind.

just Joan and Martin. People in the neighborhood didn't seem that eager to meet anyone new.

Even so, Joan did renew her friendship with Sabra Morton. They often met at each other's homes and took walks at Walden Ponds and other places.

She also got back in touch with another Wilson College classmate, Sidney Harvey, who lived in nearby Lexington with her husband. Sidney visited Joan's home four of five times, she later recalled, and if Joan hadn't disappeared, she and her children had plans to come to Sidney's house the following day.

Joan and neighbors Barbara Barker and Mary Jane Butler arranged a mutual babysitting service with each other. Each took turns watching children for the others while the women took care of shopping, ran errands, or just needed some time to themselves. Joan became closest to Barbara because her son, Douglas, was near Lillian's age, and they played together well. Often, when

Lillian was at the Barker home, and David was napping, Joan squeezed in a little time to read, write, or watch the news on television.

The Rischs lived a normal, ordinary, suburban life when Joan vanished in October 1961. Martin left the house each morning and drove or took the train to work unless he had to travel somewhere for business. Joan stayed at home with the children. She cooked, cleaned, and tried to keep herself busy with friends, neighbors, books, and outdoor walks.

There was nothing strange about the evening of October 23 – the night before Joan disappeared. The family had dinner together, the children went to bed, and Joan and Martin relaxed a bit. Two days later, Martin recalled for the police that he and Joan each had a glass of whiskey that Monday evening, which finished a bottle. The police found that bottle in the trash can the next day.

Martin had an overnight trip planned for work the following day. He'd be leaving early, so the couple didn't stay up very late that night.

Martin was up before 6:30 A.M. to get ready for this trip. Joan and the children were still in bed when he showered and dressed. He said goodbye to Joan, and she wished him good luck.

Martin would never see his wife again.

The Rischs parked their cars in the garage, and Martin backed his 1957 Plymouth onto Old Bedford Road and headed toward Boston's Logan Airport. His Eastern Airlines shuttle to New York's La Guardia left Boston at 8:00 A.M. The flight crew would later recall seeing him on the flight.

He arrived at La Guardia a little after 9:00 on Tuesday morning. He made some telephone calls and then went to his first meeting. He'd be busy for the seven hours, mostly in the company of Arthur Kaufman, with whom he'd have lunch at an Armenian restaurant. Later in the day, he checked into the Commodore Hotel. The Roosevelt Hotel, where he usually stayed, didn't have any vacancies.

Just after 11:00 P.M. that night, the telephone in Martin's room rang with harrowing news – his wife was missing.

NO ONE KNOWS WHAT TIME JOAN AND THE children got up on the morning of October 24, but by 9:15, they were dressed and had eaten breakfast. Joan made the beds, did the dishes, and straightened the house.

Something occurred that morning that put them behind schedule, but no one knows what that was. Sabra Morton called Joan at 9:20, and she said Joan was in a hurry. She and Lillian had dentist appointments at Dr. Paul J. Goldstein's office in Bedford, and they were running late. The call with Sabra was short. Joan dropped David off with Barbara Barker and hurried on her way.

Then Joan and Lillian, in her faded blue 1951 Chevrolet, backed out of the garage and drove off to the dentist's office. Later that day, Joan's car would be found parked halfway up the driveway when the police arrived at the house.

THE DENTAL OFFICE WAS FIVE MILES AWAY from the Risch home along Great Road in Bedford. It likely took them about 10 minutes to get there.

Joan had started seeing Dr. Goldstein on Sabra's recommendation. She'd had one previous appointment with him on October 6 and was probably not thrilled that he'd found 11 cavities in seven teeth, but she seemed to like him. Dr. Goldstein examined Lillian and filled one additional cavity for Joan while she was there. While he was working on Joan, Lillian played in a nearby room with some toys in it. She was on her best behavior, which made Joan happy enough to mention it to Barbara when she returned to her house a little before 11:00 to pick up David.

The police later spoke to Dr. Goldstein, and he recalled that Joan said she was happy with her new home and was getting along well with her neighbors. Nothing in the way she spoke or acted seemed to suggest she was worried or depressed.

Joan had also spoken with Betsy Lindburg, a dental assistant. She paid for the visits for herself and Lillian and made an appointment to return for further work on October 31.

After leaving the dentist's office at 10:15, Lillian and Joan did some shopping. She picked up some clothing at the local W.T. Grant store and bought a few lunch and dinner items at a supermarket. After that, they returned home.

While Joan and Lillian were gone, several routine things occurred at the house on Old Bedford Road. The garbage man stopped at the house to empty their cans, the mail was delivered, and the milkman dropped off a delivery at the side door to the

Rischs' kitchen. Their regular milkman, Bernard Socket, was on vacation, and his foreman filled in for him. In November, after Socket returned from his trip, he told police that on Thursday, October 19, he saw a strange car backed into the Risch driveway. His description of the vehicle would match one seen by another witness on the day Joan disappeared.

But not yet. When Joan returned home that morning, everything in the Old Bedford Road neighborhood seemed perfectly normal.

AFTER RETURNING HOME AT 11:00 A.M. ON October 24, Joan and Lillian walked over to the Barker house to pick up David. She stayed for a few minutes, chatting with Barbara -- who noticed nothing unusual about her friend – and then Joan took the children home, put away her groceries, and changed into a dress, a sweater, and white tennis shoes with blue piping.

At 11:15, Walton Coburn from Dud's Cleaners in Concord stopped by for a regular pick-up. He knew that Joan didn't lock her door, but he knocked on the kitchen door and she let him in. They spoke for a few minutes, and he later described the conversation as "cheerful" and "friendly" and noted nothing unusual about it. Martin had two suits that needed to be picked up, and Joan went upstairs to get them, along with two of her skirts. She handed over the clothes, and Walton left with a wave. He had only been at the house for five minutes.

After Coburn left, Joan made lunch for herself and the kids. As was her routine at noon, she put David down for a nap. He usually slept for at least two hours, which, depending on what Lillian was doing, gave Joan some time to herself.

Once David was in his crib, she cleared the lunch dishes, cleaned the kitchen, and likely went into the living room with Lillian. The police later found a copy of a book Joan was reading open and face down on the kitchen table.

At 1:20 P.M., Barbara Barker let her son, Douglas, walk to the Risch house to play with Lillian. Where Joan was during the next hour is unclear. She may have worked inside, outside in the garden, or may have been reading in the kitchen. At one point, Barbara looked out and saw her son and Lillian playing in front of the Risch garage, and she spotted Joan in the garden. The police later found fresh plant cutting in a trash barrel. Everything seemed normal up until that point.

At 1:55 P.M., Joan decided to walk Lillian and Douglas across the street to the Barker house. She brought Lillian's tricycle along with the children. She left the two children but didn't speak with Barbara.

Some have since speculated that perhaps Joan knew there was danger, got the children out of harm's way, and then returned to get David. But the fact that she said nothing to Barabra suggests to me that she had no idea her family was at risk. It's almost certain that Joan would have raised the alarm or told Barbara to call for help. The Lincoln police department was only five minutes away, and Mr. Robichaud and a friend of his were a short distance away and would have assisted her.

I don't think Joan had any idea she was in danger.

Even though she was only four years old, Lillian was carefully questioned later that day, but she didn't remember seeing a second car in her driveway or near her house that day. She also didn't see any strangers in the neighborhood.

When Joan left the children in the front yard of the Barker home, she told them, "I'll be back." It seemed she needed to do something at home that would be difficult with two children playing unattended in her front yard. However, Barbara didn't see Joan bring them over, so she had no idea they were there for several minutes.

Why did Joan bring the two children over to Barbara's house? The simplest answer is that she wanted to wake David up from his nap and either wanted to do something with him that would take her full attention, or she wanted to get him up so she could read, write a letter, or make a phone call.

Another possibility is that Joan planned to meet someone that afternoon. If she did, Martin knew nothing about it. He later mentioned Joan's dentist's appointment and the cleaning pick-up to the police but said nothing about a meeting.

What about a boyfriend? Was Joan having an affair? Everyone who knew her said it was out of character for her and denied the possibility. It also seemed unlikely she'd do so with David in the house and soon getting up from his nap. An afternoon tryst seemed unlikely, especially since nighttime – with the kids asleep and Martin out of town – would be a better time. There seemed to be nothing in Joan's past to suggest she was unfaithful, and the police never discovered anything that even hinted at an affair during their investigation into her disappearance.

Again, the most obvious answer is that Joan wanted a little time to read and relax before David woke up, so she took Lillian and Douglas across the street to Barbara's house. Why didn't she tell Barbara? It was probably because she knew they were safe there, and she had little time before David woke up. Why bother Barbara for such a short amount of time?

Knowing what happened next, it can be tempting to try and line up the events of the day in a way that makes them point toward the tragedy to come, but I don't think there was any way to predict what would occur before 4:33 that afternoon.

THE LAST TIME ANYONE SAW JOAN RISCH was on October 24 at 2:15 P.M. The Barker house directly faced the Risch home across the street, but trees at the front of both properties blocked most of the view. Regardless, looking out her kitchen window, Barbara could see the Risch house and the top of their driveway. Joan's car was parked there, and she later said she saw Joan in the driveway at 2:15.

Aside from Joan, though, we can't be sure what else she saw. From the two different statements she gave to the police, it's not clear whether she said everything the police credited her with saying. In one statement, she said she saw Joan running beside her car and something red. "I thought she was chasing a child, and the child was wearing a red jacket. She was running with her arms outstretched."

That same day, in another statement, she said that Joan ran to the car and then went back to the house again, and she saw something red.

Months later, in March 1962, in another interview, Barbara said that she'd put training wheels on her son's bicycle around 2:00 P.M. and then went into the kitchen with Douglas and Lillian. Barbara heard a sound outside. "It was Mrs. Risch, I'm sure," she said. "It was a shouting type or noise, more or less scolding or anger, rather than screaming or anguish." She couldn't make out any words.

Looking out her kitchen window, Barbara saw Joan's face and the top part of her body. She saw her for four or five seconds, running the length of her car and then stopping. Barbara told detectives, "She was hurrying, not sprinting, but she was moving fast. Then she seemed to veer away from the drive and go in – as if chasing an evasive child. That is what came to my mind at the time."

Barbara added, "I do have a recollection of something red. At the time, I thought it was the jacket of a child in front of her, and it sort of crystallized that idea of chasing the child because I thought I saw the child in a red jacket. Whatever it was, it was low and close to her."

Barbara showed enough interest in what was happening outside the window that Lillian or Douglas asked her what she was looking at. Barbara replied that she was watching Lillian's mother chasing something. One of the children said, "Oh, she's chasing David. He's run into the street." That offhanded comment planted itself in Barbara's head, she believed because she'd been thinking the same thing. She probably wouldn't have thought about the incident again if Joan hadn't disappeared.

AT 3:25 P.M., 13-YEAR-OLD VIRGINIA KEENE WAS dropped off by her school bus at the end of Old Bedford Road. On her way home, she passed by the Risch house, and when she did, she noticed a gray car parked in the Risch driveway. She identified it as a 1954 Plymouth, and it may have had Massachusetts license plates, but she wasn't sure – she just knew that it wasn't one of the cars driven by her neighbors, Joan and Martin.

A short time later, at 3:40 P.M., Hilda Ziegler was driving past and paused to allow that same gray Plymouth to back out of the Risch driveway. It passed by her car, but Hilda noticed nothing unusual about it and didn't pay attention to the occupants.

Five more minutes passed, and Barbara Barker began getting ready to leave for a shopping trip to Concord. Since Lillian was still at her house, she glanced across the street to make sure Joan was home. Barbara saw Joan's car parked in the driveway, so she sent Lillian across the street to the Risch house. Everything seemed normal. She had no reason to believe that Joan wasn't there.

Lillian entered the house through the unlocked kitchen door. She could hear her little brother upstairs crying, but the house was silent otherwise. She didn't see or hear her mother anywhere.

To four-year-old Lillian, it looked as though someone had splashed red paint all over the kitchen floor and spattered it on the walls. A small table was overturned in the hallway that led

One of the crime scene photos of the kitchen

from the kitchen to the hall steps. A trash can, a roll of drawing paper, and assorted books and magazines were scattered across the floor.

This was the kind of mess that upset the little girl. Lillian's mother never allowed the house to look like that. She finally called out nervously to her mother. No one answered. She only heard David crying – a sound that her mother would usually take care of quickly.

Lillian, showing more bravery than most adults would have under the same circumstances, went upstairs, checked on David – he was wet but safe – and spent about 30 minutes playing in the bedroom with him. She was sure that her mother would return to take care of her and her brother at any moment, but she didn't.

She waited as long as she could, but when she saw Barbara and Douglas return from their shopping trip, she hurried across the street to the Barker home.

More bloodstains are visible in a second photo of the kitchen

Barbara returned at 4:15 P.M. She had seen Joan's car in her driveway when she turned into her own and assumed all was well. After bringing her shopping bags inside, Barbara telephoned a friend and spoke with her for a few minutes. When she hung up, she was startled to see Lillian standing outside her door.

Lillian needed help. David was in his crib, wet and crying; the kitchen was a mess, and her mother was not in the house.

Knowing that Joan would never leave her children alone in the house for any amount of time, Barbara immediately became concerned. With a sense of foreboding, Barbara walked to the Risch home with Lillian, Douglas, and her oldest son, Glenn.

Barbara entered the house and was paralyzed by what she saw. Blood spattered and smeared all over the kitchen. It was on the floor, the walls, the counter, everywhere. The telephone's handset was pulled from its cradle and dangled on the rim of the trash can, which was usually stored under the sink. It was now sitting in the middle of the floor. A beer carton was resting next to it. Down the hall, Barbara saw the floor was haphazardly covered with papers, books, and magazines.

Shocked, she called out to Joan but, like Lillian, got no response. She opened the basement door and called down the stairs. Again, no one replied.

Barbara could hear David upstairs crying, and she needed to attend to him. Shaking, she gripped Lillian's hand as she walked through the house to the front hall staircase. Her heart pounded as she climbed the steps, unsure if she would be attacked by some intruder or perhaps find Joan's body lying in one of the rooms.

She cautiously looked into each second-floor room as she walked toward the nursery but found no one. Quickly gathering David, some dry clothes, and a clean diaper, Barbara and Lillian hurried downstairs. They met the boys outside and went straight across the street to the Barker home.

As soon as she could, Barbara called Mary Jane Butler to see if Joan might be there – she wasn't. At Barbara's urging, Mary Jane walked down the street to the Risch home, where she met Barbara at the end of the driveway.

The two women entered Joan's house again and searched more carefully for their friend. They agreed they shouldn't touch anything. After walking through the first floor, Mary Jane blurted out that she couldn't stand to be inside anymore and went out to the yard to look for Joan. Barbara stayed to finish the search but soon became convinced that Joan wasn't there.

Outside, Mary Jane told Barbara to call the police while she returned home to try and reach Martin at his office in Fitchburg – not knowing that he was traveling.

Barbara's hands were still shaking when she picked up the telephone at 4:33 P.M. and called the Lincoln Police Department.

LINCOLN PATROLMAN MIKE MCHUGH SPENT most of his day on October 24 doing routine traffic control for a telephone construction crew. Before his shift ended, he stopped by the police station and found dispatcher John Ciraso on the telephone with Barbara Barker. After McHugh was filled on the call, he left the station and arrived at the Risch home about five minutes later.

As he was getting out of his car, Barbara quickly approached from across the street and blurted out, "Something terrible has happened, and Joan is missing!"

McHugh walked up to the house with Barbara as she quickly explained the situation. He left her outside and entered the house, immediately seeing the same bloody kitchen scene that Barbara, Lillian, and Mary Jane had.

McHugh first wondered if he might be dealing with a suicide – although I'm not sure why – and searched the house for a body. Finding nothing, he walked the house's perimeter, looking for any clues. Aside from the mess in the kitchen, nothing seemed out of place. He returned to the kitchen and called the police station. He told William Whalen – who had taken over for Ciraso as the dispatcher – to send Chief Leo Algeo and Sergeant Daniel MacInnis to the Risch home as soon as possible. He needed more officers to search the woods behind the house.

McHugh also directed Whalen to call doctors and hospitals to see if Joan was with any of them. Whalen made calls for the next two hours, speaking to hospitals, the state police, taxi companies who might have picked Joan up, and Martin's employer in Fitchburg.

Mary Jane Butler was also trying to reach Martin. She needed him to know that Joan was missing, but his children were safe. She eventually reached Andrew Bonelli, who shared an office with Martin, but he told her that Martin was in New York on business. Later, the police finally tracked down Bob Larson, one of Martin's staff members, and he got through to Martin at 11:00 P.M. Martin was asleep in his room at the Commodore Hotel.

By that time, Lincoln's small police department was gathered at the Risch home. It didn't take long for Chief Algeo, Sergeant MacInnis, and Officer McHugh to agree that Joan had likely been abducted from her home and either taken away in a vehicle or on foot through the woods.

Barbara was interviewed by officers and gathered the details of what had happened that afternoon. Meanwhile, Chief Algeo led another sweep of the house, finding more blood on the wall near where the telephone was kept, the door frame between the kitchen and dining room, and the telephone itself. Somehow, Sergeant McHugh had managed not to smear it when he'd used the phone.

Almost all the blood in the house was dry except for a few spots where it had pooled on the floor. With the table overturned, the scattered books and papers, and the telephone receiver pulled off the hook, the chief believed it pointed to a struggle. Strangely, they found the telephone directory book was open to a page that listed local emergency numbers. There was no 9-1-1 system in 1961.

By evening, Lieutenant George Harnois and Detective Joe Ryan of the Massachusetts State Police were also on the scene, as was the county district attorney, John Droney. From the start, Joan's disappearance was treated as a high priority by all involved.

The nearby woods were searched using bloodhounds provided by the state police, but there was no trace of Joan. The dogs were followed by uniformed officers and neighborhood volunteers, but like the dogs, they found nothing. A bulletin went out to law enforcement agencies across the region, but hours passed, and no sightings of the missing woman were reported.

Joan's husband,
Martin Risch

IN NEW YORK CITY, MARTIN RISCH WAS TRYING desperately to get back to Boston and home. After dinner, Martin went to bed but was awakened by Bob Larson at 11:00 P.M. He had been trying to reach Martin at the Roosevelt Hotel, where he usually stayed, which is why it had taken so long to reach him.

Immediately, Martin called the state police barracks in Concord and was given the details about what had happened that afternoon with his wife and children. After hanging up the telephone, he checked out of the hotel and caught a taxi to the airport. He managed to get a flight and was back in Boston at 1:15 A.M. The state police picked him up, but instead of taking him home, they took him to the Concord barracks, where five state police detectives and two Lincoln police officers questioned him for the next two hours.

He offered a complete list of his activities from the previous day, from leaving home that morning to telephone calls, meetings, dinner, the hotel where he'd stayed, and everyone he'd talked with during the day. Martin described Joan as shy and quiet and said her daily routine rarely changed. He stressed that she never left the children alone. He did admit that Joan often allowed traveling door-to-door salesmen to make their pitches because she was just too nice to close the door in their faces. Aside from that, he couldn't imagine letting anyone she didn't know into the house.

Marin signed a witness statement that morning, but before he was taken home, he was asked about the contents of the trashcan in the kitchen. The police had found the whiskey bottle that he and Joan had finished on Sunday night, along with three coffee cans, a cider bottle, four applesauce jars, three baby food jars, three wax paper cups, four frozen juice cans, one peanut butter jar, a jam jar, a broken teacup, a broken plastic coat hanger, and five beer bottles. There was also an empty can of Franco-American spaghetti on top of the can and a Miller beer carton on the floor beside it. Martin could account for all of it except for the empty beer bottles.

LATER THAT DAY, THE LINCOLN POLICE contacted the FBI and notified them of Joan's disappearance. They offered their assistance with the investigation.

Samples of the blood found in the kitchen were sent to the laboratory at Harvard University, as well as more blood that was found outside in the driveway. There was a trail of blood between the kitchen door and Joan's car, including small stains on the sidewalk and the small stoop outside the door.

Joan's 1951 Chevrolet had four separate and distinct bloodstains on it: on the front and rear of the car. Strangely, a coat hanger was found sitting on top of the vehicle. It didn't appear that anyone had tried to open the doors, and nothing inside the car looked disturbed.

The blood was later analyzed and determined to be Type O, consistent with Joan's blood type. The amount of blood that was spilled in the kitchen was estimated to be less than one-half pint, even though it looked like more. While the amount of blood found seemed to indicate that Joan hadn't been murdered, the entire scene did suggest violence so that she might have been beaten or suffocated.

Sergeant Daniel Desmond, the state police fingerprint expert and photographer, found several fingerprints in the kitchen. They also found many latent fingerprints and partial palm prints – but most were later determined to belong to Martin and, eventually,

Joan. The police didn't have anything of hers to compare them with at first. However, they later found fingerprints that were on file at Joan's elementary school, courtesy of a New York law that was enacted after the Lindbergh baby kidnapping.

There was, however, a thumbprint on the loose telephone receiver and a partial print on the wall around the corner from the kitchen that did not come from any member of the Risch family or any other known source. No match to the set of unknown prints has ever been found.

THE SEARCHES OF THE SURROUNDING WOODS continued in the following days. Searchers covered nearly 15 square miles the following day, scouring the area from "dawn to dusk." In addition to dozens of volunteers, the search team included 20 state troopers, 60 air policemen from the nearby Hanscom Air Force Base, 20 state conservation officers, Lincoln police officers, and two helicopters.

Alleged psychic Peter Hurkos

Joan's body was never found, but it certainly wasn't for the lack of trying. Peter Hurkos, a psychic who had been brought in late to the "Boston Strangler" case because investigators were under extreme pressure to find the killer, also assisted in Joan's case. Hurkos told police that Joan was buried somewhere in the woods under a gray blanket but was unable to pinpoint the exact location. Although the police expected him to return to Lincoln for further investigation, he never did.

The searches continued for the next week near the Risch home. Police officers and dogs spread out through the area repeatedly, but nothing was found. They extended the search to other woods in the area, dragged ponds and lakes, and even sent almost 100 divers into the deeper rivers and reservoirs, which, according to the *Boston Globe,* was "the biggest civilian underwater search in New England history, involving 12 skin diving clubs."

The police also investigated reports of a woman being seen on two highways in different areas after Joan disappeared. The woman, who matched Joan's general appearance, was said to be "dazed and bloody," but whoever she was, she was never found.

One of the roads where a "dazed and bloody" woman was seen. It was speculated that it might be Joan, but she was never found.

By October 28, relatives in Connecticut, New York, Florida, and California had been contacted about the disappearance, but nothing had turned up. A nationwide bulletin that contained Joan's photograph and description was sent to police departments in 50 states. It included the information that she might be traveling in a "light blue or gray 1955 or 1956 sedan." But the bulletin, like the search, turned up no clues.

The police investigation also focused on Martin Risch, but they found nothing to implicate him in his wife's disappearance. There was no evidence of disagreements, an affair, or anything else that might have caused him to kill his wife or make her disappear.

He did everything he could to help with the investigation. Despite his natural desire to keep to himself, he replied to every request for police information and urged the case to move forward when it seemed to be lagging. He even sent letters to Massachusetts Governor Chub Peabody and FBI Director J. Edgar Hoover, asking for more resources to be put toward his wife's case.

His later life also seemed to confirm his innocence. While he raised his children with the help of housekeepers and relatives, Martin never remarried during the remaining 47 years of his life, and he never left Lincoln.

He wanted Joan to be able to find him if she ever came home.

THE INVESTIGATION DRAGGED ON. AS IT COOLED down, it went from a full-on run to a crawl.

On January 3, 1962, the *Boston Record-American* offered a $5,000 reward to interest the public in the search for Joan. The newspaper printed several pages detailing Joan's activities on October 24, 1961, on an hour-by-hour basis. There was an analysis of the crime scene, the blood, and the discovery of the unknown fingerprints. While the story generated no leads of substance, the police were kept busy following up on the false leads, and crank calls that seem to follow in the wake of every disappearance that gets publicity.

The police checked out a call from a woman who'd seen a two-toned blue car near Old Bedford Road on the day Joan disappeared. The driver had gotten out of the vehicle, cut some tree branches, placed them in his car, and drove away. Wasn't that odd?

A woman from a taxi company called. None of her drivers had picked up Joan when she vanished, but a man named Harold Munder had been in the office that day, trying to send a telegram to his brother and acting strangely. Munder turned out to be an outpatient from the V.A. Hospital in Bedford, and his alibi checked out.

The owner of a Bedford motel said someone fitting Joan's description had checked in at 4:00 P.M. on October 24 and then left an hour later. She was distraught, crying, and had no luggage. The story was checked out, but the woman's signature – Patricia Richardson – was not Joan's. Plus, the woman was a heavy smoker, unlike Joan. It turned out the woman really was named Patricia Richardson, and she was quickly eliminated from the case.

Another tip was called in by a cab driver who was positive that he'd picked up Joan in Boston and driven her to Lexington. He hadn't.

And so it went. The police checked each sighting, but none of the leads panned out.

TO THIS DAY, THE DISAPPEARANCE OF JOAN RISCH remains a mystery. It was one of New England's most widely covered news stories in late 1961 and early 1962, and yet, no solid evidence of what happened to Joan has ever been discovered.

As was the case at the time, most believed that an intruder abducted Joan and probably murdered her – but why? And how?

No strangers were reported in the area by neighbors. No one was seen lurking in the woods or driving up and down the roadways.

And if Joan was murdered, who did it?

Martin Risch – Joan's husband – was the first suspect, but he wasn't home at the time, and the police could find nothing that linked him to the crime. There were no marital problems, affairs, or other issues.

After finding out about Joan's accusations of her stepfather's sexual abuse, investigators looked closely at Frank Nattrass and brought him in for questioning about Joan's disappearance. During the interrogations, he denied abusing Joan and having anything to do with her vanishing. He was apparently cleared in 1963, or the police could never find enough evidence to charge him with anything. He later moved to Los Angeles and died in 1969.

The police also investigated several colleagues of Martin's at the paper company. His boss, Ben Moates, had a reputation for womanizing, and the New England sales manager, William Lawrence, had a shaky alibi. However, none of the men he worked with were ever implicated in Joan's disappearance.

If Joan was abducted and murdered, it was most likely done by a stranger, but their identity remains unknown. The police investigated over 100 tradesmen, salespeople, and service providers who visited the Risch home or worked on Old Bedford Road. They also looked at convicted burglars, sex offenders, and minor criminals in the area.

Beyond that, they interviewed Joan's neighbors, classmates, business colleagues, doctors, dentists, and insurance men. They visited taxi companies, hospitals, mental institutions, and motels and sent notices to publishing companies, restaurants, and libraries to keep a lookout for Joan. They also assisted with interviews of the thousands of officers and enlisted men at Hanscom Air Force Base.

The strangest thing about this story is that whoever the abductor and killer was, he never struck again. No one committed multiple crimes in the area, following the same general method.

Whoever this man was, he disappeared just as completely as Joan Risch did in October 1961.

IT HAS ALSO BEEN SUGGESTED THAT PERHAPS JOAN left on her own and staged her disappearance. Based on every description of her as a happy wife and caring mother who enjoyed her life in Lincoln, this seems hard to believe.

How would she start this new life under the circumstances of her disappearance? She left home without cash, credit cards, her purse, keys, or a car. The police found no evidence that she had stashed away money to fund her new life, and none of her close relatives were wealthy. Telephone records didn't indicate that Joan had sought employment anywhere, and there was no evidence that she had a secret lover or anyone else willing to help her create a new identity. Most importantly, the crime scene didn't appear to be staged. The physical evidence left at the house doesn't point to Joan voluntarily leaving her family.

Joan had no secret lover, rich relatives, or accomplices to help her, and she had no reason to leave her family. In every case, Joan was described as a "girl who lived for nothing but her home, husband, and children." Was it possible that Joan had a secret life? Of course, it is. But is it likely? No, it isn't. Joan seems to be the kind of person that what you saw with her was what you got. She loved her husband and kids, and she wouldn't leave them. If she did, leaving a bloody crime scene behind would be too dramatic for a woman like she was. I don't think she'd expose her children to that trauma, knowing what she went through herself as a girl.

Based on this, why would anyone think Joan would voluntarily disappear?

Some feel that perhaps Joan had psychological issues no one knew about that stemmed from the trauma she experienced as a child. Orphaned and then abused, maybe she kept her issues hidden until she finally just snapped one day, packed up, and left her old life behind.

It still seems unlikely, but a few insist there's evidence Joan left of her volition. Records say she checked out a book from the library called *Into Thin Air* and other mystery novels, many of which dealt with disappearances. These were not non-fiction books that offered how-to information about vanishing. The disappearances – and subsequent murders – were part of the fictional mystery. According to Martin, Joan loved detective stories and mysteries, and nothing was suspicious about them.

If we infer from her reading list that Joan planned to disappear, it's equally reasonable, based on the books she read, that she planned to solve crimes or commit a murder.

OTHERS THEORIZE THAT PERHAPS JOAN DIED from a botched abortion that occurred in her kitchen. Some believe she was pregnant with a third child that she didn't want and arranged to have an abortion – illegal at the time – performed in secret.

This theory seems to have been made up out of thin air. Not only is there no evidence it occurred, but the amount of blood also lost in the kitchen wasn't enough to have killed her. Besides that, Barbara Barker told the police that Joan would have been happy to have had a third child. Barbara and their friend, Mary Jane, had three children, and Joan had grown up with four adopted siblings.

It's also unlikely – if not impossible – that Joan could have scheduled an abortion during the very small window of time when David was sleeping and Lillian was playing across the street that afternoon. The possibility that Joan would risk an illegal procedure in her home seems remote.

BUT WHAT ABOUT SOME OTHER KIND OF medical emergency? Could she have had a miscarriage or an accident? The state police lab suggested that the blood evidence was consistent with some kind of hemorrhage, which could come from internal bleeding, external bleeding, or both.

Many medical conditions cause hemorrhaging, including hemophilia, miscarriage, heavy menstrual bleeding, or other things that are not related to violent trauma. However, there was nothing in Joan's medical history that created a heightened risk of hemorrhaging. Her doctor, Theodore Safford, stated that she was "in excellent health, both emotionally and physically." She hadn't seen him near the time of her disappearance, but there was no reason to think his diagnosis had changed.

But if it was a medical emergency and not an attack, how do we explain the unknown fingerprints in the house? And why was the telephone receiver torn away from the wall? Did Joan faint or slip and accidentally knock it down? Did she hit her head, and when she fell, it caused blood spatters and puddles in the kitchen? If so, where did she go? How did she disappear?

Even though the simplest explanation would be that an intruder left the fingerprints and ripped the phone away from Joan before hurting her, let's follow this logic for a moment.

What if Joan did call someone, then fainted, hit the kitchen floor, struck her head, and died? What if the person Joan called came to the house to help her and then, when faced with Joan's accidental death, panicked, took her away, buried her body, and never told anyone?

It's possible. Maybe.

But, if Joan needed help, why wouldn't she have called Barbara, Mary Jane, or someone else who lived nearby? Why didn't she call one of the emergency numbers in the telephone directory, which was open in front of her?

Or, if Joan was bleeding and walked away from the house on her own, why wasn't there any blood beyond her driveway? Did she stop bleeding? If a cut occurred on her scalp, it would have bled a lot initially and then slowed down. Is this why no other bloodstains were found?

It's possible. Maybe Joan wandering away from the house would explain the sightings of the dazed and confused woman walking along the roadway nearby. Perhaps she stumbled into some woods or a pond, and her body was never found.

Or maybe she ended up with amnesia. Just kidding about that one.

THIS MIGHT EXPLAIN WHAT HAPPENED TO JOAN Risch that day, even though her husband, friends, and children never believed that she wandered off or ran away.

Eventually, neither did the police. As the *Boston Globe* printed: "The Joan Risch mystery began to look more and more like a kidnapping and murder. Detectives are virtually convinced that Mrs. Risch was taken away in a car."

District Attorney John Droney agreed. "Someone has harmed this woman. We are fairly certain it is foul play."

Investigators continued to work on the case for years. It grew cold, but they never completely gave up. Many of the detectives confessed it haunted them, even after they retired. In 1993, former Lincoln police chief Leo Algeo told a reporter, "This is one of the things I would most like to see happen before I pass on, to have some resolution on that. It is sort of a stone around my neck." Unfortunately, Algeo never got that wish.

And neither did John Droney. Seven years after Joan vanished, he lamented, "It is the one case I would most like to solve." But he died two decades later without having done so.

But the regrets of law enforcement officers can never compare to the emotional loss from which Joan's family would never really recover. A woman who lost both her parents in a tragic accident when she was eight disappeared from a blood-spattered kitchen and left her children, ages four and two, without a mother.

They would wonder what happened to their mother for the rest of their lives, always believing that she was taken from them by someone – perhaps the same person who left behind those unknown fingerprints and the empty beer bottles that were found in the trash can.

They never knew the truth, and, most likely, neither will we.

Joan Risch just vanished one day – never to be seen again.

1965: THE NEWLYWED THAT VANISHED

THE STORY OF MARY SHOTWELL LITTLE

ON OCTOBER 14, 1965, 25-YEAR-OLD MARY Shotwell Little decided to go out for the evening with a friend. They were going to do a little shopping and have dinner before Mary went home and started planning the surprise party she would throw for her husband, Roy. The two had only been married for six weeks, but Roy was a bank examiner at C&S Bank -- where Mary also worked – and was out of town training to become an auditor. Mary was excited for him to come home.

Tragically, though, the party would never happen, and Roy would never see his new bride again. Mary vanished without a trace shortly after having dinner with her friend at the Lenox Square Shopping Center in Atlanta, Georgia.

MARY LITTLE WAS NOT THE KIND OF PERSON TO WHOM out of the ordinary things happened. She lived an ordinary, happy life with a happy childhood, marriage, and career as a secretary. Roy never expected her to stay home and take care of the house. He was a man ahead of his time, Mary always believed, and he was proud of everything she accomplished.

Mary Shotwell Little

She had grown up in Charlotte, North Carolina, but had moved to Atlanta with Roy just after the wedding. He put in a good word for her when she went to interview for a secretarial job at the Citizens and Southern National Bank, but even without it, Mary would've easily gotten the job. She got along well with everyone, had a friendly nature, and a winning smile. She seemed content with her job and, by all accounts, loved married life.

Roy left for his training on October 14 but would return the next day, so Mary planned a welcome home party for the night of the 15th. When she finished work, she drove her brand-new pearl-gray Mercury Comet to the supermarket, did some shopping, and then brought four bags of groceries to her car. She then drove to Lenox Square to meet her friend. The shopping center was in Atlanta's upscale Buckhead neighborhood.

They had dinner at the Piccadilly Café and, according to her friend, she was in good spirits and had glowing things to say about Roy and their marriage. They finished their meal around 8:00 P.M. and walked to the parking lot together. They waved goodbye, and Mary's friend drove off.

When she last saw her, Mary wore a white London Fog raincoat over an olive-green dress with white flowers, jewelry, eyeglasses, and flat shoes. She was carrying a set of keys and a pricey John Romain handbag.

Mary was never seen again.

THE NEXT MORNING, MARY DIDN'T SHOW UP FOR WORK. She hadn't been at the bank long, but this seemed very unlike her. Her supervisor believed she knew Mary well enough to know she would have at least called if she was sick, so she spoke with the co-worker Mary had had dinner with the night before. She told the supervisor that Mary's car had been in a parking lot near Lenox

Square and that she'd seen Mary walking back to it after dinner. She didn't see her enter it, but everything seemed fine.

Security guards at the shopping center were alerted and, initially, could not find the car. They called back to the bank, and Mary's boss decided that she'd go to the shopping center and look for herself. She couldn't explain why she was so bothered by Mary's absence – she just felt something was wrong.

Meanwhile, the security guards were still looking for the car and finally spotted it at about the same time Mary's supervisor arrived at the scene. It was in plain sight in section Yellow 32, where Mary had parked the evening before.

At this point, the police had not been called – but they soon would be.

The Comet was covered in a layer of thick, red dust as if it had been driven on a dirt road. Mary's shopping bags were inside, along with Coca-Cola bottles and a pack of Kent cigarettes.

Mysteriously, there was also a woman's slip, underwear, girdle, bra, and one stocking inside the car. Except for the bra and the stocking, everything had been neatly folded and placed on the console between the bucket seats. The panties were later determined to be Mary's, and the stocking had been sliced apart by a knife. Her dress, coat, jewelry, and car keys were missing and have never been located.

Worst of all, though, was the blood on the clothing, the steering wheel, the driver's side handle, and the front seats.

Now, it was decided that they needed to call the police.

POLICE OFFICERS WERE SOON ALSO ON THE SCENE, and it was discovered that while Mary's car was in the same parking section as it had been the previous night, it was not in the same parking space. It had been moved.

A traffic officer stated that the car had not been in the lot at 6:00 that morning. Because the engine was cold and the ignition key was missing, the police theorized that it could have been driven during the night.

Every available police officer was detailed to the case. The woods near the shopping center were searched, as were the alleys and empty buildings near the parking lot. By the weekend, hundreds of Army reservists and volunteers joined the search, checking wooded areas and creeks for 20 miles in every direction.

Crime scene examiners investigated Mary's car but even their best efforts led nowhere.

Private airplane owners offered their services, flying over Atlanta searching for the missing woman.

On October 19, the Georgia State Crime Lab issued a report that stated that the blood found in the car was consistent with Mary's blood type – there was no DNA testing in those days. The blood in the car had been described by officers as a "small amount" – about what you'd get from a nosebleed.

This led some of the investigators to believe the scene had been staged, especially since some of the blood was smeared. A fingerprint was found in the blood on the steering wheel, but it was never identified.

Even in 1965, when a wife was murdered or vanished, the husband was always the first suspect, so Roy was immediately questioned. Oddly, reports claim he didn't seem that interested in his new wife's disappearance. That might seem surprising since Mary claimed to love married life, but it didn't surprise some of Mary's friends, her former roommates among them. They'd never liked Roy, and some refused to attend the wedding because of it.

While he declined to take a polygraph test several times, he did have a solid alibi for the time when Mary went missing. He also had nothing to gain from her death, and detectives could find no signs of trouble in their marriage – aside from the fact that he seemed so disinterested in her vanishing. Roy was ultimately never charged in connection with Mary's case.

Another theory that was investigated involved Mary being connected to a sex scandal at the bank around the time she disappeared. The bank had hired a former FBI agent to investigate claims of sexual harassment and possible prostitution on the premises. Although Mary knew about the scandal, it was later determined that she was not involved, and it couldn't be linked to her disappearance.

But another, more promising, line of investigation soon emerged. Some of Mary's friends told detectives that Mary had recently expressed a fear of being home alone. This started several days before she vanished. Apparently, her uneasiness started after receiving some flowers at work from a "secret admirer." The flowers were traced to a florist near Mary's home, but the customer had paid cash and couldn't be traced.

Mary's co-workers said she had also been disturbed by some telephone calls she had been getting at work, but she wouldn't discuss them with anyone. However, a few days before she disappeared, she implied to her co-workers that she had something important she wanted to tell them, but she never did so.

Detectives wondered if the calls she'd received had been from the same "secret admirer" who sent the flowers, but they could never trace the calls.

It seems reasonable to believe that the flowers and the creepy telephone calls were the reason that Mary became afraid of staying home alone.

Could that person also be connected to her disappearance?

A FEW DAYS INTO THE INVESTIGATION, AN ESSO gas station attendant in Charlotte, North Carolina – Mary's hometown -- alerted the police that he had a credit card receipt with Mary's signature on it. It was timestamped within hours of the last time she was seen.

Then, Atlanta Detective Superintendent Clinton Chafin learned that Mary's credit card had been used again, this time in Raleigh, North Carolina. Strangely, though, the card was used the second time to get gas 12 hours after the first purchase, even though Raleigh was no more than three hours away from Charlotte.

Atlanta detective Jack Perry questioned both attendants at both stations. The man in Charlotte told him that he remembered servicing the car and that a man and a woman were inside. The man had been at the wheel, and the woman was lying slumped over in the seat, covered by a roadmap. She appeared to have an injury to her head and blood on her clothing.

After filling the tank, the attendant gave the credit card to the man driving, who handed it to the woman. She signed the receipt "Mrs. Roy H. Little."

When asked why the man didn't alert the authorities to the woman's condition, he said she'd tried to hide her face and didn't ask for help. Besides, he added, he didn't want to get involved in what he assumed was a domestic issue.

It was 1965 – when a man beat up his wife then, it wasn't a crime.

A month after Mary vanished, a young boy in Dekalb County, Georgia, found a note scribbled on the bottom half of a deposit slip from the Citizens and Southern Bank – the same bank that Mary worked for.

The note read: "Help! Mary Little ... Being held captive."

The note, along with the gas station receipts, were sent to the FBI Lab in Washington for analysis. The results showed that Mary likely wrote the notes and the receipts.

A search around the area where the note was found revealed no other traces of the missing woman.

Meanwhile, Roy Little apparently decided to get involved in the effort to find his wife. He started appearing on the radio, television, and in newspapers, pleading for his wife's return.

He announced: "This is an appeal from me and Mary's parents to the person holding Mary. Her welfare, safety, and safe return are our greatest concerns. We will do anything, go anywhere, and we will help you in any way we possibly can. I repeat, her safe return is the only thing we care about."

If the real kidnappers were listening, they never replied, but a ransom demand did come in soon after Roy's pleas were made public.

The kidnapper asked for $20,000, and an anonymous caller instructed Roy to go to an overpass in the Pisgah National Forest in western North Carolina and find further instructions posted on a sign. An FBI agent went in Roy's place and found only a blank piece of paper stuck to the sign. The caller never contacted the Little family again. The police and FBI determined the whole thing had been a hoax.

The police continued to follow every tip, potential lead, and possible sighting, but none of them led anywhere. The trail just went cold – Mary had vanished.

But then, something terrifying happened. In May 1967 – 18 months after Mary disappeared – one of her co-workers, Diane Shields, was murdered. Diane, age 22, was last seen leaving work in her blue and white Chevy Impala, which turned up at 2:30 A.M. the following day on Sylvan Road in Atlanta. Diane's body was found in the trunk. She was fully clothed, had not been sexually assaulted, and was still wearing a diamond engagement ring. She had died from suffocation after her scarf had been shoved down her throat.

The police speculated that the two cases were connected. It seemed too big of a coincidence that two women from the same office disappeared in less than two years. One was murdered, and the other was never found. If there was a connection – other than working in the same place –the police never found it.

Both cases remain unsolved.

WEEKS PASSED, THEN MONTHS, AND FINALLY, YEARS went by without new leads or suspects. Oddly, the police file on Mary's case went missing at some point in the years after Mary disappeared. The original file has never been found, although the case remains open. What happened to the 1965 file is also a mystery.

As the years passed, some investigators came to believe that Mary staged her disappearance and that she never met with foul play at all. However, no one seems to be able to agree on a reason why she would have done this.

Other detectives are convinced Mary was abducted. Soon after Mary vanished, a woman reported being accosted by a man in the Lenox Square parking lot. She said it happened the same night Mary vanished, just minutes before Mary would have been walking to her car. Could this man have been the one who took Mary? No one knows – he's never been identified.

Or was it Mary's "secret admirer" who took her? Or the person who made the harassing phone calls to her work? Or had it been a crime of chance – a young woman in the wrong place at the wrong time?

Despite the handful of clues and the many theories that have emerged over the last 60 years, it's unlikely that we'll ever know what happened to that young newlywed when she left a restaurant one night, excited to get home and start planning a party for the man she'd recently married.

1967: THE LOST BOYS OF HANNIBAL
AMERICA'S LARGEST CAVE RESCUE SEARCH

ON A WARM SPRING DAY IN MAY 1967, three adventurous boys went out into the woods near the town of Hannibal, Missouri, to explore a newly revealed entrance to a massive cave system beneath the town.

They were never seen again.

The story of the "Lost Boys of Hannibal" has continued to fascinate people ever since. Even though more than a half-century has passed since those boys vanished, their families still hold out hope that a solution may be found to the mystery of the boys who simply disappeared into thin air.

Hannibal, Missouri – often referred to as "America's Hometown"

HANNIBAL, MISSOURI, IS OFTEN REFERRED TO as "America's Hometown." Located about 100 miles north of St. Louis and nestled along the Mississippi River, the town draws its greatest fame from author Mark Twain. In the 1840s, Hannibal was briefly his home – back when he was still calling himself Samuel Clemens – but he was there long enough for the town to have laid claim to his legacy and used it to draw thousands of visitors to the town every year.

The prosperity of the river town has long been tied to its past. In a historic district along the riverfront, old brick buildings that served as brothels during the nineteenth century have been turned into tourist haunts, antique stores, gift shops, craft stores, and restaurants.

In the 1960s, families in station wagons flocked to Hannibal from all over the country. They came looking for the places they'd read about in Mark Twain's books. Several times each summer afternoon, visitors heard the calliope of a tourist riverboat as it made its way downstream from a dock just a few blocks from Twain's boyhood home. The characters that Twain created – Tom Sawyer, Huckleberry Finn, and Becky Thatcher – came to life in the place that had inspired them.

For children who grew up around Hannibal, exploring the wooded hills around the town came naturally, true to the tradition of Tom and Huck. They played on the bluffs overlooking the river, spending long,

Author Mark Twain lived in Hannibal as a boy and his books – and the characters he created – made the town famous.

carefree days that were like something from a book, perhaps one written by Mark Twain.

And then there were the caves. Missouri is known as the "Cave State" for a reason. According to the state's Department of Natural Resources, there are more than 7,300 caves in Missouri, only 20 of which are "show caves," open to the public.

The rest of them are often problematic, to say the least. Within the limestone beneath so much of Missouri are intricate systems of complex mazes and underground labyrinths. Much of this subterranean world is known for being difficult to navigate – literal mazes that have claimed numerous lives over the years.

One of the most famous caverns in Missouri – and the state's first show cave – is Mark Twain Cave, located a mile south of Hannibal. The cave served as the literary setting for Tom and Becky's escape from Injun Joe, and it remains a very popular tourist destination today.

The cave has been a source of mystery, adventure, and even grief in fiction and real life. One of the early owners of the cave was an eccentric St. Louis doctor named Joseph McDowell, who believed that the cave could permanently preserve the remains of

Mark Twain Cave is Hannibal's most popular underground attraction but there are many other caves in the area – caves that are much more dangerous.

his daughter, who'd died at a young age. He encased her in a copper tube and installed it in the cave but hadn't counted on the curiosity of Hannibal's children – including a young Samuel Clemens – who snuck into the case to peer into the glass window on the tube. He later moved his daughter to a more appropriate burial place, but the story of her tenancy in the cave stuck around – and appeared in Twain's *Life on the Mississippi*.

Today, Mark Twain's Cave and nearby Cameron Cave are safe, well-managed attractions that allow visitors to explore the area's natural wonders and the literary world of one of America's greatest authors.

The story of the "Lost Boys of Hannibal!" doesn't involve either of these caves – it's about Murphy's Cave, a cave system on the south side of Hannibal that had been discovered nearly a century before the boys vanished. In 1967, excitement surrounded this lesser-known cave because the state was rerouting and widening Highway 79 at the time, and the construction site was only a few blocks from the homes of the "Lost Boys."

Construction workers dynamited and moved millions of tons of rocks and dirt as they cut through the wooded, rocky hill that serves as the base of a scenic overlook called Lover's Leap. An entire neighborhood was wiped out as they changed a portion of the south edge of town to serve as a border for the new highway cutting through the limestone bluffs.

As the machines scraped away the earth and rock, previously unknown cave openings were exposed for the first time. The darkness behind those openings beckoned to those three boys amid the dusty and noisy mayhem caused by the road construction.

It was at one of those entrances that the largest cave search in American history began on May 10, 1967. Hundreds of volunteers joined some of the nation's best caving experts in a race against time, working heroically for days and nights, only to find nothing.

The three boys were gone.

IN 1967, JOEL HOAG WAS 13 YEARS OLD AND A dedicated amateur scientist. He loved the outdoors, was obsessed with the stars, and hoped to be the first man on the moon someday. When he found out that a new entrance to Murphy's Cave had been exposed near his home on State Highway 79, he was anxious to explore it.

After telling his younger brother, Billy, who was 11, and their friend, Craig Dowell, 14, about the entrance, he led their small expedition into the cave on May 9. He said it was just an exploratory trip so that they could make plans for a deeper look.

When the Hoag brothers' parents, Mike and Helen, found out where the boys had been that day, they forbade them to risk going into the cave again.

Mike and Helen weren't the only parents who felt that way. Joel had invited another friend, Rob Yager, to join them, but he had to decline – his father told him, "No way in hell," Rob said. Joel knew that he and Billy would get in trouble for disobeying their parents, but the siren call of the cave was too much to resist. Joel, Billy, and Craig made plans to return to the cave the next day after school.

The three boys changed clothes and hiked to the cave after school, armed with flashlights and shovels. It had been easy for the Hoag brothers to get away. Their parents had gone to the store and left their older sister, Debbie, in charge.

Joel Hoag   Billy Hoag   Craig Dowell

The three friends who soon became known as the "Lost Boys."

On the way, they ran into two girls they were friends with, Debbie Roberson and Sue Mudd, and invited them to come along. Debbie told them no – and that they shouldn't go either – but there was no stopping three boys on a mission.

Just before 4:00 P.M., the boys ran into another friend, Wes Leffert, on his green Huffy bike with its banana seat and high-rise handlebars. He was out delivering papers. The trio asked him to come with them into the cave, but he had to turn them down. He still had newspapers to deliver.

The last confirmed sighting of the boys was just after 5:00 P.M. by Louise Kohler, who taught second grade at the A.D. Stowell School in Hannibal. She was on her way home when she saw the boys on the high slope on the east side of the construction site. They had flashlights and shovels in their hands. She knew the boys from the neighborhood and had always liked them.

Even after 5:00, the road construction was still in full swing. Large bulldozers were lumbering back and forth, making the ground vibrate. The air was filled with swirling, choking dust, and the boys were gone by the time it cleared.

It would have been easy for the three boys to hurry through the dusty chaos and slip unseen into one of the cave entrances. They'd already done it once that week.

The workmen continued to grade the roadbed, oblivious to the presence of the boys, perhaps even covering the cave entrance Joel, Billy, and Craig had entered moments before, literally sealing their fate.

But we can't know that for sure. All we know is that after 5:00 P.M. on May 10, 1967, the three of them were never seen again.

WHEN THE BOYS FAILED TO RETURN HOME THAT DAY, their parents weren't concerned at first. Joel and Billy's older brother, Tim Hoag, left the house around 5:45 to find the boys and bring them home for supper. He ran into some neighborhood kids, who told him they'd last seen the brothers with Craig, and they had shovels and flashlights with them. Tim immediately knew where they'd gone and ran home to alert his parents.

Mike, Helen, and Tim drove to the construction site and found one of the newly opened entrances to Murphy's Cave. Helen shouted for the boys, but after getting no response, the family decided that more help was needed. Helen hurried to the nearby home of a friend and called the police. When officers arrived at the cave, they were just as clueless about how to proceed as the Hoags were. They shouted for the boys, but they also received no reply.

Mike and Helen Hoag were well-known in town. They had 11 children whose ages spanned more than two decades. For many years, the couple owned a family-friendly eatery and drinking establishment downtown called Hoag's Tavern -- a popular spot for tamales, meatloaf sandwiches, and homemade pies. Just about everyone in town had eaten there at one time or another, and Mike, Helen, and the kids, who often helped out at the restaurant, were well-liked by everyone.

So, when news began to spread around town about the missing brothers, people were worried and wanted to help. Groups spread out to search neighborhoods near Highway 79 or gathered with the family – and the growing crowd – around the construction area.

Bill Bridges, vice-commander of the Mark Twain Emergency Squad, heard the news and ordered the volunteer members to the scene. The squad had been formed in 1962, and while they had a lot of experience with vehicle accidents, pulling bodies from the river, and finding lost hunters in the woods, they had no experience with cave searches or rescues.

Bridges also called Mike Boudreau, a superintendent at Northeast Power, and asked him to send some heavy equipment, drilling gear, and jackhammers to Murphy's Cave. He had a feeling they'd need it.

The emergency squad began arriving at the cave entrance around 7:55 P.M., thanks to delays in the volunteers' work schedule. They brought along shovels, picks, lights, and a backhoe. None of them owned any caving equipment at the time.

The squad members split up. Some went to Murphy's Cave, and others went to the roadcut area to the south. Several of the men cautiously entered a gaping hole in the road that had been graded recently by highway equipment. They couldn't go far without digging out rocks and debris that had fallen into the cave. There was no sign of the boys from that direction.

At the same time, other squad members entered the previously known entrance to the cave, carefully exploring the immediate passages and calling out for the boys. As they moved through the narrow corridors, they marked the walls with chalk and unrolled string so they could find their way out later. The men would explore one passage only to come upon several others that branched off in other directions, and each of those passages eventually branched into others.

The cave system was massive, and the men were legitimately worried about getting lost themselves. They knew almost nothing about Murphy's Cave. They had no idea that many passages could only be traversed on all fours or hunched over for hours on end because of low ceilings. Every passage looked the same – tan, gray walls and hard-packed clay floors.

They soon realized they were literally in way over their heads.

Meanwhile, outside, the crowd was getting larger. Word spread and bystanders pushed to the front of the security line, where the emergency squad had been set up to keep people away from the cave. Mike and Helen Hoag, along with most of their children, were at the edge of the crowd. Next to them was Craig's mother, Helen, a cook at the Becky Thatcher Restaurant. She looked anxious and frustrated, dabbing her eyes with a tissue. Everyone was waiting for any information about the boys that the squad was able to offer – but they had none.

One of those who arrived at the site that evening was Milton Martin, a 20-year-old man who worked at the local Kroger grocery store. He had been inside Murphy's Cave many times as a boy, thanks to a hidden entrance that almost everyone his age in town knew about. When he heard the news, drove out to the scene, and saw the chaos, he decided he needed to go inside and help. First, though, he had to convince his father. Russell, a highway department worker and squad volunteer, that he knew the cave well enough. After some discussion, Russell reluctantly agreed to let him go.

Inside, Milton found many familiar passages and many more he didn't recognize. Most were narrow, and some were too tight to accommodate an adult. He wondered if the boys had gotten into one of these areas and could not get out.

Rescue efforts began almost immediately, searching for the three boys – although no one knew exactly what cave they'd entered.

While inside, he did come across a young caver from Quincy, Illinois, who had come to help but had gotten lost in the maze, so Milton showed him the way out.

Milton badly wanted to find the boys. He was friends with Fred Hoag, one of the boys' older brothers, but after hours of searching, he saw no sign of them. Eventually, he gave up and had to go home.

But others took his place. Bill Boltinghouse was a senior at Hannibal High School. He worked at Sandy's, a local drive-in restaurant, and would soon be joining the U.S. Air Force. That evening, he'd received a call from a cousin, Carl Nelson, who worked as a dispatcher for the Hannibal Police Department. Surprised to hear about the missing boys, he quickly drove to the cave site and joined the group of volunteers going into the cave unsupervised.

Bill borrowed a local caver's helmet and lamp and hurried into a cave he'd never been inside. He quickly realized he'd made a mistake and returned to the surface, but Bill found another way to help. As a citizen's band and ham radio enthusiast, he knew communications would be important to the search. Precious time had already been lost as rescuers relied on runners to send messages out for equipment and water.

Bill rushed home, gathered his radio gear, and set it up at the Southside Christian Church, which was adjacent to the construction site and had become the search headquarters. He set up a base station and antenna and was soon in contact with the search workers. Walkie-talkies wouldn't work in the cave, but the stronger radio broadcast allowed the searchers to circulate messages to the surface.

The radio became an important tool for the rescue party but not as important as actual cavers with real-life experience would be. On the night the boys vanished, Al Viar coincidentally hosted a regular meeting of his caving club in nearby Quincy, Illinois. He received a call from the police, who were desperately looking for cavers to help find the missing boys.

Al, who worked for a sheet metal manufacturing company, had been caving for years. He'd explored dozens of caves in the region, including Murphy's Cave. He and the rest of the club agreed to help, and by 10:00 P.M., they'd arrived in Hannibal, immediately joining the frantic search.

And then, as if things weren't chaotic enough, the sky opened up and unleashed a heavy rain that fell during the early morning hours. The construction area around the cave turned into a muddy mess and increased the chance of a ceiling collapse inside the cave or a mud and rockslide that might seal the entrances that had been opened into the hillside.

The cavers from Quincy and the group of inexperienced volunteers knew they needed to find the boys soon. It was becoming increasingly apparent that they didn't have much time.

THE NEXT MORNING, MAY 11, NEWS OF THE MISSING boys spread like wildfire at Hannibal Junior High School. Students who, only the day before, had been excited about the approaching end of the school year were now stunned by what was happening to boys they both knew and liked.

At the construction site, there were now five teams of searchers – three volunteers in each – shuffling through the cave, squeezing through narrow passages, and crawling through some areas on their hands and knees. They made arduously slow progress in the difficult cavern, worried they might get lost. The only consolation was that they had a way of reaching the outside world, food, and water – three things the missing boys didn't have.

Meanwhile, in St. Louis, Conway Christensen, the head of the Hondo Underground Rescue Team, had been following the news of the search with concern. He also served as the president of the Speleological Society of America, a new Virginia-based cave rescue organization that had just started the previous October by William Karras. He was a controversial figure because of a disagreement with the well-established National Speleological Society over the priority that should be given to cave rescues.

On Thursday morning, Christensen placed his team on alert after talking with Karras, and by noon, the St. Louis team had formally been asked for assistance by the Hannibal police. They packed up their gear and went straight to Hannibal.

Word had also been sent to Washington, D.C., to ask for help from Karras and the national group. Karras called a friend at the Pentagon, who agreed to provide Air Force Two to fly the team and their gear to Baldwin Field in Quincy, Illinois.

By then, the St. Louis team was already in Hannibal, meeting with the cavers from Quincy, who were still trying to survey Murphy's Cave. Christensen and his team donned white coveralls and helmets and entered the cave, immediately noting the maze of passageways and realizing how easy it would be for a non-caver to get lost. They found many openings so small that only boys could crawl through them. Most of the passages in the cave were filled with sediment, which meant crawling and sliding through tight areas that made the search agonizingly slow.

The experienced rescue team also discovered something else – recent collapses. They, along with the Quincy team, had found several muddy ceilings that looked as though they had recently collapsed, and Christensen feared that the boys may have entered a section of the cave, the ceiling collapsed behind them, and they were now trapped.

As one caver said, "These caves are some of the most dangerous I have ever been in."

These words foreshadowed something terrible for Joel, Billy, and Craig if they weren't found soon.

Cavers from across the Midwest – and across the country – rushed to Hannibal to try and help with the search for the three boys.

CHRISTENSEN ESTABLISHED A RESCUE CONTROL CENTER at the Southside Christian Church, which the volunteers had already pressed into service. With so many cavers and volunteers still expected, he knew they needed a process to assign tasks and track where everyone was located. A sign-out sheet was made in the center, and radios were provided for search groups. Cavers and volunteers on break or not assigned a task could rest at the church, where food and water were provided. As cavers were needed, support staff on hand would radio requests that send a specific number of people to various locations. Volunteer drivers helped get the searchers where they needed to go.

Cavers continued to stream into Hannibal. Among them were Stanley Sides, who brought along members of his Chouteau Grotto caving club, and Don Nicholson, a land surveyor, respected caver, and Hannibal native, who had assisted with a mapping expedition of Murphy's Cave in 1960. Unfortunately, a large portion of the cave was still unmapped. That section was filled with passages that were too small for adults to pass through or had been filled in with silt and debris from ceiling collapses over the years.

Each of the cavers embarked on an exhausting, energy-draining shift, crawling through uneven, cluttered passageways. The only clues they discovered were from previous searchers who had trampled the silt and scuffed the clay floors of the areas they passed through. The cavers wedged themselves into cramped, narrow areas, hoping for a sign of the boys, but found nothing.

"It was very confusing," Nicholson later said. "It would wear someone out if they got back in there and ended up panicking because they couldn't find their way out or see where they were going. It could really be a mess."

The cave teams kept working, but by late afternoon on Thursday, many were becoming skeptical that the boys were anywhere close to the construction site. Still, they brought in heavy equipment and opened up two additional entrances into the hillside to make it easier to access parts of the cave where collapses had slowed the search progress.

Around 10:00 P.M., Karras and the national team landed in Quincy and were escorted by the state police to Hannibal. When they arrived, they met with Christensen and his group and began formulating a plan for what to do next. Karras – eager to drum up publicity for his new group – also met with the press, which irritated some of the cavers, who saw the reporters as a distraction they didn't need.

A short time later, Stan Sides and his team emerged from the cave and found the area flooded with bright lights powered by generators and crowds of reporters and onlookers. They were shocked by the carnival-like atmosphere at the scene. Sides complained, "Rather than Karras and Christensen working to try and put together any semblance of an organized attempt at finding the boys, they were romancing the news media."

Stan, ignoring what was going on, met with Don Nicholson and Don Myers, who'd also helped with the mapping of the cave. They estimated that at least 70 percent of the mapped part of the cave had been searched, but there was no sign of the three boys. "I don't think they're in the cave," Nicholson said, "but the possibility can't be overlooked, so we'll continue looking."

Other cavers agreed with the three men and began to speculate that maybe the boys didn't go into Murphy's Cave at all. They might have gone to a different cave or even went exploring in the woods. The cave search had been prompted by someone assuming they'd returned to Murphy's Cave – there was no proof of it.

Stan Sides – and many others – became increasingly frustrated that William Karras refused to entertain another theory. "Nobody would listen to us," he said later. "All the emotion was directed toward a Tom Sawyer and Becky Thatcher style cave adventure."

The cave rescuers didn't listen, but the police did. With help from Captain Charles Webster, a group of rescuers planned a surface search of the area and a house-to-house search.

The police had treated the situation as a missing persons case since the first telephone call. They couldn't find any evidence that the boys had been abducted or had run away. They followed the lead provided by the parents about the boys going to the cave, but that wasn't all the police department was doing. However, as Captain Webster explained, "Once Karras and his crew arrived in town, the whole situation was turned over to the cave experts." After that, the police were left to maintain safety at the construction site and keep unauthorized people out of the caves.

When officers and volunteers began the search in town, Missouri Governor Warren Hearnes ordered 150 National Guardsmen to help. They began a massive, several-square-mile search for the boys, checking abandoned shacks, sheds, barns, railroad cars, and the river. They also checked the city's sewer system and looked for any other cave entrances.

While this was going on, Karras was busy calling other cavers throughout the region and asking for their assistance. They knew time was running out if the boys were in the cave. Soon, dozens of additional cavers were in Hannibal to join the search – and add to the chaos.

The crowd at the site was growing, fed by word of mouth and ever-increasing news coverage in the region and beyond. The construction area had almost turned into a mob scene. People were going in and out of the cave without organization, and new arrivals were being warned not to lay down their equipment because someone would steal it and go into the caves.

By now, the army of spectators had overwhelmed the local police, and the director of Civil Defense had sent men to help maintain order and keep spectators out of dangerous areas.

Searchers from all over the region had been working around the clock since Wednesday night, squirming through narrow cave passages, and found nothing. They even searched nearby Cameron's Cave, although it was blocked by a locked gate, but found no sign of the boys there either.

After their long, arduous shifts in the cramped cave passages, cavers emerged to debrief Karras and head to the church for food, water, and rest. When possible, they took quick naps before returning underground.

Karras – part seasoned caver and part showman – grew frustrated and was finally starting to agree with Stan Sides' theory about the boys. He told the press, "This will make it four times we've been through this cave, and that should convince everyone they're not in here."

But the searchers still had no other solid leads, so they kept looking underground, pressing into passable areas and digging through into areas that were not.

More cavers arrived in town, hoping to help with the search and replace their exhausted colleagues. Hour after hour, they explored new passageways, conferred with each other, reviewed the maps of the cave they had, and resumed the search.

By Friday, hope had started to wane. Karras was unusually direct that afternoon when he told cavers and family members that if the boys were trapped in a small, tight passageway with little or no ability to move, they would be unable to maintain their body temperatures in the cool cave environment and would not survive.

Karras, who wanted to raise the national profile of cave search and rescue services, was feeling the pressure. He was in charge of the largest cave rescue ever attempted in American history – and he was failing. There had never been a situation in modern history where the lost person or persons remained lost. They had always been found – dead or alive.

Karras had already made history with the size of the search, and he was about to make history again – however, it was not the kind he wanted. He feared Hannibal would be his downfall and the whole country would be watching.

BY FRIDAY EVENING, KARRAS AND THE OTHER CAVERS had become convinced that the lost boys were not in Murphy's Cave. The search teams gathered to assess the situation. They decided to focus on the immediate road cut area, where highway workers had exposed five cave openings that had since been covered over. Karras wanted the construction crew to retrace its steps and locate and reopen the entrances that had been filled.

Karras told Mike and Helen Hoag that he feared the boys had gone into one of those entrances, and then a piece of heavy equipment had dropped a load of dirt on top of them. Helen, who listened intently, closed her eyes. "It sounds so terrible," she whispered.

The search for the three boys went on for days but the searchers never found any clear evidence they had ever been inside the cave at all.

Despite their best efforts, cavers could only locate and reopen four of the five construction site openings. This gave Karras a sickening feeling in his stomach, convincing himself that the boys had slipped into that fifth opening and had been accidentally buried alive by the road crew. He told his crew to redouble their efforts to locate the opening or at least the underground passage that led away from it, but they were unsuccessful.

By now, the eyes of the entire nation were on Hannibal and the frantic search for the boys. Karras knew he couldn't afford to fail, but time and the elements were working against him.

The search continued with exhausted cavers going back and forth from the cave in shifts, unable to discover any sign of the boys.

They were soon joined by Fred Hoag, one of the older brothers of two of the missing boys. Fred and another brother, Mike, were living in South Carolina and flew home when they got the news of the disappearance. Fred joined Conway Christensen for a foray into the cave to help with the search for his two little brothers, but he didn't have any more luck than the rest of the searchers had.

It was quickly becoming apparent to most of the searchers that they were out of time. There were just too many narrow passages and unexplored sections of the cave, plus the boys had been down there too long without food, water, and warm clothing. Still, they continued to search, believing they could recover the boys' bodies, even if they couldn't bring them out alive.

Finally, in a last-ditch effort, the construction crew began working to try and uncover some of the larger cave entrances they'd found while building the road. In several places, portions of the roadbed had collapsed and had to be filled. If they could find one of those sinkhole entrances, they might be able to get access to parts of the cave they hadn't yet seen. Many of the searchers agreed with Karrass' theory that the boys had entered through an opening that was covered over behind them. Whatever section of the cave they were now trapped in hadn't been found, they believed, so perhaps finding another hidden entrance could lead them to the boys.

As the work began on pieces of land that would eventually be Highway 79, searchers examined the rocks and debris from the sinkholes, looking for clothing, body parts, shovels, or lights – any clue that the boys had been there – but they found nothing.

IT WAS NOW TIME, MANY OF THE CAVERS AGREED, to start thinking about other options when it came to the location of the boys. They were reaching the conclusion that Stan Sides had reached days earlier, that the boys had vanished somewhere else.

Only William Karras was dedicated to continuing the cave search and many of the searchers believed he was a publicity-seeker by now.

The 150 National Guard members the governor had sent had spent the weekend searching the south side of town, inspecting homes, garages, sheds, and outbuildings. As they checked the area, they found many other cave openings – usually in residential backyards – and they checked those, too. They were also sent to an

Since no trace of the boys was found in the cave, National Guardsmen searched other areas in the community, including the Continental Cement plant.

area north of town, along the River Road, and they searched the heavily wooded area there but found nothing of significance.

Another team was sent to the Continental Cement plant south of Hannibal and searched the entire 3,500 acres of the site, including a massive limestone quarry and some nearby caves. Once again – nothing was found.

Two of the stranger places searched were Riverside Cemetery, south of the road construction, and then Mount Olivet Cemetery, less than a mile from Mark Twain Cave.

These two sites were prompted by the rumors about the "mystery man" spotted around Lover's Leap for several days before the boys went missing. He was a white man, 30 to 35 years old, and he'd been seen talking to some neighborhood kids. One of the highway workers asked the man what he was doing, and he replied, "I'm watching the construction activity."

Karras and some of the other searchers had also noticed this man in the early morning hours "standing high on a hill near the highway caves looking down on the workers. Who he was or where he came from, we were never able to discover," Karras said and added that the individual had planted "false clues" – without any details – that "wasted the cavers' time."

Even in the late 1960s, people didn't automatically think of child abductions, especially in small towns – it was a more innocent time – but the man unsettled some of the searchers so much that National Guardsmen were ordered to check the cemeteries and to watch for any freshly dug areas where bodies could be buried." Nothing was found.

They also searched other cave openings in the bluffs near the construction site, even though some had been searched many times already. Again, nothing. As one of the men later put it, "We were just plowing the same ground over and over, always coming up empty."

The Mark Twain Emergency Squad extended their search to the Mississippi River, and several islands were found both north and south of the Memorial Bridge, which was connected with Illinois. Nothing related to the lost boys was found, so Civil Defence Director Bill Broadus announced they were going to drag the river for bodies. He felt the river was the only place left to search; however, it was unlikely to offer any clues. And he was right. The river search proved to be another dead end.

With a busy railroad line running only a few hundred yards from the search sites, search organizers visited the nearby railroad yard and secured a manifest of all the trains that had passed through Hannibal the days the boys went missing. The railroad took on the massive task of tracking the trains and having them searched, just in case the boys had hopped a freight train out of town.

It took five days, but no clues were found.

ON SUNDAY, MAY 14 – AFTER CONSIDERING FURTHER the idea the boys might have run away – a new strategy was attempted to try and obtain more clues. Mike and Helen Hoag were put on national television to appeal directly to their sons.

With help from the news station in Quincy, Helen spoke to the camera with tears streaming down her face, "Joey... Joey, Billy, this is Mother's Day. Please come home and make it a good Mother's Day. I had a good supper for you tonight. Your brothers and sisters all love you and have been looking so hard for you. Please come home before I have a heart attack."

Mike chimed in with his own plea: "If you hear, will you please come home or call, and we'll come get you. We love you, but we have to get to you real quick and get you home."

Even though it still seemed unlikely to the parents that the boys had run away, a lead came as a result of the television broadcast. An Interstate 55 construction worker from Overland, Missouri, named Louis Guerra – who was working just east of St. Louis – called the hotline number that was flashed on television screens. He told police that he'd seen two boys fitting the descriptions of Joel Hoag and Craig Dowell at a workhouse in the South Broadway area of St. Louis. He claimed the boys had asked him for directions to Ferguson, Missouri. He was confident that the two boys were Joel and Craig because he remembered their photos from the newspaper. He added that the boys were "very dirty." Guerra said that he hadn't seen a third boy.

The Missouri State Highway Patrol immediately responded to the tip and found the two boys Guerra had encountered – but they weren't Joel and Craig. They turned out to be 19-year-old runaways from Cape Girardeau, Missouri.

Even though the identification of the boys turned out to be wrong, it did lead to the credence of what many people believed about the situation. Hannibal's mayor, Harry Musgrove – not thrilled with this kind of national attention on his town – stated that he believed the boys weren't missing underground. He told reporters he thought they were some other place. "They could be out having fun," he said. "That's our only hope now. I'm more inclined to believe they ran away. If we keep this vigil up. The kids might never come back. You can't come back when you have 200 or 300 people looking for you."

But others were skeptical about the mayor's urgent need to put an end to the story. They insisted the boys had no money with them. Where could they have gone – other than into one of the caves?

Among those who believed the boys were still lost underground was, of course, William Karras. It was now the second week of the search, and tensions were running high. The frantic ongoing efforts and the exhaustion everyone involved felt had created some short fuses among the searchers. Mayor Musgrove met with Karras and his team to resolve the issues between the local searchers and the national team. It was finally announced that Karras' team would handle the underground search, and the Mark Twain Rescue Squad would manage all the surface search operations.

And then came more bad news. Two friends of the missing boys confessed knowing about a dangerous game that Joe, Billy, and Craig would often play, eluding construction workers along the new highway route and ducking into cave openings the crew exposed. The boys identified another area – separate from the original spot where the searches had started. There, they found a section of cave passage filled with shale that appeared to have been from a recent ceiling collapse. If the boys were trapped there, it seemed unlikely they had enough air and could still be alive.

Cavers began digging right away, trying to pull out the loose rock and reopen the passage. It was tedious work, and the men labored through the night. In the early morning, they finally emerged – just below the road cut where the search had started – but they found no sign of the lost boys.

Members of the Hoag family, Craig's mother, friends, relatives, and neighbors maintained a steady vigil at the construction site. Bill Karras and Conway Christensen walked to the Hoags' home every night to update them on the day's activities, and while the family trusted the men leading the search for their sons, it seemed the cavers never had good news.

Friends also constantly came to the house to offer support or bring meals to the family. There was always gratitude and warm hugs, but Helen Hoag would inevitably collapse into tears. They were all exhausted, and the telephone rang all night long. Friends later related that Helen put her hope into anything that came along. One night, a psychic called the house and told Helen to go to the top of Lover's Leap, open the Bible to a certain scripture, and the boys would come down from the sky. "And she did it," the friend recalled. "She was willing to do anything to get those boys back."

This was not the only psychic who got involved in the situation. A clairvoyant from Holland, Gerard Croiset, called to say that he'd studied maps and newspaper clippings and had a vision of the Murphy's Cave entrance. He claimed the boys would be found at "a sharp drop-off in one of three passages leading from the entrance." A team was sent to check out the cave but found no drop-off or any evidence of the boys.

Another psychic felt the boys would be found about 26 feet from a piece of heavy equipment, but this was an area that had been searched over and over again over the last two weeks.

One of America's best-known psychics of the 1960s, Jeane Dixon, reviewed news clippings about the boys and then traveled to Hannibal to try and help. The families hoped she could tell them if their sons were lost or abducted, but when Dixon arrived at the road cut, she was drawn to the Lover's Leap bluff, which towered overhead. She couldn't offer anything detailed, only that she felt uneasy about the town and all its caves.

America's best-known psychic in the 1960s, Jeane Dixon, tried to help in the case, but failed.

Still, another psychic had a vision of the boys in a railroad car loaded with oranges. Another claimed they were in a railcar with the word "Louisiana" prominently featured in her vision. The psychic was unclear if it represented the state or the small community near Hannibal.

William Karras later reported they'd heard from seven different psychics during the search. Some of them sensed the boys might

be in the general area of Riverside Cemetery, but none could offer specific information. Volunteers and National Guardsmen searched the cemetery – and nearby city dump – many times and found nothing.

The circus sideshow atmosphere continued when a dowser showed up at the search headquarters, claiming he could find the boys. He told Karras he had a technique that used a coat hanger with a piece of meat attached to one end.

The man was politely asked to go home.

FINALLY, ON MAY 18, WILLIAM KARRAS WAS FORCED to announce that the search was coming to an end. The reporters were gone. They'd moved on to other stories. The National Guardsman had been sent home, and the hundreds of volunteers couldn't be there any longer. They had jobs and families that needed them. A handful of cavers from the St. Louis team had agreed to stay in town a little longer in case any new leads came up. Sadly, Karras said, they weren't expecting anything.

The most experienced cavers who had traveled to Hannibal considered the caves were now too dangerous for anyone to enter. They took their concerns to the mayor -- who was as worried about the boys as he was about the unwelcome national attention. When the search concluded, he announced that all wild cave openings within the city limits would be closed.

It was a perfect example of the old adage about closing the barn door after the horses had already run off, but at least it might save other adventure-seeking kids in the future.

In the last days of the search, a final last-ditch effort to find the boys was made when construction workers removed the face of the Murphy's Cave bluff to expose any entrances that might have been missed. There was still a fear that a recent ceiling collapse trapped the boys underground.

Cavers tried once again, exploring every underground passage they could find. Another 100 local volunteers again searched the hills and valleys across the south side, but finally, after finding nothing, the search was officially called off.

Or so it seemed – it turned out it wasn't.

Even though a dinner was held to honor the search team – where Bill Karras expressed his thanks to the community and his regrets – a crowd packed into the city hall council chambers a few days later, demanding the search continue. Two cavers who had spent long hours in the cave believed the boys were trapped in a lower level near the entrance. In fact, one of them even claimed he'd seen shadows that suggested the bodies of the three boys were down there.

Bill Karras was highly skeptical. There had been hundreds of people who spent thousands of hours scouring the cave and had found nothing. He added that there was no evidence of a lower level, and if it were there, it would have to be below the water table. "It's possible but improbable," he told city officials. He challenged the cavers to show him where they thought the boys were located.

Back at the cave, the men led Karras through several passages, ending the walk in a small room that was essentially an intersection of several passages. Working on their knees, the two men dug into the cave floor but found nothing. Back at the church headquarters, Karras reported what occurred to the sheriff, and a group of curious cavers reportedly "walked away in disgust."

Despite Karras' skepticism, officials decided the claim was the only good lead they had, and on June 9, test drilling took place, looking for a lower level of the cave. Excitement swept through the community, residents hoping the boys' bodies might finally be found.

They weren't.

Drilling and digging went on for two days, and while opinions varied, they either found a lower level of the cave or they just found the same level, but all the drilling and excavation had altered it. Whichever it was, it didn't matter – the boys were nowhere to be found.

This time, the search was finally over.

WHAT HAPPENED TO JOEL, BILLY, AND CRAIG?
The simplest answer would be that they went into one of the newly-opened cave entrances that afternoon and were trapped inside, either because of an accident or because the construction work had filled in the entrance. Perhaps they went in search of another exit and became hopelessly lost.

Another theory is that there was some kind of cover-up involving an accident. In one interview, Joel and Billy's sister DeDe said the construction company building the highway suddenly sealed up some of their holes shortly after the disappearance, against the mayor's orders. "When they blasted those holes open, they didn't put any kind of caution tape around them," she said. "I think the boys got buried in one of the holes, and I think someone from the construction company who ran the equipment knew that they had buried them."

The boys' disappearing underground was the most popular explanation for what occurred in 1967 – but it definitely wasn't the only one. Many people believed the boys had run away. They'd left town, and perhaps something happened to them that made it impossible for them to contact their friends and family back home.

Or maybe they simply didn't want to come home or even talk to anyone in Hannibal. Perhaps there were things about their lives that no one knew about, and maybe there were things that made them want to flee and never look back.

Others believed the boys left Hannibal, but not on their own. People in town knew the boys. They hung out in the hills around town and had a Tom Sawyer-style desire for adventure. As one neighbor said, "They didn't have a lot of supervision because the parents were working at the tavern, so they were on their own a lot. But they were good kids, not likely to run off. They always came home for supper."

Many were starting to believe the boys had been taken. But by who?

How about aliens? Yes, that was a genuine suggestion. In his journal, Joel – who had that fascination with the stars – had written that he'd seen a UFO one night above Lover's Leap shortly before he went missing. There had been a series of alleged UFO sightings around Illinois, Wisconsin, and Michigan that spring, and there were some who believed the boys were possibly abducted by little green men.

Other suggestions were more down-to-earth and more unsettling. Many locals wondered whether the boys were the victims of abduction and murder. Since the Hoags didn't have a car, the boys were known to accept rides from strangers to get across town, behavior that their parents warned them about many times. Could there have been a stranger in town who took the boys?

Some recalled the mysterious man that had been encountered around Lover's Leap before the disappearance and then, afterward, was spotted watching the search efforts below. According to William Karras, he even inserted himself into the search operation with misleading suggestions before completely disappearing himself. Could he have been involved?

And he wasn't the only man suspected of having something to do with the disappearance. Another was a name that most readers will know – John Wayne Gacy.

Even though there's zero evidence that Gacy was in Hannibal in 1967, we do know that starting in the early 1970s, he began assaulting, torturing, and murdering at least 35 boys and young men. His known victims were murdered in his suburban Chicago home after he had lured them there by deception or force. More than two dozen of them were buried in the crawlspace under his house. Others were dumped in the Des Plaines River. Gacy was eventually caught, convicted, and served prison time until his death by lethal injection in 1994.

Not all of Gacy's victims were identified, and many detectives believed there were more victims than those named in the official count. After his arrest, the Hoag family and others wondered if Gacy had been in Hannibal in May 1967. It was a long shot, but stranger things have happened.

It was revealed that Gacy kept detailed records of his travels. In 1967, he spent time in Ladonia, Missouri, only 41 miles from Hannibal. He was living in Waterloo, Missouri, then – near Kansas City – where he managed three Kentucky Fried Chicken restaurants owned by his father-in-law. He was a

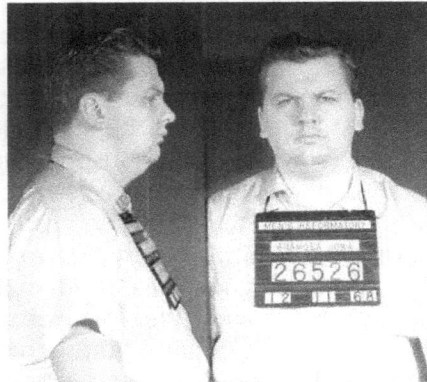

John Wayne Gacy at the time of his arrest for sodomy in 1968 – just one year after the boys disappeared. He was known to spend time just 40 minutes or so from Hannibal at the time.

successful businessman in those days, a member of the local Jaycees, and a husband and father of two children.

But it was while living in Waterloo that the dark side of John Wayne Gacy began to emerge. He cheated on his wife with prostitutes and operated a club in his basement for underage employees at his restaurants, providing them with alcohol. After getting the young men drunk, Gacy made sexual advances, and when rebuffed, he laughed it off as a joke. In 1968, though, he went too far and was arrested and charged with sodomy. He spent time in prison, but when released, he moved to Chicago, where he opened a successful contracting business, remarried – his first wife left when he was in prison – and became a leader in political and civics groups. On the surface, he was friendly and well-liked, but under the mask he wore, he was a maniacal killer.

Some wondered if Gacy could have been the mystery man who was seen lingering at the construction site, watching the work being done, talking to the boys, and misleading the searchers after the trio disappeared.

The DNA and dental records of Joel, Billy, and Craig were sent to Cook County Sheriff's detectives, but there was no match with any of Gacy's known victims. Those who believe this theory is possible suggest this isn't the story's end. They believe that Gacy could easily have killed the boys and buried them in graves that have never been found.

Possible? Sure, but it's still unlikely.

There was another suspect whose name might also ring a bell – Mike Hoag, the father of Joel and Billy.

In April 1996, an ugly rumor began making the rounds that was serious enough to get the attention of the police. The story behind the rumor began in November 1995 when retired Hannibal Police detective Charles Webster received a call from Carl Bailey, a Kirksville, Missouri, resident who had been living in Hannibal when the boys vanished. He had even volunteered and helped with the search.

The rumor he passed on to Charles Webster had come from a relative of Craig Dowell. It claimed that Mike Hoag had killed the three boys and buried them in the basement of the house where the family lived. When Mike and Helen went shopping that day, they told the boys to stay out of the caves. Then, when they returned and found out the boys had disobeyed them, Mike became enraged and began whipping the three of them. Things went too far, and they died. He buried them in the basement to hide his mistake.

According to Bailey – who'd been playing amateur sleuth – the Hoag family was never suspected, interviewed, or questioned. The house was never searched because the police never had any reason not to believe their story.

Based only on hearsay, the police wouldn't reopen the investigation. However, investigators spoke with the current house owners and asked about the basement's condition when they purchased the property. The owners were concerned about having an excavation done, not knowing who'd pay for it or how much damage it would do to the house. But, one of them told the police that the basement was intact when they moved in and ended the inquiry. "There are certainly no bones in our basement," he said. "I feel sorry for that family."

One of Joel and Billy's sisters, Lynnie, said the basement was undisturbed when her family moved out of the house years before. The lower level had three rooms, one with a large gas furnace and concrete floors. The only area with a dirt floor was under the front porch. Lynnie said it had always been dry, hard packed, and showed no evidence of any digging.

The terrible rumor was completely untrue, but it certainly upset the Hoag family. "We all heard that gossip," Lynnie said. "Daddy never whipped or beat us. There were so many cruel things said. You'd think people had better things to do."

The rumor stirred up a lot of bad memories for a family that had experienced more pain than most families could be expected to bear. The Dowell family did, too. Craig's surviving family members never spoke publicly about the tragedy.

For the Hoags, the disappearances of Joel and Billy were followed by the death of another son, Michael Jr., who was killed in a 1968 car accident in South Carolina. He was struck head-on when a drunk driver crossed the center line into his lane. He was pronounced dead at the scene. He was only 25 years old.

In October 1975, another son, Robin, who was adored by Joel and Billy and always referred to as their "little buddy," was killed in a tragic shooting when he was only 16.

Mike and Helen had lost three sons in nine months and then a fourth seven years later. It was tragedy stacked upon tragedy.

For years after the boys vanished, Helen sat in her living room at night, staring at the front door, hoping that Joel and Billy would come running in, laughing and full of life. But, of course, they never did.

Mike died in November 1989, and Helen followed him in death in 1995, ending a life of hardship and pain that had only been tempered by the love of her family.

The only good thing we can say as we end this story is that at least Mike and Helen finally discovered what happened to their sons, even if they had to find out in death.

1970: FROM THE SIDE OF THE ROAD
THE MYSTERY OF ROBIN GRAHAM

AT JUST AFTER 2:00 A.M. ON THE MORNING OF November 15, 1970, a young woman named Robin Graham disappeared from the shoulder of the southbound Hollywood Freeway near the Santa Monica offramp in Los Angeles.

What had been an otherwise ordinary night took a dark turn when a telephone call from a California Highway Patrol operator woke up Robin's younger sister and passed on a message from her sister – Robin's car had broken down, and she needed help. She relayed the message to her parents when they got home around 2:30 A.M., and they hurried toward the spot where Robin had broken down. They were relieved she was okay and knew they'd see her soon.

But they wouldn't – Robin Graham would never be seen again.

ROBIN GRAHAM GREW UP IN THE ENDLESS SUMMER of Southern California. She had good friends, a handsome boyfriend, and, unlike a lot of teenagers at this volatile time, got along well with her parents. The 22-year-old, well-liked young woman graduated from John Marshall High School. She was now attending Pierce College and working part-time at Pier One Imports – a home décor store that started with a single location in San Mateo, California, in 1962 and now had 16 stores across the Southwest.

Robin was at work on the evening of November 14, and when her shift ended, she left in her boyfriend's car, which she'd driven to work that night. Robin met up with friends, and they had a fun night out. However, after dropping off one of her girlfriends, the rest of her night went sideways when her boyfriend's car broke down on the Hollywood Freeway near Santa Monica Boulevard and Vermont Avenue.

Robin was now in a predicament. The late hour and the breakdown on the dimly lit freeway prompted her to call her parents for help. She used a call box on the highway, which connected to an operator from the California Highway Patrol. The

Robin Graham

operator called Robins' home and left a message with her younger sister. By 2:35 A.M., her parents were on the way to pick her up, but she was gone when they arrived.

Shortly after she placed the call, a California Highway Patrolman from the opposite – northbound – side of the freeway spotted Robin next to her disabled car. According to the patrol officer, another car approached and pulled to a stop behind Robin's car. He described the second car as a light-blue primer-colored 1957-1960 Corvette hardtop.

A man got out of the car. He was white, with dark hair, in his mid-twenties, about five feet, eight inches tall, and wearing a white turtleneck and bell-bottomed jeans. He walked over and spoke with Robin for a few minutes. The two of them walked to the front of the car, popped the hood, and the man leaned down out of the police officer's sight. The man directed her to get into the car, and Robin got behind the wheel, turned the key, and then laughed when the car roared back to life.

But then things got strange.

She turned off the car and got back out onto the freeway shoulder. Then, Robin, with her purse in hand, got into the passenger seat of the Corvette and drove off with him.

The patrolman – who saw the whole interaction – later said that Robin appeared to willingly get into the man's car after her own vehicle was started. This decision to leave with what is assumed to be a stranger remains one of the most puzzling and unsettling aspects of the case.

A short time later, Robin's parents arrived at the location and were baffled to find her car locked and abandoned on the side of the road. No note was left with the vehicle, and the Grahams were immediately concerned.

The CHP officer who had seen Robin and the unidentified man soon came forward and admitted that he hadn't stopped to help because he assumed this young man was the help she'd called after the breakdown.

This was CHP policy at the time, but because of Robin's disappearance, it would be changed to ensure the safety of stranded female motorists.

Unfortunately, though, the change was too late for Robin.

ASSUMING THAT ROBIN KNEW THE MAN WHO'D stopped to help her on the freeway, her parents, although annoyed, expected to see her at home – but she wasn't there. And she didn't show up in the hours that followed. Later that day, after discovering no one had heard from her, the Grahams contacted the police.

Robin's disappearance sent shockwaves through the community and triggered a thorough investigation led by the Los Angeles Police Department's Rampart Division. At first, detectives were still convinced that Robin had willingly left with the man, but her failure to contact her family and friends sent the investigation in another direction.

Detectives couldn't ignore the disturbing similarities between Robin's case and a string of other unsolved disappearances and murders involving young women in the same area over the preceding two years. The crimes involved female motorists who were attacked by an unidentified male perpetrator who targeted female drivers by offering help. None of the other cases had been solved.

Cheri Jo Bates

One of the first cases happened on October 30, 1966. Cheri Jo Bates, age 18, was stabbed to death and nearly decapitated after leaving Riverside City College. Her body was found early the next morning when a groundskeeper found her on a gravel drive near the library. She had been stabbed repeatedly after being beaten, kicked, and stomped. And then her throat was cut. She was found fully dressed and had not been robbed.

Police found Cheri's Volkswagen Beetle with the keys still in the ignition and three library books on the passenger's seat a short distance from where her body was found. The car's ignition system, which included the distributor coil and engine condenser, had been torn out. Detectives surmised that her assailant had disabled the car and then waited for her to return to it.

The murder was never solved.

On May 29, 1969, Rose Tashman, a 19-year-old Israeli-born student at San Fernando Valley State College, disappeared a few miles from the location where Robin's car was found. Rose's vehicle was found abandoned after it had broken down with a flat left tire. She left a friend's house in Van Nuys around 2:00 A.M. and was going to her apartment in Hollywood. She stopped on the Hollywood Freeway near the Highway Avenue offramp.

Her naked body was found at 6:00 A.M. that evening in a Hollywood Hills ravine, just off Mulholland Drive. She had been raped and strangled with wire.

Rose Tashman

Cindy Mellin (Below)

Months before Robin disappeared, 19-year-old Cindy Mellin vanished on January 20, 1970. She was last seen in the parking lot of the Buenaventura Shopping Center. She worked as a salesclerk at the Broadway Department Store and left work shortly after closing. She was last seen standing by her car at 9:40 P.M. with an unknown white man who was driving a "light-colored car." He appeared to be helping Cindy replace her rear left tire.

Cindy never made it home that night.

The next morning, her father drove to the shopping center and discovered her abandoned car, lifted by a jack and with the flat

Kathleen Johns

tire still in place. The spare tire was next to the car on the pavement. Cindy hadn't run over anything – a sharp object had pierced the side of the tire.

But Cindy wasn't with her car, and she was never seen again.

Two months later, on March 22, 1970, Kathleen Johns, age 22, was driving west on Highway 132 near Interstate 5 in Modesto with her 10-month-old daughter when she realized she was being followed by a light-colored car. The driver was trying to flag her down and get her to stop. After another half-mile or so, she pulled to the side of the road. The other vehicle stopped behind her. With a tire iron in hand, a man exited the car and approached Kathleen's window.

"Your wheel tire is wobbling," the man said. "I'll tighten the lugs."

Kathleen didn't move. She remained in the car as the man used the tire iron to work on the wheel. She could see him in her side mirror. After a few minutes, he stood up, waved, and told her she was all set. Kathleen returned the wave, put the car into gear, and started to drive away.

But when she did, the tire the man had been working on came off, and her car lurched to a stop with a grinding, metallic sound. Kathleen opened her door and got out – the tire was attached by only one lug nut.

The man was suddenly walking back toward her, offering to take her to a service station for help. For some reason, Kathleen got into the man's car with her daughter, and they drove away.

But he wasn't looking for a service station. Instead, he started driving around the area, taking side roads for the next hour or so. During this time, the man remained friendly and never threatened her. When Kathleen asked him if they were going to a service station, he changed the subject and started talking about something else.

By now, Kathleen was scared. She was terrified the man was going to hurt her, so she told him that she was feeling sick. When the driver slowed for a stop sign, Kathleen tightly held her daughter and leaped from the car. The driver slammed to a stop, but Kathleen was already running. A moment later, she heard the squeal of tires as the car roared away.

Fearing the man might come back, Kathleen hid in a field for a few minutes and then was able to flag down a passing police car. She was taken to the closest station where, while sobbing uncontrollably, the police interviewed her. The man was never identified, but at least Kathleen Johns was alive.

Eight months later, no one knew if Robin Graham could say the same.

WHEN THE NEWSPAPERS CONNECTED THE EARLIER incidents with Robin's disappearance, the fear that a serial predator might be stalking the area struck fear into the hearts of residents.

To make matters worse, another sinister layer was added to the investigation when someone suggested that Robin's disappearance might be linked to the notorious Zodiac Killer.

The Zodiac Killer had terrorized California in the late 1960s and early 1970s, claiming at least five victims. Most of his attacks occurred in the San Francisco area, and the killer harassed the police

Could Robin Graham – and the other women who were murdered or disappeared around the same time – victims of the Zodiac Killer?

with letters, puzzles, and cryptic clues. In those letters, he claimed to have murdered 37 victims, and since then, investigators believe he might be linked to several cold cases, some in Southern California and some in other states.

Although the Zodiac ceased written communications around 1974, the unusual nature of the case – and the fact that it has never been solved – has kept interest alive after all these years. While many theories regarding the identity of the killer have been suggested, the only suspect authorities ever publicly named was

Arthur Leigh Allen, a former elementary school teacher and convicted sex offender who died in 1992.

Why did the press and the police suspect Robin's case was linked to the Zodiac? The main thing that fueled the speculation was that Robin disappeared during a full moon, which is when the Zodiac Killer was known to strike. Aside from that, there wasn't much of anything else. Personally, I think the newspapers and the media were so focused on the Zodiac at this time that they pulled him into a case he had nothing to do with. He was the California "boogeyman," although, throughout the rest of the 1970s, Los Angeles would have a string of serial killers of their own to deal with.

It has also been suggested that perhaps Robin's disappearance could be linked to Bruce Davis, an acolyte of Charles Manson.

The possibility that Robin's case might be tied to the Zodiac Killer cast a chilling shadow over the investigation, but soon, the press would add another suspect into the mix that was tied to L.A.'s homegrown monster, Charles Manson. He had been arrested late the previous year and was charged with several murders, including actress Sharon Tate, Leno and Rosemary La Bianca, and others.

After the *Los Angeles Times* did a story on Robin's disappearance, a woman wrote a letter to her parents and said she, too, had stalled on the road, and a man driving a Corvette had stopped and offered to help her. He claimed to be an off-duty police detective. Fortunately, she declined his offer. It's unknown whether this was the same man last seen with Robin, but the description of the man seemed to match.

Later, the woman identified a photograph of Manson Family member Bruce Davis as the man she saw that night. Davis, who was born in Louisiana and attended the University of Tennessee for three years, traveled to California in 1962. He fell under the spell of Charles Mansion and three of his "girls" -- Mary Brunner, Lynette Fromme, and Patricia Krenwinkel – five years later.

Davis was present in July 1969 when Manson cut the ear of musician Gary Hinman, although he wasn't present when Hinman was stabbed to death by Bobby Beausoleil. He remained part of the group until Manson's arrest in 1969 when he went into hiding. Davis ultimately turned himself in a few weeks after Robin disappeared, which is when the woman identified him from his booking photo.

Davis is still serving a life sentence at the time of this writing, but it's unlikely that he had anything to do with Robin's case. It might be slightly more plausible than the Zodiac Killer, but not much. I think throwing these two possibilities into the mix made things more confusing and possibly kept the real killer from being caught.

Robin wasn't the last young woman to disappear from the side of a Southern California highway – under very similar circumstances – in the early 1970s.

About two months after Robin vanished, on January 18, 1971, 19-year-old Christine Eastin went missing from Hayward. She left home around 10:00 P.M. to go to a car wash and pick up a friend from a local restaurant. Her car was later found at the car wash, and her purse was discovered locked inside.

Christine Eastin

Christine was never seen again.

A year later, on April 28, 1972, Ernestine Terello, a housewife from Agoura, had to pull over in her 1969 yellow Plymouth because of a flat tire. She was trying to do some shopping at the Topanga Plaza when she had to stop. Other drivers later reported seeing her stop, and they became the last people ever to see her alive.

Later that day, she was reported missing by her husband, and five days after that, her car was found locked and abandoned near Agoura and Chesbro Roads on the Ventura Freeway.

Ernestine's body was discovered a month later, on May 27, by Boy Scouts hiking near Yerba Buena Road, off the Pacific Coast Highway, and about six miles from where her car was found. Due to the severe decomposition of her remains, her cause of death was not determined. However, authorities strongly suspected that she had been kidnapped from her disabled vehicle and then sexually assaulted and murdered.

The last woman possibly connected to Robin's case was Mona Gallegos, age 22, a part-time waitress who vanished on June 19, 1975, after visiting an auto salesman friend in Alhambra. She went to see him for advice on buying a new car. She left his home at 1:00 A.M. and was driving back to Covina when she ran out of gas near Santa Anita Avenue on the San Bernadino Freeway in El Monte. Her car was found locked and abandoned by CHP officers at 4:45 A.M.

The police theorized that a motorist had offered Mona a ride to a service station nearby that was open all night but had abducted her instead.

Six months later, her skeletal remains were found by two teenage boys who were hiking in a ravine near Riverside. Her cause of death couldn't be determined, but at least her family and friends had the closure that came with her body being found.

It was a sense of peace that the family and friends of Robin Graham never found. Despite decades of effort by law enforcement, the mystery of Robin's disappearance leaves many lingering questions.

Why did she leave willingly with the unidentified man that night? Was this man connected to the other disappearances in the area? And, if so, was Robin one of his victims, or was her vanishing a separate, yet equally baffling, tragedy?

We'll likely never know, and those questions remain to cast a long shadow over Robin's story, reminding us that some mysteries will never be fully unraveled.

1973: SEARCHING FOR A BUTTERFLY
THE DISAPPEARANCE OF JANICE POCKETT

JANICE POCKETT DISAPPEARED BECAUSE OF A BUTTERFLY.

On the late morning of July 26, 1973, Janice was walking with her family and spotted a pretty butterfly on the sidewalk. As the seven-year-old approached it, the butterfly didn't fly away. That's when she realized it was dead. Sad but still entranced by the colors of its wings, she placed it under the edge of a rock next to the path so that no one else would find it.

Janice wanted that butterfly for herself.

When the Pocketts returned to their Tolland, Connecticut, home, it was time for lunch. It wouldn't be until 3:30 that afternoon that Janice convinced her mother, Kathryn, to let her return and retrieve the butterfly she'd so carefully hidden that morning. Kathryn gave her an empty envelope to put the

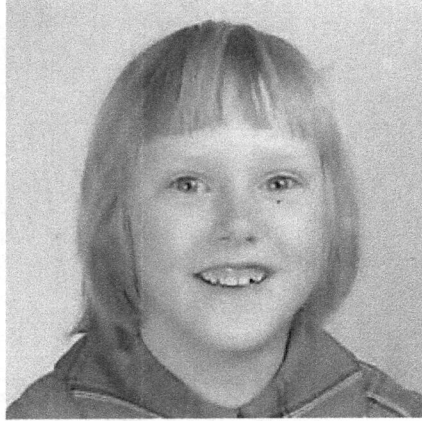

Janice Pockett

butterfly in and told Janice to come right back. It was the first time that she'd ever let her go anywhere by herself, but the rock was less than a block from the Pockett house. You could see it while standing in the front yard.

The determined little girl climbed onto her metallic green bicycle and happily pedaled off to pick up the butterfly.

And Janice Pockett was never seen again.

KATHRYN WAS BUSY IN THE KITCHEN when Janice left on her adventure, so she wasn't closely watching the clock. Suddenly, though, she realized that 30 minutes had passed since her daughter had ridden off on her bicycle. Kathryn went outside, expecting to see Janice playing in the front yard, but she wasn't there. Looking down the block, she saw something that made her heart skip – her daughter's bike was lying on its side next to the road. Janice wasn't with it.

Praying that Janice was nearby, Kathryn ran to the bike and called her daughter's name a few times but got no reply. She turned and raced back to the house. Just then, her husband, Ronald, was turning into the driveway, home from work. Together, they searched the neighborhood for about 45 minutes but saw no sign of Janice.

Finally, at 4:50 P.M, Ronald called the police. Concerned by Janice's young age, the Connecticut State Police immediately

Janice's bicycle was found next to the road, but the little girl had vanished.

began a massive search for the girl. Within hours, there were dozens of police officers looking for Janice. They were soon joined by available and off-duty firefighters from 10 different towns. They combed the streets of Tolland and scoured the surrounding woods and fields. As darkness began to fall, investigators went door-to-door, hoping Janice was at a friend or neighbor's house and had lost track of time.

But there was no trace of the little girl.

On Friday morning, July 27, the search intensified. Over 800 volunteers, including 100 U.S. Navy and Marines enlisted men stationed in nearby Groton, joined the search. Members from a local motorcycle club joined searchers on horseback and on foot as a National Guard helicopter flew above. Divers from the Tolland County fire and rescue squad searched three ponds in Janice's neighborhood, along with sections of the nearby Willimantic River.

A spokesman for the state police, Peter Walsh, told reporters they were working under the assumption that Janice was lost but admitted they'd found no clues to her location. He told the press, "Foul play is not suspected, but of course, it hasn't been ruled out. The likelihood increases with every hour the girl is not found."

The search continued around the clock, finally pausing around nightfall on Saturday. No clue to Janice's whereabouts had been discovered. Peter Walsh again told reporters that they still hadn't found any evidence that she'd been abducted, and they weren't going to stop the physical search until they were certain she wasn't in the area. He explained, "The child is in good health, and the weather has been warm, so we can't stop searching the woods until we're convinced she's not out there."

The pause on Saturday evening had been so they could scale back and redirect the search effort. Since most of Tolland had been searched, officials decided volunteers were no longer needed on Sunday. The police and military continued the search, concentrating on areas where the forest was extremely dense.

As the hours passed, clues were discovered. Footprints that appeared to have been made by a child were found, but there was no proof they belonged to Janice. There was no way to be sure. The search also turned up several articles of clothing, but her mother said the items didn't belong to Janice.

Hundreds of police officers, military personnel, and volunteers searched for the missing girl.

The searchers walked shoulder-to-shoulder through dense woodland, carefully going over every inch of ground. The Red Cross and the Salvation Army donated supplies to aid the searchers, and the ladies' auxiliary groups from several fire departments made sandwiches, provided hot meals, and gathered donations from area stores to ensure the searchers were fed and hydrated.

By Wednesday night, August 1, investigators still had not found evidence of foul play but had to admit that it was unlikely Janice was still in the area. Her family had become certain she'd been abducted. They knew she hadn't been lost in the woods because she wasn't allowed to go into the forest without her parents. Janice's godfather, John McParland – a Manchester police officer – told reporters that Janice had always followed her parent's rule about the woods. Although Ronald and Kathryn would sometimes take Janice and her younger sister on walks through the wooded area, neither girl had ever even tried to go there alone.

While the search effort was winding down, the Connecticut State Police doubled the number of detectives assigned to the case. Investigators from five different state police barracks followed up on every tip they received but were forced to admit they still had no solid leads about what happened to Janice.

John McParland told reporters that he and the Pockett family were very impressed with the way the state police were handling the investigation. The search efforts, he said, "have been the best I've ever seen in my nine years of experience."

No question they were working hard, but all the hours the detectives put in led nowhere. They had returned to the door-to-door search, interviewing everyone in the neighborhood to see if they recalled seeing anything – or anyone – suspicious in the days leading up to Janice's disappearance.

By now, they were starting to accept that Janice wasn't lost – she'd been taken. Although no signs of a struggle had been found, Kathryn was certain that her daughter would have never gotten willingly into a car with anyone.

But even with this change of strategy, the police still found no trace of the girl.

Two weeks after Janice vanished, eight area businessmen put together a reward fund of $8,000 for information leading to the arrest and conviction of whoever had taken her. The men didn't want to be publicly identified – they just wanted to see Janice returned. Peter Walsh, the state police spokesman, verified that the reward money had been deposited in a local bank and that the offer would be valid for one year.

Two months passed, and by September, the reward had grown to $10,000, but detectives were still struggling to develop solid leads. Kathryn told reporters she was trying to stay optimistic that Janie would be found unharmed, but it was difficult. She did have some sliver of hope – Janice's body hadn't been found, so it was possible she was still alive.

But Kathryn was having more trouble keeping it together than she revealed to the press. A week or so after her daughter had disappeared, she sought medical help and was given a prescription for tranquilizers. Ronald wasn't doing much better. He had taken five weeks off from his job as a truck driver because he found it impossible to sleep.

Their emotional distress had started in August after the phone calls. A man started calling their home, making disturbing comments about the disappearance. It took two months for the police to track down the caller. In October, they arrested Robert Bell and charged him with harassment for making the calls.

Around this same time, also in October, the state police surprisingly released a composite sketch of a man who was wanted for questioning in Janice's case. The sketch was based on a description given by a woman who lived near the Pocketts. She had seen a man driving a late model, medium brown car with a darker brown top in the neighborhood around the time the girl went missing. She was sure the man didn't live nearby because she'd never seen him before – and hadn't seen him in the neighborhood since that day.

Days, then weeks, passed, but the stranger had vanished as mysteriously as Janice had.

In early November, Hartford mayor George Athanson announced that he planned to ask the FBI to assist with the investigation. A public petition was circulated asking President Richard Nixon to direct the FBI to help the state police. The petition's goal was to get 50,000 signatures, but by the end of the month, they'd doubled that number. Regardless of public support, though, FBI Director Clarence Kelly stated that the bureau couldn't intervene unless there were concrete evidence of a kidnapping.

Ronald, Kathryn, and Janice's little sister, Mary Jane, had little to celebrate that holiday season. They were still trying to remain optimistic, but it was getting harder as more time passed without any progress in the search.

The case slowed, then stalled, and finally, by February, it was at a standstill. Detectives hadn't had any fresh leads in weeks. The FBI finally agreed to review the case but turned it down once again. There was no evidence, they said, that a federal crime had been committed. But that opinion quickly changed. On February 8, 1974, the U.S. Department of Justice directed the FBI to join the search for Janice.

Kathryn was thrilled that the FBI was joining the investigation. She told reporters that she had no problem with the way the state police had handled the case but stated, "The FBI is more experienced in matters like this."

It had now been six months since Kathryn had seen her daughter. She was emotionally drained. The worst part for her, her husband, and her other daughter was not knowing what had happened to Janice. Mary Jane missed her sister and couldn't understand why she didn't come home. Kathryn now prayed that the FBI could provide them with some answers.

But progress remained slow. In April, the state police announced they would conduct another search of the woods near the Pocketts' home. Reporters were assured that new information hadn't prompted the new search. It was merely another attempt to find some clues. The FBI assisted with the search – along with about 150 volunteers – but once again, nothing was found.

More time passed, and soon, the one-year anniversary of Janice's vanishing arrived. Marking the occasion, investigators announced they had two potential suspects. Both had previously been arrested on morals charges, but both had hired attorneys who refused to let detectives question them. State Police Captain Thomas McDonnell declined to name the suspects, probably because he was forced to admit they had no actual evidence that linked the men to the missing girl. There were no eyewitnesses, leads, clues, or evidence – the police were just hoping for a confession that wasn't coming. In August, the police stated that the two possible suspects had been cleared of any involvement in Janice's disappearance.

After more than a year of investigating, detectives were forced to admit they knew little more than they had on the day Janice went missing. Captain McDonnell told reporters that he thought it was unlikely that Janice was still alive, but he confessed he had no idea of what happened to her.

Thomas Leavitt, the Special Agent in Charge for the FBI in Connecticut, said that the greatest hurdle they faced in the case was the total lack of clues. He told the press, "Unless some individual is picked up on some other charge and confesses, the Pockett case will be very difficult to solve."

Janice was still gone, and to her family, it seemed that no one was looking for her anymore.

YEARS WENT BY, AND THE POCKETT FAMILY gradually adjusted to life without Janice. Detectives continued to follow up on every lead they received, but there weren't very many of them to follow anymore. What few they had soon dried up, and the case went cold.

Occasionally, something new would come up to get the attention of investigators, like the theory that Janice's case might be linked to two other missing girls – Lisa White, who vanished in November 1974, and Debra Spickler, who'd disappeared in July 1968. But it was just a theory. There was no evidence to link the cases; even if there had been, the police had no suspects in those disappearances either.

In November 1979, state police divers searched a pond in Vernon after receiving a tip that Janice's body could be found there – from a psychic. A spokesman for the police, Joe Crowley, told reporters, "We don't feel there's a great possibility that she's there, but feeling that no stone should be unturned, we're doing it." They found nothing at the bottom of the pond.

In August 1980, a former carnival worker who was behind bars in a Massachusetts prison confessed to killing Janice. Charles Pierce – serving a life sentence for an unrelated murder and sexual assault – claimed that Janice was buried on property owned by a Tolland man named Earl Beebe. This property had been searched back in 1973, but investigators returned to it and spent several days digging in the spot that Pierce had described to them. They found nothing.

Pierce still maintained he'd killed Janice, along with more than a dozen other people, but no evidence linked him to any of the crimes. On his deathbed, he admitted he'd made the whole thing up for attention.

Over the next decade, the police continued receiving occasional tips about the case and followed up on each one. Despite their efforts, though, no progress was made in finding Janice or identifying her abductor.

Then, in 2001, another announcement was made. The state police were now looking into the possibility that a man named Nathaniel Bar-Jonah – just arrested in Montana for the murder of a 10-year-old boy – had kidnapped Janice. Bar-Jonah was 14 in 1973 and lived in Webster, Massachusetts, about 20 miles from Toland. When his property was searched in Montana, investigators found human bone fragments under the dirt floor of his garage. DNA testing ruled out the possibility that any of the bones belonged to

Janice and her sister, Mary, before the disappearance. Today, Mary keeps the story of her sister alive.

Janice, but investigators refused to rule him out as a suspect in her disappearance.

Further investigation failed to find any link between Janice and Bar-Jonah. However, he was eventually convicted for the abduction and sexual assault of three other children and was sentenced to 130 years in prison. He died behind bars in 2008.

As more time passed, both Kathyrn and Ronald passed away, both going to their graves without ever knowing what happened to their daughter. Janice's sister, Mary Englebrecht, has continued to do all she can to keep her sister's case in the public eye. Despite all the time that's passed, she's still hopeful it will someday be solved, and her sister will be returned to her.

"I'm still searching for answers," Mary said recently. "Someone out there knows what happened."

And maybe someday, the person with the answers will come forward and give the little girl's sister, who only wanted a butterfly, the peace she has deserved for so long.

1973: THEY NEVER CAME HOME
THE FORGOTTEN STORY OF
MITCHEL WEISER AND BONNIE BICKWIT

EARLY ONE SUMMER MORNING, JULY 27, 1973, TWO teenagers from Brooklyn started hitchhiking toward central New York to attend one of the biggest concerts in rock history.

They were never seen again.

To this day, the disappearance of 16-year-old Mitchel Weiser and 15-year-old Bonnie Bickwit remains unsolved. Initially dismissed as romantic runaways who'd return home as soon as they ran out of money, their fate is a mystery. After decades of false leads and police bungling, investigators continue to ponder theories about what may have happened to them. Even so, they're no closer to finding them than the authorities were in 1973.

The couple was last seen leaving Camp Wel-Met, a popular summer camp in the Catskills. Bonnie, who had

Mitchel Weiser and Bonnie Bickwit before their disappearance in 1973.

been a camper there for a year, now had a job at the camp as a parents' helper. Mitch had stayed in Brooklyn that summer. He'd snagged the perfect job at a local photography studio. On the evening of Thursday, July 26, he boarded a bus in Manhattan that was headed for Bonnie's camp in Narrowsburg, a small town about two hours away.

Once they met up, they planned to hitchhike 150 miles northwest to attend the outdoor "Summer Jam" concert at the Watkins Glen Grand Prix Raceway. The lineup for the show included The Grateful Dead, The Allman Brothers, and The Band. It is still believed to have drawn one of the largest crowds in American rock history.

Of the estimated 600,000 fans who came to Summer Jam, only Mitch and Bonnie vanished without a trace.

On Friday morning, Mitch and Bonnie had breakfast at the camp and then caught a ride into Narrowsburg. With little money in their pockets, they walked along the highway, carrying sleeping bags and holding a cardboard sign that read "Watkins Glen."

What happened next, though, is at the heart of the mystery. The early 1970s was a different time in America. The case predates photos of missing children on milk cartons by more than ten years. Mitch and Bonnie vanished decades before cell phones, Amber Alerts, and social media.

They only had the police to find them, and while many investigators worked hard to solve the case, it was made more difficult by the initial bungling by the police in 1973. Police investigators in three New York counties originally ignored pleas by Mitch's and Bonnie's parents to look for them, dismissing them as two hippie runaways. Despite assurances by then-NYPD Commissioner Donald Cawley that the department would alert police agencies across the state about the disappearances, they never did. This resulted in Sullivan County – where Wel-Met Camp was located – never starting an investigation at all.

Mitch and Bonnie were lost – and on their own.

IN 1973, MITCHEL WEISER WAS A BABY-FACED, bespectacled, talented, and well-liked Junior at John Dewey High School in Brooklyn.

At five-seven and 140 pounds, he wore long brown hair parted in the middle and usually tied in a ponytail. He wore round, gold-rimmed glasses and loved Bonnie, photography, baseball, and The Grateful Dead – he even named his dog "Casey Jones" after their song. Friends considered him fearless and a bit of a rebel, only tamed by his devotion to Bonnie, who was a year younger than him. They'd met at John Dewey High.

Friends and family called him an "incredibly gifted, talented person." Susan Weiser Liebegott, Mitch's sister, still has a box that contains her brother's memorabilia collection – 1969 Mets World Series ticket stubs, souvenir trading cards from the 1964-65 New York World's Fair, his old tortoise-shell eyeglasses, a stack of his poems, and a giant birthday card from the party thrown by friends for his 15th birthday.

When he'd heard about Summer Jam, an excited Mitch and his friend, Larry Marion, were determined to go. Larry bought a pair of tickets but got the bad news that his mother wouldn't let him attend, fearing for his safety. Mitch's mother, Shirley, also asked her son not to go. She wanted to give him more money so he wouldn't hitchhike, but Mitch left with just $25 – most of which he used for his bus ticket to Narrowsburg and a taxi to the camp.

Family and friends have always rejected the idea that the couple ran away. They insisted they were too close to everyone to do something like that. Larry Marion stated with "absolute certainty" that they had no advance plan to run away. Bonnie wasn't even supposed to go – she was using Larry's ticket. The pair were going to the concert and then coming home. Mitch told everyone he'd be home on Monday, and no one doubted that – until he vanished.

WHILE MITCH WAS TRAVELING BY BUS TO Narrowsburg, Bonnie was arguing with her boss at the camp about having the weekend off to attend the concert.

At four-eleven and 90 pounds, Bonnie was sweet and highly intelligent, but she could also be a strong-willed,

The mess halls at Camp Wel-Met, the Jewish summer camp where Bonnie was working in 1973.

determined little spitfire. She had long brown hair and a freckled face and didn't look much older than the campers she was watching over that summer.

Bonnie had always been placed in gifted classes in school, but instead of continuing with traditional schooling, she enrolled at John Dewey, a recently launched experimental high school. After reading about the school, she wrote a letter to the principal and asked to be admitted. She was immediately accepted, and the principal was so impressed with her letter that he framed it.

Like Mitch, Bonnie was a free spirit. She was warm, friendly, and loved music, especially The Allman Brothers. So, when she had the chance to use Larry's ticket for Summer Jam, she was thrilled.

So, when her boss told her she couldn't take the weekend off, she quit her job and left with Mitch. Before she left, she told her employer she would return after the concert and pick up her clothes and last paycheck.

On the morning of July 27, the pair set out for the show. Both wore blue jeans and T-shirts. With an expensive camera slung around his neck, Mitch had a gray and green plaid flannel shirt tied around his waist. Concert tickets were safely tucked away in their pockets, and sleeping bags were hanging off their shoulders.

They were last seen hitchhiking along State Route 97, a 70-mile stretch of highway that runs past Camp Wel-Met. A truck driver picked them up, and they thanked him after he dropped them off a short time later when his route took him in another direction.

He was the last known person to see them.

The Summer Jam concert in Watkins Glen in 1973.

About 150,000 TICKETS HAD BEEN SOLD IN advance for the one-day Summer Jam concert. But more than two days before a single note was played, concert promoters, law enforcement, and social service providers in Schuyler County were stunned to see that nearly 200,000 fans had already started pouring into the small town of Watkins Glen in New York's Finger Lakes Region. The massive crowds had closed the roads – just as Woodstock had done four years earlier.

By the time soundchecks started, more than 150,000 people were already on the grounds, knocking down portions of the fence. The producers eventually removed all the fencing and turned the concert into a free event. By then, they didn't have any other choice.

While Woodstock featured multiple cultural touchstone performances, a bestselling double album, and an acclaimed concert film, most don't remember much about Summer Jam today. But, at one point, it held a world record for the "greatest claimed attendance at a pop festival," and it's been estimated that one out of every 350 people living in the United States at the time attended the show.

The massive crowds made it impossible to keep order at the festival – and to know who attended that weekend.

Even with all those people, though, Summer Jam was relatively crime-free. There were no violent offenses at all, and the New York State Police referred to it as "generally peaceful," mostly dealing with vehicle and traffic arrests.

The show's promoters heard nothing about Mitch and Bonnie's disappearance until they were contacted by a reporter in 2023 – demonstrating the failure of law enforcement to reach out to anyone connected to the event.

WHEN MITCH DIDN'T COME HOME ON SUNDAY, his mother, Shirley, began asking his friends if they'd heard from him. No one had.

On Monday, a day and a half after the concert ended, Camp Wel-Met telephoned Bonnie's mother, Raye, and told her that Bonnie had not returned.

That day, Mitch's father, Sidney, and his sister, Susan, drove five hours from Brooklyn to Watkins Glen. They met with the county

police and gave them photos of Mitch and Bonnie, but the missing kids were dismissed as runaways. Susan said they even went out to the concert site and screamed their names in case they were there and were hurt.

While the police in Sullivan County, Schuyler County, and New York City ignored the missing couple, their worried families scrambled to find them on their own. Bonnie's mother traveled to Monticello – the Sullivan County seat – and asked for help from the sheriff's office. They were supposed to be the lead investigative agency because it was the last place where Bonnie and Mitch were seen, but they backburned the case, already believing they were runaways. The NYPD was supposed to help because the pair were city residents, but that didn't happen.

Taking matters into their own hands, the families began distributing flyers all over Sullivan and Schuyler counties. They placed ads in underground newspapers nationwide, pleading with Mitch and Bonnie to contact them. They hired a private detective. They contacted and visited hippie communes, Native American reservations, and cult groups. Susan even went undercover and visited the Children of God cult to see if they knew anything. They didn't, and she quickly left.

Despite extensive local press coverage, the efforts made by the two families didn't get far. Without help from the police, they were unsure what to do next. Today, we have social media, private groups, and podcasts to help spread the word when the police won't, but in 1973, the families had nowhere to turn. Ignored by the cops and with no private groups to help them, they soon ran out of money and resources. Bonnie's mother, upset and exhausted, even sought help from psychics, but they weren't much help either.

The hunt for Mitch and Bonnie slowly fizzled out as their heartbroken friends and family members tried to move on with their lives. Inevitably, the story faded from the press and was forgotten by the public.

But not by the families. In 1984, Mitch's parents moved to Arizona because of his father's asthma. However, they continued to pay New York's telephone company every month to keep their name and Arizona number in the Brooklyn phone directory.

They wanted to ensure Mitch could find their new number when he finally came home.

IN 1998 – THE 25TH ANNIVERSARY OF THE DISAPPEARANCE – an investigative reporter in New York decided to look into the story of the missing teenagers. The subsequent article revealed a pattern of incompetence from all the law enforcement agencies involved. The Sullivan County Sheriff's Office and the NYPD's Missing Persons Squad lost original case files, witness lists, investigator's notes, and the teenagers' dental records, which could have been used to identify bodies.

Former Sullivan County detective Anthony Suarez admitted in the article that he'd made no attempt to find any lost witnesses after taking over the case in 1994 and said he'd never tried to contact the case's original investigator. He made no attempt to explain this.

At least the former NYPD Missing Persons Squad commander Phillip Mahoney said he was embarrassed, but that wouldn't help the two kids who'd never been found.

Schuyler County Sheriff Michael Maloney also expressed regret over the failure of the police to do their jobs, including never entering the couple's names in the FBI's national missing persons data bank.

The newspaper investigation sparked outrage from family, friends, and the public. There were calls for New York's governor and attorney general to step in and reopen the case, and finally, in June 2000, their pleas were answered. New York Governor George Pataki and Attorney General Eliot Spitzer appointed state police investigator Roy Streever and New York City detective William Kilgallon to reopen the case. After all the years that had passed, someone was finally looking for Mitch and Bonnie.

MEANWHILE, A NEW CABLE STATION CALLED MSNBC, had just started producing a true-crime series called *Missing Persons*, with Mitch and Bonnie's story among the first cases it covered.

In July 2000, they sent a video crew to Camp Wel-Met, accompanied by a psychic named Maurice Schickler, who claimed he'd received visions about the teenagers being murdered and buried in a rock quarry near the camp. He said that Mitch was murdered by a man who was a Vietnam veteran, who murdered Bonnie a few days later. Schickler said the killer's name was "Wayne, Wade, or Willie, and he is still alive."

THREE MONTHS LATER, ALLYN SMITH, A 51-year-old Rhode Island man who worked at a jewelry manufacturing company, was watching television when he came across the episode of *Missing Persons*.

He was intrigued when he saw the scenes the producers included from Summer Jam. When he saw photos of Mitch and Bonnie, he got excited and dialed the phone number provided at the end of the episode. He had trouble getting through, but after several long-distance calls to New York – no small expense in those days – he finally reached state police investigator Roy Streever.

Smith didn't know Mitch and Bonnie, but he met them randomly while hitchhiking home because he couldn't get anywhere near the concert. He recalled they looked young and heard them talk about a summer camp. He remembered Bonnie was wearing a bandana or scarf on her head.

One report claimed Mitch and Bonnie were picked up in an orange Volkswagen bus like this one.

A driver in an orange Volkswagen bus with Pennsylvania license plates picked up the three hitchhikers. It was hot, he said, and the group stopped to cool off in the Susquehanna River.

Smith said he was about 100 feet from the river's edge when the couple entered the water. He claimed he suddenly heard the girl scream and saw her flailing in the water. The boy jumped in to save her, but both were quickly swept around a bend in the river. Smith was sure they had accidentally drowned in the swift current.

His first reaction was to do nothing – he wasn't much of a swimmer and was sure he would drown, too. After the couple was out of right, Smith and the driver decided they could do nothing. It was a secluded spot, and there was no one to call for help. They returned to the van and drove off, and he recalled to the police that the driver had told him, "I'm going to be turning off to head for Pennsylvania soon. I'll call the police from a gas station."

"If he did," Smith said in 2000, "there might be a record."

Believing the driver would call the police, Smith never reported the incident himself. He was high from smoking marijuana and didn't want to deal with the cops.

Following the call, Streever and Detective Kilgallon now had to try to corroborate Smith's story Smith came to New York to try and help and went along to try and find the spot where the drowning occurred. He knew it was near a bridge, but after looking at dozens of them, he couldn't be sure which one was the right one.

Kilgallon interviewed Smith's longtime friends, and they confirmed that Smith had been talking about the drowning since he'd returned from Summer Jam in July 1972. Ultimately, the detectives found Smith to be a credible witness and accepted his story as the conclusion of the case.

Finally, after over 25 years, they had the big break that Mitch and Bonnie's family and friends had been waiting for – or did they?

There was still a big problem – no bodies were ever found.

When someone drowns, their body builds up gases over several days, pushing it to the surface. But sometimes it doesn't. A body can get tangled in debris, especially in rivers, and never be found. It's rare, though, that two bodies – or at least one of them – wouldn't surface. It was possible that they'd been carried downstream, maybe even to another state, and, if found, ended up as unidentified remains.

In 2000, Streever and Kilgallon checked three county coroner's offices along the Susquehanna for unidentified bodies but had no luck. That left 63 other counties along the river – but they weren't checked.

The family members ' reactions to Smith's story were split. Bonnie's mother and sister said the account provided comfort and closure, but Mitch's family and friends weren't convinced. There were too many unanswered questions, they said. They also wanted to find the mysterious driver of the Volkswagen bus, wondering if he'd corroborate the story.

There were other things that hadn't been done. Smith still hadn't undergone a polygraph test. Streever didn't want to do it immediately because Smith was cooperating with them. And, of course, there were still all those other coroners along the river. Plus, other theories had popped up around this time, including claims by a serial killer named Hadden Clark, who claimed he killed the pair. He hadn't – the police were able to rule him out quickly.

Tragically, before anything else could be done to verify Smith's account, two hijacked planes flew into the World Trade Center, killing 3,000 New Yorkers and triggering a national emergency. Streever and Kilgallon were quickly reassigned.

So, Mitch and Bonnie's case went back into cold storage for another dozen years.

IN 2013, TWO YEARS AFTER TAKING ON THE NOW 40-year-old cold case, a Sullivan County detective named Cyrus Barnes received a telephone call from a woman in Florida.

She had grown up in the town of Wayne – about 20 miles from Watkins Glen – and had lived there with her parents and siblings. She told Barnes that she believed that her father was involved in Mitch's murder.

She was 11 years old at the time of Summer Jam, and she was with her father in a local restaurant when she approached a young man sitting at a table and asked his name. He said it was Mitch. She recalled that the boy seemed uncomfortable and agitated.

Steuben County Sheriff's investigator Don Lewis later said that the woman's information was "detailed and pretty explicit," and she alleged that her father and other men had sexually assaulted her, her siblings, and other children. Lewis added that her father had been a "person of interest" at the time.

Her story was so convincing to detectives that Barnes asked the state police and Lewis' office for assistance with the investigation. That included securing digging equipment, sonar, and cadaver-sniffing dogs that could corroborate her account.

They searched two locations in Wayne – the family's former cottage and a decommissioned New York State Electric and Gas power plant adjacent to a private residence.

A neighbor named Sarah Saunders was home that day when the investigators arrived, telling her they needed to dig behind her property for "missing people."

Coincidentally, Sarah had just consulted with a psychic medium after losing her parents and her grandmother. The woman had asked her out of the blue, "Do you have dead bodies around your house?" Sarah was shocked, but the woman assured her they were good people and weren't there to hurt or scare her family.

"I was so freaked out," Sarah later said.

But despite a thorough search, the excavations turned up nothing. Barnes wanted to interview the woman's father, referring to him as a suspect, but was directed to

Bonnie was close with her family, and they never believed that she and Mitch had run away.

the father's lawyer, who stonewalled him. He was never interviewed by the police and died in 2022.

AFTER THAT, MORE YEARS PASSED, AND in early 2022, the case ended up on the desk of Sullivan County detective Jack Harb. He had no interest in talking to the press.

Once again, law enforcement officials, missing persons experts, and family and friends of Mitch and Bonnie are bewildered by the response from Sullivan County – comparing it to the response they got back in 1973.

The more things change, they say, the more they stay the same.

Aside from the investigators in Sullivan County, no one else seems ready to give up on the case just yet. If Mitch and Bonnie disappeared – and weren't killed – they'd easily still be alive today. If they're out there, there are many people who would really like to see them.

If they died that summer weekend, they could still be found. People have been urged to share their memories and post their photos from the concert. There are multiple websites that allow families and friends to seek information about their missing loved ones. Allyn Smith could finally be asked to take that polygraph test, strengthening the credibility of his story. A search could be coordinated for unclaimed and unidentified bodies in all the counties along the Susquehanna River, which crosses three states. New York state officials could investigate the background of the now-dead suspect, who was brought to the attention of Cyrus Barnes in 2013.

Mitch had an expensive camera that may have been given to someone as a gift, though authorities never released its exact model to use as a clue that could help corroborate a potential witness. What if there had been a partial roll of film inside that had photos of Mitch and Bonnie?

No matter how old the case might be, a lead can still be followed and treated as though it might be the one lead that could close the case.

Many of Mitch's and Bonnie's families and friends are gone now. They've died or gotten old, and their memories faded.

Bonnie's mother, Raye, developed Alzheimer's Disease in her final years. She had once asked her daughter if she'd had any other children – so she told her about Bonnie.

"I don't remember," Raye replied, "but it's just as well. It's too sad."

And she was right. It's a story that's just too sad.

1973: THE MISSING PAPER GIRL
THE MYSTERY OF SHARON PRETORIUS

IT WAS FRIDAY, SEPTEMBER 28, 1973 – an otherwise ordinary day for 13-year-old Sharon Pretorius. After finishing her weekly piano lesson, she left her home in Dayton, Ohio, to collect money from the customers on her newspaper delivery route.

Sharon worked in her own neighborhood, getting up early in the morning and delivering newspapers to readers' homes each day. Once a month, she took her *Dayton Journal-Herald* collection book and went door-to-door to collect the paper subscription fee from those who received the paper she dropped off daily.

Although it seems old-fashioned to us today – in this era of vanishing print newspapers and digital payments – back in the 1970s, no one thought twice of a young girl or boy walking to every house along their delivery route and collecting money.

It was safe – there was nothing to worry about.

Sharon Pretorius

Sharon's brother saw her leave the Pretorius home with her collection book in hand, but she never visited any of the houses on her route that day.

She never returned home.

And Sharon was never seen again.

HOURS TICKED BY. SHARON'S MOTHER CAME HOME from work, and dinner was soon on the table. But where was Sharon? Her mother, Mary Carol, called friends and neighbors, but no one had seen her. Finally, she called the Dayton police.

She told them Sharon was a very responsible young woman, and her mother insisted she hadn't run away. Even so, when she spoke to the police that night around 10:30 P.M., she was told she would have to wait at least 24 hours before she could file a missing person report.

This wasn't the truth – then or now – and, in fact, when it comes to children, the sooner the search is started, the better. All that happened in this case was that one lazy police officer managed to put off doing his job for a little while longer.

The next morning, even though she was hours ahead of schedule, Mary Carol called the police again. By now, she was frantic with worry.

The detectives who caught the case were angry about the delay in the report being filed, especially after quickly discovering that Sharon was not the kind of teenager who would disappear on her own.

Her father had died when she was seven, and she had a very close relationship with her mother. She had recently started her freshman year at Fairview High School and had always been a straight-A student. She was so smart that she'd even skipped eighth grade. She also played the flute in the high school band and was excited about performing for the football game scheduled for the night after she vanished.

A description of Sharon went out on the wire. She was tall for her age – five feet, seven inches – and looked older than 13. Despite her appearance, her mother insisted she didn't date and had never had a boyfriend. She enjoyed her paper route and spent most of her time with friends, studying and playing music. One of her friends, Holly Samuels, said, "She didn't wear makeup and always wore jeans or long skirts. She was quiet but never standoffish, and she was always friendly."

Sharon had two older brothers, but she was the oldest girl in the family, so she often helped care for her younger sister and two younger brothers without complaint. Her mother had a job and, as a single parent, needed all the help she could get. As the oldest girl in the 1970s, the job naturally fell on Sharon.

But she didn't mind. She loved her family, and there was simply no reason for her to leave home. Months before, one of her cousins confided in Sharon that she sometimes thought about running away from home. Sharon talked her out of it. She told her that she'd never felt that way. She never felt like she had anything to run away from.

That made her disappearance even more baffling.

THE VANISHING OF THIS RESPONSIBLE, well-liked young woman sent a ripple through the community. When school officials learned she was missing, they canceled the football game on Saturday night so that students could help search for Sharon.

While the volunteers combed through every inch of Sharon's Dayton neighborhood, detectives went door-to-door, interviewing residents to see if they had seen Sharon or anyone unusual on Friday afternoon. By Sunday morning, they had spoken with more than 250 people.

By that afternoon, a group of Sharon's neighbors announced they were offering a $1,000 reward for information about the missing girl. They hoped it would bring Sharon home safely – but sadly, it would never be collected.

The police weren't doing much better than the volunteers. Dayton Police Sergeant Robert Hahn expressed how hard they'd been working but with no results. He told reporters, "We've been working on it extensively, but we just haven't turned anything up. A lot of people remember seeing her, but not on Friday."

On Monday, detectives spoke with a witness who told them she had seen a young girl struggling with a man on a street corner not far from Sharon's home around 5:30 P.M. on Friday. The witness believed that the man – described as being between 30 and 40 years old and around six feet tall – had gotten out of a dark blue 1965 Ford sedan. Officer James Paxton interviewed the witness and told reporters they hadn't seen anything else. They didn't see the young woman get forced into the car or what happened after that.

He also couldn't say why the witness had done nothing to intervene.

The police released a description of the man seen by the witness but stressed they didn't know if the person was involved in Sharon's disappearance or if the young woman he was struggling with was even Sharon at all. Regardless, they did say the man had a medium complexion and a full beard and was wearing blue jeans, a dirty white T-shirt, a waist-length brown jacket, and a hat with brown trim.

As the investigation slogged on, Dayton Police Fifth District Chief G.H. Thurman stated that every police officer in the city was actively searching for Sharon. He assured the public they were running down every lead they received, no matter how small or insignificant they seemed. He encouraged anyone who thought they had any information to call the police station.

Officer James Paxton – who'd found the witness who thought they'd seen Sharon struggling with the mystery man – spent 92 hours speaking with everyone who lived within a one-mile radius of Sharon's home. He hoped to find at least one more person who'd seen something useful on that Friday afternoon.

He knocked on so many doors that he lost count of them all, but he didn't find a single witness.

On Wednesday night, several dozen people gathered at the Messiah Lutheran Church to pray for Sharon and her family. The young woman's pastor, Reverend Dale Truscott, told reporters that he planned to hold a prayer vigil every night until the young woman was found. He would ask God, he said, for Sharon's safe return.

But if he did, his god wasn't listening.

BY THURSDAY, THE REWARD FOR INFORMATION in the case had grown to $4,000. Most of the money came from private donors, including many of Sharon's classmates. The newspaper she delivered, the *Dayton Journal-Herald*, offered $1,000 on its own.

Detectives were hopeful that the increased reward would bring in some fresh leads. The case was stalling out, but Police Supervisor Harry Henry insisted that the department had no intention of slowing down the investigation.

However, as it entered its second week with Sharon's fate still a mystery, detectives were frustrated by the lack of information.

They were still leaning on the public. They asked everyone to be on the lookout for the unidentified man driving the blue Ford, asking them to write down the license number and call the police. This led to investigators running down dozens of dark blue Fords, but none of them could be connected to Sharon's disappearance.

Since Sharon had last been seen walking down Cornell Drive with her collections book, the police were convinced that multiple people must have seen her on the heavily traveled road before she vanished. They asked anyone who had been driving on the road that afternoon to call with any information they had, no matter how insignificant it seemed.

And then a call came in – just like the calls during almost every case involving a missing person. A man told the Dayton cops that he had kidnapped Sharon and was holding her captive in Xenia, Ohio. He would return her, he told them, for $150,000. When he was asked his name, the man hung up. He never called back. Detectives were confident it was a prank call. It was the first one, but, of course, it wouldn't be the last.

Weeks passed. By the end of October, detectives had followed up on hundreds of tips and distributed thousands of flyers with Sharon's information but still had no idea what had happened to her. They told reporters that tips and leads had now completely dried up. They had nowhere else to turn.

And then things got worse. The one decent lead they had and the one in which they had invested hundreds of hours – the one about the mystery man in the blue Ford -- wasn't as reliable as they'd hoped.

The young woman who claimed she'd seen the man struggling with a girl who looked like Sharon had admitted that she hadn't seen it – her aunt had told her about it. The aunt did confirm to the police that she had witnessed the event, but a man who was with her at the time said he didn't recall seeing anything at all.

Detectives had no idea who was telling the truth.

But not all of them gave up. Sergeant Robert Hahn was a neighbor of Sharon and her family, and he took a personal interest in the case, working countless hours on it when he was off duty. He clocked traffic patterns along Sharon's paper route and discovered the road wasn't as busy as investigators initially believed. He found breaks in traffic that lasted as long as 15 minutes – which meant a kidnapper would've had ample time to force Sharon into a car without being seen.

Months passed, and the case went from cold to downright freezing. By May 1974, Sharon's family and friends had resigned themselves to the fact that it was unlikely Sharon would be coming home on her own. Her mother, Mary Carol, told reporters, "I don't want to sound morbid, but I am sure she was abducted. There is no chance she would have run away. I know she didn't run away."

Police officials agreed. They had no concrete information but did not believe Sharon had run away. A spokesman admitted, though, that "if something doesn't break within a few weeks of an incident, then it is a matter of a long wait for something to turn up."

Occasional tips still came in. Detectives followed up on all of them, no matter how bizarre they seemed.

In June 1974, a self-proclaimed psychic called and provided the location of a house where she claimed Sharon's body would be found. Lieutenant Richard Schulte stated that while they hadn't used information from psychics in the past, the cops figured they had nothing to lose and searched the property. They didn't find anything.

More time passed. By September 1975, Sharon had been missing for two years, and the case was ice cold. Hoping to revive the case, her family announced they had added another $1,000 to the

Tip on girl missing 3 years fails to give police any clues

By Fred Lawson

Dayton police yesterday afternoon searched the site of a razed house on Tyson Avenue in West Dayton in a search for the body of Sharon Pretorius, who has been missing for almost three years.

Dayton Police Officer James B. Paxton, who has been assigned the case since the girl's disappearance, said last night that nothing was found and the site will not be excavated further.

He said police acted on a tip from Brookville Police Chief George E. Brown.

BROWN SAID last night his informant has been reliable in the past and he will contact the informant again. However, Brown said the informant's information was based on a second-hand report.

Brown said the informant did not mention Sharon by name, but the facts were similar to events in the case of the missing 13-year-old Dayton View girl.

Brown would not identify the informant.

Brown, formerly a member of the narcotics unit at the state's Bureau of Criminal Identification and Investigation (BCI) at London, said he has worked with the informant in the past on other cases.

The informant claimed to have just recently picked up the information, Brown said.

Brown said the informant took him and Montgomery County Sheriff's Detective Roger J. Campbell to the site Monday afternoon and said that was where the girl's body was buried.

PAXTON SAID he was told of the information Tuesday night. He said he conferred with the homicide squad yesterday morning, and a search warrant for the excavation was obtained from Municipal Judge Jack D. Duncan.

A city backhoe was used to break through a concrete slab and six feet under the site. Neighbors said the house was torn down about two years ago.

"We didn't find anything," Paxton said. "It was a big, fat nothing."

But he added:

"What bothers me is that he may have the wrong location on Tyson (Avenue)."

Paxton said that as far as he is concerned, there will be no additional searches in that area unless more information is provided.

MISS PRETORIUS, who was a Fairview High School freshman, has not been seen since 5:30 p.m. Sept. 28, 1973, when she left her home at 3024 Cornell Drive to collect on her Journal Herald route.

Neither her mother, Mrs. Marycarol Pretorius, nor any other member of her family has heard from her and long ago came to the conclusion she probably was abducted and killed.

The Journal Herald still is offering a $1,000 reward for information leading directly to Sharon's release from abduction or to the arrest and conviction of her abductor.

Police found nothing new in search

reward fund, and they didn't care about the identity of her abductor. As her uncle told the press – her family just wanted Sharon to come home.

But the reward remained unclaimed. Then, ten months later, it was canceled, and the money was donated to the Dayton Citizens Information Reward Fund. Officials first tried to give the money to Sharon's mother, but she refused. The money now would allow the police department to use the funds to offer rewards for other crimes.

Mary Carol hoped it would help other families not to suffer the way she and her other children had.

SHARON'S CASE BECAME OFFICIALLY INACTIVE, but it wasn't closed. The detectives who worked on it had been assigned to other cases, but they certainly didn't forget about it. Over the next three years, most of them had gotten to know Sharon's family well, and it pained them that they hadn't been able to bring the girl home. Privately, though, they believed she had met with foul play and didn't think she'd ever be found.

"The feeling is that she's dead," one of them confessed," but you don't want to say a thing like that."

Even though no one was actively working on the case, they did follow up on leads when they did come in. In July 1976, a tip claimed that Sharon's body was buried under a property on Tyson Avenue in Dayton. A house that had been there was razed two years earlier, and investigators used a backhoe to dig up a concrete slab that remained on the site. The tip had come from a police informant who had been reliable in the past, but he was wrong this time. Nothing was found.

In March 1977, investigators received another tip from someone claiming to know where Sharon was buried – the spot, they said, was that same house on Tyson Avenue where they'd already looked. The cops returned to the property and once again dug around the foundation of the demolished home. Once again, nothing was found. A police spokesperson told reporters there would be no more searches at that property.

Decades passed, and Sharon's fate remained a mystery. By 1998, she had been missing for 25 years, and most of the detectives who had worked on the case had long since retired. Many of them, though, admitted that they still thought about Sharon. For some, it was the one unsolved case they had to leave behind that still nagged at them.

And they weren't alone. Sharon's family still hadn't learned what had happened to her either. Eventually, Mary Carol seemed to accept the idea that she'd never have answers.

"You never forget," she told reporters when the family held a memorial service for Sharon in July 2006. "And you don't want to. But there comes a time when you have to move on."

But I'm not sure they really did. The memorial service may have allowed them to say goodbye to Sharon formally, but they could not let go of the mystery. In 2011, they announced a new $2,500 reward for information leading to Sharon's remains. This got the Dayton Police Department involved again, too. New tips were followed, now using cadaver dogs, ground-penetrating radar, and other things that hadn't been available in 1973.

Detective Patricia Tackett stated, "We believe there are people with information. Those involved may be deceased, but their families may have information."

But the re-heated investigation didn't last long. Soon, things cooled off again. The police found the same thing they found 40 years earlier – nothing.

Sadly, Mary Carol died in June 2021 without ever learning what had happened to Sharon, but her sister and three brothers continue to hope that someday, they might have the answers they've been seeking for so long.

1974: THE MISSING PAPERBOY
THE DISAPPEARANCE OF JOSEPH SPISAK

THE MORNING OF SUNDAY, JANUARY 27, 1974, WAS bitterly cold in Hammond, Indiana, but Joseph Spisak was faithful to his newspaper delivery route. Joe believed that, like the post office, he needed to make sure the papers were waiting for his customers when they got out of bed in the morning, finishing his route whether there was rain, sleet, or snow.

It wasn't snowing that morning, but it sure could be, Joe probably thought. It was so cold when the 11-year-old left home in the pre-dawn hours that he'd pulled a trench coat over his parka to make his delivery rounds. By 9:30 A.M., though, he was finished and stopped by his home on McCook Avenue to drop off his newspaper bag.

He didn't have much time to warm up. He had to hurry off toward Our Lady of Perpetual Help Church to attend mass like he did every Sunday. He closed the front door behind him and trotted down the sidewalk toward the church.

But Joe never made it to mass that morning. In fact, he was never seen again.

THERE'S NO BETTER WAY TO DESCRIBE JOE SPISAK than to say he was "a good kid." He was funny, good-natured, and had many friends. He loved sports and even kept a scrapbook of his favorite athletes, which his mother still has today. Growing up, he'd hoped to be a television or radio sports announcer.

But Joe would never have the chance to grow up.

When he didn't come home for lunch that Sunday afternoon, his mother, Monica, was slightly concerned but not too worried. Although he'd usually call if he planned to eat at a friend's house, she assumed he'd simply lost track of time. When the clock ticked a little later, and there was still no word from Joe, she called the homes of a few of his friends. She was told that Joe had been seen playing with other children at Morton Middle School, where he was in the sixth grade. Monica assumed he'd eaten lunch with the family of one of those kids.

Dinner was at 5:00 P.M. every evening at the Spisak house, and Joe knew he had to be home on time to eat with the rest of the family. It was a rule that he'd always followed – until now. When Joe didn't come home for dinner, Monica knew something was wrong. She sent Joe's two brothers, Thomas and Steven, out to look for him, but when they could not find him anywhere near their Hessville neighborhood, she immediately called the Hammond Police Department. Her oldest son, she said, was missing.

Joe Spisak in 1974

Monica was adamant that Joe hadn't run away, and his brothers agreed. Joe, Thomas, and Steven were close and shared a bedroom. They would have known if he'd been planning to run off. When police officers answered the call, they searched the house to make sure that Joe wasn't hiding in the home or had fallen asleep somewhere. He wasn't there.

Unfortunately, that was all the police would do that night. They told Monica and Joe's father, Donald, that they couldn't take a missing person report until the boy had been gone at least 24 hours. This wasn't accurate, but they left, and the family was on its own until the following day.

Steven later recalled, "When I went to bed that night, I sort of knew he wasn't coming back. I had an eerie feeling."

THE FOLLOWING DAY, THE INVESTIGATION FINALLY began. Investigators took a report and started the search for Joe, first speaking to some of his friends. Detectives still thought that Joe had left home voluntarily, despite Monica and the rest of the family insisting he wouldn't have done so. She pointed out that Joe didn't take any belongings with him when he left for mass. It was also unlikely that he would have chosen to run off on a cold January day – Joe hated the cold. She was convinced that something had happened that prevented Joe from getting home.

Detective Adam Clark, a cold case detective in Hammond, thinks she was right. "There were all these rumors he was talking about running away. But he's 11. How far could he get? We're talking 1974. All his belongings are at home."

Children from the part of Hammond where Joe lived often played around the Norfolk and Western railyards.

A few of Joe's friends said they saw him around 5:00 P.M. on Sunday, walking near the Catholic cemetery along Kennedy Avenue near the Norfolk and Western railroad tracks. A few people also reported seeing him on the same tracks, walking southeast near 169th and Arizona Streets. Those who claimed to see him said it wasn't clear where he was going. The boy wasn't carrying anything with him when he was spotted, so if it was Joe, it's possible he was heading home for dinner.

Joe's father, Donald, walked along those same railroad tracks for years after his son vanished – hoping that perhaps he'd find some sign he had been there.

The police and local volunteers braved the frigid temperatures and searched areas where Joe was known to frequent, but there was no sign of him. Local Boy Scout troops helped search along the shore of Optimist Lake and a nearby wooded area, while crews from Norfolk and Western sent an inspection car to comb the area farther down the tracks. No clues about Joe's whereabouts were found.

By now, the police had finally accepted the idea that Joe wasn't a runaway. Hammond Police Chief George Wise said it was unlikely that Joe could hide in the area for long and not be found. He had no history of running away and wasn't known to hide from his friends. Chief Wise admitted that foul play was possible, but he also thought Joe might have hitched a ride on one of the freight trains that passed through town – until detectives pointed out the boy was too short to climb into any of the boxcars that passed through Hammond. The biggest concern for investigators was that Joe might die from exposure before anyone found him.

Investigators next interviewed all of Joe's teachers and classmates, but they didn't learn anything that would help. Joe was a good student, got along with other kids, enjoyed sports, and had no behavioral problems.

While some investigators were conducting interviews, others were chasing leads from the dozens of tips they received in the days after the disappearance. Most of the leads went nowhere. However, one investigator, Charles Hedinger, received a tip claiming that Joe had been seen with a man from Southern Indiana driving a green Cadillac to Kentucky. Officers traveled to Kentucky and found the boy, but it wasn't Joe. "He was Joseph's double," Hedinger said. "A spitting-image double. But it wasn't him."

Unsure of what else to do, the police kept searching the area around the railroad tracks for the next week, but with no luck. A short time later, 40 volunteers spent more than four hours scouring the area around the Norfolk and Western tracks again, looking for any clues the police might have overlooked. The group, led by Joseph Barrios, said they believed the Hammond police were doing all they could but wanted to offer some additional help.

In the weeks following Joe's disappearance, dozens of letters arrived at the Spisak house, offering tips, clues, prayers, and offers of help. Many others, of course, were anonymous promises to reveal Joe's whereabouts if they were paid a reward. One unsigned letter, which asked for nothing, urged the family to check out an abandoned restaurant near 169th and Arizona – the same area where Joe might have last been seen. The letter noted, "There is a small window broken out, and children have gone in there. I phoned the police to check there, but I wonder if they actually went inside and checked..."

Another letter, written in reply to one sent by Monica Spisak, was dated February 22. The letter was from Jeane Dixon, the well-known psychic and newspaper columnist. Monica asked her to consult Joe's case. "Regrettably, from the information in your letter, I have been unable to pick up any vibrations, which means it is not possible to get anything psychically at this time. I am so sorry and shall keep trying," Dixon wrote, but she returned the $10 check Monica had sent her.

By April, there was still no sign of Joe. Donald said that he was still hopeful that his son was alive, but he couldn't imagine where he could be. He told reporters he was still convinced his son didn't run away. Joe had always seemed happy at home, and he'd left behind all his things, including his extra pair of glasses, money, and beloved collections of baseball cards and Matchbox cars. Donald said that Joe wouldn't have left without taking at least some of those things with him.

By now, the Hammond police had conducted several searches of the neighborhood and beyond. They hunted by air and on foot but still had no idea what had happened to Joe. By now, they were forced to admit that it was unlikely Joe was still alive. If he had run away from home, he would have been too young to have survived long on his own. They theorized that he had either been a victim of foul play or had died from exposure, but they were unable to find his body.

Captain John Kouris told the press that the Hammond police had followed leads in Kokomo, Indiana, and Kentucky, but they'd been unable to confirm that Joe had made it to either place. Kouris still believed that Joe wasn't tall enough to get into a freight car, and if he had been, he would've been spotted by railroad employees when it was unloaded.

Joe's fate remained a mystery as the years went by. His disappearance hadn't gotten much press coverage – only one newspaper mentioned his name after he went missing – and the few reporters who covered the case believed he'd run off on his own. One wrote that Joe may have had a dream to see the world or just wanted some adventure in his life – making his disappearance seem like an item that every 11-year-old boy had on his "bucket list."

No matter what happened to Joe – this wasn't exactly helpful when it came to finding him.

A DECADE PASSED, AND DURING THOSE YEARS, Joe's half of the bedroom he shared with his brother, Thomas, remained exactly as it had been when he walked out of it for the last time. When the family moved to a new house in 1986, they kept the same telephone number, hoping they'd get a call from Joe one day.

Sadly, though, that call never came.

Joe's family remained convinced he hadn't voluntarily left home. By 1998, Joe had been missing for almost 25 years and had a younger brother he'd never met. Donald and Monica continued to hold out hope that they'd be reunited with their oldest child, but all hope of finding him alive faded a little more with each passing year.

Thomas was three years younger than Joe, but the two brothers were always close. He later told reporters that he'd never considered the possibility that Joe had run away. "I still don't understand how his friends could have said he'd run away. I hung around with the same group. I was sick that week, though, which is why I wasn't hanging around them that day," he said.

Charles Hedinger, one of the first police officers to respond when Joe was first reported missing, was a detective with the Hammond Police Department in 1998 when the case was being revisited. He recalled how the case had quickly gone cold. "There was never any contact," he said. "It's one of those cases where someone is missing in plain sight. I wish I had a crystal ball. No one, except his family, wants to know what happened to him more than me."

Over the years, Hedinger started believing that Joe had been abducted. "There were a lot of transients in the area then, riding the rails. Serial killers have passed through here before," he explained. Joe might have been killed the same day he went missing, but his body was never found.

In hindsight, it was realized that when Joe disappeared, serial killer John Wayne Gacy was in the middle of his six-year killing spree. A few months after Joe had vanished, his parents had sent his dental and medical records to a police department out west when an unidentified child's body was found. Those same records were sent to the Cook County Coroner after nearly 30 bodies of young men and boys were found under Gacy's Norwood Park home. But the records didn't match any of the bodies that were discovered.

TWO MORE DECADES PASSED AND IN 2019, THE Spisak family spoke to reporters as they marked the 45th anniversary of Joe's disappearance. They were still clinging to the hope that he could be alive somewhere, maybe working as a sports announcer, as he'd always dreamed. His sister Elsa noted, 'There was no trace of him. That's why we haven't given up hope." Without a body to prove he was dead, it was easier to dream that he might be alive.

Monica said that the holidays and Joe's birthday were the hardest for her and the rest of the family, even all these years later. The passing of time hadn't done much to heal their pain, but she continued to hope someone would finally call the police with the information that would bring her son home.

Joe's brother, Steven, revealed that it had been hard to get over Joe's disappearance because of the rumors circulating at school and in the neighborhood when he was growing up. First, it was the stories that he'd run away, and then it was the ugly whispers that someone in their family – their father, in particular – was involved in Joe's disappearance.

Donald passed away in 2006 after battling cancer and congestive heart failure for many years.

Steven told a reporter in 2019, "People said Joe was buried under the garage. Well, that garage wasn't built until five years after he disappeared. My poor father had to go to his death with this, so we wanted to clear his name."

As the rumors lingered, Hammond detective Adam Clark – the lead detective on Joe's case since 2012 – contacted the Indiana State Police in 2017 to request the department's ground-penetrating radar technology.

After gaining access from the current homeowner, who was eager to help, Clark said law enforcement scanned the backyard of the house where Joe and his siblings grew up. The sonar technology scans for disturbances in the earth, as would be made when a body is buried at the site being investigated. In the yard, they found an anomaly.

"So, we got a team together with shovels, which ended up leading to a big payloader," Clark explained. "Nothing turned up. We did find a couple of toys, but that's it. I know the family's been battling with that rumor for a while, and it's just not true. The kid's not back there."

But where is he then? No one knows.

Adam Clark went to high school with Joe's youngest brother, David, so he continues to dig into the case. It's become a personal mission for him. "You just don't see a case like this very often," Clark admitted. "Usually, the person's found. In this case, Joseph went missing, and that was it. He's gone."

IN THE YEARS THAT FOLLOWED JOE'S DISAPPEARANCE, life moved forward for the Spisak family. While the children were growing up, Donald and Monica tried to keep things as normal as possible for the kid's sake. David, the brother Adam Clark had gone to school with, was born seven years after Joe never came back.

His brother, Thomas, had joined the Army and returned home to work in the steel mills. Steven also enlisted, serving four years in the Air Force and eight more in the Indiana National Guard. Steven named his youngest son after Joe and Thomas named his oldest child Andrew, which was Joe's middle name.

Elsa stayed in Hammond to be close to her parents and eventually became a mother, too. "You can't totally give up on life, you know," she said. "Even though it hurts, you still have to keep going. I mean, God willing, he will show up, whether it be alive or dead, but for me, the thing I want the most is closure for my parents."

And closure is the only thing that will satisfy Joe's mother. Indiana authorities call Monica every few years, asking the family to declare Joe legally dead. They wanted to close the case. "But I'm not going to do that," she said firmly, "not until I have proof."

1974: THREE LOST GIRLS
WHAT HAPPENED TO RACHEL, RENEE & JULIE ANN?

IT WAS ONLY TWO DAYS BEFORE CHRISTMAS 1974 when three girls in Fort Worth, Texas, decided to do a little last-minute holiday shopping. Rachel Trlica, a 17-year-old newlywed, 14-year-old Renee Wilson, and 9-year-old Julie Ann Moseley took Rachel's 1972 Oldsmobile to a local Army-Navy store to pick up some pants that Renee had on layaway. After she'd made the last payment, she changed into one of the new pairs of pants and put her old ones in a bag with the other new pair.

When they left the store, they drove next to the Seminary South Shopping Center, and Rachel parked near the Sears Department Store's upper level on the east side of the mall.

Laughing, having fun, and enjoying the holiday season, the three girls exited the car and started walking toward the Sears entrance that would give them access to the rest of the shopping mall.

We know they went into the mall – they were seen that day – but no one knows what happened next. Rachel, Renee, and Julie Ann were never seen again.

THE FAMILIES OF RACHEL AND RENEE HAD KNOWN each other for years. They hosted each other for cookouts, went camping, and even took trips together. Although married, Rachel was still a junior at Southwest High School, where Renee was a freshman.

Rachel's husband, Tommy, was a divorced father with a two-and-a-half-year-old son. They had married very young but were happy, and no one doubted they had a good relationship.

Julie Ann was a bright, happy fourth grader with a big heart at B.H. Carrol Elementary School. She and her family lived across the street from Renee's grandmother, Mrs. J.E. Swinton. Renee spent a lot of time at her grandma's house, especially when her parents were at work. She knew Julie Ann's entire family and was especially close to her older brother, Terry, who was 15. In fact, that morning, Terry had reportedly given Renee a ring, making their boyfriend-girlfriend relationship official.

The girls were expected to be at a birthday party at 6:00 P.M. that night, and Renee promised her parents they'd be back by 4:00. Though it was a Monday, school was out for Christmas break, and Renee and Rachel wanted to finish shopping. Julie Ann's mother, Rayanne, trusted Renee and let her daughter tag along with the older girls because Julie Ann had been complaining about how boring it was to sit alone at their house.

Several people later recalled seeing Rachel, Renee, and Julie Ann at the mall that day. Every report said they were having a good time, and nothing seemed out of the ordinary. That made it even more strange when they simply vanished later that afternoon.

When Renee wasn't home by 4:00, as she'd promised her parents, Richard and Judy, they were concerned. Finally, the Wilsons and Rachel's parents – Ray and Fran Arnold – went to the mall to look around. They found Rachel's car in the lot. The doors were securely locked. There was a single package on the back seat.

There was no sign of the three girls.

When the mall closed that night, and the girls didn't return to the car, the families immediately called the police. Unfortunately, though, Fort Worth law officers didn't show up for hours, finally

(Left to Right) Rachel, Renee, and Julie Ann – along with the
mysterious letter that was mailed to Rachel's husband, Tommy.

arriving at the mall around 1:00 P.M. They didn't seem to have
much interest in the girls' absence. Despite protests to the contrary
from the parents, investigators stated they had no reason to
believe there had been foul play. The three girls, they said, had run
away from home.

This made some stunning assumptions about the situation, not
the least of which was that a nine-year-old girl would run away
just before Christmas or that a 14-year-old would leave town right
after getting a ring from her boyfriend, or that a 17-year-old would
take off without her almost new car and with a nine-year-old in
tow.

The parents were shocked and angry, but the policemen said
there was no evidence of a struggle, and no one had witnessed
an abduction. They suggested that if the girls didn't run away, they
were probably with friends. They didn't bother to check inside the
car or dust it for fingerprints. They just left, advising the families
to call if any actual evidence turned up.

The next day, Christmas Eve, things took a strange turn.

A letter arrived at Rachel and Tommy's house, and it appeared
to have been sent from Rachel to Tommy, although the writing on
the envelope didn't match her writing, plus Rachel's name had
been misspelled, corrected, and rewritten.

Needless to say, it was a little suspicious.

The envelope was addressed to Thomas Trlica, although Rachel always called him "Tommy." The postage stamp had been canceled by the U.S. Post Office at the blurry zip code of "76083," which didn't exist. It's likely the "3" was a smeared "8," though, which meant it had been mailed from the Peaster, Garner, or Brock areas.

The letter read:

I know I'm going to catch it, but we just had to get away. We're going to Houston. See you in about a week. The car is in the Sears upper lot.

Love,
Rachel

Julie Ann's mother, Rayanne, said she "didn't put a lot of stock in the letter," and Renee's mother, Judy, agreed, "It just doesn't make any sense."

But to the Fort Worth Police Department, it made perfect sense and confirmed their officers' theory about the "disappearance." But that wouldn't last. Soon, the investigators would also start questioning the authenticity of the letter. They realized, as the families already had, that if Rachel wanted to leave town, she wouldn't have taken the other girls – especially the nine-year-old Julie Ann – with her.

When the police eventually did start looking for suspects, Tommy was, of course, at the top of the list – the husband always is. In this case, they discovered that Tommy was originally engaged to Rachel's older sister, Debra. After they broke up, he started dating and then married Rachel. When his wife disappeared, Debra had been staying with Rachel and Tommy following a fight with her current boyfriend. Had they decided to rekindle things and wanted Rachel out of the way? That's what the police wanted to know. The living arrangements didn't look great, but it didn't take long to rule them out. Tommy seemed legitimately worried and upset about Rachel's vanishing and immediately questioned the letter's authenticity. He knew that Rachel would not have misspelled her own name.

But the mysterious letter would not be the only strange lead that came in – many others would follow.

NEWS BEGAN TO SPREAD THAT THE THREE GIRLS were missing. They hadn't run away, so what happened?

A nightwatchman at Alcon Laboratories Inc. told detectives that he had seen two men and three girls drive up to the entrance he was monitoring on December 23, but when he approached the vehicle, it sped away. Investigators could not determine if this had anything to do with the disappearance.

A bus company employee said three girls fitting the descriptions of Rachel, Renee, and Julie Ann came into the station on the morning of December 24, asking about fares to Houston. However, they never purchased any tickets, and detectives later doubted the reliability of the witnesses.

At 1:00 A.M. on December 26, a man called Rachel's father and said that he'd seen the girls and had spoken with them at a record store at the mall on the day they vanished.

Another witness came forward who claimed they'd seen the girls in a mall security patrol car that day. Later, a truck driver called the police and said he'd seen the girls hitchhiking in Arkansas.

Meanwhile, friends and family members of the three girls were searching the area near the mall, walking local creek beds and along country roads, trying to do anything they could to help the girls.

On December 28, Renee's mother, Judy, released a letter to the press. She first addressed the girls themselves, saying that while the families didn't believe they'd run away if they had, they wanted them to come home immediately or at least call and tell them they were all right. "There is nothing we will not do for you," she added.

Then, believing the girls had been taken, she addressed their abductors: "A special plea is made to any unknown person for these girls' release if they are being held against their will so that they may be reunited with their loved ones."

Her pleas were widely broadcast, but there was only silence in reply.

On December 31, a hunter found several pairs of women's underwear in a field six miles west of Justin, Texas. When detectives arrived and investigated, they could find nothing to link them to the three girls.

Later that same day, Renee's father, Richard, received a telephone call from a young woman who claimed to be one of Renee's friends. She told the Wilsons that Renee, Rachel, and Julie Ann would be arriving in Fort Worth on a Greyhound bus from Houston at 7:25 that evening. The Wilsons immediately called the other families, and they all hurried to the bus station to wait for the 7:25 bus. It arrived, but the girls weren't on it.

On January 1, 1975, Judy Wilson and a few other family members met with J. Joseph, a Dallas psychic referred to the families by a local television personality. According to the psychic, he sensed there was something wrong with the letter that Tommy had received – no kidding – but added that he believed the girls were being held against their will and that drugs were somehow involved.

The psychic visions of J. Joseph didn't lead anywhere, but then again, neither had any of the work being done by Fort Worth investigators. They were still following up on leads, but all of them were leading to dead ends.

In mid-January, a friend of the Wilsons started a reward fund at the Forest Hill State Bank in hopes of getting information that would lead to the return of the missing girls. Two of Renee's uncles – Jesse and John McGee – began printing and distributing missing posters detailing the disappearance in towns across Texas, Arkansas, and Louisiana.

And then came the chilling telephone call.

Around 11:00 A.M. on February 7, Rayanne Moseley received a call she believed was from her daughter, Julie Ann. When Rayanne answered the phone, no one responded. She said "hello" repeatedly and started to hang up when she heard a low moan and a young girl's voice saying, "Mama."

Rayanne asked who was calling, but the voice repeated "Mama" again.

Suddenly, sure she was speaking with her missing daughter, but still wanting to be sure, Rayanne asked the caller if she was Julie Ann Moseley, and the voice said, "Yes."

Rayanne continued, "Listen, if this is someone playing a joke, please stop. I can't take any more."

She was met with silence, so Rayanne asked the caller where she was, and the voice replied that she didn't know. The caller said "Mama" one more time, and then the call was disconnected.

Rayanne screamed "Julie!" into the receiver several times, but when she heard a dial tone, she knew the call had ended. She was badly shaken by the call and later said that the girl on the other end of the line wasn't speaking "normally" – it sounded like she was sick or drugged.

But she was still willing to swear it was Julie Ann.

And then more calls followed. All three families started to get similar calls, and they alerted the police. It took the authorities three days to trace the calls, but they turned out to be coming from a 14-year-old girl in Richland Hills – well, most of them. She admitted to making calls to the families of Rachel and Renee, but the prankster denied calling Rayanne Moseley on February 7.

Was she lying? Or had the call really come from Julie Ann?

AROUND 2:00 A.M. ON SUNDAY, FEBRUARY 10, a gold sedan turned into a gas station at 3001 West Euless Boulevard in Fort Worth. Three young white girls were in the back seat. A black man drove the car. The driver asked the service attendant if he could purchase beer but was told it was after hours. As the driver pulled away, one of the girls in the back seat dropped a piece of paper out of the car window. The attendant picked it up and called the police.

The paper was one of the "missing" flyers that the families of Rachel, Renee, and Julie Ann had been distributing. What appeared to be an address had been written on it – "1714 AP R.M. BLVD."

Investigators checked the possible address and decided it referred to Randol Mill Road in Arlington. The local police assisted Fort Worth detectives by checking out the general area and keeping an eye out for a gold sedan on that road, but they quickly discovered there was no such address, no apartments, and no gold sedan.

Another dead end.

In late February, detectives received a tip that the bodies of the three girls were hidden under a bridge near Port Lavaca – they weren't.

In mid-March, three clerks at a store in the Seminary South mall told Rachel's mother, Fran, that an older woman had come into the store and claimed she'd seen a man forcing a girl into the cab of a truck, where two other girls and a second man were already seated. Fran appealed to the clerks and the *Star-Telegram* newspaper to let the woman know that if she called, they'd keep her name secret.

But the source was never heard from again.

As progress in the police investigation slowed to a halt, some of the family members of the girls hired Jon Swaim, a private detective who ran a local investigation firm called Special Services. Swaim bullied his way into the police case and the case files by making newspaper headlines. By early April, Swaim reported that an unnamed source had informed him that the girls had been murdered and their bodies were hidden, as a previous tip claimed, near Port Lavaca, under a bridge that spanned Hog Bayou along State Highway 35. The water under the area bridges was lower in April, and the resulting search party of police officers, family members, and more than 100 volunteers scoured the riverbanks and the surrounding area a second time. It was a difficult slog, but again, they found nothing.

A short time later, the families received more bad news – a fisherman in San Antonio discovered a human leg in a local lake. That led to more bodies, five in all. But only two turned out to be female, and neither were the missing girls.

Then, worse news – Rachel's father, Ray Arnold, died from cancer on July 18, 1975, at the age of only 39. Sadly, he never learned what happened to his daughter.

By August, the families had been inundated with mail from psychics, weirdos, and cranks from all over the country. Judy Wilson admitted that she'd lost three of Renee's blouses because she'd sent them off to mediums who requested a piece of her daughter's clothing so they could figure out her whereabouts. Oddly, a large percentage of the psychics claimed that a "blue hippie van" was involved in the abduction and that their abductors had taken them "north."

One psychic sent Fran Arnold a map pinpointing the location of the girls' grave near a creek outside of Mansfield. Fran and Rachel's sister, Debra, walked several miles along the creek, and when they arrived at the spot where the bodies were supposed to be, they found only a pig's skull.

Soon after that fiasco, a 15-year-old contacted Jon Swaim with a tip about a man who had been making obscene phone calls to her and her older sister for over a year. When Swaim investigated, he discovered a man who worked at a store where Rachel had applied for a job shortly before her disappearance. He had also lived in the same neighborhood as Rachel's family at one time.

Swaim coached the young woman, and she was able to get the caller to agree to meet her in person on August 12. When the man showed up, she found Swaim and some of his men waiting for him. They detained him until the police arrived. In custody, the man admitted to making numerous obscene phone calls to women who had applied at the store – he got their numbers from their applications – but denied having anything to do with the disappearance. He was given a polygraph test, which he passed.

In March 1976, a psychic in Honolulu contacted the Fort Worth police and told them that the girls were dead and that their bodies had been dumped near an oil well. The "vision" led detectives to an oil field near Rising Star, but all they found was another dead end.

Later that same year, Jon Swaim received an anonymous tip from a man insisting that he could lead the investigator to the girls, but he refused to say if they were dead or alive. He told Swaim that a friend of his could tell him where the girls were if the reward money would be paid, and, more importantly, he could get full immunity for any criminal act he may have been involved in with the girls. The unidentified party also insisted that he be able to surrender directly to the district attorney's office with no law enforcement officers involved. Swaim assured him he'd set it up, and the man ended the call.

A short time later, the informant called back – again and again. He reportedly ended up sending Swain to 17 different payphones around Fort Worth before he'd discuss a deal. Swaim tried to arrange a meeting with the caller, but the man refused. If the anonymous caller ever contacted Swaim again, he never revealed it.

If the purported 17 payphone wild goose chase seems familiar to you, it's because almost the exact same thing happened in the 1971 Clint Eastwood film *Dirty Harry*. The girls' families had seen the movie, too, and they started questioning the credibility of Jon Swaim.

And then things got weird.

On October 19, 1979, the police were called to Jon Swaim's apartment around 2:30 P.M. after Swaim's landlord found him on the floor, semiconscious. According to reports, when officers arrived, Swaim refused to be taken to the hospital, so they left.

Later that night, at 11:45 P.M., Swaim's sister and brother-in-law went to check on him after they failed to reach him by phone. They found him again on his living room floor, but this time, he was dead. The coroner later determined that he'd been dead for several hours by the time they entered his apartment.

Swaim's death was initially ruled an accidental drug overdose, but those findings were later changed to suicide. His death was allegedly triggered by the fact that his ex-wife had remarried the day before he died, and his company was struggling financially.

However, not everyone agreed with those findings. An attorney friend said that even though Swaim had called him while intoxicated several times in the weeks leading up to his death, he never sounded suicidal.

Another friend, Gary Davis, a bail bondsman who worked part-time for Swaim, said it was no surprise the company had money problems. He claimed that Swaim had spent at least $20,000 of his own money working on the disappearance of Rachel, Renee, and Julie Ann because he believed the girls were alive.

Davis claimed that Swaim kept "voluminous" files on the disappearance as well as files on members of law enforcement in Fort Worth, but where were they? Nothing was found during a search of his home and office. It turned out that, according to instructions in Swaim's will, his ex-wife had burned all the files after she learned of his death – or so said the claims of Swaim's associates.

Did he really have secret files? If so, was he murdered because of them, or did he commit suicide? Rumors swirled, adding another strange aspect to the case of the three lost girls.

OVER THE NEXT FEW YEARS, MORE GIRLS DISAPPEARED in Texas. Some were found dead, and some were never found at all. In November 1980, a woman who resembled Rachel was found on the shoulder of Interstate 45 near Huntsville. It was quickly determined that it wasn't her. In March 1981, Brazoria County authorities discovered human remains and female clothing in a swamp near Alvin. The discovery solved the mystery of two missing girls but not the riddle of what happened to Rachel, Renee, and Julie Ann.

More time passed, and the case of the missing girls went from cold to downright freezing. The story had vanished from the press long ago, but cold case detectives were still vigilant, and occasionally, the files were reopened, and new leads were checked out.

In February 1989, Fort Worth detective George Hudson contacted the television show Unsolved Mysteries to see if the producers would be willing to help with the investigation, but they weren't interested.

Detectives also continued reaching out to medical examiners across Texas and surrounding states, asking about unidentified "Jane Does" but never found a match for any of the three girls. Investigators recently obtained DNA from the letter Tommy Trlica received on Christmas Eve but never found a match.

In March 2016, James "Ice" McAlpin, a former pimp and convicted murderer doing time in Arkansas for killing his prostitute girlfriend in 1992, became part of the story. The girl he'd murdered had used the street name "Mercedes," but Arkansas investigators had never determined her real identity. After 24 years, she was only known as "Mercedes Doe."

McAlpin said he'd only reveal her name if he was paid for the information, but he did discuss her past. According to his story, she'd been on the street since she was 16 and was pimped out in Dallas and Fort Worth. He also said that she'd grown up as friends with three girls who had been kidnapped from a mall in Fort Worth in the 1970s.

He told investigators, "These girls were like sisters to Mercedes. We used to visit them. They grew up in captivity in Dallas and Fort Worth, sometimes in the same town where their parents were. By the time they were adults, they were willing members of the stable. The younger girl died giving birth to a child."

Cops who knew McAlpin warned that he was a compulsive liar and said they weren't even sure he knew Mercedes' real identity. But his reference to three girls whose circumstances could possibly match those of Rachel, Renee, and Julie Ann was worth noting – even if it sent chills up the spines of everyone who knew them, families and detectives alike.

This was ugly information – perhaps just as ugly as some of the claims that have been made that the people who took the three girls were somehow connected to the Fort Worth police department – or at least were protected by them.

Some believe that a sex trafficking ring was operating in Fort Worth in the early 1970s that was known about by the police. This was a rumor, but we do know that, around the time the girls vanished, the Fort Worth police department was dealing with corruption and scandals that became public.

In September 1974, civil service officials voided the results of the police department's sergeant's exam after discovering that several officers had been given the answers to the test in advance. By that December, civil service commissioners were pushing the incident from one department to another because no one wanted to run afoul of the police department.

So, when the girls vanished, the department was dealing with serious morale problems and rumors of corruption. This might explain the marginal newspaper coverage the disappearance initially received. The public was likely disturbed by the girls going missing, but it appears that little – or at least not enough – was done about it.

But was it all just "low morale" or something worse? If there were police officers involved with a sex trafficking operation – even if they were simply looking the other way – was that why the department was so quick to dismiss the girls as runaways?

Was it just incompetence that made the responding officers at the mall fail to check Rachel's car for fingerprints, or something worse?

Why did the disappearance of the three girls remain only a missing persons case for eight months? Why wasn't the case status changed to an abduction sooner than that?

And why did Jon Swaim's anonymous caller offer to surrender to the county district attorney but not the Fort Worth Police?

This was an interesting theory and one worth considering. Undoubtedly, the police department's dismissal of the case as being about "runaways" made it even harder to find them. It's possible that the lack of resources, time, and attention paid to the case in its early days made it unsolvable.

But this was not the only theory worth considering.

Another theory was suggested by an official investigator on the case whose name was never revealed. After working to find the girls on and off for decades, he came to believe that the most important question wasn't who took the girls but why the girls might have wanted to leave. He was convinced that the three girls had left on their own because at least two of the girls' family lives were "dressed up" for newspaper accounts to make it appear they were members of normal, happy families. But, he stated, they couldn't have been further from the truth.

Julie Ann's mother, Rayanne, had serious substance abuse issues, he alleged, while Ray Arnold was abusive to Rachel and his other daughter, Debra, who worked as an exotic dancer and had dated Tommy, Rachel's husband. Tommy was a divorced trust fund kid, and by the time he married Rachel, Ray Arnold was already dying from cancer. When Tommy bought Arnold's failing business, he received a blessing from Rachel's parents to marry her – even though she was still a high school junior. Furthermore, Rachel's medical records reportedly suggested she was pregnant when she disappeared. It was common knowledge that Tommy didn't want any more children, plus multiple sources claimed the couple hadn't been getting along.

The investigator also said that although media coverage made a special point to mention Julie Ann's older brother, Terry, giving Renee a ring, she had actually fallen for Terry's friend, Vernon Beaty. In fact, the police interviewed Beaty because the girls met him at the Seminary South mall the day they vanished. Beaty denied involvement in their disappearance.

The investigator claimed things were messier than reports made it appear. However, the newspapers and television stations preferred the "normal, happy home life" as a backdrop when discussing the mystery.

Was any of this true? And if so, did it make a difference? Maybe. This new information added some additional elements to the mix – elements that could potentially change the entire narrative.

Rachel might have wanted to escape from her marriage, especially if she was pregnant with a baby she knew Tommy didn't want. Plus, maybe Debra living with Tommy and Rachel wasn't as innocent as they made it appear.

What if Renee met Vernon Beaty at the mall that day, only to discover he didn't have the same feelings for her as she had for him? Could this have made her decide to run away with Rachel?

If Julie Ann's mother really did have a drug and alcohol problem, were things bad enough for her to have left town with the two older girls? Possibly. She'd known them both all her life.

There are still holes in this theory. To go along with it, we have to accept the idea that things were so bad in those three homes that the girls would leave and never have contact with their families again. Is it possible? Yes. Is it likely? It's hard to say.

One thing that we do know is that the disappearance of the three girls is the oldest missing persons case in Tarrant County, Texas, history – and it's one that will likely never be solved.

1975: IN THE MAINE WOODS

THE DISAPPEARANCE OF KURT NEWTON

YOU'VE SEEN YOUR PARENTS DRIVE; HOW HARD COULD it be? Sure, you're under the age of 10, but it's not like a real car or motorcycle – it's just your size. All kids had a favorite "method of transportation" when they were little. It might be a tricycle, pedal car, or scooter. For me, it was a red metal firetruck – complete with a bell my mother probably hated – that had so many sharp edges that it could never be sold today. My son had a Fisher Price car they called a "Cozy Coupe," for which I'd provide the engine and send it flying down sidewalks and around the house.

But Kurt Newton loved his Big Wheel.

When he went camping with his family over Labor Day weekend in 1975, the four-year-old made sure the three-wheeled plastic pedal bike was packed for the trip.

Kurt, along with his parents, Ron and Jill, and his six-year-old sister, Kimberly, left their home in Manchester, Maine, on August 29, 1975. They had recently bought a tent-trailer camper and were excited about spending the weekend at the Natanis Point Campground in Chain of Ponds, Maine, just a few miles from the Canadian border.

After they arrived, they set up their camping area, started a fire, and settled in for a quiet night.

The next day, Saturday, they were joined by three other young families from Manchester. The children played and raced around on their bicycles and Big Wheels while the adults cooked dinner over the fire, cracked open some beers, and enjoyed a relaxing night in the great outdoors.

It was the perfect way to end the summer – or so it seemed at the time. Their dream vacation in the woods was about to turn into a nightmare.

THE AIR WAS CHILLY ON SUNDAY MORNING, AUGUST 31, so little Kurt stayed closer to the campfire. After breakfast, he put a donut on a stick and warmed it over the fire. After he'd eaten the sticky, sweet treat, he stayed by the fire for a few more minutes and tried to decide what he wanted to do that day.

Kurt Newton

His mom, Jill, was on her way to the bathhouse – about 50 yards from the campsite – and his dad, Ron, had left in the family's Ford Bronco to get more wood for the fire. His sister, Kim, was on her bicycle, pedaling around the campground.

Kurt sat for a moment, and then he made his decision. He climbed onto his Big Wheel and took off after his father, racing as if he believed he could pedal fast enough to catch up with the Bronco.

A 12-year-old girl whose family was also camping that weekend later recalled seeing Kurt pedaling past her that morning as she was walking about a quarter mile away from the Newtons' campsite. She was surprised to see such a young boy on his own and called out to ensure he was okay, but he continued pedaling furiously past her. Kurt likely still believed he could catch up to Ron, not knowing the Big Wheel couldn't possibly go that fast.

The girl watched him go around a bend in the road, and Kurt Newton was never seen again.

Jill returned to the campsite about 10 minutes after Ron left on his errand. She was surprised when she didn't see Kurt still sitting by the campfire. He was an extremely shy little boy and didn't like going anywhere by himself. She asked the friends from Manchester who'd joined them for the weekend if they'd seen Kurt – none of

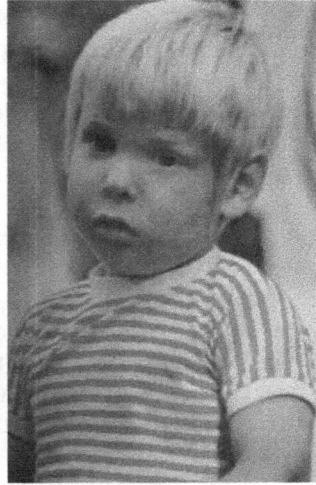

them had. Then she started walking around to check the other nearby campsites, asking other campers if they had seen Kurt.

She was starting to get a sick feeling in the pit of her stomach.

While Jill was realizing that Kurt was missing, Jack Hansen, a volunteer caretaker at Natanis Point, found a Big Wheel on the side of the road that led into the campground's garbage dump. Assuming that someone had been too lazy to carry the discarded bike into the dump, Jack picked it up and tossed it onto a trash pile.

Jack continued his rounds through the campground and ran into Jill a few minutes later. When she described Kurt and his Big Wheel, he told her about the bike he'd found near the trash area. Jill ran to the dump, and her heart sank when she saw her son's Big Wheel lying on its side in the trash pile.

She now feared the worst – Kurt had been kidnapped.

Other campers hurried to help, assuring her that Kurt had likely just wandered off into the woods, looking for his father. They'd spread out, they told her, and they were sure they could find him quickly. But Jill knew better. Kurt was afraid of the woods and would never have gone into them alone.

When Ron returned with the firewood, Jill quickly told him what was happening, and the two of them called the police. More than a dozen fellow campers quickly organized a search of the logging roads that passed through the campground. They were soon joined by Maine State Police troopers and search and rescue teams from the Maine Fish and Game Department.

Duane Lewis, a Maine Fish and Game Inspector, was at his home in Phillips, Maine – about 75 miles from Natanis Point – when he learned a missing child was in the woods. He immediately drove to Chain of Ponds to join the search. He had over 14 years of experience as a warden and had helped organize 75 searches for lost people by then – each ending successfully. He arrived at the campground around 4:00 P.M. on Sunday, fully expecting that Kurt would be found before the sun went down.

Fish and Game wardens used a helicopter and an airplane to do an aerial search around the campground. One warden used a loudspeaker to call out to Kurt from the helicopter, asking him to come toward it so he could see his mom and dad. Jill said that Kurt was obsessed with helicopters, and if he was still in the area, she knew he'd race toward it as it hovered above.

Temperatures dropped as the sun slipped over the horizon. With overnight lows expected to fall below freezing, the searchers had a sense of urgency to find the little boy before it was too late. Although Kurt was dressed warmly – in corduroy pants, jersey, sweatshirt, and jacket – he could be at risk of hypothermia if he had to spend the night outside.

Desperate, Jill and Ron also used the loudspeaker to call their son, pleading with him to walk toward their voices. After each attempt, the search group fell silent, hoping to hear Kurt's voice or some movement in the woods. As the hours went by, their fear and panic grew. They both believed that Kurt had been kidnapped, but they couldn't stop themselves from continuing to search the woods.

A lost little boy would be a blessing compared to the horror of their son being abducted by some monster.

MORE TIME PASSED AND AS WORD SPREAD OF THE missing boy, volunteers flocked to the campground, offering whatever help they could. The state police set up a temporary command center at Kern's Inn in Eustis, and from there, they set up a search grid to ensure no areas were missed. Fish and games wardens, cops, and volunteers were assigned to each section.

Ron had been a volunteer firefighter in Manchester since he was a teenager. When news of Kurt's disappearance made it back home, fellow firefighters, friends, neighbors, and community members hurried to the campground to assist with the search. By Monday morning, more than 200 people were searching every inch of the surrounding woods for any sign of the boy.

Just after sunrise on Monday, bloodhounds were brought to the campground. After sniffing a pair of Kurt's pajama pants, the dogs seemed to pick up his trail near the dump immediately. They followed it for only about 10 yards, though, then stopped. They turned in circles a few times and then sat down – the scent had disappeared. While there was a chance the dogs couldn't isolate his scent because so many people had gone up and down that road the previous day during the search – investigators feared that Kurt had gotten into a vehicle at that point.

A C-130H gunship that flew to Maine from Pensacola, Florida, joined the hunt on Monday evening. The plane was equipped with heat-seeking radar, and it was the first time it had ever been used

Maine Governor James Longley with a photograph of Kurt, asking for help from the public.

(Below) Governor Longley comforting Kurt's mother, Jill.

in a civilian search. Hopes were high that the crew could quickly locate the missing boy, but those hopes were soon dashed. It flew over the area for over three hours before the crew admitted defeat.

The temperatures had warmed up on Monday and Tuesday, but the nights were still cold. The searchers knew that Kurt couldn't survive much longer if he were still out there in the woods, cold and hungry. This prompted many of the mills and factories in the area to close on Tuesday so that employees could help with the search.

The factory workers soon learned what the other volunteers had already discovered – that the rugged terrain was making any kind of search difficult. The thick undergrowth slowed everyone down, while ledges and cliffs made it too dangerous to search in the dark. Mist, fog, and rain made it impossible for aircraft to see anything below, and the conditions made things very uncomfortable for the searchers, although none complained. By Tuesday afternoon, rain fell so hard that the search had to stop temporarily. It was raining so much that they were unable to see anything.

On Wednesday, even more people arrived at the campground, and soon, more than 300 people were searching the woods, joined by 50 soldiers from the Maine National Guard. Even after three days of searching, the police still weren't convinced Kurt had been taken. State Police Colonel Donald Nichols told reporters: "We are operating under the premise that the boy is still in the woods." He added that the search effort was the largest he had ever seen.

By Friday, the weather had cleared, and temperatures had risen, bringing another 400 volunteers to Natanis Point. Despite this massive effort, the only trace of Kurt – maybe – was a couple of footprints in the woods. It was possible they belonged to the missing boy.

Feelings of dread were already spreading among the volunteers. Many of them feared there was no way Kurt would be found alive. His parents tried to remain optimistic but weren't having much luck. Collis Ames, a neighbor from Manchester who helped with the search, confessed to reporters, "I'm afraid that if we find him, he's going to be gone. His mother is just about at the end of her rope."

Each night, after members of the massive search left to try and get some sleep, Ron and Jill continued to prowl the dark woods, using a bullhorn to call for Kurt. They were haunted by the thought of him lost out there in the dark, scared, hungry, and alone.

By Sunday – a week after Kurt had vanished – more than 1,500 volunteers gathered at the campground. They walked, shoulder-to-shoulder, out into the woods, desperately searching for anything that might tell them where Kurt had gone.

They found nothing.

The search was finally scheduled to end on Wednesday, September 10, but unwilling to give up, Maine Governor James Longley decided to extend the search effort to two more days.

Although officials continued to maintain there was no evidence to suggest to them that foul play was involved, they sent Kurt's photograph and description to police departments across the country. They weren't saying he'd been abducted, only that they hadn't ruled out the possibility of it. Soon after the photo was distributed, a tip came in saying Kurt had been spotted in southern Maine, but no one could confirm the sighting.

As the official search finally came to a close, Fish and Game Warden Robert Tribou stated that he didn't believe Kurt would be found in the woods. The fact that the search teams had found absolutely no trace of the boy led him to believe he had been taken out of the area.

If only the police had listened to him.

IT WASN'T UNTIL OCTOBER THAT LAW ENFORCEMENT officials finally, almost grudgingly, admitted that they were considering the idea that Kurt had been abducted. Once again, though, they stressed that they didn't have any solid evidence of that – they were just considering it.

It seems obvious that the reason they had no evidence of it was because they'd never looked for any. While they were organizing hundreds of people to search woods, which his mother said he'd never go into alone, no other theories had been followed. If there had been any evidence, it was long gone.

Police departments across the region had already been given information and descriptions of Kurt. Post offices have also received copies of Kurt's photograph to display in case someone recognizes him.

Over the next few months, detectives with the state police followed up on every tip they received about Kurt. There were reported sightings of him in Vermont, Florida, and across the border in Montreal. None of the tips got them any closer to finding Kurt.

In late January 1976, a child matching Kurt's description was found wandering alone through the streets of the French Quarter in New Orleans. Jill and Ron were excited when they received the news, only to be heartbroken again when it was discovered that the boy had been abandoned by a Missouri woman who wanted to hitchhike to California.

In May, state troopers and fish and game wardens returned to Chain of Ponds and conducted one final search for Kurt. There weren't any leaves on the trees yet, and with little undergrowth after the winter, they believed they could do a more thorough search of the rough terrain. Again, though, they found nothing. Chief Game Warden Alanson Noble told reporters the same thing the wardens had said months earlier: "We are convinced that Kurt Newton is just not there."

Jill and Ron, both convinced that Kurt had been abducted, still held out hope that he was alive. The fact that his body hadn't been found in the woods -- despite the most extensive missing person search in the history of Maine -- was enough to make them feel they might someday be reunited with their son. During the summer of 1976,

Jill and Ron in 1979.

they sent Kurt's photograph and description to school districts around the United States and Canada. They hoped that whoever had taken him would enroll him in kindergarten during the upcoming school year, and he might be found.

In October 1976, detectives considered the possibility that a man accused of child murder and molestation named Wayne Chapman might have taken Kurt. He had been charged the previous month with the murder of a 5-year-old in Brockton, Massachusetts, and he was a suspect in several other child abductions and murders. Chapman admitted to being in Maine only a few times, but detectives could never connect him to Kurt's case.

Jill and Ron still refused to give up hope. By that December, they had distributed more than 50,000 flyers with Kurt's picture and description. They sent them to post offices and elementary schools; some were even printed in French to spread across Canada.

But none of them brought them any closer to finding their son.

Years went by, and the investigation cooled off and then turned cold. By 1983, the U.S. was finally changing how it dealt with missing child cases – and had access to technology that didn't exist in 1975. An age progression photo of what Kurt would look like at 12 was created and distributed across the county. An updated image was created two years later, showing him at age 14. A few tips trickled in after the photographs were released, but Kurt remained missing.

In 1995, two decades after that little boy had pedaled off on his Big Wheel into nowhere, Wal-Mart and Sam's Club stores in Augusta, Maine, dedicated missing children bulletin boards to Kurt. It was a way of trying to keep his name in the public eye long after many had tragically started to forget about the little boy who disappeared and had gotten the attention of the entire state of Maine.

All these years later, time hasn't dulled the pain of losing Kurt felt by his family. On the anniversary of his disappearance, Jill would sometimes talk to reporters, reminding them again of the little boy who was lost.

State police spokesman Steve McCausland has recently admitted that no tips have come in about the boy in many years. Kurt had, he said, "virtually disappeared off the face off the face of the earth."

1977: THE BLOND IN THE YELLOW SPORTS CAR
THE VANISHING OF LOY EVITTS

SHE WAS LATE TAKING HER LUNCH BREAK AGAIN.

This happened a lot for Loy Evitts, but she knew she had only herself to blame. She loved her job, and she loved to pitch in about whatever was happening in the office, especially if it was an interesting case. Everyone in the office described the 29-year-old legal secretary as an eager and conscientious worker. She often worked through her lunch – or left late for it – or stayed after work when a project needed to be finished.

So, on February 28, 1977, none of her coworkers were surprised when she was late returning from lunch. She'd certainly put in the extra time, and no one was watching the clock where Loy was concerned. She was completely justified in taking some extra time after all the hours she'd put in.

She'd left early that afternoon, around 2:00 P.M. – more than an hour later than usual – and said she wanted to do some shopping. She drove off in her bright yellow MGB GT sports car and headed for some shops about four blocks from the office in downtown Kansas City, Missouri. She was seen there, browsing in a few stores but she never returned to the office.

At some point, after she finished her shopping, Loy Evitts disappeared without a trace.

IT WAS AROUND 4:00 P.M. WHEN LOY'S COWORKERS realized she'd never returned from lunch. They assumed she'd taken some extra time, but Loy would never miss that much work. Some of them worried she'd been in a car accident. Their concerns grew when the workday ended, and Loy hadn't returned by 6:00. When they checked the parking garage, they found Loy's car was parked in its usual spot. They searched for Loy but then called her husband, Don, and told him they didn't know where Loy was.

Loy Evitts

Don Evitts knew something was wrong as soon as he received the call. Although his wife often worked late, she always called to let him know. He called several of her friends, hoping that one of them had seen Loy or knew where she was. None of them had spoken to her all day. Worried, Don's next call was to the Kansas City Police Department to report that his wife was missing.

The police met Don at the Country Club Plaza parking garage, next to her office. The bright yellow car was in its usual parking space, but there was no sign of Loy. Later that day, Kansas City Police Sergeant John Wilson told reporters, "Nothing we have at this time would lead us to believe she left on her own accord. Everything leads us to believe there is a possibility of foul play."

Loy's assigned parking space was in a dark corner on the fourth floor of the building. Once she parked, she had to walk about 50 yards to get to the nearest stairwell that led down to her office. She never expressed any fears about her safety, but after looking at the spot, the police couldn't help but wonder if she had been grabbed in the quiet, isolated garage.

Don was baffled by the situation. He and Loy had been married for four years and had a great relationship. He was sure that she wouldn't have taken off on her own.

Country Club Plaza in Kansas City.

Unsure of what to do and unwilling to go home without his wife, Don wandered around downtown Kansas City for hours, searching for any sign of Loy. Finally, around midnight, he reluctantly went home. He was exhausted but unable to sleep. Instead, he sat by the telephone, hoping it would ring and bring news about Loy.

The following day, detectives interviewed Loy's coworkers and others who worked in the same office complex. Several reported that Loy's distinctive car hadn't been in the parking garage around 2:00 P.M. the previous day but said it was back in its normal spot by 3:00. No one had seen the car return, so they couldn't confirm who'd been driving it.

Officers canvassed the shops in the area and were able to retrace Loy's steps in the hour leading up to her disappearance. After leaving her office, she stopped at a local jewelry store. Don had recently given her a new watch, and she wanted it adjusted. After that, she went to Macy's and looked around the women's clothing department before going to Skagg's Drugstore, where she purchased an umbrella. Her shopping was apparently completed, and she was seen getting back in her car. After that, it was assumed she drove herself back to the parking garage – but then, her trail came to an end.

While detectives were conducting interviews and retracing Loy's movements, Don remained close to the phone, hoping for a call from Loy to say she was okay.

He and Loy had dated for seven years before getting married in 1972. After the wedding, they moved to Kansas City from Coffeyville and enjoyed everything the larger city had to offer. They didn't have any children, and both worked full-time. Loy worked at the law firm, and Don was recently promoted to a management position at Fireman's Fund Insurance Company. His much larger salary allowed Loy to indulge in her favorite pastime – shopping. She had graduated from Kansas State University with a degree in clothing and retail design and loved buying clothes and antiques.

Don never cared about the money Loy spent, but he sometimes worried about her shopping alone. Loy laughed at his worries, assuring him that nothing bad would happen. He was now distraught that one of his few fears had seemingly come true.

As the investigation entered its second week, Don struggled to stay positive. Friends and relatives took turns staying with him, so he wasn't alone, but it didn't make him feel any better. He tried staying busy by bringing extra work home but struggled to concentrate. Night after night, he imagined he heard her car pulling into the driveway, even though he knew deep down that it was already sitting empty in the garage.

Like Don, Loy's coworkers were stunned by her disappearance. The other secretaries started walking back and forth from the parking garage in pairs, terrified there was a madman on the loose. They all loved Loy and prayed they would hear something from the police soon.

Detectives were working hard on the case. They dug into Loy's background but found nothing to suggest she would have walked away from her life. Everyone who knew Loy and Don described them as a happy couple – genuinely in love and content with spending time together. They couldn't even find anyone who'd seen them disagree. Loy's close friends assured detectives that she had never given them any indication there were problems in her marriage.

They spoke to everyone associated with Loy and could not find anyone who had a bad word to say about her. Sergeant Wilson noted, "This is the first saint I've ever seen. Everyone says she's perfect, and I haven't been able to disprove it."

Although Don was never a serious suspect in his wife's disappearance, he was asked to take a polygraph examination that could clear him of all suspicion. He readily agreed, and after the three-hour test concluded, the examiner was sure he was telling the truth – Don was not involved in his wife's vanishing.

Investigators were baffled. In most cases, a marriage like the Evitts' had would seem too good to be true, and they'd assume one of them was hiding something. But this time, cops admitted, they could find nothing out of the ordinary. Loy and Don seemed to be just what they appeared – a happy, loving couple.

In the days that followed Loy's disappearance, detectives followed up on more than 50 tips, but none led to substantial leads. Sergeant John Wilson admitted to reporters that the case was frustrating because they had exhausted almost every lead. "They've all come to a closing end right now. We have two or three more to work on, and then we'll start all over."

But then, ten days after Loy vanished, a new and disconcerting clue was discovered that changed everything.

ON MARCH 10, three children searching for their lost dog found Loy's purse under a bridge in the southeast side of Kansas City. It was about 12 miles from where Loy was last seen. That part of the city was sparsely populated in 1977, with the closest house at least a quarter mile from the bridge.

The kids didn't initially realize what they'd found. It wasn't until their father saw them playing with the purse that he realized there were credit cards in it that matched the name of a missing woman on the news. He immediately called the police and reported the discovery.

Although slightly damp, the police found Loy's purse undamaged. Her checkbook and credit cards were inside, and when detectives searched the area around the bridge, they found some papers with her name on them, a pack of cigarettes, and prescription medication that she used and wouldn't have willingly left behind.

It seemed obvious that the purse had been thrown into the creek from the bridge above. Because of its remote location, the area was known throughout the city as a popular "lover's lane." It was a common dumping spot for trash.

Detectives feared what else they might find dumped there.

Over a dozen officers spent hours scouring the creek and the surrounding area for clues, finally calling off the search when the sun went down.

More than 75 officers and recruits were called in the next morning to help widen the search parameters. A helicopter searched from above, hoping to find something the ground search couldn't see, but no clues to Loy's whereabouts were discovered.

Unsure where to go next, Sergeant Wilson asked for the FBI's assistance with the case. Since it had been classified as a potential kidnapping, they alerted agencies in the surrounding states but didn't get any further with the case than the Kansas City Police had.

On March 15, the law firm where Loy worked announced they were offering a $1,000 reward for information leading to her whereabouts. Several new tips trickled in, but none of them led to Loy.

Four days later, Jackson County Sheriff Robert Rennau ordered another search of the area around the bridge where Loy's purse was found. He said that since it had been raining when the first search was conducted, he wanted to make sure that no potential clues had been missed. Officers on foot and horseback spent hours going over the wooded area along the creek again but found no new evidence.

The next day, March 20, brought a startling turn of events. A 34-year-old man was arrested after it was discovered that he had made an anonymous phone call about the location of Loy's body. Unsure of whether it was a prank call or if the man had actual knowledge of the crime, he was brought in for questioning, and his home was searched. But they found nothing. He was just another of that strange group of people who want so desperately to be part of a story that they insert themselves into it in disturbing ways. He was eventually released without charges.

But another turn of events occurred a few days later. This time, investigators from the police department in Lee's Summit, Missouri, obtained a warrant to dig in a construction area for Interstate 470. They had received a tip that Loy's body could be found there. The immediate search turned up nothing, so a helicopter with infrared photographic equipment flew over the area and obtained images of the ground. Experts identified one area where a body might be buried, but it turned out to be nothing but a rock that had retained heat from the sun. After three days of further searching, the dig was called off.

By April, detectives had spent over 5,000 hours working on the case, but little progress had been made. They sorted through over 1,000 tips and interviewed at least 300 people. They had searched every single body of water in the area, including wells and cisterns. They dug up a section of the newly constructed highway and searched 12 miles in every direction from where her purse had been found. Despite the long hours of grueling work, what happened to Loy remained a mystery.

To put it bluntly, they'd run out of leads and ideas.

Sergeant Wilson confessed that the case had become an obsession to him. He hadn't taken a day off since Loy had gone missing. He told reporters, "I'd just like somebody to give me a call to say that she's alive or that she's dead – alive, mainly. There's still a possibility that she's alive, and that's the way I'd like to find her."

By the time the search had gone on for three months, Loy's friends and family were forced to face the fact that it was likely she wasn't coming back. Don was devastated. Although he said he no longer expected his wife to return, he continued hoping for a miracle. He left the house exactly as it was on the day Loy disappeared and made sure her beloved sports car remained in perfect condition so she could drive it when she came home.

Investigators felt the same way Don did. They knew that, realistically, it was unlikely that Loy would be found, but they still refused to give up. If nothing else, they were frustrated by the fact that her body hadn't been found. Sergeant Wilson admitted that he kept a shovel in the trunk of his car so he could quickly follow up whenever anyone reported seeing anything resembling a grave.

By August 1977, Loy had been missing for six months, and the investigation was at a standstill. Don was still struggling to cope with his loss, and Sergeant Wilson – two men joined together by the same woman but in different ways – still actively worked the case, even with no new leads. There was simply no trace of Loy, and though he was sure she was dead, he had no idea who killed her – or where she was.

Loy's case, of course, faded from the headlines, and the investigation turned cold. By the time the first anniversary of her vanishing arrived, those who cared for Loy had resigned themselves to the fact that they'd probably never have answers. Don told the press, "I have prepared myself mentally and accept that I will never see her again."

Sergeant Wilson offered his own grim statement to reporters. "I suspect she is buried in a shallow grave somewhere in the area where her purse was found, but if you don't

Don Evitts never recovered from the loss of his wife. He never remarried and never dated again, burying his grief in model-training building and loneliness.

have a body, you don't have a homicide."

As the years passed, many different detectives reviewed Loy's case file, hoping to find something that was missed back in 1977. But no solid evidence of what happened to her after she left the drugstore and returned to the parking garage has ever been discovered.

It remained the most puzzling case of Sergeant Wilson's career. He said sadly, "She just vanished. It was like she just left the face of the earth."

In 1984, seven years after his wife disappeared, Don had Loy declared legally dead. It wasn't for his own peace of mind. He only did it so her estate could be settled. He also didn't consider it closure. He told a friend that he'd said his goodbyes years before.

After Loy vanished, Don built model trains to stay occupied and deal with his grief. All these years later, the house he once shared with Loy is filled with the model trains he has so carefully built.

His brother, David, has said that Don never got over the loss of his wife. "Don never remarried," he said in an interview. "He never even dated again. Loy was the one-and-only love of his life."

1977: A PITCHER OF ICED TEA
THE VANISHING OF EVA DEBRUHL

IT WAS A HOT AFTERNOON.

Well, of course, it was, Eva likely thought to herself – it was the end of June in South Carolina. It's always hot.

Eva DeBruhl, 15 years old, had just finished mowing the grass at her home in Catawba, in the north-central part of the state, not too far from Charlotte. She started in the morning when the heat wasn't so bad, but by the time she finished at 11:00 A.M., the day had turned into a scorcher.

Eva left the lawn mower and went into the house to make some iced tea. The telephone rang, and she answered. Then, she told her father, Willard, that it was his supervisor at work calling to see if he'd come in. Willard, who worked for Suburban Texaco, agreed to take the extra shift and left for work a few minutes later. Eva was still in the kitchen making tea when she said goodbye.

Eva's mother, Opal, had worked an overnight shift and was still sleeping when her husband left. She didn't wake up until noon, and when she came downstairs, she noticed Eva was gone. This was strange – she always woke Opal to let her know before going anywhere. The television had been left on a religious show that Eva liked to watch, but otherwise, the house was silent.

Opal entered the kitchen and saw a fresh pitcher of iced tea on the counter. A glass was sitting next to it. Pieces of ice were inside of it, all of them starting to melt.

Eva was gone – and she was never seen again.

All she left behind was that pitcher of iced tea from which she never had a single sip.

EVA WAS BORN ON MAY 25, 1962, and was the youngest of the DeBruhl children. Her oldest sister, Elaine, was married and didn't live at home, and her sister, Tami, was 17 years old.

Eva could probably be described as plain with her long, straight blond hair and glasses – until she smiled. It was a smile that lit up her face, and, let's face it, Eva was usually smiling.

She had recently graduated from Castle Heights Junior High School in Catawba and was looking forward to starting at Rock

Hill High School in the fall. She was described as a friendly but shy young woman who enjoyed singing in the choir at Providence Baptist Church and had a close relationship with her family. She had no boyfriends and was usually at home when she wasn't at church or school.

And there was a good reason for that. Underneath her shy smile, Eva was haunted by a time just four years earlier when she'd had no reason to be happy. In 1973, the DeBruhl family had been wrecked by the death of their 14-year-old brother and son, Willard. He was walking with friends near his home when he was hit by a car and killed. The tragedy brought Eva even closer to her parents and sisters, which was one of the reasons she usually stayed home – and why she always told them where she would be.

Eva DeBruhl in a school photo taken the same year that she vanished.

But not this time, Opal must have thought.

When she realized that Eva wasn't in the house that June 29 afternoon, she went outside to look for her; the lawn was freshly mown, and Eva's flip-flops were on the porch near the front door.

Eva's grandmother, Eva Maree, lived in a trailer on the property, about 40 feet from the house, and Opal asked her if she'd seen Eva leave. She told Opal that she'd seen a new-looking Jeep or Scout enter the family's circular driveway about five minutes after Willard had left for work. The man driving it had been medium height, wearing a light green shirt and dark green pants, like a utility worker. He had walked up to the front door and seemed to be talking to someone through the screen door. After that, he returned to his vehicle and drove away, but he returned about 10 or 15 minutes later.

Eva Maree didn't see her granddaughter leave or hear any screams, shouts, or sounds of a struggle. Even so, Opal immediately called the police. The call was taken seriously, and officers were soon at the scene. They listened to Eva Maree's story and noted

that the man may have had a legitimate reason for being in the area. They had no idea if he had anything to do with the girl's disappearance. Captain Eugene Ervin of the York County Sheriff's Department admitted that there was nothing to indicate Eva had been taken by force, but he was concerned. He couldn't rule out an abduction. For now, though, Eva was simply a missing person.

Eva's friends and family members were certain that she hadn't run away. She got along well with her parents and with both of her sisters. They knew she wouldn't leave voluntarily. Eva had spent the previous night at Elaine's house and was in a great mood when she left. There was nothing to indicate anything was wrong.

Opal pointed out that Eva hadn't taken anything with her and had been barefoot when she went missing. Besides the shirt and shorts she'd been wearing when she mowed the yard, all her clothes were still in her bedroom. She had $54 that she'd saved from babysitting, which was left behind, too.

Willard and Opal feared the worst. Eva was the kind of girl who called home when she was at a friend's house and would be a few minutes late getting home. She had never gone anywhere without letting one of her parents know where she would be.

Eva's family, friends, and neighbors spent hours searching the area for her but found no sign of her. None of her friends from school or church had seen her after she finished mowing the grass that morning.

The search widened the following day. Detectives from neighboring Lancaster and Chester Counties and parts of nearby North Carolina assisted with the search, trying to find anyone who might have seen Eva. York County Sheriff W.E. Sutton told reporters that he contacted the FBI but that they were unable to assist in the investigation because, so far, there was no evidence the young woman had been abducted or had been taken across state lines.

Worry spread through the entire community. It was a small town, and most people knew the DeBruhl family. Those who also knew Eva reinforced the fact that she would never have run away from home.

Rick Vaughn, who worked at a neighborhood store, said Eva was always with her mother or her best friend, Jane Cassidy. He'd never seen her anywhere alone. When Eva vanished, Jane was on vacation with her family in North Carolina, but reporters were able to reach her mother. She told the press that Eva often spent the night at their house, and when she did, she always called her mother before bed to tell her she loved her. She was a genuinely sweet girl, Mrs. Cassidy said, and would never do anything that might worry her parents.

Now, Opal was waiting by the phone, afraid to go too far away from it, praying that Eva would call her again.

ON SUNDAY, JULY 3, MORE THAN 100 VOLUNTEERS spent the day combing the woods and along the banks of the Catawba River, searching for any clue that might lead them to Eva. They returned home that night disappointed.

On Monday, another 200 people joined the search as it spread beyond the town's limits. Volunteers used motorcycles, ATVs, and boats to cover more ground, but once again, nothing turned up.

Although Willard and Opal tried to stay optimistic, their fear grew daily. Eva would have called them if she had been able to do so. They knew in their hearts that Eva would never run away from home, but they almost would have preferred that to the horror growing in their minds with each passing day.

Willard had taken time off from his mechanic job to join the search for his daughter. He told reporters he hadn't been able to sleep and was growing increasingly desperate for some word about Eva. The family had received several crank calls from people since she'd disappeared, but there were no reliable leads about where she might be.

Detectives were still stubbornly saying that they had no evidence that Eva had been abducted but were forced to admit she didn't seem to be the kind of girl to leave home on her own. They made several public appeals to help identify the man Eva Maree saw at the DeBruhl home when Eva disappeared. However, despite offering as many details as they had, no one could identify the driver.

On July 8, the case took a turn with the arrest of a man named Daniel Boulware. He was charged with extortion and blackmail after calling the DeBruhl house five times and demanding a $2,000 ransom in exchange for Eva's return. Boulware wasn't involved in the disappearance; he was trying to exploit the family's desperation. The police searched his home in Great Falls, South Carolina, but no evidence of the girl was found. He eventually pleaded guilty to the charges and was sentenced to spend seven years behind bars.

As mentioned to reporters by Willard DeBruhl, the family had been taunted by many crank calls. Once, someone called and claimed to have Eva and then pretended to beat her while they were on the phone with Opal. Another caller spoke with Tami and told her they had her sister and would take her next.

But a few calls seemed to offer solid leads. Over the next two weeks, Willard spoke to at least four people who believed they saw Eva and her abductor traveling in a blue and white Jeep Wagoneer with a South Carolina license plate. The vehicle was seen on Interstate 95, heading toward Florence, South Carolina. Hoping to find his daughter, Willard traveled to the area on July 20, but with so few clues to follow, he could not find any trace of Eva.

In late July – a month after Eva vanished – her parents announced that they were starting a reward fund for information about Eva or her abductor. They started the fund with $200, and donations from the public quickly doubled it. Several stores in the Catawba and Rock Hill area agreed to allow the family to place donation jars near their registers to make it easier for people to donate. By the end of August, they had raised more than $700 – a substantial amount in the lower-income area.

However, the reward fund didn't get the family or the police any closer to finding Eva.

By November, detectives still had no leads in the case. Frustration led Willard to quit his job so he could focus only on searching for Eva. He was certain she'd been kidnapped, and he became obsessed with finding the man responsible.

Meanwhile, the York County Sheriff's Department still classified Eva as a missing person. They maintained there was no evidence that she had been taken by force and couldn't be certain she was abducted. Investigators continued to follow up on every tip they received about the case but confessed the number of calls had dropped to almost zero, and they had no new leads.

But Willard and Opal refused to give up. They sold their home to finance the search for Eva and moved into a mobile home in Catawba shortly before Thanksgiving. As Christmas approached, no one in the family felt like celebrating. Eva had always been the one who had the most fun decorating the tree each year, and without her there to enjoy it, Opal didn't bother putting one up that year. The family had a quiet holiday and then returned to searching for the missing girl.

By the start of 1978, it was clear that the official investigation into Eva's disappearance had stalled. Investigators had exhausted every available lead and were no closer to knowing what happened to her than they were on the day she first went missing. While Willard and Opal continued to insist that Eva had been kidnapped, detectives still insisted there was no evidence of foul play.

Eva was simply gone.

Her case went cold and faded from newspaper headlines.

But then, two years later, in February 1980, Eva's case was back in the news. Investigators learned that an unidentified body had been found near Lumberton, North Carolina, on June 1, 1978, almost a year after Eva disappeared. The missing girl's dental records were sent to a forensic dentist so they could be compared with the teeth of the unidentified body. The authorities were cautiously optimistic that a match would be made and even told reporters they believed Eva had finally been found.

On February 15, however, Captain Ervin announced there was no match – Eva was still missing. For her parents, the news meant there was still hope that their daughter was alive. Opal told reporters that she didn't want to believe that Eva was dead, although if she was, she prayed her family would be able to give her a proper burial and not be left wondering forever about her fate.

The DeBruhls kept searching. They consulted a series of psychics as they looked for answers, only to be disheartened when at least three of them claimed that Eva was dead. All believed her remains would be found in a heavily wooded area near where Eva was last seen. For years afterward, Willard spent two Sundays each month combing the woods around town, hoping to find something that would lead him to his daughter.

By this time, Willard had done everything he could think of to do to find Eva. He quit his job, sold his home, spoke with psychics, traveled to nine states following up potential leads, and spent over $18,000. Nothing he did brought him any closer to her. He finally told reporters, "I don't think she's alive. I don't think she was alive two hours after she left the house... I'd just like to bury her."

Two more years passed, and then, in July 1984, Eva was back in the news again. Infamous serial killer Henry Lee Lucas claimed that he had been responsible for Eva's kidnapping and murder – one of the 600 people that he confessed to killing.

Investigators would eventually determine that most of his confessions were false – including the one about Eva's murder. He claimed he'd picked her up while she was walking along a county road, killed her, and dumped her body in a wooded area.

Nothing he said matched the known facts surrounding Eva's disappearance, but search teams still spent weeks wasting their time and combing through Landsford Canal State Park in Chester County. This is where he claimed her body had been dumped. Not surprisingly, nothing was found to substantiate his story, and detectives managed to eliminate him from having any involvement in Eva's case. Lucas later died in prison, and the exact number of people he killed remains a mystery.

As does the fate of Eva DeBruhl.

BUT EVA'S STORY ISN'T OVER.

In July 1997, two decades after her disappearance, officials from the York County Sheriff's Department told her family that they were going to take a fresh look at the cold case. Willard was thrilled and told Opal he believed they were finally getting close to some answers.

But for Willard, they never came.

He died in his sleep on July 5, just two days after the announcement from the sheriff's department. Those who loved him said he'd never really recovered from Eva's disappearance, and his broken heart had finally given out.

As part of the new initiative, an age progression photograph of Eva was created, and new missing person flyers were sent out across the country – and met with silence. Detectives were unable to develop any new leads.

More years have passed since then, and the case has remained cold. On June 29, 2017, Eva's family gathered to mark the 40th anniversary of her disappearance. Her mother and sisters remembered the shy teenager who vanished without a trace.

Tami told a reporter that the passing years hadn't lessened the family's pain. "Some days, it's like it was yesterday, but it has been

40 years. I think about her every day. She was such a sweet, wonderful, beautiful young girl. We just want to bring her home."

Opal continued to hope for the same thing, always wondering what happened to her daughter in 1977. But like her husband, Opal never got the answers she desperately wanted. She passed away in May 2022 – never discovering how the story of the missing Eva would finally end.

1977: A VANISHING HITCHHIKER
THE DISAPPEARANCE OF SIMONE RIDINGER

SHE HITCHHIKED ALL THE TIME.

There was nothing out of the ordinary about this Labor Day Weekend in 1977. Simone Ridinger needed to get from her job in Natick, Massachusetts, to Martha's Vineyard, where she was meeting up with her family for the holiday weekend, and hitching a ride was the easiest way to do it. The 17-year-old was very independent, and even though friends and family warned her about getting into cars with strangers, she had never had any trouble before.

And she didn't expect to have any on that Friday afternoon. But, unfortunately, she did. Simone never made it to Martha's Vineyard, and she's never been seen again.

SIMONE STEPHANIE RIDINGER WAS BORN on January 5, 1960. Her father, George Barrett, died when she was very young, leaving her mother, Jane, to survive as a single mother. Simone was still a child when her mother moved them to New York. There, she met a widowed neighbor, John Ridinger, who had a young daughter of his own, Betsy. The two families became close, and Jane and John were married. John adopted Simone, and she took her new father's last name.

In time, the Ridingers moved to Sherborn, Massachusetts, preferring the smaller town as a place to raise the two girls. But if they were hoping to tame the rebellious Simone, they failed. She was an artist and a free spirit who sang and played multiple instruments. She was extremely smart, meaning she was easily bored and was always looking for something new. She was in and

Simone Ridinger

out of high school before ultimately dropping out. The assistant principal at her school later recalled her as "a delightful girl who wasn't fond of school and seemed to be rebelling against something." Simone was working on her GED at some point but never finished it.

But Simone was never a troublesome or difficult girl. She just marched to the beat of her own drum, so to speak. To her friends, she was a "gifted pianist, free spirit, and fiercely independent."

The marriage of John and Jane Ridinger didn't last, and they eventually divorced. Simone moved with her mother but, in early 1977, decided to get an apartment of her own in Framingham. She started working at the Rainbow Restaurant on South Main Street in Natick and was, by all accounts, enjoying her new life as a young woman on her own.

On September 2, 1977, Simone was working her shift at the restaurant. It was the start of Labor Day Weekend, and she knew her mother and relatives were spending the weekend on Martha's Vineyard. Simone told coworkers she had decided to hitchhike to Cape Cod and planned to take the ferry to Martha's Vineyard. Everyone recalled her excitement about her travel plans, and she seemed eager to spend a few days with her family.

Her excitement was why a few of her coworker friends hated to discourage her plan to hitchhike to Cape Code, which was about 70 miles away. Simone dismissed their concerns. She hitchhiked all the time, so this was nothing new to her. But, they pointed out, she didn't hitch rides that far – she usually only hitchhiked from work to home. Her sister, Betsy, offered to drive her to the bus stop, but Simone declined the offer. She was perfectly comfortable with thumbing rides and insisted this was the best plan.

As soon as her shift was over at 3:00 P.M., Simone changed out of her work clothes and went outside the restaurant to start looking for a ride. A couple of her friends from the diner checked on her a few minutes later, but Simone was already gone. None of them had seen the vehicle that picked her up.

And none of them ever saw Simone again.

WHEN SIMONE DIDN'T ARRIVE ON MARTHA'S Vineyard, her family wasn't too concerned at first. Though it wasn't like her to be late, her mother thought she might have run into friends at Hyannis Port or had been delayed and missed the ferry. Or perhaps she'd decided to skip the weekend altogether.

The problem was that there was no way for them to know. They were staying at a house in Chappaquiddick, which was a little off the beaten path and didn't have electricity or a telephone. They couldn't call home and check on Simone or receive a call from her to say she was late.

Worse, back home, Betsy assumed that Simone had made it to Martha's Vineyard and had no idea she hadn't arrived.

Simone was missing for the next nine days – but no one knew about it.

Her mother, Jane Barrett, arrived home on September 11, and she discovered that her daughter wasn't at her apartment in Framingham and that no one had heard from her since she left work on September 2. Jane and her family began making calls, trying to track her down. They called every friend they could think of, but no one had seen her. The last known sighting of her was outside the Rainbow Restaurant after her shift. After that, no one knew what had happened to her.

Jane went to the police station that day and reported Simone as missing. It was a small-town station with only a few officers, and she was initially dismissed as a runaway – even though she lived independently, was employed, and had nothing to run away from. Jane's concerns weren't taken seriously. The cops believed Simone would turn up – until she didn't.

Finally, a missing person investigation was started, and flyers went out to the surrounding area. Simone was five feet, two inches tall, and weighed 115 pounds. She had strawberry blond hair, brown eyes, a birthmark on her lower back, and a small mole on her forehead. When she'd left work on September 2, she'd been wearing spoon rings, bracelets, and a necklace with turquoise stones.

Officers visited the Rainbow Restaurant and spoke with some of Simone's coworkers. On September 17, the police visited the Billerica House of Correction to talk to Simone's boyfriend. I haven't been able to find out why he was in jail. He told investigators that Simone had stopped writing, which concerned him. She was also supposed to visit him the same day the police showed up, but she missed her appointment. He said this wasn't like her because she'd been given special permission to see him that day.

By October 4, the investigation was finally in full swing. Even the detectives who assumed Simone had taken off on her own were taking things seriously. She had been missing for more than a month at that point. Any clues that may have existed were gone by that time.

They vanished – just like Simone.

YEARS PASSED. THERE WERE NO LEADS IN HER disappearance, and her case was completely cold. Her social security number was never used, and she never accessed her bank accounts again. The police had checked pawn shops, hoping that Simone – or someone – had pawned her jewelry, but they came up empty.

Then, nine years after she vanished, there seemed to be a break in Simone's case. An older man – whose name has never been released – came forward to the authorities. He said he had seen an article in a local newspaper with Simone's photo, and he was sure she had been the girl in his car back in 1977.

The man said he was on his way to Osterville, Massachusetts, on September 3 to pick up some clock parts when he was pulled over for speeding by a state trooper on Route 128 at 6:45 A.M.

The trooper had a teenage girl in his car, and once he heard where the man was traveling, he asked if the man would give the girl a ride since that was where she was heading, too. He agreed, and the young woman switched vehicles, and they drove toward Cape Cod. He later dropped her off at the Hyannis Airport Rotary Club. If it had been Simone – the girl never offered her name, and he never asked -- she could have easily caught a flight from there to Martha's Vineyard. He saw her walk to a nearby restaurant and then drove away.

That was the last time he'd seen her until he spotted her face in the newspaper article saying she'd been missing all those years.

The police found the man's story credible, especially after he described Simone, her clothing, and the things she had with her that morning. The man said the girl he picked up was wearing a blue blouse, blue jeans, and white sneakers and was carrying a grayish-colored duffle bag.

Detectives went in search of Simone's former coworkers at the Rainbow Restaurant who were with her on the day she went missing. When they successfully found two of the employees, they recalled Simone was wearing a blue vest-style blouse, blue jeans, and white sneakers and carrying a gray duffle bag that had her work uniform in it when she was last seen.

One more piece had been added to the puzzle of Simone's disappearance, but the police were no closer to that puzzle being solved.

IN 2014, SIMONE'S CASE WAS TAKEN OVER by Detective James Godinho, who worked on it for years. When the cold case file landed on his desk, he started back at the beginning, tracking down surviving witnesses from the records and trying to clear up some existing inconsistencies.

He was interested in the witness account from the man who believed he'd given Simone a ride and wanted to try and confirm it. He decided to review traffic stop records from 1977 to track down the trooper and ask him some questions, but he quickly learned that no records of old traffic stops existed.

He next tracked down the man's son and spoke to him about his father's story. The son couldn't recall his father ever telling him about driving Simone anywhere. This didn't mean it never occurred; he just never mentioned it to his son, who was a teenager at the time. Regardless, Godinho thought this was a little strange and made him rethink the man's statement. Had he really given Simone a ride?

And stranger yet, Simone left work on September 2, but the man claimed to have driven her to Cape Cod on the morning of September 3. Where was she all that time?

Just as detectives had in 1986, Godinho tracked down some of Simone's coworkers from the diner, and they also described her changing out of her work uniform, getting dressed, and looking for a ride. Once again, the description of what she'd been wearing matched what the man had said when he came forward with his statement in 1986.

It seems that Simone did make it as far as Cape Cod, but what happened then? And where had she been the night before?

No one knows.

In the years that have passed since she vanished, her parents have died, as have many of her friends. Life has moved on, and her story has been largely forgotten. Her sister, Betsy, still does interviews now and then, hoping that by keeping Simone's story out there in some small way, there's a chance the mystery might someday be solved.

1978: VANISHED FROM CAMPUS
THE DISAPPEARANCE OF JUDY MARTINS

THERE WAS NO DOUBT ABOUT IT – JUDY WAS excited about her plans for Memorial Day Weekend. The 22-year-old junior from Kent State University in Ohio was going to New York to spend the holiday weekend with two of her best friends. She couldn't wait!

But she still had the rest of the week to get through. It was only Tuesday, May 23, and Judy still had responsibilities. She was the resident assistant at her dormitory, Engleman Hall, and there were things to do as the semester ended.

But on that Tuesday evening, Judy didn't feel like doing them. She smiled as she left her dorm and headed towards nearby Dunbar Hall to visit friends. They ordered a pizza and hung out for a few hours, and then Judy left to make the five-minute walk back to her own dorm. By then, it was around 2:30 A.M., but the campus had always been safe, and she didn't think twice about walking back alone.

The campus may not have been as safe as she thought. Judy never made it back to Engleman Hall and has never been seen again.

JUDY WAS BORN ON JULY 15, 1955, THE OLDEST daughter cf Arthur and Dolores Martins. She also had a younger sister and younger brother. In 1973, Judy graduated from Avon Lake High School and enrolled at Ohio University in the fall. She spent two years there before deciding to take some time off and move back home with her parents. After a few years, Judy got her life back on track and decided to go to Kent State.

She had always been a good student but had now become more serious about her education. She became an art major, minoring in women's

Judy Martins

studies at Kent State. She hadn't ruled out graduate school but planned to become a therapist. She enjoyed helping people, even serving as a volunteer counselor at the university's Pregnancy Information Center.

Judy had a winning personality and was a friendly and outgoing young woman. She made friends easily, was popular on campus, and loved to have fun.

Judy walked back to her dormitory on the night she was last seen. One of the perks of her position as resident assistant was that she had a single room – but this meant she had no roommate to raise the alarm when she didn't show up.

So, her disappearance initially went unnoticed.

More than 24 hours went by before one of her friends reported her missing to the campus police. This was on Thursday night – but officials didn't call Judy's parents until Friday afternoon. They didn't take it seriously. They thought she'd gone off alone and would probably be back after Memorial Day weekend. Although they told Judy's family that they had searched the campus for her, it is unknown whether they really did so. Most of Judy's classmates had already left for the weekend and weren't around to be questioned.

Those who had seen Judy in the hours before she vanished told police that she had been in a good mood when she left Dunbar Hall and said she was going straight back to her room. The friends had been celebrating the fact that the semester was almost over. They also noted that Judy had pranked the other girls by wearing a curly red wig when she showed up to hang out with them.

Although campus police insisted that Judy would return when she was ready, her family and friends didn't agree. Her parents were just as insistent that Judy wouldn't just take off and not tell anyone where she was going, especially since she had plans with her friends. Besides her friends, Judy was also very close to her sister, Nancy. The two talked on the phone almost daily, and she had never mentioned going anywhere before the planned trip over the weekend.

No one did anything when Judy vanished. Her parents believed the Kent State police were trying to downplay her disappearance. They felt the university was still trying to overcome the public relations nightmare caused by the Kent State shootings in 1970 and didn't want the negative press caused by a missing student.

So, Arthur and Dolores Martins didn't wait. They went around the campus police and contacted the local police department, who also did nothing. Since the disappearance occurred on campus, they claimed it was out of their jurisdiction and had to wait for the school to contact them.

A week after Judy was last seen, officials for the campus police finally made a public appeal for information about her whereabouts. It was noted that she was "reliable and dependable," and her family didn't think she had vanished voluntarily. At this point, they contacted the local authorities, but they didn't organize any area searches.

Another week later, Kent State Police Chief Robert Malone announced that detectives had reason to believe Judy had gone to Mexico. He reported that Judy had been spotted at a garage sale in town on Memorial Day – days after she disappeared. She allegedly spent an hour looking through items for sale before buying some clothing. She told several people there that she planned to hitchhike through Mexico. The witnesses were shown photos of Judy and told investigators they were certain she was the woman they'd seen.

Although Chief Malone was confident that he'd solved the mystery, he told reporters they still planned to conduct an aerial search of the campus and the surrounding area. In addition, the Kent State University Foundation was offering a $1,500 reward for information leading to Judy's whereabouts.

Judy's family scoffed at the news. They knew she wouldn't hitchhike anywhere. She'd never done it before, and she had her own car. They believed this was a case of mistaken identity – the witnesses had seen someone else.

And they were right.

On June 5, the woman from the garage sale was spotted again. This time, she was getting a passport photo taken in preparation for her trip to Mexico. Although she resembled Judy – it wasn't her. Investigators spoke to her and confirmed she was not the missing woman.

More time had been lost – and Judy was still missing.

FINALLY, THE NEWS OF JUDY'S DISAPPEARANCE began reaching a wider audience. Her parents appeared in newspapers and on television, asking for help finding her. Dolores stressed that all her daughter's belongings had been left in her dorm room – her clothing, books, makeup, and eyeglasses. Judy had been wearing her contacts when she vanished, but at that time, contacts were not meant to be worn overnight. Judy almost certainly planned to take them out when she got home. She had problems with her eyesight due to a flattened cornea, and she never would have traveled anywhere without taking her glasses with her.

The public eye was now on the university, and Kent State officials were forced to admit they had no idea what had happened to Judy. After more than two weeks of delays, they were now starting to search for her. A helicopter with heat-seeking radar was used to search the campus and a nearby wooded area, but there was no sign of Judy. All of Judy's friends and acquaintances had now been questioned, and four people – including a man that Judy had dated on and off – took and passed polygraph exams. No one who knew her could offer any clues about where she might be.

A Kent State detective named Tim Brandon was assigned to Judy's case, but he told reporters he didn't have much to work with. "We are investigating minor leads, but nothing has turned out to be significant."

And thanks to the delay, Judy's case failed to attract much attention from the media, which meant that very few tips came in. Before the summer was over, the investigation had stalled, and Judy's case had gone cold.

NEARLY TWO YEARS PASSED.

Although investigators with the campus police claimed they were still actively working on the case, they said they hadn't received any new tips in months.

Needless to say, the lack of progress was brutal for Judy's family. Dolores noted, "We've had some bizarre rumors from time to time, but they have led nowhere." One persistent rumor had been that Judy was working as a prostitute in Cleveland, Ohio. "We checked it out...it's unfounded."

Every week, Dolores called the campus police and asked for any updates on Judy's case. Detectives, though, never had anything new to report.

In January 1980, Nan Abdo, a friend of the Martins family, announced that she was offering a $10,000 reward for information leading to Judy's return. Her father had passed away and left her a small inheritance. She wanted to do something solid with it to help find Judy. "It's a long shot," she admitted," but maybe this will do the trick."

Just a few weeks later, Kent State Deputy Chief John Peach had an announcement of his own. He stated that detectives were looking into the possibility that a man named William Posey might have been involved in Judy's vanishing. Posey had been arrested and charged with the murder of a woman in Illinois, and detectives had become interested in him when they learned that he lived in Kent from June 1978 to September 1979.

Once again, the campus police jumped to conclusions they couldn't prove. It was like Judy's "hitchhiking trip to Mexico" all over again. They had no evidence to connect Posey to Judy. Not only did he deny having anything to do with her disappearance, but detectives had to admit just two weeks later that they couldn't place Posey in Kent at any time during May 1978 – you know, when Judy actually vanished. As a result, Posey was never charged in connection with Judy's case.

The failures of campus police detectives did nothing to lessen the desperation of the Martins to find their daughter. Eventually, they decided to speak with a psychic. Although neither Arthur nor Dolores had ever believed in spirit mediums, they were willing to try anything.

Dolores explained, "We brought this woman an article of Judy's clothing, and she told us things about Judy, personal things about her that were never in any newspaper, things that only we could know."

Sadly, though, the psychic didn't have good news for them. She said that Judy had been abducted and murdered by three men. She told them that Judy's body had been thrown from an airplane that was flying at a low altitude. The body could be found on a heavily wooded, uninhabited island at least 50 miles northwest of Kent.

When they contacted the police, detectives reluctantly admitted there were islands on Lake Erie that fit the psychic's description and assured the Martins they would search some of them as soon as the weather got warmer.

The psychic seemed to think they would be successful. She told the Martins: "The earth will give up Judy's body in April or May."

But by the end of May, it had become clear that the prediction about the recovery of Judy's body was wrong. She remained missing, and her case soon went cold again.

AS THE YEARS PASSED, JUDY'S CASE was largely forgotten. In the following decades, no articles or news reports were written about her or the case, and it was unclear if any detectives were still working on it. Then – as if they hadn't screwed up the case enough – Kent State University destroyed all the files concerning Judy's disappearance. Officials didn't feel the need to keep the case active, even though she had never been found. When contacted, they told Judy's family that throwing out records after a certain time was "campus policy."

You see, Judy's disappearance had never been classified as a crime. The authorities still insisted that Judy might have left on her own.

In the years since Judy went missing, both of her parents have died. Her sister, Nancy, always believed that Judy's vanishing cut their lives short. Arnold was just 57 when he died; Dolores was 71.

Unlike Kent State University, Nancy and her brother, Steve, have not given up on their sister. They both submitted DNA samples to the Ohio Bureau of Criminal Investigation so they could build a profile for Judy and check for matches with unidentified bodies across the United States. They have come to terms with the idea that Judy is likely dead, but they'd still like to give their sister a proper burial. Steve said in an interview, "The not knowing is very difficult, and it would be much better to know what happened, no matter how tragic."

Unsurprisingly, bitterness remains about how the university's police department handled Judy's case. Nancy believes that no one there ever really cared – always suspecting that Judy had just taken off. She added, "That Kent State destroyed its files on Judy's disappearance is probably the most painful part."

And, I'd add, the most irresponsible.

No one knows if Judy Martins will ever be found. Too many years have passed for the closure the family still wants and deserves. If only someone had bothered to look for her when she first disappeared, perhaps her story would never have had to appear within these pages.

1979: "SHE LEFT NO TRACE"
THE DISAPPEARANCE OF LORRAINE HERBSTER

IT WAS ONE OF THOSE LATE WINTER DAYS when you knew Spring was just around the corner. It had been cold in Mount Holly, New Jersey, when the sun came up on March 9, but the day had turned warm by afternoon.

It was just after 4:00 P.M. when 17-year-old Lorraine Herbster walked out of the Microcircuit Engineering Corporation, where she'd recently started working as a lab technician. Lori, the name she usually went by, loved the job, which surprised her a little, but part of it was how well she got along with her coworkers. Lori didn't have her driver's license yet, but one of those coworkers was happy to give her a ride home each evening.

Lori lived in the Tarnsfield housing development in Westhampton Township, New Jersey, which had only been started one year before. She lived in a new home with her parents along one of the housing addition's confusing streets. Lori only lived a short distance from Microcircuit, and her friend dropped her off at the entrance to the development. She waved goodbye and started making the six-block walk to her house on Whitlow Drive.

But Lori never made it home – and she was never seen again.

LORRAINE REA HERBSTER WAS BORN ON January 16, 1962, in New Jersey. Family and friends described her as a shy girl who liked spending time at home. She enjoyed playing the flute and riding her bicycle and had attended the Burlington County Vocational and Technical School at one point. However, she dropped out during her junior year.

At that time, she was engaged to her high school boyfriend and was already planning their wedding. However, when the couple broke up in December 1978, Lori decided to get a job instead of returning to school.

Lorraine Herbster

She still lived with her parents, Terry and Betty Herbster, and was very close with them. On Friday, March 9, Lori had promised her mother that she would come straight home after work so they could go together to their local bank and cash the paycheck Lori received the previous day. When she failed to arrive at home, Betty wasn't too concerned. Lori often babysat for one of their neighbors on Friday nights, so she assumed Lori had forgotten about their plans to go to the bank and had gone straight to her babysitting job instead.

But when Terry and Betty got up around 7:00 A.M on Saturday, they realized Lori wasn't home. Betty called the neighbor she often babysat for and learned that Lori hadn't been there the previous night. They hadn't seen her at all.

Immediately, Betty and Terry began calling Lori's friends, but none had seen her, spoken with her, or had any idea where she might be. After two hours of increasingly worrying calls, the couple started to panic.

At just after 9:00 A.M., they called the Westhampton Township Police Department and reported that their daughter was missing.

While waiting for officers to respond, Terry and Betty went outside and started walking up the street, following the route Lori would have taken from the housing development entrance to their home.

But they didn't have to go far – they found Lori's purse abandoned in the front yard.

When the police arrived, they assured the officers that Lori was not the type of teenager who would run away. She was close with her parents and loved her new job. She was also excited about getting her driver's license, and Terry had already bought her a new car to drive when she passed the exam. It was sitting untouched in the driveway.

Westhampton Township detectives took their concerns seriously and started an investigation. They spoke with Lori's friends and coworkers, but none of them could offer any clues about her whereabouts. They canvassed the homes along the route Lori walked each afternoon and found one witness who recalled seeing her walk past their home just before 5:00 P.M. However, no one saw her arrive home, and it was unclear how her purse ended up in the Herbster's front yard.

A few days later, on Tuesday, March 13, the police set up a roadblock outside the neighborhood's entrance. They stopped each vehicle that entered or exited the development, handing out missing person flyers with Lori's photo and information on them. They asked the occupants of every car if they had seen or heard anything unusual around the time Lori went missing. Despite spending many hours on the street and talking to dozens of people, no one could provide the investigators with any substantial leads.

Detectives were baffled by Lori's case. They'd found no evidence of foul play, but the teenager had no history of running away, and her friends and family were convinced she didn't leave voluntarily. They'd done extensive interviews with everyone who knew her, yet no solid clues had emerged. The coworker who dropped her off that Friday afternoon voluntarily took a polygraph exam to confirm his version of events and passed with flying colors. He was never suspected of playing any part in Lori's disappearance.

On March 15, Lori's loved ones were shocked to hear that the body of a young woman had been discovered on the side of a road near the Deptford Mall. Responding officers feared that it was the missing, but it was soon determined to be the body of an older woman – not Lori. Betty and Terry were sympathetic for the family of the unknown woman but breathed a sigh of relief that it hadn't been their daughter.

Over the next few days, the police conducted extensive searches of the housing development and the surrounding area using volunteers, search dogs, and even a helicopter, but they found nothing connected to Lori.

Westhampton Police Detective Gary Stephens told reporters he feared Lori met with foul play. She had never, he said, spoken to friends about being unhappy at home, and besides, she had left all her belongings behind. Even the paycheck from work she'd picked up the day before was still sitting on her dresser in her bedroom.

The investigation continued but soon stalled out. Days passed, then weeks, and then Lori had been missing for a month. Hoping to generate new leads, the Herbsters announced they were offering a $1,000 reward for any information leading to their daughter's safe return. Sadly, even a reward failed to bring in new leads, and the case was finally considered cold.

Six months passed, and there were still no leads regarding Lori's whereabouts. Terry and Betty left New Jersey and relocated to Alabama, where Terry had a job offer. "I had to get out of that house," Betty told reporters. She stayed in regular contact with Westhampton Township detectives, though, but they never had anything new to report.

Months turned to years, and the case remained cold. No clues about what happened to Lori that Friday afternoon after she left work had ever been found. When a local newspaper did a "cold case" story about Lori, Betty was interviewed and told the reporter, "This is something you don't get over. You still miss her. You're still waiting for any word. It's not knowing that drives you crazy. It doesn't get any better."

In March 1987, Westhampton Township Police Chief Russell Minuto took a fresh look at Lori's case – and he had good reason. He explained that he'd received four telephone calls from men who claimed they knew what happened to Lori during the past three weeks. None of the men would give him their name, but each agreed to come to the police station and talk to him.

But none of them ever showed up.

Although Chief Minuto was discouraged by their failure to show up, he refused to let the case go. Energized by the new interest in the story, he told the press, "I got to thinking that somebody must know something about what's going on. I want to encourage these people to come in so we can solve this case once and for all."

Chief Minuto was certain four men had made the calls and noted that all of them had been made just before the eighth anniversary of Lori's disappearance. He said, "My gut feeling is that these calls are not pranks."

Betty was encouraged by the news that the case had been re-opened. She had given up calling detectives a few years earlier because they never had anything new. She had stopped believing her daughter was still alive, but she needed to know what had happened to her. She and Terry needed some peace.

Chief Minuto, like his predecessors, believed Lori had been abducted. "I fear the worst happened," he said. "I doubt very much she ran away." Lori's case was the only long-term missing person case in the small department's history. Every officer that worked there wanted nothing more than to be able to solve it finally.

In 1989, two friends of Lori's – Diane Truitt and Liz Royers – paid for a billboard in hopes new information would come out about their friend's disappearance.

Unfortunately, though, if the four men who called the chief did have information about Lori's disappearance, they never called back to share it with him.

The case soon turned cold again.

LORI HAD BEEN MISSING FOR A DECADE IN 1989. A couple of her friends wanted to ensure the public knew she had not been forgotten. Lori's best friend, Diane Truitt, and another close friend, Liz Royers, knew Lori hadn't run away from home. They were convinced she'd been taken and likely murdered. So, to mark the tenth anniversary of her disappearance, the two women paid for a billboard to be put up at the spot where Lori had last been seen, at the corner of Rancocas and Holly Roads.

The billboard had a photo of Lori on it, along with the words:

MISSING BUT REMEMBERED.
LAST SEEN HERE ON MARCH 9, 1979

It also included a telephone number that people could call if they had information about Lori. Diane and Liz were hopeful it might encourage someone to finally come forward with the needed information to bring their friend home. In an interview, Diane said, "I hope all this will come to something. At least one person has got to know something."

Liz explained that they just wanted to have some closure. She told a reporter, "It hurts. It hurts so much. If we just knew what happened to her, bad or not. Sometimes, I feel I wouldn't want to know, but now I feel like it needs to be known."

Reporters also interviewed officials from the Westhampton Township Police, who were still discouraged by the lack of leads in Lori's case. They hadn't had anything new come in since the anonymous calls two years earlier.

Sadly, the billboard failed to produce anything new.

In 2001, Chief Bruce Reed told reporters he continued to work on Lori's case. He had a personal interest in it because he was working as a patrol officer when Lori went missing, and he was one of the cops who had taken the initial report. He noted, "We work on the case actively, all the time. Any time a body is located anywhere, and it's anywhere close to a match, we get a teletype. We've probably had at least 300 or 400 possibilities over the last 20 years, but none of them were her."

To this day, Lori Herbster is still the only unsolved missing person case in the township, and her file remains open. Tragically, though, no additional information has been added to that file in almost two decades.

As Chief Reed noted years earlier, the police wanted to know what had happened to Lori. "We have no idea," he said. "She left no trace."

1981: LAST SEEN AT HIS LOCKER
THE VANISHING OF ROGER ELLISON

THE MORNING OF TUESDAY, FEBRUARY 10, WAS a cold one in Cedaredge, Colorado. But that was pretty common for the Rocky Mountains in the winter, as Roger Ellison knew. Roger didn't mind cold weather and loved snow – mostly because he loved skiing. He'd been on skis since he was a little kid and hoped to qualify for the U.S. Olympic team at some point.

Roger was up early that day and got himself ready for school. He was a senior at Cedaredge High School, and his eighteenth birthday was only a month away. After that, it was only a few more months until graduation, and then he would go to college.

He had a lot to look forward to, so what happened later that morning remains baffling after all these years.

After getting dressed, grabbing breakfast, and zipping himself into his parka, Roger caught the bus to school like he did every other morning. He arrived with plenty of time to stop at his locker before he had to be in his homeroom.

Roger spoke briefly to one of his friends while spinning the combination for his locker and then grabbed the books he needed for his first-period class.

And then...

Well, no one knows what happened then. Roger didn't show up for any of his classes that day – not even the first-period class he'd picked up the books for – and what happened to him after he spoke to his friend remains a mystery.

He simply vanished from his locker, his high school, and off the face of the earth. Roger Ellison was never seen again.

ROGER WAS BORN ON MARCH 11, 1963, the youngest of the five children of Ernest and Evelyn Ellison. He'd always been a good kid, reliable, dependable, and a straight-A student. He'd already been accepted at Western State College in Gunnison and had already picked out and paid for his dormitory room.

Classmates later described Roger as quiet with only a handful of close friends. He didn't socialize much because he spent most of his free time skiing, but everyone seemed to like him. He was always friendly but never went out of this way to be noticed. He had a close relationship with his parents, especially his father, who had been forced to retire early after suffering a stroke and then undergoing open-heart surgery.

Roger Ellison

That close relationship caused Ernest and Evelyn to become very concerned when Roger didn't come home after school that day. After he was several hours late, they called Cedaredge High School and were surprised to learn that he'd missed all his classes that day. Roger had never skipped school before – he'd had a perfect attendance record before that day – and they couldn't imagine where he might be. Evelyn started calling all of Roger's friends, but none of them knew where he might be. Ernest and Evelyn spent a sleepless night waiting by the phone for a call that never came.

Early on Wednesday morning, they called the Delta County Sheriff's Office and tried to report their son missing, but a deputy told them – incorrectly -- that Roger hadn't been missing long enough. According to Evelyn, "He told us we had to wait 48 hours before he could begin a search." This, of course, is not true, especially with a missing person who is under 18.

Ernest and Evelyn were unwilling to wait. They started driving around the area, searching in vain for any sign of their son. They found no trace of him – no one had seen him or had any idea where he had gone after he was seen at his locker on Tuesday morning.

Roger's case was finally assigned to Delta County Detective Keith Waibel on Friday. He initially assumed he was dealing with a runaway but quickly learned things that made him rethink the idea that the young man would vanish voluntarily. He was a model student and a skilled skier who dreamed of the Olympics.

Roger's parents informed him that their son had participated in a skiing competition in Telluride the weekend before he went missing. He had hoped to score high enough to earn a spot on the U.S. ski team but fell a little short. Although disappointed with his results, he took things in stride and was convinced he'd do better when he competed in Aspen the following weekend.

He'd been in a good mood when he left for school on Tuesday. When he entered the kitchen for breakfast, he looked out the window and told his mother that it might snow. He commented that a fresh layer would be a good omen for his upcoming ski competition. He couldn't wait to get to Aspen, she said.

In other words, Roger had no reason to disappear – which is why what Detective Waibel did next is so puzzling.

Even after speaking to Roger's family and friends – all of whom told him that Roger had not run away from home – he told reporters that he suspected that Roger had gone to a ski resort to look for a job.

Evelyn was beside herself. She knew this wasn't true. "He always called when he would be late or left a note if he was leaving for someplace and we weren't home." She knew he wouldn't have left home without telling her and wouldn't have thrown away college and his ski competition to go off and look for a job.

She pointed out to investigators that Roger hadn't taken anything with him when he left for school that day besides his books and the clothes on his back. He'd had $3 in his wallet. All his ski equipment had been left behind, and his savings account, which contained $1,000 he had planned to use for a car or motorcycle, was untouched. Evelyn noted that if he'd planned to run off to a ski resort, he certainly would have taken his skis. As she told a reporter, "He was such a good boy. He wasn't a runaway. But how do you convince people?"

ROGER SHOULD HAVE BEEN CELEBRATING HIS birthday on March 11, but he was still missing. His parents noted that since he was now legally an adult, there was no reason he wouldn't contact them. They couldn't make him come home if he didn't want to. Although they hoped they'd hear from him once his birthday arrived, they weren't surprised when they didn't. They knew Roger hadn't run away. His failure to call was more evidence that something bad had happened to him.

Ski season ended, and spring came to the Rockies. Roger was still missing. Another month passed, and Roger's classmates gathered on the school's football field for their graduation in May. Ernest and Evelyn were too distraught to sit in the stands and watch as one of Roger's friends accepted his diploma in his place. They sat in the parking lot instead – and wept.

More time passed, and in July, the Ellisons announced they were offering an $8,000 reward for information that led to Roger's whereabouts. They were desperate for information – especially since the police still believed he'd run away – even though Evelyn feared that Roger was no longer alive. "We think there was foul play. He would've let us know by now. Maybe somebody's holding him, or he saw something in Telluride that he wasn't supposed to see."

Detective Waibel, though, still disagreed. He didn't think Roger had been hurt or abducted. "I think he's out of the state. I think he just got fed up and left... I can't find any indication of foul play." But he had no answers when asked where he believed Roger might be.

Sadly, Ernest never learned what happened to his son. After Roger disappeared, his health deteriorated, and he suffered another stroke. He died on August 21, 1981, at the age of only 58. Evelyn vowed to continue the search, supported by her daughter and three other sons.

It took over a year, but in May 1982, Detective Waibel finally conceded that Roger's parents had been right all along – Roger hadn't disappeared on his own. As he told the press, "There was absolutely no evidence of a drug problem, no hint of mental illness, nothing to indicate Roger had been the slightest bit depressed."

While this admission did nothing to find the missing young man, at least it gave him a new direction to take with the case. Even though a year had passed, he hoped he might find some answers.

Evelyn shared his hope. She was willing to do just about anything to find Roger, but she confessed that she had been overwhelmed with calls from "self-proclaimed psychics, amateur detectives, and a lot of weird people." At one point, she hired a private detective, and while he was happy to take her money, he never turned up any leads about what happened to Roger.

Years went by without any progress. In 1989, Delta County Sheriff Bill Blair, who had been a detective when Roger went missing, told reporters that the case was still a complete mystery. "We have followed lead after lead after lead, but nothing has panned out. It's real tragic that we can't come up with something." He believed that something terrible had happened to Roger, but he had no evidence to prove it. Hesitantly, he added, "I have this little thing in my stomach that says he didn't get out of Cedaredge."

Tragically, Evelen shared the sheriff's bad feeling – she also believed that Roger had been killed and was somewhere close to home. She worried that his body had been dumped in one of the many abandoned mines in the area, but the family lacked the resources to launch an extensive search.

She continued to hope that some clue would emerge that would lead them to Roger, but sadly, like Ernest, she never got the answers she'd been seeking since 1981. Evelyn died on February 9, 1992, at the age of 70. It was just one day before the 11th anniversary of her son's disappearance.

Although Ernest and Evelyn were both gone, detectives from the sheriff's department didn't give up on the case. In March 1994, they brought in a team of experts to dig up a large section of lawn that belonged to the Taylor Mortuary, which was located next to Cedaredge High School.

When Roger vanished, the property was a private home belonging to John Pash, one of Roger's teachers. Sheriff Blair had received a tip from one of Roger's classmates that suggested a search of the land would be worthwhile.

Pash taught psychology at the high school and was the wrestling coach. Evelyn had been suspicious of him from the start. After Roger had disappeared, Pash had come to see her and Ernest and told them that Roger had been suicidal and had probably killed himself. This opinion wasn't shared by any of Roger's friends or any of his other teachers, all of whom reported that he'd been a friendly and happy teenager who'd never shown any signs of depression.

But Pash claimed he knew more about Roger than anyone else because he had been counseling him at his home. Evelyn told detectives she believed this was untrue. In fact, Roger told her that he didn't like Pash, who'd made Roger drop homework off at his home on at least one occasion. She was certain that Roger would never have agreed to therapy with him, especially without telling his parents.

Family members had stressed to Sheriff Blair that shortly before Evelyn passed away, she had reiterated her suspicions about Pash, telling them that she'd always suspected he knew more than he was saying about Roger's disappearance. She also believed that some of Roger's classmates knew more than they were saying. Sheriff Blair took this seriously and ordered detectives to reinterview some of Roger's old friends, which led to the tip about the former Pash property.

Two years after Roger vanished, Pash moved to California and his property was purchased by the funeral home. The house was later torn down, but the section of land where it stood was still empty.

While detectives declined to name Pash as a suspect, they first searched the property in March and then returned in April 1994. This time, they used ground-penetrating radar to look for possible burials. They identified six anomalies, including two that were under concrete.

Investigators dug up four of the sites but found nothing. Officials said that more investigative work would have to be done before they could search the areas under the concrete. Sheriff Blair told reporters, "We need to do more interviewing and go another direction before digging up the whole countryside."

Eventually, they dug up most of the yard and uncovered a bone they initially thought was human. More testing revealed it was an animal bone, however. Nothing else was found, and no further investigation was directed toward John Pash as a suspect. However, in my opinion, there should have been more.

Roger's case lay dormant for the next four years, although investigators did what they could with no new information to work with.

Then, in September 1998, Detective Dave Duncan received a call from a man who claimed to know what happened to Roger. The man, who claimed to be dying, said that he wanted to clear his conscience before he passed away.

According to Detective Duncan, the man, and a friend were in the Cedaredge area in early 1981 when they saw a young man they came to believe was Roger being held at gunpoint by another man.

The dying man's friend came forward and corroborated the story. Both said the other man was threatening to kill Roger. The friend told the police that it was because of a bad cocaine deal. Apparently, Roger had stolen some money and given it to friends. As the two men left the area, they heard gunshots and assumed that Roger had been killed. The dying man was given a polygraph exam about this story, and, according to detectives, he passed.

Investigators searched the woods where the men claimed Roger had been shot – looking for bones or bullets – but found no sign of anything. This didn't mean the witnesses were lying, they told the press. If any skeletal remains hadn't been buried, scavengers could have dragged them away.

The story seemed hard to believe to those who knew Roger. He didn't seem the type of person to associate with drug dealers or users, but perhaps he'd stumbled onto something that he wasn't supposed to see. His brother, Roy, did say that Roger had been acting strange the last time he'd seen him. Perhaps Roger saw or did something that led to his murder.

But who can say? The truth may never be known. It's been more than four decades since Roger walked away from his locker that day and vanished without a trace.

In 1982, Detective Waibel admitted that the case seemed impossible to solve. "It looks like Roger Ellison just disappeared into thin air," he said, "but I know that can't happen. We've never had a single solid lead. We can't find a trace of where he went."

1982: IT WASN'T DELIVERED IN 30 MINUTES
WHEN SHERRY EYERLY WENT MISSING

FOR READERS WHO WERE BORN AFTER 1995, you likely don't recall how travelers used to get from one destination to another when they didn't know how to get there. There were no cell phones, GPS devices, or internet back then. We'd marvel a few years later when we could print out directions from a website and get from place to place like latter-day pirates with a treasure map.

But this tragic story takes place years before even that was possible. In 1982, if you needed to find an address, you had to know where you were going or at least use a city map to get there, even if it didn't have addresses on it. At least you'd be heading in the right direction.

But what about when the address you were given didn't exist, and you went to that address anyway?

That's exactly what happened to 18-year-old Sherry Eyerly in 1982 when she worked part-time as a delivery driver for a growing pizza chain called Domino's. She was new to the job and had only been working for the Salem, Oregon, store for about a month when an order came in on the night of July 4.

Sherry recently graduated from Sprague High School and lived in an apartment on the city's south side with a cousin. The pizza delivery job was just supposed to be for the summer.

Sherry didn't know it was the last job she'd ever have.

Ironically, Sherry wasn't even supposed to be working that holiday night. One of her coworkers wanted the day off to spend with family, and Sherry agreed to cover her shift.

It would be that one twist of fate that resulted in Sherry's disappearance that night -- creating an unsolved mystery that has continued for more than four decades and has included a ghost, a psychic, strange confessions, and a lot of unanswered questions.

SHERRY WAS BORN ON DECEMBER 6, 1963, the daughter of Steve and Linda Eyerly. She was a well-liked, friendly young woman with plans to attend college in the fall of 1982. The summer after graduation, the independent teenager decided to move in with her cousin and share an apartment with her until she left for college. The job of delivering pizza for Domino's was a lark; it was just a way to make some extra money and pay her share of the expenses with the apartment.

Sherry went to work that evening, not expecting anything out of the ordinary. The store's manager didn't plan on them being busy since most people attended family gatherings or congregated for fireworks shows. It seemed like Sherry would have an easy night, and she was happy about that since she was just there to cover for her coworker who went to a party.

Around 9:00 P.M. that evening, an order came in from a customer named "Dunbar." The worker who took the call later said he sounded like a "middle-aged man."

The customer placed his pizza order and then, before hanging up, mentioned to the store employee that he'd recently received pizza delivery from a young woman who drove an orange Volkswagen. She'd been on time and had been to his house before. Sorry, he added, it's hard to find, but she knows where it is.

Once the caller hung up, the employee realized the girl he described wasn't working that night – she was the one that Sherry was covering for. So, he called the customer using the number he'd given with his order – a call-back number that went to the City Center Motel. The customer said he was on his way home from the motel now and would be at his address on Riverhaven Drive, near Brown Island Road. He said whoever delivered the pizza would be fine, but it might be tough to find since this was a heavily wooded area near the Willamette River.

In another twist of fate, it was Sherry's turn to deliver when the man's order was ready. She took the two pizza boxes, went out to her Ford Pinto in the parking lot, and was soon on her way to the address the man had provided.

In those days, Domino's Pizza had a motto that it stuck by – "delivered in 30 minutes or less, or it's free." But while the pizza was apparently delivered on time, it was never paid for, and Sherry was never seen again.

TIME PASSED – MORE THAN ENOUGH TIME FOR A pizza to have been delivered and for Sherry to have returned, but there was no sign of her at the Domino's store. She hadn't come back from the "hard to find" delivery. After over an hour, the store's manager

Sherry Eyerly

decided to go to the delivery address to see if she'd had car trouble or something.

Sherry's car was found on the side of Riverhaven Drive with the engine running and the driver's door open.

He quickly found the car, but Sherry wasn't in it. Her car was on the side of Riverhaven Drive. The engine was still running, and the driver's side door was open. Her Domino's uniform hat was on the ground next to the car. The two pizza boxes she'd left the store with were lying a few feet away. One of the boxes had a tire track on it, and the other had been stomped on. A clear boot print was visible on the white box.

The manager drove immediately to the closest payphone and called the police. It was obvious, even to a pizza store manager, that Sherry had been abducted. The police officers who soon arrived at the scene agreed, and on that same night, the search for Sherry began.

Initial inquiries were made to try to track down the caller who lured Sherry to the spot. Telephone records were much harder to track then, and all that could be determined was that the man had given a false name, and his address didn't exist.

When news of the abduction spread, a handful of tips came in – and so did the prank calls. On July 5, someone called the Domino's store with a ransom demand for Sherry's safe return. But whoever it was, they didn't call back, and investigators deemed it a hoax.

The police found several witnesses who saw an older model truck parked on the side of the road around the time of Sherry's abduction. It was described as a four-wheel drive vehicle with large tires and two spotlights on the cab's roof. It was parked at an angle with its front pointed toward the shoulder and the back end facing the road. No one had gotten a look at its license plates

– or had failed to remember the number – and the truck and driver were never located or identified.

The case quickly turned cold. There was simply nothing to work with. Detectives did what they could – speaking to Steve and Linda, Sherry's family, and her friends and learning all they could about her day-to-day life – but they'd found no clues. No one seemed to have a grudge against Sherry. She hadn't been in trouble and didn't run with a bad crowd.

Worse, it seemed the abduction had been by chance. She hadn't even been the customer's requested driver – that was her coworker. The police also looked into the coworker's life but discovered nothing unusual. The caller had apparently targeted the young woman for unknown reasons, and when she didn't show up with the pizzas, Sherry was taken instead. The police were completely baffled.

And then, a month after Sherry vanished, her case took a very strange turn.

JOHN CATCHINGS
Psychic Investigator

John Catchings during a television appearance about the case.

IN EARLY AUGUST, A PSYCHIC FROM DALLAS, TEXAS, named John Catchings, woke from his sleep at 3:00 A.M. and later stated that he saw the ghostly figure of a young woman standing in his bedroom. She didn't speak to him, but he said he strongly felt she was there for a reason.

Then, four days later, he received an envelope in the mail from Salem, Oregon. It was a packet of information about Sherry's missing person case, apparently sent by either a friend or an anonymous person at the police department. A note that was included asked if he might be able to provide some answers for Sherry's family.

John said that when he opened the package and saw Sherry's photograph, he realized she was the ghostly figure he'd seen in his bedroom a few nights earlier.

He also knew that Sherry wasn't missing – she was already dead.

After looking over the file and tracking down other information about the case, John took a flight to Oregon to see if there was anything he could do to help.

His first stop after arriving in Salem was the spot where Sherry's car had been found abandoned. He wanted to go there and see if he could determine where she had been taken, but when he arrived, he said that he received visions of what happened that night. According to what he saw – or later told the police and Sherry's family – Sherry had been driving down the road, looking for an address she couldn't find. She was approached by a pickup truck with several lights on it. The driver flagged her down and told her that he had been the one who'd ordered the pizzas but accidentally gave the store the wrong address. As Sherry exited her car to give him the pizzas, the man grabbed her and pulled her into his truck.

John walked up and down the road where Sherry's car had been found, and then he asked the police officer who had accompanied him to the location if he would read aloud the names of the possible suspects. As the officer read the names, John interrupted him – was there anyone on the list who drove a green pickup truck?

There was one – a man named Darrell J. Wilson.

Wilson had ended up on the suspect list because of an informant. His sister-in-law had called a police tip line because she knew the police were looking for a pickup truck driver. She said Wilson had a green truck he'd suddenly decided to paint brown just days after Sherry's abduction. Not only that, she said, but Wilson knew Sherry. When questioned, though, Wilson had denied this. Now, a few weeks later, Wilson's name had come up again.

On August 21, detectives returned to Wilson's home to question him again, and this time, they allowed John Catchings to come with them. When they arrived, John said he'd had a vision of that house. He even described things about the house that he couldn't see from outside despite never having been there before.

During the interview with Wilson, investigators asked him if he'd be willing to take a polygraph exam to clear him as a suspect.

Wilson refused, but strangely, he said he would talk with John Catchings.

During this interview, Wilson claimed that he had been camping with friends at Elk Lake when Sherry disappeared. This was about two-and-a-half hours away from Salem, but there were still eight hours during the period that Wilson was unable to account for – including the time during which Sherry was abducted.

John was certain that Wilson was responsible for taking Sherry, but aside from his feelings about him, there was no actual evidence that investigators could use to link him with the crime. They did assure John, however, that they would keep working on Wilson's alibi and see if he could have been in the area where the abduction occurred.

But they never got that chance.

Less than two hours later, the police were called back to Wilson's home. He had committed suicide.

WITH THE LEAD SUSPECT NOW DECEASED, investigators weren't sure where to turn next. They had no idea where Sherry – or her body -- could be found. If Wilson had been involved in her disappearance, he took whatever information he had with him to the grave.

Sherry's case ended up in the "open and unsolved" file and likely would have stayed there permanently if it hadn't been reopened a decade later by cold case investigators. When they started their new investigation, they immediately felt that Wilson didn't fit the behavioral profile of the abductor. Wilson had no criminal history, aside from some minor drug offenses, which didn't seem to fit the methods of Sherry's abductor. Detectives felt Wilson was simply a troubled man – not a kidnapper and killer.

They believed that Sherry's abductor likely committed similar crimes in the past, so they went searching through other cold cases to see what they could find.

And while they didn't discover anything before Sherry's abduction, they did find a very similar murder that occurred one year after she vanished. The victim was a young woman named Katie Redmond, and she disappeared one night after leaving a college party.

Her car was discovered on the side of a road with its motor running, the driver's door was open, and there were signs of a struggle. It was nearly identical to Sherry's abduction scene, but unlike Sherry, Katie's body was later found in a river, and her killer was caught.

His name was William Scott Smith, and he was convicted for Katie's murder as well as the murder of another young woman, Rebecca Darling.

Soon after he'd been arrested, he was questioned about Sherry's abduction but denied involvement. He claimed he'd been driving a truck in Washington when she disappeared.

Cold case investigators, though, took another look into Smith's story and found that he'd actually been stopped and questioned by police near Salem within hours of Sherry's abduction. This broke his alibi of being in another state at the time. They also talked to some of his cellmates and learned he'd mentioned being involved in an incident with a "pizza girl." Unfortunately, though, he'd never mentioned Sherry by name.

In 2007, investigators interviewed Smith again. He initially refused to talk but then changed his mind when he was offered the chance to transfer to a different prison in exchange for cooperation.

And he confessed to Sherry's kidnapping and murder.

He told detectives that a friend named Roger Noseff had ordered the pizzas, and they waited for Sherry to arrive together. When she did, Smith flagged her down. When she got out of her car to hand him the pizzas, they grabbed her and dragged her into their truck. They took her to a place near the home of Smith's parents and strangled her there. Her body was dumped into the Pudding River – the same place he'd dumped his later victims – but he knew it often flooded, so there was likely no way her body would ever be found.

Smith's description of the kidnapping matched the physical evidence that had been found at the scene. He also gave investigators information about the crime that had never been released to the public, including the toppings on the pizzas that had been ordered and that he and Noseff had planned to abduct the delivery driver that Sherry was filling in for that night. He also told them that Noseff had been the one who made the ransom call to the Domino's store the following day and added that he had asked for $50,000 for Sherry's return. That was another detail that hadn't been released to the public.

Conveniently, though, Roger Noseff died in 2003, four years before Smith's confession. Smith had done his best to make it sound as though it had all been his friend's idea and that Noseff committed the actual murder. Smith claimed he hadn't killed Sherry; he'd only helped abduct her and hide her body. Regardless, Smith took a guilty plea in December 2007 and was given another life sentence in prison, which was tacked on to the years he was already serving for the murders of Katie and Rebecca.

So, was the kidnapping and murder of Sherry Eyerly solved? It certainly seems to have been. If Smith was telling the truth, then at least her family and friends had the cold comfort of knowing what happened along the dark road that night.

But as for Sherry herself, she remains missing. To this day, her body has never been found.

1982: "LIVE, LOVE AND LAUGH"
THE DISAPPEARANCE OF KELLIE BROWNLEE

IN THE 1980S, YOU WOULDN'T FIND VERY MANY high school-aged girls who didn't want a job at the local shopping mall. The mall was the place to be in those days – hanging out with friends, buying records, trying on clothes, grabbing an Orange Julius, and just being seen. If you worked at the mall, too? Those were the jobs that everyone wanted.

And Kellie Brownlee knew this. The 17-year-old was anxious about finding a good summer job before all the area college kids came home for their break.

Kellie's boyfriend, Mark Graves, later said this was all Kellie talked about as the end of the school year started to loom closer. In fact, as they rode the bus together to Walled Lake Western High School on the morning of May 20, 1982, Kellie told him she was thinking about skipping class that morning and going to the mall to fill out some job applications. Mark assured her she had plenty of time to find something, but Kellie didn't want to take a chance.

After the bus arrived at school, Kellie told Mark she would either see him at school later in the day or would catch up with him that evening. She kissed him, then waved and walked away.

Even though Kellie turned 17 the previous fall, she hadn't gotten her driver's license yet, and her preferred way of getting around was to hitchhike. She quickly found a ride and was dropped off five miles from the high school at the Twelve Oaks Mall in Novi, Michigan.

Several people spotted Kellie that morning, filling out applications in various clothing

Kellie Brownlee

stores, and around 11:00 A.M., she ran into Judy Mehay, the mother of one of her close friends. Judy asked Kellie if she needed a ride back home, but Kellie said she wanted to fill out a few more applications before leaving the mall. Judy gave her a quick hug and told her she'd see her soon. Then, she took her shopping bags, went to her car in the parking lot, and drove home.

Judy didn't know when she left the mall that day that she would be the last person known to see Kellie alive.

KELLIE BROWNLEE WAS BORN ON NOVEMBER 5, 1964, and had a complicated childhood. Although well-liked and regarded as a genuinely nice young woman, she'd developed a bit of a wild streak by the early 1980s. Like many of her friends, she loved big hair, tight jeans, army jackets, heavy metal bands, and smoked Marlboro reds. They sometimes skipped school and hung out in local diners to drink coffee. Kellie loved parties, too, and she and her friends drank more than their share of booze when they could find someone to buy it for them. She told her mother, Loretta, that her motto was "live, love, and laugh," and she tried to live by it.

But Kellie also took her responsibilities seriously and wasn't lazy. She worked hard, got good grades, and received good reviews from her past employers. She might have been a bit rebellious, but aside from her habit of hitchhiking, she didn't take many risks in her life.

The complications in Kellie's life in the spring of 1982 weren't caused by anything she had done. Six weeks before she vanished, Kellie had moved in with her boyfriend, Mark, and his family. She loved her mother dearly, but she didn't get along with her stepfather and had recently admitted to friends that he had been abusing her.

Most people assumed that Paul Brownlee was Kellie's father because she'd always used his last name, but he wasn't. Loretta married Paul when Kellie was very young, and he raised her and her older sister, Kim. From the outside, they appeared to be a happy, stable family – but for Kellie and Kim, nothing about their situation was happy or stable.

In 1977, Kim had accused Paul of sexually abusing her. He eventually pleaded guilty to fourth-degree criminal sexual conduct. Soon after the accusations, Kim moved to California to live with her biological father. Although Kellie considered moving with her, she was extremely close to her mother and didn't want to leave her behind. She made what turned out to be a fateful decision to remain in Michigan.

Kellie never told her friends why Kim moved to California, but many of them suspected that bad things were happening at the Brownlee home. Kellie often had bruises on her, and once, friends counted them and found 32 marks on her body. But even while staying quiet about what was happening at home, Kellie left and stayed with friends for weeks at a time over the next few years. She couldn't stand being around Paul but refused to abandon her mother completely and stayed in touch with her no matter where she might be.

In April 1982, Kellie reached her limit with Paul once again and moved out of her West Bloomfield home to the Graves home in Walled Lake.

Loretta was very upset about the move, begging her daughter to come home, but, this time, Kellie refused. She said she would only return when her mother got rid of Paul. Loretta had a long list of excuses for why she'd stayed with Paul, but the main reason was always financial. By now, though, she was almost finished with nursing school and knew she could soon support herself and her daughter without Paul's help. It was simply a matter of time.

Kellie had every intention of moving back home once Paul was gone, and she obviously believed that would happen soon. When she filled out all those job applications on May 20, she listed her mother's house in West Bloomfield as her home address.

Mark wasn't surprised when Kellie didn't return to school before classes ended that day, but when there was still no sign of her that evening, he started to worry. By 9:00 P.M., his worry had turned into fear. He started calling Kellie's friends, hoping she'd run into one of them at the mall and had gone to their house, but none of them had seen her.

Mark called everyone he could think of over the next two hours, but no one could offer any help. He called back a few of Kellie's closest friends, and they decided that one of them needed to call Loretta. Even when she wasn't living at home, Kellie always stayed in touch with her mother. Her friends hoped that she'd called Loretta from the mall and had decided to go home with her for the night.

One of Kellie's best friends, Carrie, offered to make the call. Her heart sank when Loretta told her she hadn't heard from Kellie all day. Carrie, unsure of what to say, blurted out that Kellie was missing, stunning Loretta. She immediately knew that something was terribly wrong and called the police.

They took things seriously, and an investigation immediately began. One of the first to be interviewed by detectives was Mark Graves. He explained that Kellie had skipped school that day to look for a summer job. It wasn't something she did regularly, he assured them. He was certain she wouldn't have voluntarily run off. All her belongings were still at home, and the only thing she had with her was her purse. Investigators searched Mark and his parents' house but found nothing that suggested anything had happened to Kellie there. Mark was ruled out as a suspect very early in the investigation.

From there, detectives traced Kellie's movements the day she was last seen. They verified that she'd made it safely to the mall that morning, and witnesses had seen her there as late as 11:00 A.M.

After that, however, there was no trace of her.

They knew she might have been abducted from the mall by a stranger. They were aware that she often hitched rides and feared she might have met with foul play after accepting a ride from the wrong person. Detectives only hoped someone had seen something. The mall had been crowded with shoppers that day. Perhaps someone would remember seeing Kellie if they could get the word out.

Detectives also believed there was a possibility that the answer to Kellie's disappearance might be closer to home.

There was speculation – by both law enforcement and Kellie's friends – that Paul Brownlee had done something to her. He certainly had a motive. The two of them didn't get along, and they knew Kellie was pressuring her mother to divorce him. They also knew that Kellie had finally started telling people that he'd abused her. He had a lot to gain if Kellie went away and never came back.

But when questioned, Paul insisted that he was nowhere near the mall during the time Kellie was there. He also swore that he'd never do anything to hurt her – which was a lie. He claimed he'd spent his morning visiting his father-in-law's grave and working out at the gym. Detectives asked him if he'd be willing to take a polygraph exam concerning his stepdaughter's disappearance, and he initially agreed. But then he decided to hire a lawyer and stopped cooperating with the investigation.

Although Paul was still considered a person of interest, the detectives grudgingly admitted they had no evidence against him. Even Kellie's allegations of abuse hadn't been substantiated before she vanished. They kept him on their list of suspects but continued with other aspects of the investigation.

Word had spread about Kellie's disappearance, and dozens of tips and possible sightings flooded police headquarters. Detectives checked out all of them. There were several alleged sightings of Kellie after she had been seen at the mall, but none of them could be confirmed. They visited numerous places and spoke to dozens of people but could not come up with any solid leads about where Kellie might have gone.

The only thing they felt with any certainty was that Kellie had met with foul play – and, most agreed, her stepfather was probably involved.

Paul still refused to be interviewed by detectives, but he called frequently with tips about potential sightings and his own theories. He also offered a $1,000 reward leading to Kellie's safe return. As you might imagine, investigators were suspicious of how he kept inserting himself into the investigation, but they had no hard evidence against him. Without it, there was nothing they could do.

Days passed, and the case stalled. Days turned to weeks, then months, and Kellie's disappearance went cold.

KELLIE'S VANISHING HAD A BRUTAL EFFECT ON her mother, and Loretta finally divorced Paul – but not until 1985.

Even after the divorce, Paul continued to call detectives and offer tips about potential sightings of Kellie. In 1991, he showed up at the police station with a swimsuit catalog gripped in his hands. He insisted that one of the models in it was Kellie and even provided detectives with a contact number for the person who hired the models for the catalog. They believed he was trying to get them to update him on the investigation status, so they sent him on his way after pointing out that Kellie would be 26 years old in 1991 and that the model in the catalog appeared to be about 12.

Kellie's case – cold and on the back burner – has never been forgotten. In 2018, the police investigated the possibility that suspected serial killer Arthur Ream might have killed Kellie. He was already serving a life sentence for the murder of Cindy Zarzycki, a Michigan girl who went missing in 1986. Ream claimed that he'd killed others the police hadn't found yet, so they tried to find a link between Ream and Kellie but found nothing.

Over the years, detectives have followed up on scores of possible sightings from all over the country.

One tipster claimed Kellie was playing the character of Snow White at Disneyland in California. Another said she was a topless dancer in New York City. Sightings came in from Illinois, New Mexico, Indiana, and beyond. All of them were dead ends.

Despite this, authorities still consider Kellie's case an active investigation and hope it will be solved one day.

Until then, we can only wonder what happened to the young woman who only wanted three things out of life – to "live, love, and laugh."

1982: ONE LAST DRINK

THE LEGEND OF CHARLIE HOPE

ON APRIL 1, 1982, CHARLES HOPE, WEARING A blue Hawaiian shirt and carrying a plastic container of mustard greens under his arm,

Charles "Charlie" Hope, the businessman and realtor who went from being a character to a legend in Southwest Florida.

walked out of the Redfish Seafood and Steak House after having a drink with his uncle and vanished into the night, becoming an indelible part of local Tampa, Florida, legend.

Disappearances of middle-aged, recently divorced men are not unheard of. However, Charlie's notoriety in the community and absolute lack of hard evidence about his fate made it impossible for even more than four passing decades to end the interest in his case completely.

Charlie was a business leader, held a political appointment, and sought elected office. He was the scion of a pioneer Florida family – he wasn't the kind of guy to vanish.

And yet, he did.

The investigation into his vanishing failed to discover what became of Charlie or why he disappeared. After all these years, this bizarre case has more questions than answers. It has inspired many theories – some more believable than others – including a drug-related homicide, a private island, a jealous husband, burial under the floor of a Kmart, a dead man being fed to the fishes, a living man hiding out in Belize, or maybe the federal witness protection program, and more. At one point, investigators even considered the possibility that a serial killer was targeting realtors.

So, what happened to Charlie Hope? You decide.

"A MAN AROUND THE CAMPFIRE AND A GENTLEMAN AT the dinner table" – that's how close friend Albert Richardson described Charles David Hope, who was born on September 30, 1940, in Brookville, Florida, to parents William "Buck" and Geraldine Hope. The Hope family had resided in the region for generations and could trace their ancestry back to William Hope, one of the first white settlers on the west coast of Florida.

One of six children, Charlie loved being outside, fishing, hunting, and spending time on the water. He knew the swamps and wooded areas better than most, and when not spending countless hours traipsing through the wild, he excelled in school and sports.

Charlie married his first wife, Alice, at 17, and the couple had three sons and one daughter together. At that time, he had finished school and worked in supervisory roles for three construction companies and a lime rock mine. In 1972, he ran an unsuccessful campaign for

A wedding photo of Charlie and his first wife, Alice.

a County Commission seat, losing a Democratic primary race by only 307 votes. In 1979, Charlie changed career directions and went into real estate, becoming a prominent and successful businessman. He was also elected chairman of the Hernando Valley Port Authority, a board of commissioners in charge of maintaining navigable waterways.

Two months before he disappeared, Charlie resigned from the board. The fact that he had headed the Port Authority would later fuel speculation about connections to the tons of marijuana known to have been smuggled through the marshy areas along the coast.

But Charlie was also a Shriner, president of the Lions Club and member of the Hernando County Board of Realtors. He was outgoing, known to almost everyone in the area, and was well-liked by most. He was described as a kind and generous man who would do just about anything for anyone.

Well, he was described that way by most people. But not everyone had a great impression of the trim, tanned, good-looking Charlie, who was always very outspoken, played sometimes harsh practical jokes, and loved women – a lot. He was a well-known figure in local nightspots, where he performed the nearly impossible task of juggling multiple romantic relationships in an area where everyone knew everyone else.

"He had no conscience when it came to women," said former Hernando Circuit Clerk Karen Nicolai, who, with her husband, Joe, was a close friend Charlie had visited a couple of hours before his disappearance. In fact, Charlie left Karen's and Joe's house to visit one woman but stopped off at the Redfish to look for another before he vanished.

Adele Wright, Charlie's second wife, who'd divorced him shortly before he disappeared, said in the weeks after he disappeared that she was convinced an angry girlfriend or jealous husband had murdered him. Charlie and Adele had only been together three years before she'd had enough of his womanizing.

Yet Charlie was devoted to his four children and remained a close friend of their mother, Alice, who believed he'd never have left his family willingly.

"Alice was his best friend. If she called him at three in the morning and needed something, Charlie was up and gone," said Albert Richardson, one of Charlie's closest friends.

People who knew him said that his failure to contact Alice or their children made them believe he was dead.

CHARLIE MAY HAVE CARRIED ON WITH TOO MANY women and rubbed a few too many people the wrong way, but there was little to suggest that trouble was coming his way in the spring of 1982.

Although he had just been through a costly divorce, his financial situation was fine. Carol Schmalzreid, Charlie's secretary and friend, said he was working on a $450,000 commercial real estate deal when he vanished. Glenn L. Harris confirmed her statement. "I was negotiating with him to buy half of his business," he said. "We'd had a couple of meetings on it."

Glenn recalled that the last time he'd seen Charlie, he'd waved at him and said, 'I'll get with you on it again in a couple or three days.' He also didn't believe that Charlie would have voluntarily skipped town.

Charlie wasn't having problems with women either. His love life was no more chaotic than usual, and he hadn't told anyone he was worried or afraid of anything.

His uncle, David Hope, who sat and drank with Charlie that night at the Redfish, said Charlie didn't appear to be particularly upset about anything, and the only concern he seemed to have been getting those mustard greens to his girlfriend's house.

Even so, those closest to him noted – in hindsight – that perhaps something was bothering him.

David Pointec, another friend of Charlie's, talked to him on the phone the night he disappeared. "He had asked me to join him for a drink that night, and I couldn't because I have a family and small children. But I often wonder if I let him down. I didn't sense any urgency in his voice, but I wonder."

Most of his friends and relatives wouldn't recall any signs of depression in Charlie. However, when he traveled to Georgia to see his son, Scott, who was graduating from military boot camp, he made a point to say that if anything ever happened to him, he wanted Scott to know that he'd be taken care of. Scott remembered that his father seemed upset when he said this to him.

On March 30, Charlie stopped by Alice's house to see his one-year-old grandson. She later remembered him spending more time than usual during the visit. "I should have known something was wrong. He was just sitting there, not saying anything. I caught tears in his eyes a couple of times. I should have known," Alice said.

Charlie also reportedly received a phone call while at her house, during which she said he sounded agitated and agreed to meet with someone. The identity of the caller, as well as the reason for the meeting, remain a mystery.

The next morning, March 31, Charlie called his parents' house. "He didn't talk too much. He wanted to see his mama," Buck Hope later recalled.

Unfortunately, Geraldine was busy with guests and unable to speak to her son that day. Charlie asked Buck to have her call him that evening. "We had a house full of people that night, and I never called him. That was my last chance to talk to him," Geraldine later remembered with regret.

Later that evening, Charlie went to the home of friends Joe and Karen Nicolai for dinner. They were surprised to see him. He hadn't been over for a while. While there, Charlie played with Dan, a friendly pit bull he'd gifted to Joe two years earlier.

Later, the couple would wonder if Charlie's visit had been a goodbye of sorts, though he never mentioned anything was wrong.

Charlie later met his Uncle Dave at the Redfish. He spoke to a staff member soon after arriving, asking where a particular waitress was. While chatting with his uncle, he also mentioned he was going to his girlfriend's house when he left, with the mustard greens, of course.

Strangely, no one would recall the boisterous Charlie – who never exited anywhere quietly – leaving the restaurant that night. Sources vary as to when exactly someone noticed he was gone, but most agree that it was sometime after 1:00 a.m. Also, going against character, he left a half-finished drink behind.

Charlie Hope would never be seen or heard from again.

GERALDINE HOPE'S BIRTHDAY WAS APRIL 2. Something occurred that day that had never happened before – she didn't get a call or visit from Charlie. He never missed his mother's birthday, but this time he did. You can call it a mother's intuition, but Geraldine knew something was wrong. She and Buck tried to contact him, but their calls went unanswered.

Then, on April 6, Charlie's secretary, Carol, arrived at the real estate office and saw his truck parked outside. That in itself wasn't odd, but when she went inside, she found Charlie wasn't there. She contacted his parents to see if they knew where he was and discovered they couldn't locate him either.

Charlie was reported missing that day.

The police investigation began with an examination of Charlie's truck. Officers discovered it was locked – something Charlie never did – and that he had about $2,000 worth of guns, fishing equipment, and other stuff inside. There were no signs of foul play.

Next, detectives took on the monumental task of interviewing everyone who knew Charlie but quickly found that no one had seen him since April 1 at the Redfish. None of them could offer any idea of his current whereabouts.

They even tacked down the waitress he'd been looking for at the restaurant that evening. They learned she'd gone on a canoe trip with Charlie a few days before he disappeared. According to her, they were just friends, and investigators ultimately concluded that she had no connection to his disappearance.

Searches began for Charlie and went on for weeks. Investigators, volunteers, family members, and friends searched on land, by boat, and in the air by helicopter. They combed the marshes and woods of the county while detectives were still conducting the dozens of searches that became part of the investigation.

Ironically, there was no real evidence that a crime had been committed. It is legal for adults to disappear if they want to, as long as they don't try to profit from their "deaths." Charlie's estate was limited, and the people who eventually benefited from it had been the ones who worked the hardest to find him.

But all the searches turned up nothing. Charlie was still missing, and no one was getting closer to why.

AT THE SAME TIME CHARLIE DISAPPEARED, something else frightening was going on in Southwest Florida. In the spring of 1982, two other realtors also went missing from neighboring counties, which led residents to fear there was a serial killer on the loose.

And some believed Charlie was one of his victims.

In what became one of the case's eerie but unrelated overlaps, Charlie's parents – Buck and Geraldine – were picking blackberries on their land and discovered a human skull on May 23. Initially, they feared the skull, which they found in some brush about 250 feet away from the highway, might be Charlie's, but it wasn't. It was later identified as belonging to 39-year-old Margo Delimon, another real estate agent who went missing in 1981. Investigators eventually learned that she had been murdered by a serial killer named James Winkles – who had no connection to Charlie.

Detective Thomas Blackman from the county sheriff's office said there was "no end to the tips coming in," which had no value until he heard from detectives in neighboring Pasco County and learned that another realtor had also gone missing.

This third realtor, Roman Stangherlin, was a locally beloved former Catholic priest. Strangely, he was sighted all over town when he was supposedly missing but hadn't been seen since.

Frightened calls poured into the various sheriffs' offices, suggesting connections between Charlie and Roman. Most intriguing were the suggestions that drug smugglers commonly used the local roads and airstrips near where both men went missing.

Even before that angle could be pursued, though, investigators received a phone call from an attorney representing a man named Stanley Modzelewski, who subsequently was granted immunity from prosecution in exchange for his testimony against others involved in Roman's murder. He and his son confessed to burying Roman's body on their farm. While another suspect suggested that Charlie might be buried there, too, Modzelewski denied any knowledge of Charlie's fate. The police exhaustively searched the farm anyway but failed to find any additional remains.

Of the three realtors who went missing, two of the cases were solved. Both had intersected with Charlie in strange ways, but ultimately, there was no connection between them.

Charlie's case stalled for a while, and then, eight months after he vanished, another strange piece was added to the puzzle.

A man walking through an area overgrown with palmettos discovered a stack of neatly folded clothing. He was only about 100 yards from the building where Charlie's office had been located. The clothing – shorts, a beige Hawaiian shirt, shoes, and underwear -- was clean and had no blood on it. Although the shirt wasn't the blue Hawaiian shirt that Charlie was last seen wearing, the Hope family were "pretty well positive" that the clothes belonged to him.

However, there was no explanation for why his clothes would have been there or who placed them there. Like so many other elements of this case, it remains a mystery.

OVER THE PAST FEW DECADES, CHARLIE'S DISAPPEARANCE has inspired countless theories, rumors, and wild tales. Many of them are throwbacks to the days of Florida during the "War on Drugs," *Miami Vice*, and Glenn Frey's "Smuggler's Blues," which is likely why people seem to delight in keeping the stories alive.

One theory is that Charlie disappeared on his own. He took off one day to become an expatriate on some private island or in some tropical spot like Belize. It's an intriguing idea, right out of a Jimmy Buffett song, but there's no clue what Charlie would have been running from to make him want to disappear.

His son, David, later stated, "We know he talked to the man at Scuba West that day about the island off Belize. It was a place where you could just go and disappear."

The problem is that it's unclear where this story came from. No one at the dive shop remembered Charlie stopping by that day, much less having a lengthy chat with him. Two of the shop owners were away on a dive trip when Charlie vanished, and the third owner, who was at Scuba West that day, said he didn't remember Charlie coming into the shop.

But even if the conversation did happen, nobody knows if it was a serious attempt to get information about a good place to disappear or whether it was just musings among adventurous and suddenly single middle-aged men.

In addition, it's unknown if Charlie even had a current passport. No one found one in his belongings. His ex-wife Adele said that his passport had been stolen years before when they visited her family in Colombia, but she didn't know if he'd ever replaced it.

THERE'S ALSO THE THEORY THAT CHARLIE'S DISAPPEARANCE had something to do with drugs. There's no question that the remote marshes in the area were known to be a haven for drug smugglers. Many wondered if Charlie was involved in that business or if he'd perhaps witnessed something he wasn't supposed to see.

Charlie's attitude toward drugs is hard to pin down because his friends and family have very different opinions about the subject. According to his close friend Albert Richardson, Charlie "was as adamant about that stuff as I am. He hates it and wouldn't have anything to do with it." Alice and several others agreed with this sentiment.

Yet other friends of his claimed that Charlie wasn't staunchly anti-drugs at all and even smoked marijuana on occasion. Maybe he was only against hard drugs, but it's impossible to say at this point.

For their part, Charlie's kids felt certain that the narcotics business had something to do with their father going missing. "We all have believed that drugs were involved in Dad's disappearance, whether Dad was selling drugs or undercover investigating," said Charlie's daughter, Tami.

But again, it is unclear where this theory came from, other than knowing that smuggling was widespread in the area. Charlie certainly didn't seem to have the lifestyle of a drug dealer, and no hidden cash was discovered after his death.

It's also not clear who he'd be "investigating" for. Charlie sold real estate; he wasn't a police officer or even an informant. Like every well-connected man in rural Florida counties in the early 1980s, Charlie did carry a "special deputy" card, which gave him no authority but implied the person was at least known to the local sheriff. Again, it didn't make him a cop.

And it also wouldn't have landed him in the witness protection program. Sheriff's detectives never found that Charlie had a connection to any law enforcement agency. This makes it unlikely that he was an undercover agent tied to a massive local drug bust that happened less than a year before he disappeared. He also didn't testify in the trial that followed the arrests, and the authorities seldom go to the expense of creating new identities for people who don't testify.

AND NOW, THINGS GET WEIRDER.

About a year before Charlie went missing, a young couple named Ricky Merrill and Dori Colyer were shot up with drugs and then burned to death in Ricky's car in downtown Brooksville. While the authorities didn't think this had any connection to Charlie's later disappearance, at least one person wasn't so sure.

Cindy Crane, a woman who described herself as "working" on the investigation of Charlie's vanishing with a Hernando County sheriff's detective, came up with a theory that had nothing to do with drugs or women.

In a note that was written in 1984 on a Jesse Jackson campaign brochure, she told detectives she "literally fell into something" that she said was "relative to tying three felonies together."

During a later interview with sheriff's deputies, she said that those three felonies were what she described as the arson of the Redfish, the death of Charlie Hope, and the murder of Roman Stangherlin, the former priest who was beaten, strangled, and buried on the local farm. She also mentioned "those burned-up kids," a reference to Ricky Merrill and Dori Colyer.

Cindy claimed the information that connected the cases came from a business associate of Charlie Hope named Charles Haggett, who sometimes told her that Charlie was "fish bait." At other times, he'd say that Charlie was merely visiting a girlfriend in Mexico.

Haggett reportedly also claimed that the reason Charlie was murdered was because he knew too much about an arson plot involving the Redfish, the restaurant where he was last seen. Cindy spun a convoluted story about how Charlie had known about the arson plot and even spoke about it at the Redfish on the night he vanished. For this, he was murdered, and the arson plan was put on hold. Haggett supposedly told Cindy, "They snuffed him, and they couldn't burn it until the investigation was real old."

He also allegedly said that Charlie had been buried under a nearby Kmart, which, interestingly, a construction permit had been issued less than a month before Charlie vanished.

The Redfish did have a fire -- although it's unclear exactly when this happened -- but it was determined to have been accidental, caused by faulty wiring in the ceiling. An attorney for the owners stated that the restaurant was underinsured, and no one benefited from the fire.

It's also worth noting that investigators never believed the fire -- or any of the other crimes mentioned by Cindy Crane – had anything to do with Charlie's case. They believed the connections were concocted by Cindy, the amateur sleuth who, sheriff's detectives clarified, was neither employed nor affiliated with their office in any capacity.

It was suggested that Charles Haggett still be questioned about what he knew about Charlie's disappearance – but they wouldn't be able to follow through.

Five months after Cindy gave his name to detectives, a realtor who was preparing to show Haggett's house to prospective buyers found his badly decomposed body in a locked bedroom. It had nothing to do with Charlie Hope, though. A man who rented a room from Haggett in his house later pleaded guilty to killing him.

SO, WHAT DID HAPPEN TO CHARLIE HOPE?

Given his notoriety as a womanizer, some, like his ex-wife Adele, believed he was killed by a jealous husband, a boyfriend, or one of the women he wronged. But, as with other theories, nothing was found to support this.

"I keep thinking that there's somebody, in fact we know there's somebody, who knows what happened to him. He didn't walk from his office to South America. Somebody knows what happened to him," said Charlie's mother, Geraldine, who died in 1991.

Charlie himself was declared legally dead in 1992.

His children never gave up on finding out what happened to their father. His son, David, spearheaded a successful campaign to reopen the case in the 1990s, but nothing new was discovered.

When the case was reopened, the Redfish was a vacant lot, and Charlie's old office had become a barbecue joint.

Even Hernando County Sheriff Tom Mylander was frustrated by the lack of evidence in the case. "Unfortunately, things were done differently here back then. Records were kept haphazardly at best and not centrally. It wasn't unusual for an officer or detective to just keep things in his head, and if the detective left, so did the information."

He also noted that they could no longer request Charlie's medical or dental records for potential identification purposes. "Nobody bothered to obtain them, and they were purged by the doctors or whoever had them," he explained.

CHARLIE'S CASE IS STILL OPEN TODAY, although it remains at a standstill. It's unlikely it will ever be solved.

And that may be because many things about Hernando County haven't changed even after all these years. Back in the 1980s, mentioning drugs to some of the locals invited nods, winks, and index fingers laid quickly across tightly sealed lips. Out among the salt marshes and inlets that fringe the coastal edge of the county, not much has changed. Even all these years later, it's still a place where boats sometimes run at night without lights and where the cargoes are things that no one talks about.

There are plenty of places along that ragged coastline where a person can disappear – sometimes with a little help.

A strange blend of businesspeople, fishermen, retirees, and sun-leathered natives can still be found in the area's bars and taverns. And late at night, when an empty glass can be filled by telling a good story, talk still sometimes turns to what happened to Charlie Hope – that long-ago local who vanished without a trace.

But if anyone knows what really happened, they're not the ones doing the talking.

1984: ONE MORE PAPERBOY
THE DISAPPEARANCE OF EUGENE MARTIN

DON MARTIN WAS JARRED AWAKE BY A RINGING telephone at 7:15 on the morning of August 12, 1984. It was a Sunday and his day off, and he certainly hadn't planned to be up so early. Who in the world would be calling at that hour?

He reached for the telephone receiver next to the bed and grumbled a greeting into the receiver. He didn't recognize the voice on the other end of the line, but his name sounded familiar. It took a moment, and then he realized what the man was telling him. It was the manager for his boys' newspaper delivery route.

Apparently, a customer on the route had called and complained that she hadn't received her paper that morning. When the route manager went to the corner where Don's sons had picked up their papers, he found a bag with ten folded papers inside. But the boys were nowhere in sight. He'd delivered the rest of the papers himself, but he thought he'd better call and speak to the boys' father about their responsibilities.

By then, though, Don had stopped listening. He placated the route manager, hung up the telephone, and woke up his wife. He knew something was wrong.

His son, Eugene, and his stepson, David, had the paper route – and neither boy would have failed to do their job. But David, Don knew, spent the night with friends, so Eugene went alone that morning.

The route had the boys delivering papers on Southwest 12th Street and Highview Drive in Des Moines, Iowa. He was last seen in that area between 5:30 and 6:00 A.M.

It would later be determined that the 13-year-old Eugene's first stop that morning was at 5:15 A.M. He arrived at the usual pickup spot for the newspaper delivery driver at Southwest 14th and Highview Streets and grabbed his bag of papers from the driver. He sat down and started folding them.

Multiple witnesses later reported seeing Eugene talking to a man that morning, having a normal, friendly conversation. The man was described as clean-cut and in his thirties – but he was never identified.

When Don hung up the phone after speaking to the paper route manager, he woke his wife, quickly dressed, and went out looking for his son. He walked the entire route, stopping to speak to the people he saw outside, even knocking on the doors of some of the neighbors he knew were Eugene's customers.

No one had seen his son.

Eugene Martin

Eugene Martin had disappeared off the streets that morning and would never be seen again.

EUGENE MARTIN was born on August 17, 1970, in Des Moines. He was the third of three boys, and Rick and Don were a little older than he was. His parents, Donald and Janice, were divorced soon after Eugene was born. His father remarried, giving Eugene four new siblings – Kim, Mike, Don, and David – and Eugene moved in with his dad and stepmother, Sue.

By all accounts, he was a happy kid. He got along well with Sue and his stepsiblings. He was a quiet boy, described as shy and polite, and he loved video games and books, fishing, football, and skating. He'd only recently started the paper route with his stepbrother to make some pocket money. The Iowa State Fair was quickly approaching, and he wanted extra money to spend there.

After Don called the authorities that morning, detectives immediately went into action – for good reason. Two years before, another paperboy named Johnny Gosch had disappeared. Because the police had been criticized as slow to act in that case, they quickly got organized around Eugene's disappearance.

No one wanted a repeat of Johnny Gosch's case.

Johnny was one of the original "milk carton kids." When the 12-year-old disappeared while on his paper route in West Des Moines, Iowa, on September 5, 1982, America was just beginning to understand there was a problem with missing and exploited children in the county.

There had been a handful of others that made headlines around this time. Etan Patz, 6, vanished while walking to his school bus in New York City. Adam Walsh, also 6, was abducted in 1981 from a shopping mall in Hollywood, Florida, and later found murdered. Kathy Kohm, abducted in 1981 at age 11 from Santa Claus, Indiana, was raped and murdered. More than two dozen children, including 9-year-old Yusuf Bell, were abducted from 1979 to 1981 in what became known as the "Atlanta Child murders."

When Johnny vanished, he had just started his Sunday morning paper route, setting off into the pre-dawn hours accompanied by his dog, Gretchen. His parents – Noreen and John -- only found out he was missing after one of Johnny's customers called to complain that he didn't get his Sunday paper.

Johnny's father left the house and found his son's red wagon abandoned and still filled with bundles of the *Des Moines Sunday Register*. The police initially said they believed Johnny had been abducted, but after the community turned out to help search for him and no trace of Johnny was found, they began to think he'd run away.

Much too late, they'd realize they were wrong.

Despite the striking similarities between Johnny's and Eugene's

Johnny Gosch, one of the original "Milk Carton Kids," also disappeared from the Des Moines area but no connection could be found between the two boys.

cases, law enforcement could never connect them. Despite decades of searching, there was nothing to link the two boys – absolutely nothing.

And they wouldn't be able to connect the other disappearance either.

Marc Allen, 13, vanished on his way to a friend's house in Des Moines on March 29, 1986. Although Marc was not a paperboy, all three cases occurred in the same general area in the 1980s – and all three remain unsolved.

LOCAL GROUPS BEGAN SEARCHING FOR EUGENE right away. Soon, teams of volunteers were scouring the area while the police were working on their end of things. They decided to call in the FBI early in the investigation, hoping things would move faster than they had two years earlier. They'd already stumbled once – suggesting Eugene had run away because he'd argued with his stepmother – but quickly determined his disappearance had been foul play.

Local newspapers posted notices about Eugene's vanishing, including photos and descriptions of what he'd been wearing on Sunday morning. They asked anyone with information to come forward and requested that their paperboys keep an eye out for Eugene or anything suspicious. The newspaper ordered supervisors to start monitoring the paper routes.

The paper Eugene delivered – the *Des Moines Register* – announced a $5,000 reward for information that brought Eugene home. The reward would later be increased to $25,000, but it would never be collected.

The police began looking for possible witnesses and questioning those who knew Eugene or had seen him that morning, trying to get all the information they could. They talked to everyone on his paper route, including his supervisor and other paperboys who delivered in the area.

During the interviews, they did get some new information. Witnesses described seeing a green car idling near 14th Street, first spotted around 5:00 A.M. The driver was described as a white male with short, dark hair. He was in his twenties or early thirties. Recently, other witnesses reported a man with a similar description following some young girls in the same area.

And then there was the witness who'd seen Eugene talking to a man that morning at the same corner where he took delivery of his newspapers. This was around 5:45 A.M. The witness hadn't heard their conversation but said it appeared to be friendly. This man was also reportedly in his thirties and was clean-cut. A few other witnesses corroborated this sighting, offering the same description.

Detectives were able to track down the man in the green car, and he was questioned about his possible involvement in Eugene's disappearance. The man said he'd been in the area because he was dropping his wife off for work. He knew nothing about Eugene and hadn't been following young girls in the neighborhood. His alibi was checked, and he was ruled out. The man in the green car had nothing to do with the case.

But what about the other man – the one seen talking to Eugene? The FBI was convinced that Eugene had been kidnapped and that this man knew something. In a nationwide bulletin they sent out, seeking information, they described him as a loner, about 30 to 40 years old, with a medium build and short hair.

But he wasn't the only suspect. Another man, Sam Soda, also became mixed up in the case. Soda was a Vietnam veteran who'd been working as a private investigator. In 1984, Soda had exposed a pedophile named Frank Sykora, who worked at the *Des Moines Register*. Sykora was fired and later pleaded guilty to sexual abuse charges. The police could not connect Sykora and Eugene's case, though, so he was never a suspect.

The same couldn't be said for Sam Soda.

Bizarrely, Soda had spoken to Noreen Gosch – mother of the missing Johnny Gosch – a few months before Eugene disappeared and told her that another kidnapping was going to take place. He said, "The kidnapping would take place the second weekend in August 1984, and that it would be a paperboy from the southside of Des Moines."

Soda had already crossed paths with the police, passing himself off to witnesses as a member of law enforcement and inserting himself into Johnny's investigation. He was soon doing the same thing with Eugene's case. He'd go on to become a person of interest in both cases, especially after allegations were made that he was involved in sex trafficking. Unfortunately, the cops could never make anything against him stick, and he was never charged.

This was just a bit of strangeness mixed into the baffling case – and it wouldn't be the last.

BY THE END OF THE SECOND DAY, THE area around Eugene's home and his entire paper route had been thoroughly searched by the police and volunteers. The authorities decided to expand the search into a wider area, using police officers, 16 FBI agents, volunteers, friends, and family members. They searched warehouses, parks, riverfronts, ditches – anywhere the boy could be. Others handed out flyers and made posters that soon papered telephone poles, bulletin boards, and blank walls all over Des Moines.

It rapidly became clear to the police, and to everyone involved in the search, that Eugene was not in the city. They decided to expand things again, this time focusing their attention on the rural areas surrounding Des Moines. The authorities implemented air searches and brought even more support and volunteers to continue hunting for Eugene. Once again, though, there was no sign of him.

By now, theories had started pouring in about the disappearance. Most would have assumed he'd run off if it had been an isolated incident. There would have been no similar crimes to connect it to in the area. Most people, however, had a hard time not pointing out the similarities between Eugene's disappearance and that of Johnny Gosch. Johnny's vanishing had gotten a lot of media coverage, and even though more than two years had passed, no one had forgotten it.

Much of the speculation about Johnny's disappearance was that he had been abducted by a pedophile ring, which allegedly kidnapped young children and sold them at "auctions" to various buyers. There was now speculation that Eugene had suffered a similar fate, having been abducted by the same sort of people for nefarious reasons.

For Eugene's family, none of these possible explanations were good news. Eugene had been just days away from his fourteenth birthday on August 17. A big party had been planned, but it was now canceled. The new bicycle he was supposed to receive to help with his paper route now gathered dust in the family's garage.

Eugene's father, Don, vowed the party would be held when his son returned home. He also vowed that his new bike could be used for anything he wanted – his days as a paperboy were over.

Instead of celebrating a birthday with their son, Don and Sue were praying and sitting near the telephone, hoping for news from the investigators. The FBI had instructed them to wait by the phone, keeping a vigil, because they wished for good news. Don, a maintenance man for an apartment complex, had been given as much time off as he needed – hoping he'd be home when his son returned.

Several days after Eugene vanished, the phone finally did ring. A potential sighting had come in. A witness had seen a boy fitting Eugene's description near the town of Ankeny. The report was so convincing that the police rushed to the Ankeny Industrial Park – where the boy was spotted – with a helicopter and searchlights. They spent two hours searching the area, but whoever the boy was, they didn't find him.

The Martins firmly believed their son was still in Des Moines. The police had acted quickly when he disappeared. Their response had been nothing like how they reacted when Johhny Gosch had vanished. They had been reluctant to search two years earlier, telling the family they had to wait 72 hours to file a report since they were sure he was a runaway. But Johnny's mother had worked tirelessly to make changes in Iowa, making sure that missing children's cases would be immediately investigated. This changed things during Eugene's disappearance, but speed hadn't helped at that point.

The Martins had their own ideas about what happened to Eugene. They knew he would never follow a stranger into danger. They suspected someone had stopped him and asked him for directions when delivering papers. When Eugene tried to help, he'd been grabbed.

The search continued in the area. Teams of local volunteers continued to hand out flyers and scour the streets, hoping to find someone who'd seen Eugene. The police continued searching rural areas. The reward fund kept growing, eventually reaching $64,000.

But still, they found nothing.

Eugene Martin's disappearance had cooled off within a few weeks, and then it turned completely cold.

IN FEBRUARY 1986, AN ARREST WAS MADE THAT breathed new life into the case. A 43-year-old man named Wilbur Millhouse was arrested and charged with six counts of third-degree sexual abuse. Two 15-year-old boys had reported him to the police, claiming that Millhouse had abused them. During the investigation that followed, the police discovered a sexually explicit phone call that Millhouse had made to a 14-year-old boy. It was enough to get them a search warrant.

While searching his house, they found a massive list of more than 2,200 names and telephone numbers for young boys living in

Wilbur Millhouse, the former newspaper circulation manager who was arrested for assaulting young boys.

the area. The notes, written by hand, had notations in the margins with information about the boys. Some of them also had school yearbook photos attached. Some of the boys' baseball rosters were also clipped to the pages of notes.

Millhouse was on disability and didn't work outside his home. He'd previously been employed at the *Des Moines Register* but had suffered a heart attack in 1983. Millhouse had been a circulation manager at the newspaper, recruiting new paperboys for the routes. The list had been compiled when he'd worked at the newspaper, stealing the information from their files. He confessed to the police that he'd used various fake names when he called the boys and tried to engage with them in sexual conversations.

Millhouse had been using a "GAB" line to make the calls. Northwestern Bell provided this type of party phone line for teenagers in 1985. However, the service was shut down because there had been an outcry from parents when they discovered that teens were allegedly using the GAB lines for sex and drug sales. When Millhouse had his line, he managed to rack up a monthly bill of as high as $383, the equivalent of over $1,100 today. They were all calls made to young boys in Des Moines.

The police responded by sending out hundreds of letters, warning parents in the area that their children may have had contact with a pedophile. There was no way of knowing if Millhouse had been in contact with all the boys on the list, but they wanted to ensure families knew the situation. The notifications ended up convincing other victims to come forward, telling the police about their own encounters with Millhouse.

One was a former paperboy for the *Des Moines Register*, whom Wilbur Millhouse had supervised. He reported that while delivering newspapers, he was approached by a man in a Ford Fairmont who asked him for directions on several occasions. He believed the man was a pedophile, using the ruse to talk to young boys on their paper routes. Later, he saw Millhouse talking to a man on the street, and he recognized him as the man in the Ford – apparently, they knew each other.

He told the police that Millhouse had propositioned him multiple times and once, in conversation, said he'd known Johnny Gosch. He also claimed that Millhouse told him, "Nothing would have happened to Johnny if he would have just kept his mouth shut."

Wilbur Millhouse was charged with the six crimes for which the police were able to gather evidence – but he denied any links to Johnny Gosch or Eugene Martin. There was no hard evidence to link him to either abduction.

And despite the hopes that the arrest of Millhouse had raised, Eugene's case turned cold again.

And this time, it stayed that way.

EUGENE'S FATHER, DON MARTIN, DIED IN 2010. He was never reunited with his son, and he never found out what happened to him. The strain of dealing with his son's disappearance had destroyed his relationship with Sue, and they later divorced.

Eugene's new bicycle remained in Don's garage until the day he died.

Today, two of Eugene's siblings keep the search for him alive. His older brother, Donald, has made numerous requests for information in the media, believing that someone in Des Moines knows something about what happened to Eugene. He continues to urge them to come forward.

Eugene's stepsister, Kim Dellaca, has also been interviewed many times about her brother. She has long stated that her parents never gave up on finding Eugene. "As long as they thought he was still out there, I assume the same thing," she has said.

And hopefully, she's right. Maybe one of these days, Eugene – or perhaps one of the other two boys who vanished from Des Moines around the same time – will finally come home.

1985: NOT THAT TYPE OF GIRL
THE VANISHING OF JENNIFER SCHMIDT

THE EVENING OF AUGUST 6, 1985, WAS A WARM one on the Purdue University campus in West Lafayette, Indiana. But even if it hadn't been, Jennifer Schmidt would've likely been walking anyway. She was an active, fit young woman who was part of the Air Force ROTC at the university. She planned to join the Air Force as soon as she graduated.

That summer, the 19-year-old had been taking summer classes, hoping to get a jump on her sophomore-year studies. She was majoring in electrical engineering, and she worked hard. She was a conservative, religious young woman, serious about classwork, and rarely socialized. So, when she didn't return to her apartment that evening, her roommate immediately sensed something was wrong.

Jennifer met with one of her professors in the afternoon, and a friend spotted her around 5:00 P.M., walking in her neighborhood, likely on her way home.

And then she was gone.

What happened to Jennifer Schmidt that day remains a complete mystery that remains unsolved four decades later.

ON WEDNESDAY, AUGUST 7, WITH NO WORD from Jennifer in 24 hours, her roommate called the police and reported her missing. Detectives with the West Lafayette Police Department realized right away that Jennifer wasn't the type of girl who was likely to disappear on her own.

Born on May 1, 1966, to parents Donald and Johnni Schmidt, Jennifer was raised in a religious home, and her childhood values stuck with her. She'd come to Purdue from Beavercreek, Ohio, near Dayton, and didn't have a car. She didn't want one. She lived close to campus and loved

Jennifer Schmidt

to walk. She was described as "dependable and reliable," she didn't drink alcohol or socialize much, and never dated. She was engaged to a young man who was currently in New York.

According to her father, Donald, she was intelligent and always aware of her surroundings. He found it hard to believe that anyone could have abducted her, but he was certain she hadn't run off on her own. The Schmidts tried to remain optimistic that she would be quickly found. "We're all praying for her safe return," he told the press.

Within a day of opening the case into Jennifer's vanishing, Harry Martin, the West Lafayette department's captain of detectives, told reporters that he suspected foul play. Jennifer had missed a final exam on Wednesday, which everyone agreed was completely out of character.

According to her friends and family members, Jennifer hadn't had any problems with anyone on campus. She looked forward to finishing summer classes and seeing her relatives before the fall semester started. She had a very close relationship with her parents and wouldn't have left town without telling them where she was going.

Donald and Johnni had seen Jennifer less than a week before she vanished. The entire family had attended her older brother's U.S. Air Force Academy graduation. She'd been in a great mood then and was excited about an upcoming family reunion in Butternut, Wisconsin. The flight had been scheduled for August 7 – Jennifer missed that, too.

A full-scale search was launched using law enforcement, volunteers, and state conservation officers, who assisted the police with searches of the nearby Wabash River. A helicopter crew conducted an aerial search of rural Tippecanoe County while teams searched alleys, dumpsters, backyards, and abandoned buildings all over Jennifer's neighborhood, hoping to find the missing young woman or at least some tangible clue as to where she might be. But the searches led nowhere.

West Lafayette Detective Curtis Cunningham admitted that he had no idea what had happened to Jennifer. "Nobody knows anything or where she could have gone. She just disappeared."

Detectives decided to create a timeline for what Jennifer had been doing in the hours leading up to her disappearance – which was harder than they thought it would be. She had vanished just as the summer semester was ending, and most of her friends had already left campus because class was over. It would be at least two weeks before they returned for the next semester.

The timeline didn't seem to offer much help. A young man named David Dippon, who knew Jennifer through ROTC, was one of the last people to speak to her that day she went missing. He saw her around 5:00 P.M. at the intersection of Grant Street and Northwestern Avenue. David was walking toward campus, and Jennifer was walking away from it. They paused only for a moment to chat. "The only thing we were talking about was exams that were coming up on Wednesday," he told investigators.

The search continued, but it wasn't getting anywhere. On August 16, Tippecanoe County Crime Stoppers announced a $1,000 reward for Jennifer's location or information that led to the arrest of the person responsible for her disappearance. Detectives were hopeful the reward would bring in some tips. "Somebody out there has information that can help us get our daughter back," Donald said.

The previous April, Jennifer had organized a candlelight vigil at Purdue to raise awareness about missing prisoners of war and members of the military who were still listed as missing in action from the Vietnam War. In August, a candlelight vigil was held for Jennifer, with friends and classmates praying for her safe return.

Jennifer had been active in the Arnold Air Society, the honorary student group on campus that had organized the vigil. Major Vernon Zink, the group advisor, described Jennifer as "motivated, enthusiastic, and quick to volunteer for extracurricular projects." Like everyone else, Major Zink hoped Jennifer was safe but acknowledged that time was the enemy. "It isn't looking good," he said. "Every hour that goes by is to our detriment -- and hers."

On Saturday, August 31, Purdue students who were returning for the start of the fall semester spent the day hanging missing person posters of Jennifer all over Lafayette. In just three hours, they distributed over 500 posters, hanging them on telephone poles, store windows, bulletin boards, and in the bus station. The poster included Jennifer's photograph and a number to call with information.

West Lafayette police officer Gary Rockhold said he appreciated the students' help. "It's more exposure. It might jog the memory of somebody, someplace. Not everybody has television and newspapers."

By now, though, almost a month had passed, and detectives admitted they were running out of leads. Gary Rockhold told reporters, "There's nothing new on Jennifer. We need something to break the ice. In the past week, there have been helicopter checks and the river's been checked again with the airboat -- nothing."

On September 11, Donald and Johnni traveled to Lafayette from their home in Ohio to make a public appeal for help finding their daughter. Johnni fought back tears as she spoke. "If anyone knows anything, please, let us have peace of mind. If she's no longer with us, it's important for us to know so that we can do what we can to have a Christian burial."

But her plea went unanswered.

Then, in October, the police received a call from a man who claimed he'd killed Jennifer. He was taken into custody while detectives investigated his confession, but it led nowhere. It was quickly discovered that the man had a long history of mental instability and had nothing to do with Jennifer's case. It turned out to be the first false confession, and it wasn't the last. Captain Withers noted, "In any crime, you'll get volunteers who want to get the credit."

Months passed without any trace of Jennifer. Detective Harry Martin told a reporter that the case was eating at him. He had three daughters, and he could understand the pain and frustration that Jennifer's parents were feeling. He admitted, "You try to walk a thin line with the family between the reality of the seriousness of their missing loved one, and yet try to give them some ray of hope."

Even so, Martin knew the odds of finding Jennifer alive were slim. He knew that her parents knew that, too, and had accepted that they would likely never see their daughter again. They just wanted to bring her home, and he desperately wanted to give them that chance, but the investigation was at a dead end – and it stayed that way.

Seven years after she disappeared, Jennifer's case was the only unsolved missing person case in West Lafayette. There were still no leads or suspects. Detective Martin was later promoted to Captain Martin, but he never forgot about Jennifer's case. "It's a tragedy," he said in 1994. "It's a tragedy for the family, and it's a tragedy for the community."

Martin said it was still hard to comprehend how someone had just disappeared from a busy street corner in broad daylight. With no evidence, investigators had nothing but theories. Jennifer might have been forcibly abducted from the street, but it seemed more likely that she'd accepted a ride from someone she knew – a ride that ended badly.

No matter what happened that day, none of the detectives who worked on the case believed that Jennifer was still alive.

Tragically, her parents agreed. In May 1993, Jennifer's parents filed a petition to have their daughter declared legally dead. The request was granted. Officially, Jennifer was gone for good.

Captain Harry Martin retired from the West Lafayette Police Department, but he took the memory of a few unsolved cases – including Jennifer's – with him. "You get involved with the families," he shrugged. "Sometimes, you've got to stand back because you're too involved."

Larry DeWayne Hall

ALTHOUGH JENNIFER'S CASE REMAINS ACTIVE, there have been no new leads in years. It's believed she met with foul play, but who took her? None of the suspects named over the years have panned out.

Back in March 1987, detectives suspected that Jennifer might have been abducted by William Michael Gable, a 31-year-old man who shot and killed himself when the police tried to arrest him for kidnapping a young woman from the Purdue campus. They believed there might have been other victims, so investigators searched his property and dug up his backyard but found nothing to connect Gable to Jennifer.

Another suspect was possible serial killer Larry DeWyane Hall, an Indiana man who has confessed to committing at least 35 murders throughout the Midwest and the eastern United States – and then has slowly recanted them all. Regardless, the FBI currently suspects he may have committed at least 50 murders.

Thanks to Hall's notoriety, multiple investigators across Indiana have considered Hall a suspect in homicide, missing persons, stalking, and kidnapping cases. The problem they've had with charging him? Lack of evidence.

"If Hall did everything that Hall's been accused of, he's one of the most prolific serial killers in the Midwest, if not the most. But he's made all these claims and withdrew them," said Detective Joey Laughlin with the Fayette County Police Department, who has investigated the case of Denise Pflum, who disappeared in 1989.

Hall grew up in Wabash, Indiana. The socially timid son of a gravedigger and his school years were spent in the shadow of his more outgoing identical twin brother, Gary. Acting out, Hall committed a series of thefts, arson, and petty crimes during his high school years. He eventually found employment as a janitor.

Then, in the 1980s, he began pursuing his passion for the Revolutionary and Civil Wars by dressing up in costume and attending historical reenactments across the country. The authorities now believe – based on investigations and Hall's confessions – that he committed murders close to reenactment sites from about 1981 until 1994 when he was arrested for the kidnapping of 15-year-old Jessica Roach.

Jessica went missing in September 1993. Six weeks later, she was found dead in Perrysville, Indiana, which was only 20 miles from her home in Georgetown, Illinois.

More than a year later, two girls in Georgetown reported that a van was stalking them. The number on the license plate was traced back to Larry Hall. Illinois investigators went to Wabash to interrogate Hall, who confessed to tying Jessica up with a rope, raping, and strangling her.

He was booked into the Grant County Jail on November 16, 1994, and recanted his confession the next day. He was eventually found guilty on one count of kidnapping and for transporting Jessica across state lines for sex. They couldn't prove that he'd killed her.

Despite multiple attempts at parole, Hall remains behind bars, serving a life sentence. After all this time, he has still never been convicted of a single murder – but this hasn't stopped the authorities from trying. He has been suspected in many murders and disappearances over the years – including that of Jennifer Schmidt.

"I just think that based on his suspected involvement in numerous homicides that, as a general course of action, his name came up. I don't know how much they explored that other than his name hit everybody's radar," Detective Jonathan Eager with West Lafayette Police Department said in a 2022 interview.

Authorities considered the possibility that Hall had been in the West Lafayette area because of the popular historical reenactment festival, Feast of the Hunters' Moon. But that theory never really held up for Eager because the reenactment wasn't held until October – today and in 1985.

"Her disappearance was way too early for that," he said. "I don't know that there would have been any reenactors in the area for anything at that time that I was aware of."

Detective Eager, who took over the case a few years ago, has remained in contact with Jennifer's family and said her disappearance isn't something they've gotten over. "Her mother told me that she thinks about it and has thought about it every day of her life since it happened," he said sadly.

"It's nothing that people ever get over," Eager said.

1986: VANISHED FROM THE COUNTY FAIR
THE DISAPPEARANCE OF JEREMY BRIGHT

ON AUGUST 14, 1986, JEREMY BRIGHT AND HIS SISTER, S'te (pronounced ESS-TEE), did what average American kids had been doing for decades – they went to the fair.

It was the week of the 75th annual Coos County Fair and Rodeo in Myrtle Point, Oregon, which Jeremy and his sister looked forward to every year. This summer was particularly special since the pair had moved with their mother, Diane Beatty, to Grants Pass, Oregon – about two hours away -- after Diane had separated from their stepfather, Orville, the previous year.

Orville, along with their grandparents, aunts, uncles, and cousins, still lived in Myrtle Point, and Jeremy and S'te had been allowed to spend the week in town with the family before 14-year-old Jeremy started his freshman year of high school.

By all accounts, it was an ordinary day, but at some point in the evening, things went horribly wrong, and Jeremy vanished without a trace. His last credible sighting was that night when he stopped by his grandmother's tavern for some money.

And he was never seen again.

JEREMY DOLAND BRIGHT WAS BORN IN BALTIMORE, Maryland, on May 25, 1972. After his parents split up, his mother, Diane, moved to Myrtle Point, Oregon, where Jeremy was raised. She later remarried Orville Beatty, but Diane moved Jeremy and his sister to Grants Pass after their relationship dissolved.

Jeremy was, by all accounts, a happy kid. He was well-liked and popular in school and was looking forward to starting high school after the summer ended. He struggled academically, thanks to his parents' divorce and moving to a new town, but he excelled in basketball and planned to join the freshman team.

Jeremy Bright

At 14, Jeremy was already six feet tall and seemed a shoo-in for a starting position.

The trip back to Myrtle Point had turned into a great week, especially with the county fair kicking off. He'd enjoyed spending time with his family and reconnecting with friends.

On August 14, Jeremy took his nine-year-old sister to the fair. He and S'te met with some friends and purchased day passes. At first, the siblings stayed together but then split up around 1:30 P.M. They made plans to meet up at the Ferris Wheel at 5:00.

S'te would show up – Jeremy wouldn't.

She waited for him and then got worried when he didn't show up when he said he would. She found a police officer and tried to tell him something was wrong, but the officer wasn't interested. He told her, "Don't worry, he's probably just off with friends. He'll turn up eventually."

But as the evening went on, there was no sign of him.

It was later discovered that Jeremy was seen in a few places that afternoon and evening, so it's unclear if he was actually

missing when S'te reported it to the police officer. He was supposed to be with his friend, Johnny Fish, but the timeline of when the two boys were together is also unclear.

In fact, a lot about this story is unclear.

There are conflicting reports about whether S'te saw her brother near the Ferris Wheel or if she saw him getting into a pickup truck that afternoon.

And then there's the telephone call to his mother. There are two versions of this – one that he called from a payphone at the fair and one that claimed he used a payphone somewhere else. Wherever the call was made, Diane said it was at 4:45 P.M., just 15 minutes before he was supposed to meet his sister. They talked about her coming to Myrtle Point to pick them up in two days. She later stated that Jeremy seemed fine, and nothing seemed unusual.

There are also conflicting accounts from family members that Jeremy was doing other things during the day and was safe that evening when he was supposed to be missing.

One of those reports claims that after splitting up from his sister, Jeremy left the fair and went to his aunt's restaurant, where he helped out for a few hours. Then, he called his mother, telling her he was going to meet S'te at the fair.

But he didn't go straight back to the fair.

Instead – according to this version of events – Jeremy stopped by a tavern owned by his grandmother and asked his stepfather for some extra money. When he left Orville, Jeremy said he was returning to the fair.

But he never made it. That evening, Jeremy went missing and has never been seen again.

ON AUGUST 16, DIANE DROVE TO MYRTLE POINT to pick up Jeremy and S'te as planned. She went to Orville's house, expecting they'd both be there – but Jeremy was gone. Diane found that her son's wallet, watch, and keys were all sitting on top of the television in the living room – but no Jeremy.

Worse, she discovered no one knew where he was. Diane found that Jeremy had been missing for two days, and nobody knew where he'd gone.

Once again, it's unclear why Orville – or any of Jeremy's other family members – hadn't notified Diane or called the police. Apparently, the family had been worried about Jeremy since the night he didn't return to get his little sister at the fair, but they'd assumed he'd turn up.

He didn't.

Diane immediately went to the police and reported Jeremy as a missing person. Initially, the police suspected foul play, but once the investigation began, they started receiving calls from locals who had spotted Jeremy around the area. After multiple reporters, they decided that Jeremy hadn't been abducted – he was a runaway.

The case was put on the back burner. Detectives surmised that Jeremy had used the fair as a place to hide out and then had left town. They believed the separation of his mother and stepfather was a good reason for him to run away.

Diane was angry, pointing out that Jeremy's wallet and watch had been left at his stepfather's house. The watch was new and very important to him. She didn't believe he would have left those things behind. The police used this to suggest further that Jeremy had run away and would undoubtedly come back soon.

The delay from the police department caused a delay with the media, too. There was little coverage for the first several days, and then finally, a small piece ran on page two of the local paper on August 19 – five days after he vanished. The headline simply read "Youth is Missing" and briefly described Jeremy and the circumstances surrounding his disappearance.

Meanwhile, the Coos County Sheriff's Office made it clear that they didn't share the opinion of the local police. When he was brought into the case, Sergeant Steve Dalton ran down every lead he could find and stated firmly that he didn't believe Jeremy had run away. "He was not the type of kid who would have struck off on his own," Dalton said after conducting extensive interviews with Jeremy's family and friends.

The sheriff's department began looking for suspects and returned to a report made by J'te about seeing Jeremy getting into a pickup truck. She wasn't the only one who made this claim. Several others said they'd seen Jeremy grabbed and dragged away from the fair by an unknown man. Unfortunately, none of those witnesses could be sure that the boy they'd seen was actually Jeremy, so the sightings were never confirmed.

As the case finally started to get attention, rumors began to spread all over town. There were stories, rumors, and lies making the rounds, including that Jeremy had ducked out of the fair to go to a party and had been given a beer spiked with drugs. He had a heart murmur, and this could have caused his death, the rumor claimed. He overdosed, and the other partygoers decided to get rid of his body.

Another story claimed that Jeremy and some friends had gone swimming in the Coquille River, where a group of men approached them with guns and began using Jeremy for target practice – seeing how close they could shoot at him without hitting him. But one bullet struck Jeremy, so they pulled him out of the water, then took him to a nearby cabin to try and patch him up. But once Jeremy died, they buried his body in a shallow grave.

There was also a rumor going around that claimed Jeremy had decided to run off with the carnival and when it left town a few days after he disappeared, he went it. The sheriff's department even followed up on a tip that a man named Jeremy Bright was with a traveling circus in Florida, but it turned out to be a different Jeremy Bright.

And there were more – a lot more. So, the authorities decided to follow up on some of the rumors and theories, and they started searching for the properties where people claimed Jeremy's body was buried. They investigated buildings, barns, and patches of land. They dug up backyards and drained several wells, checking the bottom for clues, but every search came up empty.

The Coos County Sheriff announced that he feared Jeremy had died the day he'd disappeared. Investigators were convinced he hadn't left town on his own. He had no money and no spare clothes. Jeremy was also extremely close with his sister, and they didn't believe he would have abandoned her. But they confirmed the case was still ongoing and asked anyone with information to come forward.

And someone did. Her name was Cecelia Fish, and during the early morning hours of August 15, she was leaving her sister's apartment when she saw a teenager who had blood all over his clothing. When she'd expressed concern, the young man had laughed. "This happened hours ago," he said and kept walking.

About 30 minutes later, Cecelia said her brother, Johnny, came home. Johnny was one of Jeremy Bright's best friends, and they had been hanging out all week while Jeremy was back in town. But Cecelia said that when she saw Johnny that morning, he had been shaking and seemed traumatized. When she tried to talk to him about what had happened, he refused to talk about it.

Over the many nights that followed, Johnny suffered from terrible nightmares but never spoke to his sister, the police, or anyone else. But whatever happened, it changed him permanently. He spent years suffering from substance abuse issues, became homeless, and died without ever revealing what he knew in 2011.

Another tip came in claiming that the driver of the pickup truck that Jeremy got into that night was Jeremy's former babysitter, a man named Terry Lee Steinhoff. A few witnesses claimed to see Jeremy in Steinhoff's truck that afternoon, too, before he vanished.

And the men who shot at Jeremy in the river? One of them was Steinhoff and his cousin, David.

And the man Cecelia Fish had seen the night after Jeremy disappeared, wearing the bloody clothes? That was the cousin David again.

Obviously, many locals believed that Steinhoff – and probably his cousin – were responsible for Jeremy's death and that they'd hidden his body.

The authorities searched Steinhoff's property. They tried to question him about Jeremy's disappearance on multiple occasions, but Steinhoff refused to cooperate with them. If he was involved – or knew what happened to Jeremy that night – he kept it to himself.

But Steinhoff was certainly capable of violence. Two years after Jeremy vanished, Steinhoff was convicted of murdering a 32-year-old woman from Coos Bay. The victim, Patricia Morris, had been stabbed 15 times in the throat and left for dead behind a local bar.

Detectives believed that people in Myrtle Point had information about Steinhoff's involvement in Jeremy's case but had been too scared to come forward. They hoped that once Steinhoff was behind bars for the murder, they might be willing to talk, but no new information was revealed.

In 2007, Terry Lee Steinhoff died in prison while serving a life sentence for Patrica Morris' murder. Investigators had approached him about Jeremy's disappearance several times, but Steinhoff refused to cooperate. Whatever secrets he had, he took them with him to his grave.

Over the years, the Coos County Sheriff's Department has continued to work on Jeremy's case. They hope they'll eventually find his remains and bring some closure to his family and friends. The sheriff's office has an entire filing cabinet used solely for Jeremy's case. There is even a photo of Jeremy hanging on the wall, a reminder that his case is still unsolved – that his story has no conclusion.

Even after all these decades, the case still draws theories and speculation. When asked about the many rumors that surround Jeremy's case after all these years, his mother, Diane, said, "Every time I'd hear a new one, I'd have nightmares for a week or so."

Diane moved to Florida a few years after her son vanished, but she returned to Myrtle Point every summer to look for Jeremy. While she has long assumed that her son died on the day he disappeared, she still holds out hope for closure. She believes his body is still in Coos County somewhere but has yet to be discovered.

Jeremy's sister, S'te Elmore, spoke out in an interview, stating that she believes there were Myrtle Point residents who knew what had happened to her brother all those years ago. "Everybody knew each other, everybody knew what was going on with everybody else, and I just can't believe that Jeremy just you know, vanished, and nobody knows anything," she said. "Justice would be nice. But in the end, I just want to know where Jeremy is."

S'te says that even though Jeremy had been gone for years, he remains a part of her family's daily lives. She has told her children about their Uncle Jeremy and has his photos on the wall, keeping his memory alive.

They'll continue to be haunted by the memory of their lost son, brother, and uncle until their hopes are finally realized – when whatever happened to Jeremy on that long-ago summer day is finally revealed.

1989: OVER A FENCE – AND GONE
THE DISAPPEARANCE OF PATRICIA MEEHAN

SOMETHING WAS BOTHERING PATTY IN APRIL 1989.

Her friends and family thought it was obvious, and when she offered no information about what was wrong, they asked her about it. But Patty insisted she was fine. She wasn't. She hadn't been acting like herself. She seemed distracted and slightly disoriented at times, forgetting about things and not showing up for plans she'd made. It wasn't like her – it was very odd.

It took a couple of weeks – maybe it was the constant asking by others – but Patty eventually began to see what everyone was talking about. She had started to get concerned and agreed to see a psychologist. She wasn't sure what was happening but realized she needed to see a professional.

She made an appointment for April 21 – but she never arrived for it.

Patty vanished one day before she was supposed to see that psychologist, and while 5,000 alleged sightings of her were reported in the months and years that followed, Patty Meehan has never been seen again.

PATRICIA MEEHAN WAS BORN ON NOVEMBER 1, 1951. Her parents, Thomas and Dolly Meehan, raised her in Pittsburgh, Pennsylvania, where she grew up and attended school. Patty moved to Oklahoma City for college, and since she'd always enjoyed being around children, she decided to get a degree in early childhood development. Her initial plan was to open a daycare center back home after graduation, but things changed while she

Patty Meehan

was in college. She decided she liked working with animals more than kids, and her life went in another direction. She dropped out of school without obtaining her degree and moved to Bozeman, Montana, where she found work on a ranch.

Although Patty loved her work – she loved horses – she quickly found she wasn't making enough money to make ends meet. She started doing odd jobs for her landlord, making extra money and getting a break on her rent, and while it wasn't a lavish lifestyle, she always seemed happy with her life.

Until one day, in early 1989, when she wasn't.

Patty became easily distracted. She forgot about the jobs she was supposed to do, forgot about plans with friends, and telephone calls back home started to slip her mind. When anyone asked what was bothering her, she initially shrugged off their concerns. After a few weeks, Patty noticed it, too. She wasn't feeling right, and it had become obvious to her. She needed to do something about it. That was when she called and made that appointment with a therapist.

Then, oddly, two days before the appointment, Patty's mother, Dolly, received a call from her daughter. On the evening of April 19, Patty called home to Pittsburgh and asked if she could come home. She said she wanted to return to Pennsylvania and asked if she could stay with her parents for a while. Dolly assured her it would be fine, and Patty promised to call back the following day to work out the details.

But that call was never made.

On April 20, Petty spoke with her landlord for about five minutes as he was doing maintenance on her building. She mentioned to him that she was going away for a few days – not that she was moving back to Pittsburgh. She didn't say where she was going, and he didn't ask. He did say later that Patty didn't seem like herself that morning. She appeared "hyper," he said, and very distracted.

He didn't question her, though, and Patty climbed into her Chevy Nova and left her Bozeman apartment for the last time. Considering she had an appointment with a psychologist the next day, the trip's timing seemed odd, but her landlord knew nothing about that as he waved to her and went back to work.

It's unclear if Patty had a particular destination in mind that day. She might have been heading toward Pittsburgh, but no one knows for sure. She got onto Montana Highway 200, going east, and started driving. By 8:15 that evening, she was almost 400 miles from Bozeman.

Around this time, Patty arrived just outside Circle, Montana, and seemed to lose control of her car. Driving west on the same highway, Peggy Bueller was startled to see Patty's car had crossed the center line and was headed directly at her. Peggy quickly swerved and barely managed to avoid Patty's car. Stunned and shaken, she promptly pulled over to the side of the road to catch her breath. She glanced into her rearview mirror and saw Patty collide head-on with the car behind Peggy.

The driver of the second car, Carol Heitz, was an off-duty police dispatcher, and she hadn't seen Patty in time to get out of the way of the vehicle hurtling directly at her. The resulting head-on collision totaled both Patty's Nova and Carol's Monte Carlo, and yet – against all odds – both women survived the crash.

Carol suffered a blow to the head and had a few bruises, but she managed to get out of the twisted wreckage of her car without assistance. She saw Patty climb out of her crushed Nova, and Carol stumbled toward her and asked if she was okay.

Carol later reported that Patty seemed to look right at her, but it was as though she didn't see the other woman. She didn't respond or even acknowledge that Carol was there. Then, more bizarrely, Patty walked over to a fence alongside the road and climbed over it. She stood there, motionless, looking at the wreck.

Peggy Bueller, who had now exited her own car, saw Patty climb over the fence and stand there, staring at the highway. She later reported, "As I looked out across the accident, I noticed someone on the other side of the fence. She was standing there like a spectator - not like it had happened to her."

Peggy watched the unidentified woman stand silently on the other side of the fence for several moments before turning and walking away into the empty field behind her. Patty vanished into the night.

Noticing that Carol needed medical help, Peggy's father, who had been with her in the car, stayed with Carol Heitz while Peggy drove into town to call the police. The police arrived within 30 minutes, and an ambulance took Carol to the hospital, where she spent the next several days recuperating.

By then, there was no sign of Patty.

Peggy and Carol provided the police with a description of the woman in the other car. They described her as around 35 years old, 110 pounds, five feet six inches tall, with a freckled face and reddish-blonde hair. They weren't sure if she had been injured in the crash but said she had appeared to be in shock.

The authorities ran the license plate and registration for the wrecked and abandoned Nova and determined it was owned by Patricia Meehan, who lived in Bozeman. However, they had no idea if she was the woman driving it at the time of the accident. A search occurred immediately after the police arrived on the scene, and they found a set of tennis shoe tracks leading out into the field. They were later discovered to be the same size shoes that Patty wore. Tracking dogs were brought in to aid the police, and the trail was followed for hours until both the scent and the prints were lost around 3:00 A.M. The search was suspended until morning.

After more investigation, the police confirmed that Patty had been driving the Nova when the accident occurred but had no success locating her. Although they first assumed she had fled the scene out of fear, after speaking to family members, they became more concerned that Patty was suffering some mental distress prior to the crash. It was even surmised that she was suicidal and had intentionally caused the wreck, although no evidence of this existed to support or disprove the theory.

After the sun came up on April 21, a plane began conducting flyover searches of the area surrounding the crash site, hoping to spot something from the air that those on the ground might miss. Two different pilots conducted searches throughout the day but saw no sign that Patty was hiding or injured in the nearby fields.

While this was happening, a large-scale ground search was conducted by the Montana Highway Patrol, the police from Circle, ambulance crews, local ranchers, and an area work crew, but they found no sign of Patty.

The following day, the temperature dropped, and rain began falling. Until then, the weather had been dry and fairly mild, but now, if Patty was still outside without shelter, she needed to be located quickly. A team of search and rescue personnel, accompanied by dogs, continued to scour the area. Overhead, pilots conducted more flyovers, increasing the radius of the search each time. By the night's end, investigators had begun to believe that Patty had likely left the immediate area. If she had hitched a ride with someone along the highway, there was no way to guess where she might be.

Regardless, the area search continued. As a storm dumped rain, wind, and hail on them, search teams moved into Circle, checking vacant buildings, basements, alleys, and anywhere else someone could get away from the weather. Nothing was found.

Once the sky cleared, the search planes returned to the skies, but, as with the earlier searches, they found no sign of the missing woman.

Several members of Patty's family traveled to Montana to help with the search. They still hadn't been able to process what the police were telling them. It seemed inconceivable to them that Patty would simply walk away from the scene of an accident. She had always been responsible and reliable and had a firm idea about right and wrong. So, what happened? Her siblings had started to agree with the police – Patty must be in the midst of a mental health crisis.

It soon became clear that Patty wouldn't be found in the area around Circle, so her family began traveling along the major highways in the region. They distributed missing person posters at truck stops and rest areas, and while there were several potential sightings of Patty, none of the tips led to their missing sister.

On May 25, 1898, Patty's parents, Tom and Dolly, arrived in Montana to join the search. Patty's brother, Terry, came with them. They were devastated by the disappearance but tried to stay cautiously optimistic. There had already been several possible sightings of Patty – and soon there would be more – and they vowed to follow up on all of them. They printed more flyers and brought along photos and videos of Patty to pass out to the media. They hoped that having additional images of the missing woman would help people be sure if they had seen her or not.

Right away, Tom and Dolly started following the leads still coming in – all from people who believed they had encountered Patty. Using the photos and video to eliminate false sightings, they identified five credible people who were convinced they'd seen Patty.

The first was on May 4, when a police officer in Luverne, Minnesota, claimed to have seen Patty sitting inside a Hardee's restaurant. She had been drinking water alone in a booth for over five hours. When the restaurant closed, she left and walked to a nearby all-night diner. When the officer questioned her, the woman refused to give her name and claimed to be from Colorado and Israel.

The next day, May 5, a waitress at a diner in Murdo, South Dakota, reported seeing Patty between 10:00 and 11:00 P.M. with a man who looked to be in his thirties.

The following week, on May 11 and May 13, Petty was allegedly seen in Billings, Montana, and then back in Bozeman on May 19 – or so the witnesses claimed.

Not only was this pattern of sightings unlikely, but they were almost impossible without a vehicle. In addition, these were not the only "credible" sightings that were reported at the same time – they were just the ones that Tom and Dolly believed were the most believable.

There had been another sighting of Patty on May 5. This one came from Sioux Falls, South Dakota, where a waitress in another diner claimed to see her drinking coffee around midnight – less than an hour after when she was supposed to be in Murdo, which was three hours away by car.

On May 19, another restaurant waitress said she saw Patty in Bozeman, where she ordered breakfast, ate quickly, and said she had to go shopping. She was gone by 9:00 A.M. Another server on duty that day said she seemed disoriented and was talking to herself.

Later that same week, Patty was allegedly seen at a horse auction in Billings, Montana.

More than two weeks later, on May 30, a woman who resembled Patty was spotted by a passing truck driver on Interstate 90 in rural Washington. The driver offered her a ride, which she declined. A short time later, the same woman told a passing female motorist that her car had broken down and that she was going to find a phone.

Another reported sighting of Patty occurred the following week in Tacoma, Washington. She was allegedly seen by a Port of Tacoma employee who claimed she was at a truck stop on Interstate 5 asking strangers for directions to Aberdeen.

By June, more than 25 sightings of Patty had been reported, three of which were confirmed by the police. And they kept coming in. Law enforcement officials received dozens of sightings throughout the Pacific Northwest, many of them from truck stops between Montana and Seattle. Detectives believed she may have been in Washington during this time because she had a sister in Seattle and an ex-boyfriend, Kurt Fletcher, who lived in Spokane.

But if that was true – and Patty really was in the area – she didn't contact either of them.

The people who encountered the woman they believed was Patty all reported that she was soft-spoken and polite but appeared tired and unkempt. She tended to be in fast food restaurants and diners, where she sat quietly and never bothered anyone. When asked, the woman mentioned not having much money and often used change to pay for whatever she ordered. She always lingered in those places for hours at a time, as if she had nowhere else to go.

However, If it was Patty that these people were seeing, she did have someplace to go. She had family members and friends who were looking for her.

Had Patty suffered some mental break? Her parents believed she had. Not only had she seemed unlike herself before leaving Bozeman, but they thought she'd suffered amnesia after the crash and was wandering aimlessly around Interstate 90, likely hitching rides with truckers.

By the second week in June, Tom and Dolly had expanded their search area, following up on several reported sightings in Idaho and Washington. They continued focusing on Interstate 90 since almost all the sightings seemed centered around it.

They spent weeks looking for Patty but eventually had to give up and return to Pennsylvania. They left the search in the hands of professional investigators, holding out hope that their daughter would eventually be found.

MORE TIME PASSED AND WITH PATTY STILL MISSING. In September, her case was featured on the television show *Unsolved Mysteries*. After the episode aired, detectives received a flood of tips from people who claimed to have seen her. Some were more promising than others, and every new lead was checked.

One report particularly excited the investigators. It came from a woman who had picked up a hitchhiker in Victor, Montana, in late September. The woman said she was looking for a ride to Missoula. Because it was late and nothing was open, the woman allowed the hitchhiker -- who said her name was Patty -- to spend the night with her and her husband at their home in Lolo, Montana. The witness said the hitchhiker matched the missing woman's description, had a soft voice, and talked about her love of horses.

The couple dropped her off at a Missoula truck stop the following morning. From there, the woman planned to hitch a ride to Whitefish, Montana, where she claimed she would stay with a friend.

The police received other tips that Patty was seen in that area around the same time, which added more legitimacy to all the sightings. But unfortunately, whoever this woman was, she was never found. If she was Patty, she'd vanished once again.

It's probably no surprise that the television show brought in other kinds of calls, too – ones that weren't as helpful. After seeing *Unsolved Mysteries*, detectives received a call from a psychic in Florida who said she didn't think Patty had ever made it out of the Circle, Montana, area. She stated that Patty's body would be found in a cave or mineshaft near the accident site. The Dawson County Search and Rescue Team was brought in to comb through the more than a dozen abandoned mines in the area, but they found nothing to indicate any truth to the psychic's vision.

Soon, interest in Patty's case started to cool, but a handful of new sightings came in during the later months of 1989. And there were a couple of sightings that got a lot of attention but turned out to be disappointments.

In December 1989, a man was so convinced that he ran into Patty at a bar in Kalispell that he not only called the police to report the sighting, but he also grabbed the woman and refused to let her leave the bar before police got there. The woman angrily insisted she was not the missing woman, but the man didn't believe her. When the police arrived, the responding officer was also so sure she was Patty that he took her to the station to be questioned. She wasn't Patty – and once she proved it, she was allowed to leave.

In August 1990, a transient woman was arrested by police in Coeur d'Alene, Idaho, for littering. The woman bore a resemblance to Patty, and the arresting officer initially believed she was the missing woman. On September 1, the woman appeared in a Kootenai County court, claiming before the judge to be a missionary traveling between Montana and Washington. Even the judge didn't believe her. He was also convinced she was Patty Meehan. Sadly, she wasn't Patty either, as her fingerprints finally proved.

Since then, there have been numerous sightings of Patty – some claim as many as 5,000 – but none of them have ever led the police, her family, or her friends to wherever she might be. Her family remains convinced that she was struck with amnesia and simply couldn't find her way home.

Unfortunately, it's also just as likely – probably more likely – that she was badly hurt in the accident and died from her injuries. Although the authorities conducted a massive search for her, there's always a chance that her body remains hidden somewhere in that sparsely populated area of Montana. Or worse, that animals disposed of her remains many years ago.

No matter what happened, Tom and Dolly never gave up on their search for Patty. They spent years traveling the country and looking for her. Tragically, both have since died without knowing what happened to their missing daughter. The rest of her family remains hopeful that her case will finally be solved one day.

1991: LAST SEEN AT A PAYPHONE
THE DISAPPEARANCE OF ANGELA HAMMOND

IT'S TOUGH TO IMAGINE FOR YOUNGER READERS, but it wasn't that long ago when no one had a cellphone. There was no texting or calling from anywhere with a signal. If you needed to make a call, your phone was attached to the wall or sitting on a counter. If you were lost, you bought a paper map. If you wanted to take photos, you needed a camera.

And if you had an emergency, a flat tire, a broken-down car, or needed help, you had to find a payphone. Of course, today, a payphone is a relic from another time, and few of them still exist, but in the early 1990s, they were still used every day and could be found just about everywhere – including in the town of Clinton, Missouri.

On April 4, 1991, Angela Hammond vanished while talking with her boyfriend on a payphone in that small town southeast of Kansas City.

Angela had never been seen or heard from again.

What happened to her? Well, that's one of the spookiest mysteries that still haunts western Missouri to this day.

Angela Hammond

ANGELA WAS BORN IN KANSAS CITY, MISSOURI, on February 9, 1971. Her parents – Chris and Marsha – decided to move about 80 miles southeast to Clinton to be closer to Marsha's parents when Angela was still a baby. Their second child, a son, was born shortly after moving to Clinton.

Everyone who knew Angela described her as fun, smart, and clever. She was well-liked, popular in school, and eager to do great things in her life. When she was 19, she began dating 18-year-old Rob Shaffer, a former football star from Angela's high school. Friends considered them a great couple – popular, outgoing, smart, and likable. So, in January 1991, when Angela found out she was pregnant, Rob proposed, and Angela said yes.

Besides marrying Angela and becoming a father, Rob planned to enlist in the military. Until he left for boot camp, though, he worked a series of odd jobs. Angela attended Central Missouri State University during the day and worked evenings at a bank as a processor. They rented a home together, but money was tight as they tried to prepare for the baby's arrival.

That April night, Angela was four months pregnant but feeling good with most of the morning sickness she'd experienced behind her. She and Rob decided to go to a barbeque at the home of Angela's mother, Marsha. Her parents were now divorced, but it had been amicable, so she also expected to see her father that night.

They had a nice time, but around 9:00 P.M., Rob had to leave. He'd promised his parents that he'd babysit his little brother, so he drove to his parents' house after saying goodbye.

Angela left soon after, picked up her best friend, and drove around with her for a while, chatting and simply hanging out. At 11:15, she dropped her friend off at home and stopped at a payphone to call Rob. Angela and Rob couldn't afford a phone at home, so they frequently used payphones. Angela was supposed to meet Rob at his parents' house, but she was tired and wanted to go home and sleep. She needed to let Rob know about her plan.

Rob had no objections. He knew how tired she'd been with the pregnancy. They chatted for a bit on the phone, only interrupted by a truck that pulled into the empty parking lot where the payphone was. It started driving around and around the lot, annoying Angela, and she mentioned it to Rob. As she described it, the truck left the lot and drove away.

A few minutes later, though, it was back. The truck pulled into a nearby spot and stopped. A man then got out of the truck and went to the phone booth next to the one where Angela was sitting. Angela mentioned this to Rob, but this was 1991, and everyone used payphones, so it didn't seem strange.

Not yet, anyway.

The man didn't stay in the booth for long. He left, went to his truck, grabbed a flashlight, and then walked around the parking lot like he was looking for something. Angela was now starting to feel unnerved. It was late; it was an isolated spot, and this seemed very strange. Why was the man hanging around? Rob suggested that maybe the other phone didn't work, and he was waiting for Angela to finish so he could use hers.

Rob heard Angela lean out of the booth and ask the man if he needed to use the phone, and he replied that he didn't.

Now, Rob was starting to feel uneasy, too. Angela described the man to him – a white man wearing overalls and a baseball cap. He also had a beard and was very dirty. He was driving a green Ford truck. It was a slightly older model, probably from the mid to late 1970s.

Suddenly, Rob heard a chilling scream – it was Angela! He heard the man say, "I didn't need to use the phone anyway." And then the line went dead.

Rob frantically ran out of his parent's house, got into his car, and drove quickly to the payphone's location. It was only minutes from where his parents lived. As he sped along the dark streets, he saw a truck like the one Angela had described approaching him. As it flashed by, he saw a man driving and a woman in the passenger seat, leaning over the driver and screaming. He immediately recognized Angela. As the vehicles zipped past one another, she heard Angela scream, "Robbie, Robbie..." trying to get his attention.

Angela was abducted by a man driving a truck like this one, described by Rob.

Rob slammed on the brakes, quickly pulled a U-turn, and chased after the truck. He followed closely for more than two miles, but when the truck turned onto a side road, Rob tried to follow, but his car died. As it rolled to a stop, he saw the truck's taillights disappearing into the darkness.

Panicked, he jumped out of the car and tried to follow on foot, but it was a lost cause. The truck quickly vanished. Rob returned to his car and tried to start it. The engine cranked but refused to turn over. He ran back to the main road and managed to flag down a passing car. They drove Rob directly to the police station.

When Rob burst into the quiet, small-town police station, the officers on duty didn't know what to think of his story. It took some convincing, but soon, they started searching for the truck. They also worked up a composite sketch of the man Angela had described to Rob – but it looked nothing like what Rob told them. He said the man had a beard and was wearing a baseball hat, but the sketch left both of those things out.

When asked about this, the police told Rob they thought the man might have been wearing a fake beard. They didn't explain this and refused to release an alternate sketch.

This would be one of the many things about this story that continues to bother investigators today.

In any case, they did a better job with the truck's description. Rob was able to add that a decal of a fish jumping out of the water was on the back window. He also spotted an X and a Y on the license plate, but the rest was too rusty to read.

The search started for Angela, but not surprisingly, Rob became the number one suspect in the disappearance. The Clinton police department only had one detective on staff, but he was determined to find Angela. He had doubts about Rob's story – it sounds like something out of a movie – but Rob passed a polygraph test with flying colors. Angela's parents insisted that Rob loved Angela and didn't believe for a second that he could have been involved. He was eventually cleared of any involvement in Angela's disappearance. But this didn't make him feel much better. His fiancé was still missing, and he was desperate to find her.

Angela's car was found in the parking lot near the phone she'd used. Her purse was still inside. Witnesses came forward and reported seeing the green truck – and the woman screaming inside. Rumors around town pointed toward Angela's former boyfriend, Bill Barker, but he also passed a polygraph test. Even Rob spoke up for Barker, insisting that he wouldn't have hurt Angela either.

But none of the reports led to any clues. The investigation went nowhere, even after the state police and the FBI were brought in to assist.

Angela's disappearance stunned the small town. Volunteers led searches, hung flyers, and went door to door, trying to help the police find information.

The Missouri State Police tried to track down the green truck but found over 1,500 vehicles that matched the partial description that Rob had given them. Volunteers pitched in from other police departments in the region, but the investigation stalled again.

And this time, it went cold – for years.

Over the decades, several theories have emerged about Angela's case, including that she was taken by mistake because the kidnapper thought she was someone else.

The theory was that the kidnapping was tied to testimony offered in court by a confidential informant in a massive illegal drug operation. When the identity of the informant was revealed during a preliminary hearing, he received a cut-and-paste ransom note – like one from a kidnapping movie – in the mail. The note addressed the informant by name and the code number

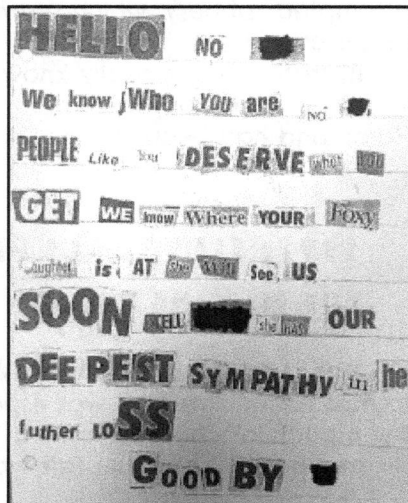

he'd been given to protect his identity. It also mentioned the informant's estranged wife by her first name. The letter had been mailed on April 4 – the same day that Angela Hammond was abducted. The note read:

HELLO NO. (informant's code number)

WE KNOW WHO YOU ARE. PEOPLE LIKE YOU DESERVE WHAT YOU GET. WE KNOW WHERE YOUR FOXY DAUGHTER IS AT. SHE WILL SEE US SOON. TELL (name of wife) SHE HAS OUR DEEPEST SYMPATHY IN HER FURTHER LOSS. GOOD BY

The informant's estranged wife and his daughter –also named Angela – lived in Clinton at the time. She even bore a striking resemblance to Angela Hammond. Investigators believed the meth dealers wanted revenge against the informant and kidnapped his daughter – but got the wrong girl.

It's theorized that when the mistake was discovered, the dealers killed Angela rather than have her reveal any details of their operation. Tragically, this is a very likely theory. A major drug problem remains in western and southwestern Missouri even today, several decades later.

This isn't the only theory that exists, however. Others believe a serial killer took Angela, or perhaps it was a random attack or an attempted robbery, which seems unlikely since her purse was still in her car.

In truth, no one really knows anything for sure.

More than 30 years after she vanished, no trace of Angela Hammond had been found.

1992: SIDETRACKED BY LIES

THE MISSING PERSON CASE OF MISTY COPSEY

THE FAIR CAME TO TOWN TWICE A YEAR, but Misty didn't want to miss either date. She was especially excited about this fall. She'd been back in school for only a few weeks but already wanted the distraction she knew the fair would bring. It was, without a doubt, the biggest attraction in Puyallup, Washington, and there was no way she'd miss it.

She spent days begging her mother, Diana, to let her go to the fair with friends, and eventually, Diana relented. Misty could go on September 17, she said, as long as she had a safe ride home. Diana worked the night shift and couldn't pick her up. Misty promised her mom she would take the last bus from the fairgrounds that night.

But Misty didn't catch that last bus. She missed it, and she hasn't been seen since. More than 30 years later, what happened to Misty remains a mystery that no one has been able to solve.

MISTY COPSEY WAS BORN ON MARCH 10, 1978, and had a bumpy childhood. Her parents separated and divorced when she was young, and she mostly lived with her mother, who'd later be described as a functioning alcoholic. Diana Smith had a history of DUIs and a conviction for welfare fraud – she'd been collecting food stamps while employed. She was doing her best to raise her daughter, but her somewhat sketchy past would get in the way of her search for her daughter.

Misty Copsey

On September 17, Misty went to the fair with her 15-year-old friend, Trina Bovard. They spent most of the day doing what normal teenagers do – they rode the rides, consumed a large quantity of lemon shake-ups, and ate a lot of sugary and deep-fried food. At the end of the evening, the two girls had already agreed to find their own rides home. They split up. Trina would walk a mile-and-a-half to her home, and Misty would catch the bus to her home in Spanaway.

But she missed that 8:40 P.M. bus.

The last known sighting of her was by a Pierce Transit bus driver who encountered her as she was looking for a bus home. Unfortunately, the buses had stopped running by that time. He gave her instructions on how to catch another bus that ran later, and with that information, she walked away, found a payphone, and called her mother about her predicament. Diana worked at night as a caretaker for an older woman and could not leave.

Knowing this, Misty told her she might get a ride from an 18-year-old friend named Rheuban Schmidt, but her mother objected. Diana didn't trust Rheuban and told Misty to find someone else to help her. She asked Misty to call her back and let her know whom she was riding with.

But Misty never called.

As far as we know, Misty decided to walk the eight miles home. Perhaps she had called around but had no luck with other rides – no one knows. But we know that a witness spotted her around 10:00 P.M. in downtown Puyallup, walking along Meridian toward the westbound onramp of Highway 512.

After that, she vanished.

When Diana got home the next morning, she discovered Misty wasn't there. She had never come home after she'd talked to her the previous night. She began making telephone calls to family members and friends, but none of them had heard from Misty, and none of them knew where she was. Diana's next call was to the police – who had little interest in a girl they quickly assumed had run away.

It didn't help that the Puyallup police were familiar with Diana Smith. They'd arrested her a few times for drunk driving, plus there was the incident a few months earlier when Diana had called to report Misty missing the first time. Diana couldn't find her daughter one day earlier in the summer and had filed a missing person report with the authorities. She later found Misty asleep in her bedroom but never called the police – likely because there was liquor involved – to let them know her daughter wasn't lost.

Now, when Misty really had vanished, her report wasn't taken seriously. It was assumed that she had run away from home, and Diana was told that if she didn't return within 30 days, she should call back.

At some point, though, an officer did ask around about Misty and was told by a classmate that Misty had called her and told her she was okay. Another classmate claimed to have seen Misty on September 21 at a concert. Because of this, the police were convinced their initial suspicions were correct – Misty had run away. It would later be discovered that neither classmate knew Misty well, and one of them admitted that she had made up the story because she wanted to be popular.

However, based on what they told the officer, the authorities never opened a case and falsely told the media that Misty had been found.

It wasn't until December that the police grudgingly accepted the idea that Misty met with foul play. Months had passed, and they still hadn't interviewed the two people who had been with or may have talked to Misty that night – her friends, Trina and Rheuban.

When they finally spoke to Trina, they discovered an arrangement had already been made with Rheuban to pick her and Misty up from the fairgrounds. The bus had been a backup plan, and Misty had lied to her mother. But when the time came, Rheuban said he couldn't do it because he didn't have enough gas. Misty called him back and told him how to get inside her house so he could get money and buy some gas, but Rheuban still refused to come. He said he didn't even have enough gas to get to Misty's house, which was six miles from his own.

So, the girls parted ways – Trina walking home and Misty catching the bus, she said. But this didn't line up. Misty had already missed the bus by then, which was why she called her mother.

Later, the police would discover that Trina had lied to them about how she got home that night. She hadn't walked. She'd gotten a ride home from her boyfriend, 23-year-old Michael Rhyner. Trina tried to get Misty to go with them, but Misty declined. She didn't like or trust Michael. Although he didn't have a criminal record as an adult, he had been accused of kidnapping an 11-year-old girl when he was 16. He hadn't been charged, but there was no question he was a creep – and Misty knew it.

Detectives speculated that Michael returned to the fairgrounds after dropping Trina off at home and convinced Misty to get in the car with him. Michael denied this, passed a polygraph, and was eliminated as a suspect.

Investigators interviewed Rheuban Schmidt next. He admitted that Misty had called him on the night of her disappearance and asked for a ride home. He confirmed all the aspects of Trina's story but then added something else – he said he'd suffered from blackouts for most of his life and couldn't remember anything after that second phone call from Misty. He said he woke up the next morning alone at his grandmother's farm near Enumclaw, Washington.

When detectives asked if it was possible he'd blacked out and hurt Misty, he answered, "I don't know." Rheuban was given a polygraph exam, but the results were inconclusive. Investigators believed he was trying to influence the results by attempting to put himself to sleep.

Rheuban seemed to have something to hide, investigators believed, especially after they spoke to his roommate, James Tinsley. According to James, Rheuban had left their apartment with his uncle soon after the second phone call from Misty. He assumed they were going to pick her up. Rheuban – who'd initially lied about leaving the apartment – now admitted that he'd left, but he and his uncle went to a party, not to pick up Misty. What about his blackout? He now claimed that happened later.

At that point, the already sluggish investigation slowed down even more, and balls continued to be dropped. For instance, the woman who allegedly last saw Misty at 10:00 P.M. in downtown Puyallup was never questioned by police, and no record of her tip exists today. The woman is still unidentified, which leads many to wonder if the sighting ever occurred and, if it did, if the girl was even Misty.

Rheuban Schmidt, who remained a person of interest in the case, sold his car to a wrecking yard for unknown reasons in the middle of the investigation. No one bothered to check it out. Michael Rhyner also sold his car in April 1993, but the police forensically examined it. The results of the exam, though, are unknown.

While police investigators conducted periodic searches for Misty throughout the last days of 1992 and into early 1993, her mother and volunteers organized most of the searches. One of these private groups made a chilling discovery on February 7, 1993, nearly four months after Misty vanished.

Covered in mud and rolled up in a ditch near the intersection of State Highway 210 and Weyco Road near the Mud Mountain Dam area, they found Misty's underwear, jeans, and one of her socks. The items looked like they'd been exposed to the elements for a long time. Laboratory analysis showed there was no blood or semen on the clothing, but there were three red paint chips on the jeans.

Of course, those paint chips have since been lost.

In 2009, a DNA test was performed on the jeans, and curiously, the DNA profile didn't match Misty but came from an unidentified male instead.

Then, on February 20, Misty's hair pick and toothbrush were found a half-mile from where her clothes were discovered. These were items that she always carried in her purse.

Misty's mother, Diana, confirmed that the clothing, hair pick, and toothbrush belonged to her daughter. Tragically, she became convinced this meant that Misty was dead – although she never stopped looking for her daughter. After 27 years of searching, Diana died in 2020.

Meanwhile, lies told by various people mixed up in the case continued to keep Misty from being found.

WHILE MISTY'S CASE WAS STILL DRAGGING ON, Rheuban Schmidt continued to be a menace. He had been telling co-workers that he knew where Misty's body could be found – six miles from where searchers discovered her clothes.

What else was six miles from the site? His grandparents' farm, where he said he woke up the day after Misty vanished.

When investigators got wind of his claims, they questioned him, and Rheuban admitted that he'd made the statements. He said they were untrue, though, and he'd made them up to get people "off his back." He agreed to take another polygraph exam, and this time, he passed.

But that didn't take him off the list of persons of interest in Misty's case. In the years that followed, Rheuban was accused of rape by a friend of Misty's, but after two weeks, she dropped the charges. He was convicted of theft in 2000, and his wife obtained an order of protection against him in 2006, saying he'd threatened to kill her and burn down her house.

Rheuban Schmidt remains a wild card in this case. His numerous lies and different versions of his alibi seem as though they should have been major red flags to any competent investigators – and perhaps they were. However, if so, many questions about him remain unanswered.

When Rheuban woke up at his grandparents' farm the next day, was his car there? And if so, did it have gas in it? Did the police ever search it? My guess would be no since it was not searched before he sold it to the wrecking yard, which destroyed it.

Was the grandparents' property ever searched? Were they interviewed? Who was the uncle he "went to the party with?" Was he ever questioned?

A tip that was received by the police in 1993 – that was likely never investigated – claimed that Misty was spotted getting into a yellow Chrysler Cordoba with an older man who had a history of sexual assault on young women. The man was never publicly identified, but in December 2015, an anonymous person who claimed to be a relative of Rheuban Schmidt said there was a closely held family secret about Misty's disappearance. They claimed Rheuban and his uncle were in the yellow car that night, and they picked up Misty. Was this true? No one knows. The anonymous tipster was never heard from again.

There seems to be a lot missing from the records, and little information is available about the interviews that investigators conducted.

It's almost impossible to consider this case "thoroughly investigated," which is likely the reason – or at least one of the reasons – why it remains unsolved.

THERE HAVE BEEN SOME WHO HAVE SUGGESTED that perhaps Misty's disappearance was a crime of opportunity for a predator or serial killer. In 1992, hitchhiking was still common enough that people did it every day. It wasn't seen as dangerous as it is today. Picking up a young woman walking along a highway wasn't hard to do back then.

This theory should've put a potential suspect named Robert Leslie Hickey on investigators' radar – but it didn't. Hickey had abducted and raped a young girl on January 10, 1993. He'd picked her up not far from where Misty was last seen near the fairgrounds. When he was finished with her, he dropped her into a ravine, but fortunately, she survived, and Hickey was arrested and sent to prison for the next five years. A few years after he was released, he tried the same thing with another woman, who also survived. He was convicted again and, this time received a life sentence.

So, we know that Hickey did the same thing twice – picked up a young woman, raped her, and then tried to kill her and dispose of her body at the same time. Were there other incidents when he was successful? Perhaps the young woman he attacked in January – just a few months after Misty disappeared – wasn't his first victim. What if Misty was? And what if his success emboldened him to try it again?

We'll never know. Despite the proximity of the January 1993 crime and the possible link to another young woman being lured into a car, Hickey was never questioned about Misty's case.

AND THEN THERE'S CORY BOBER, A TRUE CRIME fanatic who was obsessed with the infamous Green River Killer, a serial murderer who was responsible for the murders of numerous girls and women in King County, Washington, in the 1980s.

Cory Bober

Bober had spent years researching and investigating Green River Killer suspects, and he persistently harassed law enforcement with his ideas. He was convinced the killer was a man named Randy Achziger, who was later charged with child rape, but, as we know, he was not the Green River Killer. Gary Ridgway pleaded guilty to 48 of the Green River killings in 2003.

Prior to this, though, Bober claimed that Achziger told him a vital piece of information regarding the Green River killings that only the killer would know – information he, of course, never revealed. Bober personally investigated Achziger, going so far as to sneak onto his property looking for clues and having Achziger's ex-girlfriends record phone conversations to try and trap him. The police didn't take him seriously and dismissed him as having some sort of undiagnosed mental illness.

In the late 1990s, Bober linked Misty's case to the murders of Kimberly DeLange, 15, and Anna Chebetnoy, 14, believing that all three of them were connected to the still unsolved Green River killings. Kimberly had disappeared in 1988, and her body was found later that year. Anna had vanished in 1990, and her remains were discovered in 1991. Both girls had gone missing from the same Puyallup shopping mall, and their bodies were found within 100 feet of one another.

Because those girls were killed two years and one month apart, Bober suggested that another victim would be murdered two years and one month after Anna – and yes, Misty disappeared exactly when he predicted another girl would vanish. Bober later claimed he had tried to warn the police before that, but the authorities had no record of the call. This is not surprising since they never took him seriously.

Bober, though, had plenty of notes. Kimberly and Anna were taken from the same place and found along Highway 410, where Misty's clothes were found. The bodies were located about a 10-minute hike into the woods, though, and were not in relatively plain sight as Misty's clothing had been.

Eventually, Bober contacted Misty's mother, Diana, and told her everything he knew and explained his theories to her. They worked together for a while, and Bober suggested searching the area where Misty's clothes were found.

But it wasn't long before Bober's strange behavior – and his obsession with the Green River Killer – caused Diana and the police to suspect he might have been involved in Misty's disappearance and possibly the murders of the other two girls. He had a partial alibi for the night she disappeared and maintained his innocence. He had no criminal history of violence or sex offenses but did serve jail time on drug charges after Misty went missing. When questions about his guilt came up, he agreed to a polygraph exam but then canceled it at the last minute.

Cory Bober was certainly an odd individual but his true crime obsessions didn't make him guilty of anything other than annoying the cops. It's too bad they didn't listen to him, though, especially about the pattern created by the earlier murders. It's possible that Misty's disappearance could have been prevented if they had, but again, who knows?

In the end, it's possible that Cory Bober might have had some good ideas about the cases of the three girls, even if he was wrong about the Green River Killer. The evidence that connects Kimberly,

Anna, and Misty is compelling, and it seems possible that a serial killer could have been at work. Was it Randy Achziger? Did he fail twice but succeed with three other victims?

Maybe. I think it's certainly possible, even likely, that a killer was active around Puyallup in the late 1980s and early 1990s, kidnapping and killing vulnerable young girls.

But until we know for sure, the search for Misty goes on.

1993: LAST SEEN AT PIZZA HUT
THE VANISHING OF ANGELA FREEMAN

IT WAS AROUND 1:00 A.M. ON THE MORNING OF Friday, September 10, 1993, when Angie Freeman left the apartment of her friend Paula for the last time.

Angie left behind a note that said she'd be back soon, though she didn't mention where she was going. At 1:30, she stopped by Pizza Hut in her hometown of Petal, Mississippi, and spoke briefly with a former boyfriend, the store's assistant manager. A few minutes later, she left the restaurant alone.

Angie never returned to Paula's apartment and was never seen again.

Early on Friday afternoon, Angie's uncle, Randy Freeman, was driving on Mahned Road outside the nearby town of New Augusta when he spotted Angie's silver Honda hatchback. The car was empty, parked close to the Old Mahned Bridge, a historical landmark that spanned the Leaf River.

Randy stopped behind Angie's car, got out, and walked up to look inside. The driver's window was rolled down, but no one was inside or around the vehicle. Concerned, Randy quickly got back in his truck and went home. As soon as he arrived, he called Angie's mother, Debra Stewart, and told her what he'd seen. When Debra could not reach her daughter, she instantly knew something was wrong. She called the police and told them that Angie's car had been found abandoned and she was missing.

And the police did nothing. After all, it was obvious to them that 17-year-old Angie had run away.

Angela Freeman

But they didn't know Angie – and they didn't know about the baby she was carrying at the time she vanished. If they had, perhaps things would have turned out differently.

ANGELA FREEMAN WAS BORN ON JANUARY 16, 1976. She grew up close to her mother, which isn't surprising since Debra was only 17 herself when her daughter was born. Plus, Angie's father was never involved in her life. This meant that the mother and daughter – both just children – learned to depend on each other.

When Angie was three, Debra married, and a second child – a son named Nicholas – soon followed. The marriage didn't last, though, and two years later, the couple divorced, leaving Debra a single mother of two. Nicholas later said that Angie was always very protective of him growing up. They were half-siblings, but neither acted like it. They loved each other. "She was my big sister. She never let anyone mess with me," he laughed. "She let people know, 'You don't mess with my brother.'"

Friends said Angie was a homebody. Although she enjoyed going out with friends, she preferred spending time at home. Her mother recalled that she'd come home from work and go straight to her room and watch television.

In her sophomore year, Angela dropped out of high school and started working at Crystal's, a local restaurant. But she loved people and loved children and started studying for her GED so she could become a nurse – and then her plans were partially derailed.

Four months before she vanished, Angie discovered that she was pregnant, which meant big changes were coming into her life. It's unclear whether she still planned to pursue her studies, but friends and family were adamant that she was excited about becoming a mother and was looking forward to the future. She had been doing everything possible to ensure that her pregnancy was healthy, and no one, especially Debra, believed she would have voluntarily run off while pregnant.

Or would she? It would turn out that Angie's personal life was a little complicated. The relationship with her baby's father had recently fallen apart. He had started dating someone else and told Angie he was not interested in raising a baby with her. In addition, it would be revealed that Angie was trying to get back together with an ex-boyfriend, who also told her that he wasn't interested.

Would Angie have run away, as the police believed? Her family and friends insisted that she wouldn't have, but it is understandable why some would feel it was possible.

DEBRA HAD LAST SEEN HER DAUGHTER ON Wednesday, September 8. Angie, Nicholas, and their mother were all at home that afternoon. Debra and Angie were chatting in the kitchen, and Angela told her that she was going to stay with her friend Paula for a few nights. Angie and Paula had recently been discussing getting an apartment together.

Debra remembered those last moments very well. "She said, 'I'm going to Paula's,' and she left. When she got to the door, I said, 'Be careful.' And she said, 'I love y'all.' And she walked out of the house."

That was the last time Debra ever saw her daughter.

Two days later, on Friday, September 10, Angie's boss called the house to see if she was home. She hadn't shown up for her 6:00 A.M. shift at the restaurant. Worried and knowing that Angie never missed work, Debra called around to see if anyone had seen her. One of those calls was to Angie's ex-boyfriend, Steven Lindsay, who worked at Pizza Hut but told her he hadn't seen Angie that day. At the time, he didn't mention that he'd seen her hours before. Apparently, that didn't seem important at the time.

Later that afternoon, Angie's uncle spotted her car while driving near the abandoned Mahned Bridge. Angie was nowhere to be found. He called his sister, Debra, and she rushed to the scene. She had no idea why Angie would have been out in that area. As far as she knew, her daughter had no friends nearby. The bridge was about 15 miles from Petal and was in another county. The old bridge was in Perry County, while Petal was in Forrest

(Above) The Mahned Bridge

(Left) Angie's car was found parked near the bridge, even though she had no reason to be there.

County – which would cause the investigation to become even more complicated.

After making more calls, hoping someone knew where Angie was, Debra and Randy contacted the Perry County Sheriff's Office.

But Perry County sheriff's detectives weren't all that concerned at first. According to Debra, they dismissed Angie's disappearance as a runaway case. "Forrest County was ready to put dogs out there right then, but Perry County wouldn't let them. The sheriff told us to just take the car home. We asked them if they needed fingerprints or anything, and they said no."

"At the time, we didn't see any indicators of foul play," said one sheriff's detective. He asked Debra if Angie could have been partying or drinking, but Debra had to explain that this was impossible – she was pregnant. The cops didn't seem to take that seriously either.

Angie's stepfather, Bill Stewart, came to help get the Honda home. He pointed to a small red puddle near the car and asked deputies if it was blood. One of the deputies poked at the puddle and assured Bill it was just transmission fluid.

Perry County Sheriff Carlos Herring refused to comment on the case, only saying, "We don't just go on rumors around here."

Meanwhile, investigators with the Petal Police Department – who'd learned of the disappearance and were trying to lend a hand – were never even notified that Angie's car had been found. They weren't given a chance to search for potential evidence before it was moved. They believed that Angie's disappearance seemed suspicious.

Petal Police Sergeant Kent Wade told the press, "She didn't take a toothbrush, make-up, clothes...nothing. She didn't have any extra money. There was nothing that said she was planning not to come back." He also noted that, shortly before she went missing, Angie had made her car payment and stocked up on groceries. She'd also bought baby clothes and had a paycheck waiting for her at work. These weren't things a person planned to do if they were running away.

By Monday, there was still no word from Angie, and her loved ones were growing increasingly concerned. She was a very responsible young woman, and after missing several shifts at work, everyone started to fear the worst.

Over the weekend, the police departments in the two different counties continued to work against each other. Officers in Petal were busy investigating the case while the Perry County Sheriff's Office continued to do nothing.

Finally, around 5:00 P.M. on Monday, a reporter called Perry County and asked what was being done to find a 17-year-old girl who had gone missing from their jurisdiction. The threat of bad publicity finally seemed to get Sheriff Herring moving. He sent officers with search dogs to the bridge area, and the dogs immediately went to the puddle that Bill Stewart had pointed out to deputies on Friday afternoon. The puddle was dry at this point – thankfully, there'd been no rain – but the dogs' handler collected a sample to be sent for analysis.

On Tuesday, a search and rescue team brought in from Louisiana scoured the area for any possible clues to Angie's whereabouts. The only thing they found was her shoes – a pair of white Keds sneakers. One shoe was found in the tall grass near her car. The other was discovered on a nearby private road.

Divers with the Forrest County Sheriff's Office – the counties were finally cooperating -- were sent into the river to search for any sign of Angie's body but found nothing.

On Wednesday, investigators with the Petal Police Department were finally able to search Angie's car, which had been sitting at her mother's house. They processed the car for fingerprints, finding only one they couldn't identify. In the car's ashtray, though, they found two bullets. Since Angie didn't own a gun, how they got there was a mystery. On the back windshield of the car, investigators saw what appeared to be blood. It had dripped down to the back fender. They took a sample and sent it away for analysis.

Petal detectives were working the case from their end, interviewing Angie's friends and relatives. They found no one who had any idea what had happened to her. Police Chief Wayne Murphy had become convinced that Angie wasn't the kind of person who would disappear without contacting anyone and directed his investigators to trace Angie's last steps as closely as possible.

Investigators determined that after leaving her mother's house on Wednesday afternoon, she had gone to stay with her friend Paula, as she'd told her mother she would do. On Thursday evening, Paula left Angie at the apartment and went to visit a family member. When she arrived home later, she found Angie's note. In it, Angie said she was going to visit her ex-boyfriend at Pizza Hut, where he worked. She also wrote that she'd be back later and asked Paula to leave the chain undone so she could get back into the apartment.

Angie had gone to Pizza Hut to speak with 23-year-old Steven Lindsay, her former boyfriend. He was the restaurant's assistant manager, and Angie occasionally stopped by to visit him while he was at work. He claimed she wanted to get back together with him, but he wasn't interested.

Other employees at Pizza Hut confirmed that Angie had stopped by the restaurant to see Steven, and they said they'd last seen the couple talking outside around 1:00 A.M. as the rest of the staff was leaving for home.

According to Steven, while talking to Angie, he suddenly remembered that he had forgotten to reset a computer program so it would be ready when the restaurant opened the next day. He went back inside to take care of it and told detectives, "When I came back out, she was gone, which was typical of her. I didn't think anything about it."

Just five hours later, Angie would fail to show up for her shift at work.

Detectives also questioned another of Angie's ex-boyfriends, 21-year-old Larry Posey. He and Angie had dated briefly and still spoke occasionally, but he had nothing to add to the investigation. However, he told a reporter that he thought Angie had staged her disappearance. "I think she's trying to get attention," he said. "I hope she's okay."

Investigators also spoke with dozens of Angie's friends, trying to determine where she had been in the hours leading up to her disappearance and why she would have been in Perry County. Friends said that while Angie did have some relatives in Perry County, she had only recently started driving and likely wouldn't have known how to get to the area around Mahned Bridge.

Suzanne Lindsey - who had gone to high school with Angie and was the younger sister of Angie's former boyfriend, Steven - didn't understand how Angie had gotten there and doubted she could find her way around that area. She knew Angie well but admitted to reporters that they hadn't always gotten along. "I had some iffy feelings about her, mostly because she was dating my brother. But I could really talk to her about a lot of things." Suzanne initially thought Angie left on her own. "At first, I thought she was just hiding out, trying to get some attention, but now I don't know."

Suzanne said she knew that Angie's life hadn't necessarily worked out the way she'd hoped, but she still had dreams for the future. "She talked a lot about wanting to be a nurse. She had things planned out so she could do it. She tried to get her life back on track and it never really worked out right. I think mostly she just wanted somebody to love her."

As the search continued, Angie's family became more and more convinced that she was a victim of foul play and were angry about the way the Perry County sheriff had initially handled the investigation.

As Debra bluntly said, "I guarantee you if it were the sheriff's daughter, he would have done it differently."

ANGIE HAD BEEN MISSING FOR A WEEK WHEN the search for her was scaled back. The dive teams who dragged the Leaf River found nothing, and the search dogs had no further luck. Perry County investigators said they would continue to walk the banks of the Leaf River in case anything new surfaced, but there would be no more large-scale searches unless new information were received. The river hadn't been high at the time, officials said, and the current wasn't swift. If a body had been placed in the water, they believed that searchers would have found it.

On September 19 – always willing to try and show up the Perry County sheriff – the Forrest County Search and Rescue Team returned to Mahned Road. Using search dogs, they pinpointed an area of the river where they believed Angie's body might be found. Crews searched the river in that area but found no trace of Angie.

The official searches may have been called off, but Angie's family and friends continued to look for her near Mahned Bridge. They spent countless hours combing the riverbanks and the nearby woods for Angie's purse or car keys. Those items had not been in the car when it was found, and search teams had been unable to locate them. Bill Stewart maintained they walked the area "inch-by-inch" but found nothing.

Grim news arrived on September 24. Detectives learned that the red substance found on Angie's car and in the sand near it had been positively identified as human blood. Although additional testing would be needed before officials would know if it was Angie's blood, the finding was an ominous one.

Two days later, Petal and Forrest County search teams returned to the Leaf River for another search. This time, they moved a large blockage of tree logs in case Angie's body had snagged underneath them. Although cadaver dogs indicated there was a body in the water, the search again came up empty.

Three weeks after Angie was last seen, Bill and Debra were forced to admit to reporters that they believed Angie was dead. They feared she'd been murdered and her body thrown into the river. The cadaver dogs continued to alert on the area, but the searches that followed discovered nothing in or around the river. Bill and Debra had been a constant presence at the bridge, watching as the search teams combed the area for clues each day. They continued this silent vigil until September 30, when they decided it was time to return to their jobs.

But Debra would be unable to stay away. By March 1994 – when Angie would've given birth to her baby – Debra quit her job so she could devote all her time to the search for her daughter. Even though detectives told her the investigation was at a standstill, she was convinced that someone knew something. Hoping to raise money to offer a reward, Debra decided to organize a massive rummage sale, which turned into two – one in May and one in July. She managed to raise $5,000

She continued to do whatever she could to find answers. As the first anniversary of Angie's disappearance drew close, Debra contacted a psychic who told her that Angie's body was buried in the woods within a few miles of where her car was found. The psychic believed Angie had been stabbed to death. Debra's brother, Randy, went out to the area with a friend who had a trained search dog, but they didn't find anything.

Years passed, and Debra eventually resigned herself to her daughter's not coming home. She hadn't gotten over the bitterness about how the investigation had been handled when Angie was first reported missing. She felt that if the Perry County Sheriff's Department hadn't waited four days before starting the search, Angie would have been found. "I'll always believe that," she said. "If they had done their job and brought those dogs out there, I just believe we'd have known something."

However, the search continued with or without Debra's knowledge, even though the case had long grown cold. In June 1997, investigators searched a gravel pit in Perry County after a tip that Angie's body might be buried there, but they didn't find anything. Sheriff Herring admitted that the search had been a long shot. Most of the tips they received were nothing more than rumors, but it was worth checking out. Debra wasn't notified of the search until after it took place. As you can imagine, she wasn't happy about that.

Other bloody events in the area grabbed the public's attention, and many wondered if they could be connected to Angie's case. In May 1995, a young couple – Robbie Bond and William Hatcher – were brutally slain at Mahned Bridge, but authorities were quick to assure the public that there was no link between the crimes.

Cousins Kenneth and David Moody were arrested and charged with the murders and sentenced to life in prison.

By 1999, Angie had been missing for six years, and investigators still had no idea what had happened to her. However, cold case detectives resubmitted the blood collected from the side of the road and Angie's vehicle for DNA analysis. The tests proved what Debra had suspected all along -- the blood belonged to Angie. While those few drops of blood couldn't confirm that Angie was dead, those close to the case had suspected as much for years. They knew they were most likely dealing with a homicide.

In 2001, those suspicions seemed to be confirmed. Human skeletal remains were found along an old logging road in Perry County, and the first thought was that Angie had been found. DNA testing proved otherwise, however. The remains were not Angie. Forensic analysis determined the skeleton was that of a woman between 20 and 35, but she has never been identified.

The fight to find Angie continued for Debra in the years to come. In 2002, she held a memorial service for her daughter. "I don't want people to think I'm giving up," she explained. "I'm not. But it's been more than eight years, and I need to give her something."

In November 2011, she raised money to have a billboard about the case placed in Perry County and continued to offer a reward for information leading to Angie's recovery. She hoped this might bring in some new tips, but Angie's case remained unsolved.

But not for the lack of effort. 2006, the Pine Belt Cold Case Unit was formed to assist local law enforcement agencies with unsolved cases. The unit was headed by Southern Mississippi Police Assistant Chief Rusty Keyes, who prioritized Angie's case. "We continue to work on the case, and we hope in the near future to have enough information to submit a case to the District Attorney's office. This case is an active case. I believe it's a very solvable case."

Detective Keyes stated in 2021, "We have interviewed everybody in her life." But they hadn't. Neither Angie's family nor the authorities knew who the father of her unborn child was. The police are unable to say, even now, if he's a person of interest because his identity remains unknown.

Even so, Detective Keyes was confident that new leads were still being tracked down. He said the threads were still loose, and he just needed to find a way to tie them all together. He felt they were on the verge of clearing the case.

And in November 2021, it seemed he was right.

Perry County Sheriff Mitch Nobles announced that Angie's case had been turned over to the county district attorney for evaluation. Although he didn't want to say much for fear of jeopardizing the investigation, he believed the case would finally be solved.

It wasn't.

Unfortunately, it turned out that they didn't have enough evidence to prove that any one person was responsible for Angie's disappearance, so no charges were filed.

The case once again went cold, but in 2023 – the 30th anniversary of Angie's vanishing – Detective Keyes remained hopeful. "The case continues," he said. "We have worked on several leads over the years. We hope we're going to get some resolution and some conclusion."

As time goes on, Debra Stewart has said that even though more than 30 years have passed since she last saw Angie, she is still haunted by her daughter's disappearance.

"It's something that never goes away," she said. "You wake up thinking about it. You go to bed thinking about it. You have good days, and you have bad days. The only thing that really keeps you going is that she's in a better place than we are."

1998: LOST AT SEA

THE DISAPPEARANCE OF AMY LYNN BRADLEY

HAVE YOU THOUGHT ABOUT TAKING A CRUISE SHIP VACATION?

If you have, no one can blame you. They seem a fun and luxurious way to knock a few locations off your world travel bucket list. Plus, they're filled with interesting people from all walks of life, all-you-can-eat buffets, all-you-can-drink bars, dance clubs, and every kind of off-the-boat activity you can imagine on tropical islands and in exotic cities.

Booking passage on a cruise ship is like getting a ticket to paradise on the sea. Right?

Well, not always.

Even if we leave out the seasickness, claustrophobic cabins, overflowing sewage, secret morgues, bedbug infestations, and failing grades from the Centers for Disease Control, I've got some facts for you that may make you want to stay on land.

The chances of a ship sinking are slim, but it's not an impossibility. And I'm not talking about *Titanic* in 1912. I'm talking about recently – several dozen cruise ships have sunk since 1980. One of the worst was in 1994, when 800 people died on a ship that sank in the Baltic Sea. In 2012, a cruise ship hit some rocks off the Italian coast, partially sinking and killing 32 people. Its captain was found guilty of manslaughter in 2015.

Even more common than a ship sinking is a ship getting stranded somewhere. In March 2019, more than 1,300 passengers were left stranded when a Viking Sky luxury cruise ship ran into engine trouble off the coast of Norway. Over 400 people had to be rescued from the boat, and 28 ended up in the hospital.

People die during cruises, too – and more often than you might think. There were 623 deaths on cruise ships between 2000 and 2019. That count stopped *before* the COVID-19 pandemic, during which cruise ships became a hotbed for outbreaks. For passengers, the most common causes of death before the pandemic were cardiac arrests, followed by suicide.

But don't worry, there's a plan for when it happens. Ships are legally required to carry body bags and maintain a morgue – not visited during shipboard tours – and they typically have room for three or four bodies. Need more space than that? The contingency plan is the kitchen's walk-in freezer.

Cruises seem to be an escape from reality, but crime happens on board, too. Most reported crimes are, unfortunately, sexual assaults. But other things can happen, just like anywhere, when you put that many people into one confined space.

Of course, that's not to say that all cruises are bad. Hundreds of thousands of people take trips on cruise ships every year and have a great time. They come home with wonderful memories and souvenirs from faraway places.

But what about those people who don't come home at all?

On March 24, 1998, a young woman named Amy Lynn Bradley vanished from a Royal Caribbean cruise ship while it was on its way to Curacao.

She has never been seen again.

AMY BRADLEY WAS 23 YEARS OLD IN MARCH 1998, when she and her brother, Brad, agreed to join their parents, Ron and Iva, for a cruise that would take them from Puerto Rico to Aruba and then to Curacao in the Caribbean islands of the Dutch Antilles.

Amy had been reluctant to go along on the trip when her parents first asked her about it. She was just about to start a new job at a computer consulting firm, and it wasn't the best time for a getaway. After some convincing, though, she agreed, accepting the trip as a nice way to get some downtime before she started working.

Amy Lynn Bradley

Amy was born in 1974 in Petersburg, Virginia, and was the oldest of Ron and Iva's two children. Her younger brother's name was Brad – so yes, he was Bradley Bradley – and the family was very close. In fact, Amy and Brad were more like best friends than siblings, doing almost everything together.

Amy was described by all who knew her as friendly and outgoing with short, brown hair, green eyes, and several noticeable tattoos – like the Tasmanian Devil on her shoulder, the sun on her lower back, and a tribal-style gecko lizard that curled around her pierced navel.

She had always been athletic and earned a degree in physical education from Longwood University. She had attended school on a full basketball scholarship. Beyond that, she had worked as a lifeguard for many years and was a very strong swimmer, even though she feared open water, which is surprisingly common for swimmers.

The trip started great, and on March 23, the third day of the cruise, the family rented a Jeep in Aruba and enjoyed the sights. Later that evening, they had dinner together, but Amy and Brad left the restaurant early to return to the ship.

Amy with her brother, Brad, and parents, Ron and Iva, before her disappearance.

The pair spent the evening visiting many of the bars on board. There were seven of them in 1998, along with numerous restaurants, two massive pools, hot tubs, spas, fitness centers, game centers, and more. They reportedly enjoyed drinking and dancing with other passengers and even members of the ship's band, Blue Orchid. Amy spent a lot of time with the bass player, Alister Douglas, who went by the nickname "Yellow." This was later confirmed when the authorities looked at a video from that night filmed by a camera crew making a promotional video for the cruise line.

Around 1:00 A.M., Amy and Brad called it a night. They returned to their family's cabin together. Brad recalled, "The last thing I ever said to Amy was 'I love you' before I went to sleep that night. Knowing that's the last thing I said to her has always been very comforting to me."

Brad never saw his sister again.

AROUND 5:30 ON THE MORNING OF MARCH 24, Amy's father, Ron, glanced out at the cabin balcony and saw Amy relaxing on the deck. He looked out again a half-hour later, and she was gone. Ron went to his daughter's bedroom to see if Amy had gone back to sleep, but she wasn't there. Aside from cigarettes and a lighter, it didn't appear that Amy had taken anything with her. She hadn't even taken her shoes.

Concerned, the family searched the common areas of the ship. Amy was nowhere to be found. They became increasingly worried and begged the cruise ship staff to postpone the docking at Curacao, but the request was denied. They couldn't halt the ordinary operations of the entire ship for one young woman who could be anywhere onboard. The crew even refused to page Amy until the ship was in port. The gangplank was lowered, and passengers and staff members were allowed to leave the ship.

Did Amy leave with them? If so, this would have been her chance to disappear. She could have left the ship on her own. After the public was alerted to her disappearance, several people came forward after seeing her photo and reported seeing her that morning. None of those sightings, though, were ever confirmed.

The Bradleys refused to believe she would run away. Amy had a new job, a new apartment, and a beloved dog, Daisy, back in Virginia. Nothing in her life suggested that she was unhappy, and she was not the type to frighten her parents by just leaving without telling someone.

But if Amy hadn't left on her own, then she must have been kidnapped. This meant that her abductors had the same chance to leave the ship when the passengers did – unnoticed, unseen, and with Amy in their possession.

The Bradleys essentially conducted their own investigation on the ship without the crew's help. They continued to search and speak to fellow passengers, and most were eager to help.

Several witnesses said they had seen Amy around 6:00 A.M. with bass player Alister Douglas near the ship's dance club. One of the witnesses said that Douglas handed Amy a cup of what looked like coffee. Douglas denied that this encounter occurred.

One passenger tracked down a cab driver who said he saw Amy off the ship. He later reported that she had approached his cab that morning and said she urgently needed a phone. This sighting was also never confirmed.

Meanwhile, the Bradleys were still frantically searching the ship – and the crew remained unhelpful. Although they did agree to page Amy over the intercom once the ship docked, they refused to announce her disappearance or even hang photos of her on board because they didn't want to upset the other passengers.

By afternoon, the captain had eventually – and reluctantly -- ordered the ship to be officially searched, but only to a degree. He allowed only a search of the common areas, not the passenger or staff cabins.

The crew suggested that Amy had fallen overboard. But even if she had, Amy was a strong swimmer and a trained lifeguard. There was no evidence that she had fallen or been pushed, but the Dutch Antilles Coast Guard offered to search the ocean near the ship anyway. After four days, though, they found no sign of a body in the water. Ultimately, the local authorities believed the most likely conclusion was that she fell overboard, whether accidentally or because she jumped.

Amy's family refused to believe that. They knew there was something more sinister about her disappearance than someone merely lost at sea. When she disappeared, the ship had been very close to shore, and no one had seen or heard anyone falling overboard. She hadn't vanished by accident – they were sure of it.

The Bradleys began to suspect that some staff members knew more than they were saying. They believed some of them had given their daughter "special attention." At one point, before the ship had gotten to Aruba, Ron remembered one of the servers asking for Amy's name, saying he wanted to take her to a bar called Carlos and Charlie's when they docked there.

Carlos and Charlie's in Aruba, one of the last known locations of Amy – and of American tourist Natalee Holloway a few years later in 2005.

When he asked Amy about it, she said, "I wouldn't go and do anything with any of those crew members. They give me the creeps."

Ron didn't think much of the incident then, but he'd remember it later. It turns out that Carlos and Charlie's was the bar that American tourist Natalee Holloway disappeared from a few years later in 2005.

But the investigation into Amy's whereabouts – both the family search and the official one – went nowhere. On March 29, the Bradleys had to return home without her, but they were nowhere close to finishing the search.

In the following days, weeks, and months, the Bradleys wrote to members of Congress, foreign officials, and the White House. With no official help at this point, they hired private detectives, launched a website, and started a 24-hour hotline. Even with the promise of rewards for information, no worthwhile leads appeared. Similarly, when the FBI got involved in the case, every lead seemed to be a dead end.

And then, in August 1998 – five months after she went missing – the first new sighting of Amy was reported to the Bradley family. That first alleged encounter wasn't all that strange, but the ones that followed would be much more unusual and frightening.

THOSE WHO SAW HER IN AUGUST 1998 – IF IT really was Amy, of course -- were Canadian tourists on vacation in Curacao. The couple, David Carmichael and his wife, were on the beach when they noticed a woman with two men nearby. The woman reacted to hearing the Carmichaels speaking English and walked toward them. The woman appeared to be terrified, they later said. It looked as though she was about to say something, but suddenly, one of the men she was with signaled for her to walk away and gave the Carmichaels a threatening look.

The woman and the two men walked over to a nearby café, so the Carmichaels followed and grabbed a table near them on the patio deck. David later reported that the woman continued to stare at them as if trying to get their attention, but eventually, the trio left.

It wasn't until the Carmichaels were back home and saw a story about Amy Bradley that they became convinced she was the woman on the beach. They were even positive that she had the same tattoos that Amy had.

David called the FBI and the Bradley family, and they worked with him to try and confirm the sighting. He even submitted to a polygraph exam and passed it with flying colors. He was interviewed multiple times, trying to glean all the information out of the incident that was possible, but unfortunately, it led nowhere. No one could track down the woman, but it gave the Bradleys hope that Amy was alive.

Then, five months later, in January 1999, a second sighting of Amy occurred which was much more disturbing than the first. Unfortunately, though, no one would know about it until several years later.

A Chief Petty Officer in the U.S. Navy claimed that he encountered Amy at the Stellaris Hotel in Curacao. According to his story, he was sitting in the hotel bar when a woman approached him because she recognized him as an American. She told him that her name was Amy Bradley and that she was being held against her will. Could he help her? The officer later claimed that he didn't understand what she was trying to tell him. He didn't know who Amy Bradley was or that she was missing, and he brushed her off. Then, two men approached the woman and demanded she go back upstairs.

The officer returned to his ship and didn't think much about the encounter – until July 2001. That was when he saw the face of the woman who'd asked him for help on the cover of *People* magazine. He was stunned when he realized she had been the missing Amy Bradley.

Even so, he said nothing. He didn't call the FBI or report the sighting until he retired from the Navy. The Stellaris Hotel was off-limits to U.S. military personnel. He wasn't supposed to be there because it was a known brothel. Rather than risk getting in trouble to help a woman in danger, he'd stayed silent until he was out of the service.

Years had passed when he finally came forward.

As upset and disappointed as they may have been, the Bradleys refused to give up hope, sadly allowing people to take advantage of them. In the fall of 1999, Ron and Iva received an email with another promising lead – or so it seemed at the time.

A man named Frank Jones claimed to have information about where Amy was. He was a former member of the U.S. Special Forces, and he said that Columbian gangsters were holding Amy hostage on Curacao. He had a team of ex-Army Rangers and ex-Navy Seals ready to go in and rescue her – for a price. The Bradleys were taken in by the ruse because Frank kept feeding them what seemed to be solid information.

He told the Bradleys that he had an eyewitness who'd recently seen Amy in person. The witness, a cook, had noticed Amy's unique tattoos and recalled hearing Amy sing a song that her mother used to sing to her when she was little.

Frank told them two of his soldiers knew exactly where Amy was right now, but he needed money to get a team in to rescue her and get her back to the States.

Wisely, the Bradleys wouldn't blindly turn over the kind of money that Frank said he needed. They asked for proof of life, and he sent a photo. It wasn't great, but it looked like Amy, so they were in. They wired him $210,000 to bring their daughter home --

$24,000 of their own money and $186,000 from a fund established for Amy's search by a group called the Nation's Missing Children Organization.

The money was sent, and Frank told the Bradleys to fly to Florida and wait for further instruction. They waited a week at their hotel before discovering the whole thing was a hoax. One of the hired soldiers in Curacao became suspicious. He was being fed the same story by Frank and was instructed to keep up surveillance on a house where Amy was supposedly being held. He never saw Amy or anyone who looked like her the whole time he was there. Eventually, the story fell apart, and one of the soldiers called the Bradleys in Florida, exposing the scam.

Frank Jones was a con artist. He had never located Amy, and the woman in the photo was an acquaintance photographed with a blurry lens. Not only had he ripped off the Bradleys, but he'd cheated a charity for missing children.

Frank was arrested and eventually pleaded guilty to mail fraud. He was forced to pay back the money he'd scammed but only received a five-year jail sentence, which didn't make up for the pain and anguish that he'd caused Amy's family.

But more seemingly legitimate sightings were still to come.

AMY'S CASE WENT QUIET FOR THE NEXT SEVERAL YEARS. No new leads were coming in, and while the Bradleys tried to remain hopeful that Amy was still alive, they were struggling.

Then, in 2005, a woman named Judy Mawer was on vacation in Bridgeton, Barbados, and while using a bathroom stall, heard two men and a woman enter the bathroom and loudly start to argue. She waited a few minutes until she was sure the two men had exited the bathroom before she came out of the stall. She found a woman at the sink who was very upset and crying. She said her name was Amy, and she was from Virginia and needed help. Before Judy could do or say anything, the two men barged back into the bathroom and forcibly removed the young woman.

Judy contacted the FBI but couldn't offer any evidence or clues to help find the woman she'd met. She could only say that she was sure "Amy from Virginia" matched the photos she'd seen of Amy Bradley.

And then came the photographs.

The photo of the sex worker obtained by the Bradleys in 2005. Members of an organization that located sex trafficking victims believed it was Amy.

That same year, the Bradleys received an email from a member of an organization that locates sex trafficking victims on adult websites. It contained two photos of a woman who strongly resembled Amy, aside from the fact that her hair was longer and she looked older, as would be the case since nearly a decade had passed since she vanished.

In the photos was a woman identified as "Jax." She was wearing lingerie and was posing on a bed. It had been found on a website that advertised "all-inclusive erotic vacations" to the Caribbean. A single package was about $3,000 and included free access to sex workers.

At first, the family was unsure if the woman was Amy. She looked distressed, sad, and tormented, but when they hired an independent forensics expert to examine the photos, he told them numerous markers in the images were a perfect match for their daughter. This is subjective evidence, though, and there's no definitive proof this is Amy – but even so, it was unsettling.

It also seemed to confirm a fear that the Bradleys had since the day Amy vanished – that she had been taken off the cruise ship that morning and sold into the sex trade industry. Based on some of the other sightings of Amy – and now these photos – they couldn't help but believe the worst.

Once again, though, this unsettling clue led nowhere.

In 2010, a human jawbone washed up on a beach in Aruba. Initially, it was feared that it belonged to Natalee Holloway, but a single tooth that remained on the jawbone ruled out any connection to Natalee. However, examiners were able to determine that it came from a Caucasian woman – although they never tested it against Amy's DNA or anyone else's. It's become one more missed opportunity in this tragic case.

It was in 2010 – 12 years after she vanished – that Amy was legally declared dead. While there is no active investigation, the Bradleys still hope that someday they'll find out what happened to their daughter. They continue to believe she didn't fall overboard that morning, she didn't jump, and she wasn't pushed.

They hope that she is still alive and may someday return to them. If she is alive, Amy would be in her early 50s at the time of this writing, which sadly is likely far longer than a sex worker under slave-like conditions would be kept alive.

But hope remains alive for the Bradleys. If there is even the smallest chance that they can ever bring Amy home, they'll keep trying and praying that the mystery of her vanishing will someday be solved.

1999: OKLAHOMA'S TWO LOST GIRLS
LAURIA BIBLE AND ASHLEY FREEMAN

OKLAHOMA IS NO STRANGER TO GHOST TOWNS.

Scores of formerly bustling small towns across the state died when the local industry – usually mining or drilling – went bust, leaving no money or reason for anyone to stay. There are dozens of towns like this in Oklahoma, with a few scattered buildings, which are the only reminders of what once was a thriving community.

But the town of Picher is different.

It was once a bustling mining town near the Oklahoma-Kansas border. Built around zinc and lead mining, the small town contributed to war efforts during World War I and World War II. For years, the materials mined ensured Picher had a booming economy. It was once home to nearly 20,000 people, and at the time, the residents had no idea that their town was slowly killing them.

The hills of what appeared to be gravel that loomed over the town consisted instead of waste from the lead and zinc mines that were filled with toxic chemicals. As the years passed, the waste

The abandoned town of Picher, Oklahoma played a chilling role in the disappearance of two young girls.

from the hills and the mines seeped into the water supply and became hazardous to the town and its residents.

And where there weren't poisonous hills and bad water, there were sinkholes. Mine tunnels slowly began to collapse, opening cavities so large that in 1967, a sinkhole consumed nine houses on a single street. The highway into town had to be closed to large trucks after one driver was killed when the street opened beneath him.

After the Environmental Protection Agency declared Picher the most toxic town in America, authorities issued a mandatory evacuation – which some residents chose to ignore despite the risks to their health.

But it gets worse. A devastating tornado hit the town, killing six people and injuring 150 others. More than 20 blocks in town suffered extreme damage from the storm, destroying most of the struggling businesses that were left.

The local school closed, the homes fell silent, and soon, there was little left in Picher but overgrown foundations, some crumbling buildings, a rusted water tower, and a lot of crude, spray-painted signs that marked some of the structures as government property.

The abandoning of the town went on for years, and even while sitting there eerily among the empty lots and crumbling structures, a few families refused to leave. Lights burned in their windows, satellite dishes could be seen in their yard, and children's toys and bikes were in their driveways.

Picher eventually breathed its last, but not before the ghost town played a role in one of the most tragic disappearances in the region.

In December 1999, two 16-year-old girls – Lauria Bible and Ashley Freeman -- vanished during a sleepover to celebrate Ashley's birthday. By the following morning, the Freeman house was in flames, Ashley's parents were dead, and the girls were gone. Friends and family have been looking for them ever since, although years later, one of the killers in the case confessed to what he'd done with the bodies of the two girls.

He claimed he'd taken them to Picher, and they were never seen again.

Lauria Bible and Ashley Freeman

IT WAS WINTER IN OKLAHOMA, A TIME OF year that long-time residents like to call "relentless." The days are short, the nights are long, and the wind can be punishing across the flat, wide, gray land. For newcomers, it's miserable, maybe even unbearable, but for natives, it's ordinary. It's the same thing every year, or so it seems.

That's why, on a cold December morning in 1999, when a fire engulfed a home in Welch, no one could have predicted how out of the ordinary the rest of that winter would be.

On December 29, 1999, 16-year-old Lauria Bible made plans to spend the night at the home of her best friend, Ashley Freeman, for the second night in a row. The two spent the day together, celebrating Ashley's 16th birthday with her mother, Kathy Freeman, who took them to get pizza.

Ashley and Lauria had been best friends for years. Lauria was about six months older than her friend. She was born on April 18, 1983, and her mother, Lorene, said that once she started, she never stopped. Lauria also never met anyone she didn't like. She wasn't a fan of sports, but she loved cheerleading. She even started a babysitting service and created a kit filled with coloring books, crayons, Disney movies, and all sorts of activities for the kids. When Lauria came to babysit, the children always knew she'd bring "the kit."

She was a sweet girl, always funny, always fun to be around, and, according to her mother, rarely in trouble. "I never had a problem out of her," Lorene later said.

After pizza that day, the girls returned to the Freeman home, where Lauria left her car. But knowing that Lorene and her father, Jay, didn't like her to drive after dark, Kathy took Lauria by her house to ask her mom if she could spend one more night with Ashley. Lorene didn't think twice about it. She just made Lauria promise she'd be back in time for her dental appointment the next morning. She kissed her mom, hurried back out to Kathy's car, and they drove off into the night.

But the next morning never came; that was the last time Lorene ever saw her daughter.

THE CALL CAME IN AROUND 5:30 A.M. A passerby called the Craig County Sheriff's Office and reported that the Freemans' home was on fire. By the time the firefighters arrived, it was completely engulfed in flames. They quickly went to work, and the flames were out within an hour. Officials began poking through the charred ruins, looking for signs of possible victims.

Lorene Bible was at work when the fire occurred. She was surprised when she saw a deputy waiting to speak to her. She told him she'd been to the Freeman house and explained its layout, including where the parents' bedroom was and the bedroom the girls should be in.

"So, how bad is it?" she asked. "Have they found anybody?"

Lorene was informed that a body had been found in the home's front room. The body was that of a woman who had given birth and wore a ring.

It was Kathy Freeman.

At the scene, Agent Steve Nutter from the Oklahoma State Bureau of Investigation, Undersheriff Mark Hayes, deputies from Craig County, firefighters, and other officials searched through the smoldering rubble for the two girls and Ashley's father, Danny. Three cars belonging to Lauria, Danny, and Kathy were parked in the driveway.

Once they arrived at the Freemans' property, Jay and Lorene were forced to wait with curious bystanders, hoping for information about their daughter. But the authorities didn't have any. They'd found no other remains in the house – only Kathy's. At one point, Lorene asked one of the investigators if they were certain there were no other bodies in the fire. She was told they were 100 percent certain that only Kathy's body had been found.

At that point, officials assumed Kathy had died from the fire. They were unaware that she'd been shot in the head and murdered before the house was burned to the ground.

THROUGHOUT THE DAY, THE AUTHORITIES SEARCHED the property for clues about where Danny and the girls might be but found nothing. Agent Nutter released the scene to Danny's stepbrother, Dwayne Vancil. Since they found no other remains, investigators left the scene with a working theory – that Danny killed his wife and then fled with Ashley and Lauria.

In less than 24 hours, they'd find out they were wrong.

Meanwhile, reported sightings of Danny and the two girls came pouring into the sheriff's office. But instead of looking for the girls, investigators spent the night questioning friends and family, planning to follow up on the sightings the next morning.

That would seem like a strange choice to most of us, but the Freemans, as it turned out, were no strangers to law enforcement.

Rumor had it that Danny was involved in both the marijuana and the meth business, and there were also reports that his temper had caused several previous brushes with the law.

To make matters worse, the story of Danny and Kathy's son, Shane, was well-known to local law enforcement officers. After several run-ins with the law and a short crime spree, Shane had developed his own reputation in the area. On January 8, 1999, Shane was shot to death by a sheriff's deputy after stealing a car. The shooting was ruled to be justified, which angered friends and Freeman family members, who disagreed with the version of events offered by the authorities.

This led to rumors of a feud between law enforcement and the Freemans, who had threatened to file a wrongful death lawsuit against the sheriff's department. Danny's stepbrother, Dwayne, later claimed that Danny confided in him that deputies harassed him and attempted to intimidate him.

Danny and Kathy Freeman

True or not, rumors were swirling, and it's believed that law enforcement was treading very carefully with the investigation into the fire and the missing man and the two girls. Of course, that led to frustration from family members, who wanted to know what was being done to find the girls. However, all they found were answers that led to more questions.

The following day, after being questioned by the police, Jay and Lorene returned to the fire scene to search on their own for clues that could lead to their daughter, Ashley, and Danny. By then, the crime scene tape had been torn down, and all that remained of the house were piles of charred rubble and the lingering smell of smoke.

Moments after they began searching through the ash and debris, Jay made a shocking discovery. Covered in shoe prints – having obviously been stepped on dozens of times the previous day – was another burned body.

It was Danny, and he'd also been shot in the head.

Unable to get a signal, Lorene went down the road and called 911. She identified herself and told the dispatcher to send the OSBI and sheriff's deputies back to the Freeman property because she had found another body.

The woman on the other end of the line asked Lorene to repeat what she'd just said. She repeated, "There was another body in that fire." She hung up and returned to the ruins of the Freeman house.

The authorities rushed back to the scene, hopefully feeling as incompetent as they seemed to be. Trying to regain control of the scene, they ordered Jay and Lorene to go back down to the road and stay out of the way, but Lorene refused to go. "This no longer your scene," she told them. "It's ours. You turned it over to the family last night."

This put Lorene and Jay right in the middle of the investigation that followed. What some dubbed the "Bible Bureau of Investigation" began searching for Lauria and Ashley alongside law enforcement investigators.

In the days that followed, tips that came in prompted searches in nearby bodies of water – and even in some mine shafts in Picher. The case was also featured on both *America's Most Wanted* and *Unsolved Mysteries*, but the authorities were no closer to finding the girls than they were in the house after the fire.

Lorene was adamant that she wouldn't give up. She told *America's Most Wanted* host John Walsh that she would go wherever she needed to go and do whatever she needed to do to get her daughter back.

What no one knew at the time, though, was that no true answers would be revealed in the story until 2017 – or that most of the pieces of the puzzle were found in the days right after the girls vanished, including the identities of the men who took them.

TO WEAVE THIS TOGETHER, WE HAVE TO INTRODUCE two more characters into the story – private investigator Tom Pryor and his friend, a bounty hunter named Joe Dugan.

While combing through the Freeman property, looking for clues, they came across a woman's car insurance verification card. Not wanting to cause trouble, Pryor tried to give the card to sheriff's deputies, who were also at the scene. They weren't interested, although they might have been if they knew that this card would break the case wide open in the years to come.

The insurance card belonged to a woman who was the girlfriend of a man named Warren "Phil" Welch, a dangerous criminal with a long rap sheet who ran around with two other lowlifes named David Pennington and Ronnie Busick.

Since the officers on the scene didn't take possession of the card, Pryor and Dugan tracked down the car to which the insurance card belonged. It led them to a salvage yard, and, with permission, they searched the vehicle. Soon after, Pryor reported the vehicle and his finding to law enforcement but was told the car had gone through too many hands to be processed for evidence.

So, once again, Pryor and Dugan continued to investigate on their own. Within a few weeks of the fire, they interviewed the woman whose name was on the insurance card. When asked about Welch, she "clammed up," saying that she was scared Welch would kill her if she talked.

Two weeks after that, they interviewed Welch, and this interview led them to believe that Welch, Pennington, and Busick were involved in the murders and kidnapping of the Freemans, Ashley, and Lauria.

Once again, Pryor tried to take what they'd discovered to law enforcement, and this time, they were told to stop investigating the Freeman case. They were interfering in police business, he was told, and if they didn't end the investigation, his private investigator's license would be revoked.

There was nothing more that Pryor and Dugan could do. Unfortunately, there wouldn't be anyone competent involved in the case until 2011 when Gary Stansill, an investigator for the Craig County District Attorney, took over the search for the killers and kidnappers.

He would later learn that after Joe Dugan died in May 2009, one of his relatives took his box of investigative material pertaining to the Freeman case to the Craig County Sheriff's Office, and they refused to take it. It was eventually destroyed.

It would turn out that the answers everyone had been looking for were right under their noses all the time – just like the killers were.

AFTER GARY STANSILL TOOK OVER THE CASE, HE began digging through all the old files, which eventually led to the insurance card that had been recovered by Pryor and Dugan a few days after the fire. He'd eventually get help from Pryor in wrapping up the case, but at this point, he was on his own.

The insurance card led him to the same suspects named by Pryor and Dugan and would take him into Kansas and to the nearly abandoned town of Picher.

In January 2011, Stansill interviewed another of Welch's girlfriends who reported that Welch cooked methamphetamine and confirmed his association with Pennington and Busick. While living together, she had overheard conversations between the three men about the people "who were killed in Welch, Oklahoma."

During these conversations, it was stated that they "had owed them money and had been murdered for that debt. They had taken the two girls that were missing from Welch with them and eventually killed them. Pennington and Busick indicated they had set fire to the home of the murdered people."

Even more horrific, the woman stated that Welch kept a briefcase containing Polaroid photos which showed both girls "bound and gagged with duct tape and lying on a bed," with Welch lying next to the girls in some of the photographs. A bedspread in the photographs was identified as one belonging to Welch, further linking him to the missing girls.

The girlfriend added that a missing poster of Ashley Freeman and Lauria Bible had been hung on the wall in Welch's house in Picher. After the woman saw the poster, she was certain the girls in the Polaroids were the same as the girls on the poster.

She added that the three men had claimed to have raped and tortured the girls before disposing of their bodies "in a pit" or mine shaft in Picher.

The interview with the woman offered Stansill some leads, but as far as evidence goes, it was all hearsay. He needed a lot more, but it would be years before he found it.

It wasn't until 2016 that he finally received more information and leads about Welch, Pennington, and Busick. The bad news was that two members of the trio were dead -- Welch died in 2007 and Pennington in 2015. But there was still Busick and, of course, two missing girls.

Stansill's information came from one of Pennington's former girlfriends, who told him that Pennington had threatened her on many occasions and promised to "throw her in the pit with the girls" if she ever told anyone what she knew. She had been too afraid to talk while he was alive.

Another witness interviewed in 2017 told investigators that Busick "started running his mouth" about his involvement in the Freeman murders, as well as the kidnappings of Ashley and Lauria. According to Busick, the girls had been kept alive for several days before they were killed. And though he claimed he hadn't shot the Freemans, Busick did admit to staying behind with Pennington and setting the house on fire. Welch had allegedly been the one who shot Danny and Kathy.

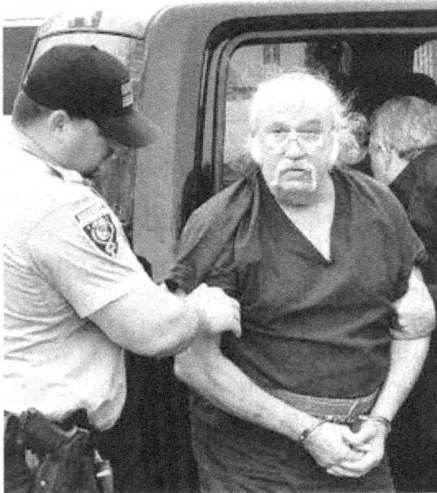

Ronnie Busick was arrested for his part in the murders in 2018.

Stansill also took an affidavit from Tom Pryor, who recounted the information he and Joe Dugan had collected years before and had attempted to deliver to the authorities.

Finally, Stansill and OSBI Special Agent Tammy Ferrari brought in the last living suspect, Ronnie Busick. They interrogated him three times, and despite the evidence and statements against him, Busick tried to maintain that he didn't know where Ashley and Lauria were but admitted to "hanging around" with Welch and Pennington back in the day.

On April 23, 2018, Busick was arrested and charged with four counts of first-degree murder, two counts of kidnapping, and one count of first-degree arson.

After his arrest, Busick told reporters that he wanted to speak with the Bibles, and on April 26, Lorene confirmed that she met with him, but he denied knowing Lauria and Ashley's whereabouts.

A competency hearing was held for Busick in 2019. The jury deliberated for only 45 minutes before finding him able to stand trial for the murders of Danny and Kathy and the kidnapping and presumed deaths of Lauria and Ashley.

But the case never went to trial. On July 15, 2020, Busick pleaded guilty to being an accessory to first-degree murder in the deaths of Danny and Kathy Freeman, the burning of their home, and the presumed slayings of the two girls. He was sentenced to 15 years for his crimes – 10 in prison and five on probation.

Believe it or not, Busick was released early for good behavior and was released on May 19, 2023, after serving just 38 months of his 10-year sentence.

The light sentence he received, though, was supposed to be dependent on leading investigators to the bodies of the missing girls.

"Our hope is just to find the girls," Jay Bible said. "All this time, we've sat here and waited on him. He started out, 'I don't know nothing about it.' Now, he talks like he knows something. So, let's find out what he knows."

It turned out he didn't know much. Or he claimed he didn't, anyway.

In October 2021, a new search was conducted in the root cellar of a home

Despite the arrest of Ronnie Busick, Ashley and Lauria have remained missing. Many of the searches for their remains have occurred in Picher. Investigators are shown here at the sealed entrance to one of the old mines.

formerly occupied by David Pennington. Investigators claimed that Busick kept repeating "the root cellar," and Pennington's stepdaughter alleged that he had forbidden anyone from going down there.

But the search turned up nothing. The two lost girls were still missing.

BUT EVEN AFTER ALL THESE YEARS, LORENE Bible has refused to give up. She has led the way to ponds, sinkholes, basements, and even to the Mexican cartels.

After she heard a rumor that the girls had been sold as sex workers in Mexico, she found a source to investigate the tip for her. The source told her that one day, a visitor would find her, without notice and seemingly at random, and give her answers. A year and a half later, Lorene was at work and turned around when someone asked for her by name. She confirmed that she was "Mrs. Bible."

"Are you Lauria's mama?" the person asked.

She said that she was.

Lorene Bible's search for her daughter continues today.

"She's not there," the person said, and they were gone before Lorene could ask any questions. The source had come through – the girls were not in Mexico.

But Lorene remains fearless and undeterred. Since that terrible night in December 1999, she had been dismissed, threatened with arrest, warned about retaliation by associates of the three killers, justifiably added to the controversy about how the investigation was initially handled, and been part of the debate about Busick's sentencing.

Lorene isn't worried about any of that. Her focus is still on the same place it was in 1999. "I want the focus to be on the girls. When you take the focus off the girls, then it isn't about the girls. So, all about the rest, that will come when I'm done. But the main focus is the girls," she has said.

Gary Stansill's investigation continues, too. Over the past several years, numerous searches have been conducted for the missing girls using ground penetrating radar, excavation crews, dive teams, and cadaver dogs -- all with the hope of bringing those girls home.

Far too many of those searches have taken the investigators to the desolate ruins of Picher. On several occasions, they have used drones and high-tech cameras to go into the mine shafts, many of which have been closed off for years.

So far, all the searches have come up empty.

But Gary Stansill, Lorene Bible, the investigators, friends, and family – everyone involved in the case – are convinced that someone out there knows something. The case has haunted the people involved, much like it has been haunting what's left of Picher since 1999.

This nearly forgotten town should give up its secrets before there's nothing left of it, and the people who know what happened to those girls are as dead as Picher will soon be.

This mystery deserves to be solved, and it is a story of two girls – Lauria and Ashley – that deserves an ending.

2000: ON THE ROAD

THE VANISHING OF LEAH ROBERTS

IN DEATH, HE BECAME A LEGEND.

His name was Christopher McCandless, and in 1991, he left the real world behind and began wandering the American West, working when he needed money to support his simple lifestyle and exploring the world outside of the normalcy of everyday life. He aimed to make it to the Alaska wilderness, where he planned to live off the land and become one with nature.

It turned out to be Chris's final journey.

Four months after he left civilization, hunters found his painfully thin body huddled in a sleeping bag inside an abandoned bus that had been used for shelter. Chris likely died of starvation, but whatever happened, he died there after walking into the wild.

A young woman named Leah Roberts walked off into her own oblivion almost a decade later. After losing both her parents and surviving a near-fatal car crash, the 23-year-old became determined to live her life to the fullest. For her, that meant dropping out of school and embarking on a soul-searching journey inspired by Beat Generation writer Jack Kerouac, who spoke of a simple life on the road.

Without telling anyone, Leah withdrew money from her savings, left her hometown of Durham, North Carolina, and began a cross-country trip toward the Pacific Northwest – where she eventually vanished.

Did she end up like Chris McCandless, sacrificing her life for an unattainable ideal? Or is she still out there somewhere, living her best existence under another name or somewhere off the grid?

No one knows. Her family and friends maintain that Leah Roberts has never been seen again.

LEAH ROBERTS WAS BORN ON JULY 23, 1976, to Stancil and Nancy Roberts. The youngest of three children, she grew up in Durham, North Carolina.

The Roberts kids had an ordinary life growing up in the 1980s and '90s. Durham was a nice town, and Leah did well in school, had many friends, and was close to her family, which made the

Leah Roberts

events that began when she was 17 even worse. That year, her father was diagnosed with a life-threatening respiratory disease that put him in and out of the hospital for most of the year. Two years after that, her mother, Nancy, unexpectedly died from heart disease.

Leah, who was then a sophomore at North Carolina State University, was shattered by her mother's death. She took time off to be with her family and didn't return to school until fall 1998.

Soon after returning to school, Leah was involved in a near-fatal car accident when a large truck turned in front of her. Unable to stop quickly, she slammed into the truck at full speed. She was so badly hurt that she narrowly pulled through, suffering a punctured lung and a femur that was broken so badly that she had to have a metal rod placed in her leg.

Leah considered the accident to be a life-changing moment for her, and she spoke of it as her "second chance."

She was still attending North Carolina State University and threw herself into her studies and as many outside activities as possible. She played soccer and spent a semester studying abroad in Spain. When she returned, she signed up for a field study program in Costa Rica and planned to leave when tragedy struck again. Her father, Stancil, who had been dealing with his condition for years, passed away in 1999.

Once again, Leah was devastated, and it's unclear from her later actions if she ever really recovered from the loss of both parents in such a short amount of time.

But she announced that she would continue with her trip to Costa Rica, saying that it was what her father would have wanted. She packed her things and left for the study program, returning months later as a different person. She was now interested in "life's adventure," she said, and wanted to see the world. She had started writing poetry, began keeping a journal, and ultimately decided to drop out of school, even though she only had six months to go before graduating with degrees in Spanish and anthropology.

Although already a private person, Leah's trip to Costa Rica changed her. She pulled herself away from her core friend group and spent much more time alone. She learned to play guitar and took up photography. She also adopted a kitten that she named Bea.

On the morning of March 9, 2000, Leah received a telephone call from her sister, Kara, who wanted to see how she was doing. They spoke briefly, and Kara later said she seemed fine. Around 11:00 A.M., she also confirmed plans with her roommate, Nicole Weeks, for a babysitting job the next day.

When Leah didn't show up to babysit, Nicole didn't think much about it. The two young women had very different schedules and often went without seeing each other for a day or two. But by March 12, Nicole had become concerned. She'd had several calls from friends who'd been trying to get in touch with Leah. It didn't look like Leah had been home, and no one seemed to know where she was. The white Jeep Cherokee that Leah drove was missing from the driveway. Around noon that day, she called Kara, and the two of them spent the next 24 hours calling everyone who knew Leah, but to no avail.

On March 13, several of Leah's friends met Kara and Nicole at their house. Kara went through her sister's room and noticed what was missing – including her new kitten, Bea – and determined that she'd left voluntarily.

But there was still a problem – how was Leah's emotional and mental state when she took off? Kara worried that her sister, who'd been dealing with their parents' deaths and her own issues with the accident and school, might be suicidal. This prompted her to call the Raleigh Police Department and report her sister missing. It is, of course, not illegal for an adult person to voluntarily disappear, but given Kara's concerns about her sister's mental stability, the police took it seriously.

On March 14, Kara returned to the house shared by Leah and Nicole to take another look at her sister's room. She wanted to double-check and ensure she hadn't missed any clues about where she'd gone. During this second search, she found a letter Leah had left behind for Nicole. The note was pretty cryptic but had an upbeat tone, and with it was a drawing of the Cheshire Cat's grin and enough cash to pay Leah's portion of the rent and bills for a month. This led Kara and Nicole to believe that Leah would return soon.

The note left behind read in part:

This is enough to cover bills for while I am gone. Remember – everyone is together in thoughts and prayers and time passes quickly. Have faith in me, yourself.

No, I'm not suicidal. Remember Jack Kerouac?

The reference to Kerouac jogged Nicole's memory. She and Leah recently had a conversation about taking a cross-country road trip, like in his book *Dharma Bums*, which chronicled a trip to Whatcom County in Washington state.

Now that Kara had confirmation that her sister had gone off alone, she decided to check her bank accounts to see where she'd gone. When Leah had gone to Costa Rica, she'd given Kara access to all her accounts, and now, Kara put that access to use.

She discovered that Leah had withdrawn $3,000 from her bank account around 6:00 P.M. on March 9. She saw a motel charge in Memphis, Tennessee, the following day. A string of additional charges traveled west on I-40 until she hit California. At that point, she turned north on I-5.

The last transaction on her account was shortly before midnight on March 13 at a gas station in Brooks, Oregon.

While Kara had been scouring Leah's bank account, Nicole and her friends were busy canvassing the area closer to home. They came across a woman who regularly talked with Leah at the Cup 'O Joe coffeehouse. She said that Leah had recently discussed her wish to visit Desolation Peak in Whatcom County, Washington – the same location that Kerouac wrote about in *Dharma Bums*.

Leah Roberts had seemingly gone off to "find herself" without telling anyone where she was going. This wasn't a big surprise, especially in her recent state of mind. But her sister and her friends worried about one thing – what would Leah do when she finally reached this place she'd been dreaming of visiting?

WHILE LEAH'S SISTER AND FRIENDS WERE TRACKING HER journey on one side of the country, on the other side, a couple were out for a morning run in the Mt. Baker-Snoqualmie National Forest in Washington. They rounded a curve in Canyon Creek Road and discovered a white Jeep Cherokee that had been driven off the

Desolation Peak in Whatcom County, Washington – the same location that Kerouac wrote about in *Dharma Bums.*

road and down an embankment. They quickly called 911.

When deputies arrived on the scene, they initially suspected it had been abandoned by a drunk driver, which was somewhat common in the area. The Jeep had been badly damaged when it left the road. Windows were broken, the headlights were shattered, and the front fender had been badly twisted and bent. But on further examination, they found the scene was more unsettling than they first believed. They found that the now-broken windows had been covered with towels and clothing as if someone had shaded them so they could sleep in the vehicle. They also found clothing and other items, including a passport, checkbook, guitar, driver's license, and a pile of CDs.

The name on everything in the Jeep was Leah Roberts.

The authorities called in the license plate number on the Jeep to North Carolina and discovered it was linked to Leah's missing person report. Officers contacted Kara and put her in touch with the Whatcom County Sheriff's Office.

Kara was faced with the grim news that Leah wasn't just off on a journey – she was now truly missing.

As more Whatcom County Sheriff's deputies arrived on the scene, they began investigating the site and estimated that Leah's Jeep would've had to have been traveling between 30-40 MPH when it went off the road. That meant whoever was in the vehicle at the time would – or should – have been badly hurt. However, there were no signs of blood in the Jeep, nor were there any footprints leading away from the scene.

Even so, investigators wondered if perhaps Leah – or whoever was driving – wandered away from the scene after hitting their head or being injured in some other way. A check of area hospitals revealed no records of treating an injured or disoriented woman.

The forest was searched for at least a mile in every direction, but there was no sign of Leah or anyone else that could be connected to the wrecked and abandoned Jeep.

On March 21, Kara and her brother, Heath, arrived in Bellingham, Washington, to begin their search for their sister. Sheriff's deputies took them to the area where Kara's Jeep was found and allowed them to look at items found in the Jeep. Both noticed that while Bea's empty cat carrier was still in the car, the kitten was missing – along with Leah. Investigators also showed them a small keepsake box, and they discovered a movie ticket stub from a theater at Bellis Fair Mall in Bellingham. It was timestamped at 2:10 P.M. on March 13, 2000, and was a paid admission for the film *American Beauty.*

No one recalled seeing Leah at the movie theater, but Kara visited a mall restaurant, where two patrons remembered seeing her. One said she was open and kind and left the restaurant alone after eating.

The other customer had a different story. He was a mechanic with a military background and recalled that he'd chatted with Leah about Jack Kerouac and the reason for her trip to Washington. But he claimed Leah left the restaurant with a man he only knew as "Barry." He didn't know anything about him, but he did offer investigators an extremely detailed description. A sketch was released to the public, but investigators could not track him down, leading them to wonder if "Barry" existed at all. When they confronted the witness about this, he fled to Canada.

As missing person flyers were being plastered all over Bellingham, sheriff's investigators and FBI agents were doing a more thorough search of Leah's Jeep. They found a pair of jeans with $2,400 in one pocket and discovered her mother's engagement ring under one of the floormats. Kara assured them that Leah never took it off, leading investigators to theorize that she'd met with foul play.

A little less than a week after the Jeep was discovered, a man called the police claiming that he and his wife had seen Leah after the crash at a Texaco gas station in Everett, Washington. He said she seemed disoriented and didn't seem to know who she was. Unfortunately, the man ended the call before investigators could get additional details. Detectives believed the sighting was valid and that the man panicked during the call for unknown reasons – or wanted to help but didn't want to interact with the authorities.

During this time, searches took place in the Mt. Baker-Snoqualmie National Forest. Starting from Canyon Creek Road, an area was mapped out based on how far an injured person could travel on foot. Search dogs, ground personnel, volunteers, and helicopters were brought in to scour the area, but nothing was found. Investigators now began to theorize that Leah either wasn't in the Jeep when it crashed or that she hadn't been hurt in the accident.

As the search continued, other investigators began working backward through the charges on Leah's account. This brought them to the gas station in Brooks, Oregon, where Leah had stopped before going missing. Surveillance footage from the station showed her alone, but she continually looked out the door while waiting for the clerk to ring up her purchases. Unfortunately, no cameras were pointing outside, which means there's no way to know who or what Leah might have been looking at.

After the search of the forest was finally called off and tips and leads dried up, Leah's case started to cool off and then turned cold. Kara and Heath returned to North Carolina, and while they stayed in touch with investigators, detectives had little to offer them.

In 2006, cold case investigators decided to re-examine the Jeep to see if anything had been overlooked. The first thing they discovered was a clear fingerprint under the hood that had not been documented in 2000. They also found signs of tampering, including cut wires on the starter relay, which would have allowed the vehicle to accelerate without a driver at the wheel. Tampering could've been easily accomplished by a mechanic or someone with a knowledge of cars. This brought investigators back to the second witness at the restaurant, who'd been a military mechanic.

Working with Canadian authorities, they obtained his fingerprints and DNA. There was no match with the fingerprint under the hood, and in 2010, the DNA was tested against male DNA that was recovered from Leah's clothing. Once again, though, there was no match.

Then, in 2014, a body was discovered in rural Whatcom County. The remains had been exposed to the elements for years and had become partially mummified, making identification difficult. However, measurements revealed a person around five feet, five inches, only an inch shorter than Leah. More compelling, though, was the metal rod that had been inserted in the right leg of the body to repair a shattered femur. The serial number on the rod was traced to 1998, which lined up closely with Leah's accident.

But the problem with the discovery? The coroner and sheriff's investigators stated that the remains were of a man over 35, not a young woman.

Numerous people have theorized that the police made a mistake, claiming the remains had deteriorated too much to be properly identified, but there is no evidence of this. Deteriorated or not, science seems to make it pretty clear that the body doesn't belong to Leah Roberts.

SO, WHAT HAPPENED TO LEAH?

This is a case that is open to many theories, although they really fall into two categories – Leah was murdered, or she wasn't.

If she did meet with foul play, the main suspects seem to be the mechanic she chatted with at the restaurant or "Barry," if he was real. That doesn't necessarily mean that either one of them killed her. They just happen to be the only men found by the police who have any contact with her.

But regardless of who killed her, someone tampered with her car. Someone was under the hood of the Jeep and left a fingerprint there. They either caused her accident or cut those wires so that the Jeep could run off the road with no one inside, making it appear that an accident had occurred.

And that gives us two more options – that someone harmed Leah and then wrecked the car or that someone helped Leah to wreck her own vehicle so she could disappear and start a new life.

Based on how Leah had cut herself off from people after returning from Costa Rica, plus the death of her father and dropping out of college, it's possible she just decided to chuck everything and start over somewhere.

Of course, this also means we must consider that Leah came to the woods for one last adventure before ending her life. She stated that she was not suicidal, and if she did plan to die, why did she bring so much stuff with her to Desolation Peak, a place she was inspired to visit by her literary hero? It seems more likely that she was running away – or at least taking a long trip – than ending her life.

But, of course, the suicidal mindset isn't always logical. It could have been a goodbye trip, a place she'd always wanted to see before she died. After abandoning her Jeep, Leah could have walked off into the woods to die, and her body was simply never found.

Or maybe it was what it looked like all along. Maybe after wrecking her car, she was disoriented, wandered into the woods, lost her way, and succumbed to the elements. But why was there no blood in the car? If she'd hit her head hard enough to become confused, she'd have likely bled everywhere – as head wounds usually do. With the condition of the glass in the Jeep, it seems unlikely Leah could have escaped without at least some scratches.

Leah's case remains open today, and her story is filled with questions. Her fate remains a mystery, but hopefully, it's one that will someday be solved.

2000: TAKEN FROM HIS BED
WHAT HAPPENED TO ZACHARY BERNHARDT?

SOME KIDS JUST CAN'T CATCH A BREAK.

No matter how well-behaved they are, how well they do in school, and how much the neighbors like them, their situation, environment, and home life always seem to drag them down. All we can do is hope they manage to get free from the place where they're stuck and the people dragging them down by growing up and leaving it all behind.

But some kids never get to grow up.

That seems to be the case for Zach Bernhardt, a Clearwater, Florida, kid that everybody liked. The eight-year-old was an all-around good kid, cheerful, polite, and at the top of his third-grade class at Eisenhower Elementary School. He got good grades, his teachers raved about him, and he always had a smile on his face.

But behind that smile was a boy whose home life was filled with turmoil, drama, and constant upheaval. He had no relationship with his father, and his mother stayed just one step ahead of bill collectors and eviction notices by moving from one cheap apartment complex to another all over town.

Zach was a kid trapped in his mother's chaotic life of booze, cigarettes, late nights, and a string of assorted men. She loved him, but since she couldn't save herself, there seemed to be little chance she could save her son.

Eventually, he paid the price for the chaos.

Leah Hackett and her son, Zach, about two years before he vanished.

LEAH HACKETT WASN'T A MORNING PERSON. Her life seemed to start around 9:00 P.M. when her son Zach was on his way to bed. She worked at night when she had a job, but on Sunday, September 10, 2000, she didn't have anywhere to go and, feeling restless, couldn't fall asleep. According to her story, she decided to go outside and smoke a cigarette around 3:00 A.M. She said she glanced into Zach's room to make sure he was sleeping soundly, then went out onto the patio behind the apartment.

It was a hot, humid night in Florida, so Leah made a spur-of-the-moment decision to take a dip in the pool in the center of the apartment complex. She didn't have a suit on but shrugged that off, stripped off her shorts, and slipped into the water. She swam a few laps back and forth before getting out and walking back to her apartment. She opened the unlocked door and quietly re-entered the apartment, removing the wet clothes and changing into something dry. When she left her bedroom, she pushed open the door to Zach's room to check on him again – but he was gone.

Leah was horrified. She'd only been out for a few minutes. How could he be gone? She rushed into the bedroom, sure that he had rolled out of his bed, but he wasn't there. She cried out his

Zach Bernhardt in 2000.

name, searching frantically through his bedroom. She yanked open the closet door – he wasn't there either. She raced through the rest of the cramped apartment, calling out his name. He wasn't there! In a panic, she called 911 and reported Zach missing.

The police responded quickly, and when they did, Leah admitted that she had left her apartment unlocked when she left for the pool. She knew she wouldn't be gone long and was sure it would be okay since she wasn't leaving the apartment complex. She insisted that Zach wouldn't have left on his own. He always asked for permission before going anywhere. He was a very responsible boy with no history of wandering away from home.

As the blinding red and blue flashing lights of the police cars were bouncing off the complex's buildings, residents began gathering on the patios and sidewalks to see what was happening. Officers began asking questions and conducting a door-to-door search. No one objected. Those who knew Zach liked him – and probably felt sorry for him – and wanted to do what they could to help. Investigators searched empty apartments, looked into empty dumpsters, and scoured other apartment complexes in the area but found no sign of Zach.

Around 4:00 P.M. that afternoon, Deputy James Kaen from the Manatee County Sheriff's Office arrived at the complex with his search dog. The dog, Lonzo, was given several of Zach's items, and he followed a trail to a different apartment complex but lost the scent almost immediately. Lonzo spent an additional hour trying to pick up Zach's scent again but had no luck.

Detectives interviewed Zach's teachers, classmates, friends, and neighbors, but none of them offered any insight into his disappearance. Susan Dalton, a friend of Leah's who lived in the same Savannah Trace complex, said that all the neighborhood children knew and liked Zach and played together often. She told detectives that Leah was a good mother, noting, "She takes real good care of Zach. He's always polite and friendly. He always speaks to you when he passes and smiles."

But detectives probably should have talked to other neighbors, not just ones who were friends of the missing boy's mother. They would, but maybe not soon enough.

Jean Eubanks, the principal of Zach's elementary school, told investigators that Leah was very involved in Zach's activities and often volunteered to help at school events. "He was her whole world. We had no indication that anything was wrong."

Clearwater Police Sergeant Wayne Andrews told reporters that while they hadn't found any evidence of foul play, Zach's young age made finding him a top priority. Zach had only been wearing a T-shirt and boxer shorts when he was last seen and was mostly likely barefoot. He didn't have a bicycle, so he would've been on foot if he had left the apartment alone. Although he had no history of sleepwalking, investigators were open to every possibility.

At this point, the police hoped he was still nearby and would be quickly found.

Officers from six different agencies, including the FBI, the Florida Department of Law Enforcement, and the Tampa Police Department, assisted in the search for Zach. A helicopter crew was also dispatched to the area, and they spent hours flying over the county but found no sign of the missing boy.

While officers and volunteers continued pounding the pavement, detectives were quietly compiling an unnervingly lengthy list of the area's registered sex offenders. These "usual suspects" were rounded up and questioned, trying to find out if one of them was near Zach's apartment when he went missing.

They were grilled for hours, but nothing was found to suggest one of them had been involved in his disappearance.

On Wednesday, September 13, Leah made a tearful public appeal on television, asking the public for help finding her son: "He is a beautiful boy, inside as well as out. Anyone who has ever met Zach has loved Zach. We miss him. We love him very much. And we want him to come home."

Later that afternoon, the apartment complex and surrounding area were searched again, this time by cadaver dogs. Investigators were starting to fear the worst and thought it might be possible that Zach's body could be hidden near his home. Luckily, though, nothing was found.

Detectives also – for the first time since Zach was reported missing – searched Leah's apartment, taking fingerprints and DNA swabs and looking for any clues about Zach's fate.

Clearwater police spokesman Wayne Shelor told reporters that investigators were mystified by Zach's disappearance and noted that while they couldn't find evidence that a crime had been committed, they also didn't believe he'd run away or wandered off on his own. They'd found no signs of a struggle inside the apartment, and Zach's belongings seemed undisturbed.

Shelor also wanted to reassure residents of the Savannah Trace complex that police didn't think there was a threat to public safety at that time. He spoke through the press, saying, "There is absolutely no reason for anyone there to be fearful of an abduction or something like that. We have no evidence a crime was committed. We don't know why Zach is missing."

As the investigation dragged on and Zach remained missing, Leah fell apart. Hoping to raise her spirits, some of Zach's friends and young cousins sent her notes of encouragement. One read, "Zach was always good at hide and seek! Never stop hope! Our prayers are with you! As Zach always says, 'Don't worry, be happy!'" They could only hope that Zach's fun, playful, and sunny outlook on life would help him with whatever he was facing.

On Thursday, police officers, firefighters, and community volunteers gathered at the Eddie Moore baseball field in Clearwater. They broke up into small groups and searched through more than 500 acres of woods, trees, mangroves, and underbrush, looking for Zach. A few groups used boats to search the shoreline of Old Tampa Bay – but the entire day was spent in vain.

Zach was still missing.

By Friday, September 15, more than 1,000 acres of land surrounding the apartment complex had been searched, but Zach's whereabouts remained a mystery. Detectives spent the day reviewing the hundreds of tips they'd received and continued interviewing everyone associated with Zach and his mother. Many neighbors who hadn't been home when the incident occurred were finally tracked down, and many of the residents received second and third visits from detectives.

And that was when the focus of the investigation began to change.

ON MONDAY, SEPTEMBER 18, IT SEEMED THAT investigators were no closer to finding Zach than they had been a week earlier when he'd initially disappeared.

Leah's mother, Carole Bernhardt, spoke to the press, saying that Zach's family was frustrated and growing increasingly desperate for answers. She was terrified that the case would get cold, and she wanted to make sure no one forgot her grandson was still missing. The case had been in the headlines for the first few days, but now, the publicity was starting to fade after days had passed with no progress. She demanded to know, "No one is putting his picture out anywhere now… but how else will they find him if they don't keep getting his picture out?"

Meanwhile, police spokesman Wayne Shelor was also talking to the press. It was true that things had slowed down, but after spending the weekend talking to Leah's friends and neighbors, Shelor made an announcement that seemed to have an unusual tone to it.

The first thing he told reporters was that Leah was definitely *not* the subject of their investigation, even though they had just impounded her car so it could be processed for potential evidence. He assured the press that this was routine and didn't mean she was a suspect. He added, "We have spoken to her many times about the disappearance of her child. We haven't discounted what she has told us. We found nothing that disproves what she's saying."

Aside from the one public plea that Leah made for Zach's safe return, she had otherwise stayed out of the public eye during the past week. She hadn't commented on the case and had spent most of her time in her apartment with her mother and sisters, praying someone would call with the news that her son had been found. Denal Donnelly, one of Leah's sisters, told reporters that Leah believed someone abducted Zach while he was sleeping.

It seemed possible, but why wasn't Leah telling people this?

A little over a week later, on September 27, Wayne Shelor was back in the news with another statement that reversed what he'd earlier told the press.

The police were now taking a closer look at Leah.

Though Shelor refrained from coming out and calling Leah a suspect, he did express some issues. He told reporters, "From the beginning, the officers have had any number of concerns about the circumstances of his disappearance. Investigators don't believe they have the whole story from Zach's mother."

There was no question that almost all of Leah's friends and neighbors said that she was a dedicated mother who loved her son. However, a few of them had other things to say. They stated people were often coming and going from Leah's apartment, and she kept late hours with Zach at home. They also said Leah liked going out to bars at night when she wasn't working and usually left Zach alone at home when she did so. This was a common thing – including on the night Zach disappeared.

One neighbor told detectives that Leah couldn't have been smoking on the patio and taking a dip in the pool that night because she wasn't home. They said they saw Leah's car pulling into the parking lot after 3:00 A.M, insinuating that she had been at a bar when Zach vanished. Leah claimed this wasn't true – still insisting she'd been home all night.

But the more detectives dug into Leah's past, the more concerned they became. It turned out that Zach wasn't Leah's only child. She also had a six-year-old daughter with another man. Leah initially had full custody of the girl, but she was later removed from Leah's home and sent to live with her father in Michigan. He'd alleged that Leah went out drinking too much, leaving her children alone. A judge agreed and granted him full custody of his daughter.

Zach, unfortunately, had no father in his life and no one to look out for him.

While living with his mother, they'd stayed in several different apartments all over Clearwater before landing at Savannah Trace the previous year. Leah had been evicted from five different apartments for failure to pay rent. Five days before Zach disappeared, she received another eviction notice because she failed to pay rent again. Three weeks after Zach vanished, Leah quietly moved out of the Savannah Trace complex and moved in with one of her relatives.

Within a few weeks, the investigation into Leah was dropped. They couldn't find any evidence that she'd harmed Zach and, no matter what they may have believed, couldn't prove she wasn't home when he was taken.

Zach's case was featured on an episode of *America's Most Wanted* that fall. Investigators were hopeful that some national exposure would bring new life to the case, but even though several tips were received after the show aired, none of them led to the missing boy.

Soon after that, leads in the disappearance began to dry up, and most of the detectives assigned to the case initially were now working on other things. Officials confessed they still weren't sure what had happened to Zach. Despite an intensive investigation, they had no clues about his current whereabouts.

Zach had disappeared into thin air.

ON DECEMBER 18, 2000, ZACH SHOULD HAVE BEEN celebrating his ninth birthday but, instead, was still missing. Detectives had followed more than 700 leads but had never found a trace of the boy. Although there was still no evidence found suggesting that he was a victim of foul play, there had been no confirmed sightings of him since he'd been reported missing.

By the end of the year, Zach had also vanished from newspaper headlines. As the first anniversary of his disappearance approached, his family hoped to generate enough publicity to jumpstart the investigation. Preparations were made, interviews were arranged, and detectives announced that Zach's case would be featured on a billboard and on a flyer that would be sent out to 800,000 West Florida homes.

But none of that ever happened. The one-year anniversary of Zach's disappearance fell on September 11, 2001, and the story of the missing nine-year-old was overshadowed by the terrorist attacks that occurred in New York City that morning.

And then, another tragedy occurred.

On December 31, 2001, a five-year-old boy was playing outside his apartment at the Savannah Trace complex when he was abducted by a man in a white pickup truck. Witnesses quickly called the police, but the man and boy were gone by the time they arrived. Hours later, the boy was found 56 miles from Clearwater. He had been thrown into a dumpster behind a fast-food restaurant in Sumter County. The boy managed to escape from the dumpster and was found by a passerby, who alerted the authorities. The boy, although in good physical health, had been sexually assaulted by his kidnapper.

Detectives weren't sure if the abduction was connected to Zach's, although both had disappeared from the same apartment complex. Unfortunately, though, the kidnapper of the five-year-old was never found, so he was never questioned about Zach's case.

More time passed, and Zach remained missing. In August 2003, an age-progressed photo of Zach was placed on a billboard along U.S. 41 in Pasco County. Zach's grandmother and two of his aunts attended the press conference where Florida Governor Jeb Bush unveiled the billboard. There was no explanation as to why Leah didn't attend.

One of the aunts, Billie Jo Jimenez, told reporters, "Any one of us standing here would give our right arm to see Zach again." They hoped the new billboard would bring in some fresh tips about the case, which had been stagnant for the past two years.

More time passed, and in August 2009, Zach's photo was featured in a deck of cold case cards distributed to jail inmates by the Florida Department of Law Enforcement. The decks were passed out in hopes an inmate might have information to offer about the featured cases and speak up with a promise of lightening their sentence. Carole Bernhardt, wearing a T-shirt with age-progression photos of what her missing grandson might look like between the ages of 10 and 14, was on hand at the press conference announcing the cold case deck. She said sadly, "It's terrible...you have to watch him grow up on a T-shirt."

As the years passed, Zach's family tried to remind people that he was still missing. His case had never gotten much publicity outside of Florida, and by the time he'd been gone for a decade, even Florida news outlets had forgotten about him. His grandmother and his aunts continued to attend missing children rallies and marches, however, and did all they could to support the families of other missing children.

Leah, though, remained silent and out of sight. She later moved to Hawaii, got married, and changed her name. While her family continued to search for Zach and bring awareness to his case, Leah never spoke about him again.

In September 2020, Zach's grandmother and aunts marked the 20th anniversary of his disappearance. Billie Jo told reporters that the passage of time had done little to diminish the grief they felt. She remained convinced that the story told by her sister was true – that someone had entered the apartment while she was at the swimming pool that night and had taken Zach while he was sleeping.

She remains hopeful that the family will one day be reunited with Zach. "I do believe that my nephew is still out there... there's a big world out there and he could be anywhere."

The Clearwater Police Department continues to consider Zach's vanishing to be suspicious but maintains they have no evidence to suggest he is dead. In 2022, a spokesman stated that the case remains open and active.

The truth behind what happened to Zach that night remains a mystery. Leah never spoke publicly about the case again, and while detectives are still skeptical of her story and believe she was never truthful with them, they never officially named her as a suspect in Zach's disappearance. If Leah was out at a bar that night, it would have been for hours, not minutes. If she was gone for an extended period, Zach could've disappeared hours earlier than detectives were led to believe.

As many have also pointed out – if your son was abducted, wouldn't you continue to keep his name out there and never stop looking? Most people wouldn't refuse to do interviews, let alone move away, change their name, and never speak about the missing boy again. But then again, if you already knew what happened to him, I suppose "closure" wouldn't be something you'd need.

Personally, I don't think Leah played a direct role in Zach's disappearance. I believe the cause of his vanishing was neglect – a mother who maybe loved her son but couldn't be bothered to take good care of him when she wanted to be out partying, drinking, and having fun. She didn't want responsibility – she wanted a good time.

And she never considered what might happen when she chased after that good time at the expense of her son.

2001: THE AFFAIR HE DIDN'T WANT TO REMEMBER

THE DISAPPEARANCE OF PATRICIA ANN ADKINS

THE TELEPHONE RANG AGAIN AND AGAIN.

Marcia wasn't going to wait for the call to go to voicemail again and punched the "end" button on her cellphone. After days of calling her sister and receiving no answer, she'd started calling Patti on her mobile line incessantly. It didn't matter that her sister told her she wouldn't have service on her vacation – she should be home by now.

Marcia hadn't spoken to Patti for a week, and Patti should have been home hours ago to pick up her daughter. On June 29, Patti had arranged for Marcia to help keep an eye on her daughter while she was away. She was always on time to pick up seven-year-old Michaley – she loved that little girl with all her heart – but it was now July 8, and there was no sign of Patti.

What happened next would seem like something from a Hollywood script. Such things weren't supposed to happen in blue-collar Ohio, yet they did.

And Patti Adkins was never seen again.

PATRICIA ADKINS WAS BORN ON MAY 4, 1972. She grew up in Marysville, Ohio, close to her family. She married, had a daughter, and divorced while holding down a full-time position at the Honda automobile factory in town. She was 29 years old in 2001, and by then, she'd been working at the facility for a decade. She worked her way up through the ranks to become a supervisor on the assembly line.

Between being a single mother and being in a high-pressure position at the plant, she had a busy life with little time for much of anything else, especially a love life. But you could sort of say

Patti Adkins

that love came looking for her. A year before she went missing, she began an affair with a married co-worker and fell head over heels in love with him.

It goes without saying that the relationship had to be kept quiet. Not only would an affair at work be frowned upon by the company, but Patti also didn't want friends and family to know she was involved with a married man.

The only person who knew about the secret affair was her sister, Marcia. Patti explained to Marcia that she adored the man, and he'd promised that he would soon leave his wife and children for her. He said they'd start a new life together and have children of their own.

Let me know if any of this sounds familiar.

When Marcia expressed skepticism about the situation, her sister assured her that the only reason he hadn't already filed for divorce was that he and his brother-in-law owned a business together. He wanted to buy him out before the divorce so there'd be no retaliation.

He asked Patti to loan him the money for the buyout, and since she believed it was an investment in their future together, she agreed. Patti took a second mortgage on her home and even withdrew money from her 401K. Altogether, she gave her boyfriend $90,000 with the promise that he would pay it back in July.

July 2001 was, by the way, the month that Patti went missing.

In late June, Patti began making plans for "shutdown week" at the factory, when all employees received a week of vacation over the July 4 holiday. She told Marcia that she and her boyfriend had plans for a romantic getaway in Canada. Marcia agreed to keep her daughter, Michaley, for part of the week; her ex-husband would have her for the rest of the time, and her cats were being boarded at her vet's while the plant was closed. As far as Patti was concerned, the stars had aligned.

Marcia wasn't thrilled with her sister's affair, even though she did seem happy. And nothing about it made her fearful until Patti mentioned one more detail—her boyfriend told her not to bring any clothes on the trip. He was going to buy her all new things in Canada.

On the night of June 29, she packed only a small overnight bag, got a lift from a friend to work, and clocked in at the Honda factory. She could barely contain her excitement during that last shift. She told many co-workers she couldn't wait to leave when her night ended. At 19 seconds after midnight, she clocked out and walked out of the plant.

And this is when it gets worse.

She explained to Marcia that the plan was for her to get into the back of her boyfriend's pickup and hide under the bed cover he'd bought just for their trip. That way, she wouldn't be seen by their colleagues or the friends he was dropping off at their homes before the vacation started.

Marcia tried to tell her how ridiculous and suspicious it sounded, but Patti assured her it was fine. He loved her, she promised, and would never hurt her. She'd see her sister on July 8 when she came to pick up Michaley. She reminded Marcia about the lack of cell service where she was going but promised to call as soon as possible.

And Marcia never heard from her again.

AS EXPECTED, NO ONE HEARD FROM PATTI FOR THE next week.

But when Sunday, July 8, came and still Marcia heard nothing, she had a nagging feeling that something was wrong. She called Patti several times, but there was no answer. She tried to shrug it off, telling herself that her sister was just running late, but as she continued to call her landline and cell phone every half hour for the next several hours to no avail, she began to worry. She tried calling some of Patti's friends, but they hadn't heard from her either.

After a few hours of this, she finally dialed the married boyfriend's house. His wife picked up the phone and said he was out of town and hadn't returned yet. Marcia was relieved. This meant he and Patti were running late. She was sure that she'd hear from her sister soon.

But she didn't.

By 5:00 P.M., she'd waited long enough and called the boyfriend's house again. This time, he answered the call, and to Marcia's dismay, he said he had no idea where Patti was – and why would he? He barely knew her and then only as a co-worker at the factory. She knew this wasn't true, but he insisted that he hadn't gone on vacation with her, and she was not his girlfriend. He was married, he said.

Marcia knew he was lying and asked him flat out, "What did you do to my sister?"

He denied having anything to do with Patti or her disappearance and ended the call.

Marcia was now in a panic. She called her other sister, who was at their mother's house, and told her that something wasn't right. Patti was missing, and she was worried. By 7:00 P.M. that evening, Marcia had filed a missing person report with the Marysville Police Department.

But Marcia couldn't sleep that night, still hoping she'd hear from her sister. As she tossed and turned, she decided she wasn't going to leave her sister's disappearance in the hands of the authorities. She needed to do something on her own.

At 3:00 A.M. on July 9, Marcia called the boyfriend's home again. When his wife answered, Marcia told her all about the affair her husband had been having with her sister. She told her about the gifts Patti had bought for him and even provided intimate details about their marriage, which was information she could only have gotten from Patti.

But the wife turned out to be as deeply under the man's spell as Patti had been. She began asking her own questions when, finally, the boyfriend took the phone out of her hand and started talking to Marcia. She quickly realized that while trying to get information from him, he was doing the same to her, trying to find out how much Marcia knew. The conversation continued for nearly 45 minutes, with Marcia demanding to know where her sister was and the boyfriend denying everything.

He claimed he barely knew Patti, he was not having an affair with her, and he refused to change his story.

The official investigation kicked off later that same morning. When detectives arrived at Patti's house, they found nothing out of place. Her car was still in the garage, and all her personal belongings seemed to have been left behind. They confirmed she had caught a ride to work with a friend, was present for her entire shift, and clocked out at midnight.

What happened after that, though, was a mystery.

It didn't appear that Patti had been forcibly removed from her home, but investigators were assured that she would not have abandoned her daughter.

Marcia quickly steered investigators toward Patti's boyfriend. He allowed them to search his home and business, which seemed helpful, but he continued denying the relationship with Patti. They also spoke with his wife, who was still dubious about the alleged affair. According to her, with work, the side business, and the children, he didn't have time for an affair. It just wasn't possible, she insisted.

When detectives began tracing the boyfriend's movements on June 29, he claimed he was home by 2:30 A.M. His shift had ended at midnight, too. He said that after leaving work, he had driven a co-worker to Burger King, where they waited 45 minutes in the drive-through. After they got their food, he drove the co-worker home. His wife corroborated the story – at least about him getting home at 2:30 – and said he'd spend the rest of the weekend with her and their children. They'd even gone on a short fishing trip. He didn't have time for anything else.

However, the Burger King manager told the police it wasn't a busy night. They'd only had eight or nine orders, and there was no way anyone was kept waiting for 45 minutes.

Not only that, but the police found a birthday card in his house that they asked about. Though he claimed it was from several of his colleagues at Honda, the only name written inside the card was Patti Adkins. They also found a phone that Marcia told police Patti had bought for him and a T-shirt from the Hard Rock Café that Marcia remembered Patti buying for him during a sisters' trip to Florida months earlier.

Then there was the letter. Hidden in the man's house was a letter from Patti about how much she loved him and couldn't wait to be with him.

Detectives were now realizing the affair was real. It wasn't the figment of a young woman's wild imagination, as the boyfriend tried to claim. But there was one thing they hadn't been able to locate – the money Marcia told them Patti had loaned to the boyfriend.

During the search of Patti's house, the police had found more than a dozen money bands, which had been wrapped around large bills. A banker corroborated that Patti had taken out another mortgage on her home and removed money from her 401K account, but she'd taken the money in cash. The money was never deposited in the boyfriend's account, so there was no way to connect him to the cash.

But what about his truck? The police noticed that all the parts for the weatherproof cover for the truck bed were intact, but the cover itself was missing. Speaking to some of the man's co-workers created more questions than answers.

One of them told detectives that the cover was installed on the truck on June 29, the day Patti went missing. The problem was that the truck was a company vehicle, and the bed was needed to haul items, so having a cover made it unusable.

A week after police questioned the boyfriend, the bed cover appeared in the company's storage area. The boyfriend claimed he'd used it for his fishing trip the weekend before the July 4 holiday.

A forensic examination of the cover showed cat hair and a small drop of blood. DNA was still limited in 2001, and the amount of blood found wasn't enough for a conclusive analysis. Any test carried out would require the destruction of the entire sample, which was unlikely to have been enough for a match at that time. The blood was never tested, and I assume it's in storage somewhere, but the records are unclear.

At some point, it might finally reveal the truth.

MORE THAN TWO DECADES AFTER PATTI VANISHED, there are still many unanswered questions and leads that couldn't adequately be followed.

Where was the boyfriend during those two hours after work when he lied and said he was in the Burger King drive-through? Did his co-worker confirm this alibi? There seems to be no record of this, or even that they were asked.

Where did the boyfriend tell Patti he was taking her on their trip? And if he told her not to bring any clothing since he would buy her all new ones, why wouldn't there have been cell phone service in a town large enough to buy a wardrobe in?

What happened to Patti's $90,000 if the money was never deposited in a bank account? The police were convinced she gave it to her boyfriend – just as they were convinced the affair was real – but they had no way to prove it.

And perhaps the most important question of all – who was the boyfriend? Officials have refused to reveal his name for more than 20 years, probably because they have no solid evidence to build a case against him.

Although Patti was legally declared dead many years ago, her body has never been found. Her case is considered cold but active, and her mystery remains unsolved.

And the only person who can probably solve it will likely never reveal what he knows.

2002: "IT'S ALWAYS THE HUSBAND"
THE VANISHING OF BRANDY WILSON

ANYONE WHO HAS EVER WATCHED A DETECTIVE SHOW, a true crime documentary, or read a book about murder, whether truth or fiction, knows that when a woman disappears, the police always first suspect the bad guy is her husband or boyfriend. This is a common trope. You see it all the time. But it exists for a reason.

The reason is because it's usually accurate.

It would be the husband that the police came looking for when Brandy Wilson vanished in 2002 – the husband who waited an entire day to call the police to report her missing and the one who was so disinterested in where Brandy was that he moved and didn't bother giving the police his new number and address.

But did he make Brandy disappear?

We don't know, but we do know that Brandy Wilson has never been seen again.

BRANDY WILSON'S HUSBAND KENNY ALWAYS CLAIMED she was home when he got there. He finished working the third shift at his job on the morning of Tuesday, June 4, 2002, and Brandy was at their rural Colfax, Indiana, home as she usually was.

They didn't have much to say to each other, so he went to bed soon after getting home. When he woke up around 2:00 P.M.,

Brandy Wilson

Brandy was gone. She was supposed to work that afternoon, so he wasn't surprised until he saw both of their vehicles still sitting in the driveway. He thought she must have gotten a ride with a friend but noticed Brandy's purse on the kitchen counter. That was weird but not as odd as the $420 he later claimed was missing from the house.

He'd have something to say about that when she came home.

Brandy worked at Donaldson Company in Frankfort, Indiana, and was scheduled to be there at 4:00 P.M. that day – but never showed up. Right away, her co-workers were worried that something had happened to her. She'd told everyone that she and Kenny had been having problems and even went so far as to say that if she disappeared someday, Kenny would likely be responsible.

As for Kenny, he didn't bother to report Brandy missing until the following day. He went to work on Tuesday like normal, but when he came home on Wednesday morning – and Brandy wasn't there – he decided to make some calls. He told the police that he contacted her friends first to see if she was with any of them, although the friends would never confirm this. He said he could not locate her, so he called the police.

When Brandy's mother, Pam McGuire, eventually discovered her daughter was missing, she knew she hadn't gone anywhere voluntarily. She had an eight-year-old son from a previous marriage and, with Kenny, had a second son born in late 2001. Pam insisted Brandon wouldn't willingly abandon her children, who had been staying with Kenny's parents while the couple tried to resolve some recent marital problems.

Friends also said Brandy would've never voluntarily vanished, but Clinton County Sheriff's detectives weren't so sure. They were initially under the assumption that she'd taken off and would return when she was ready. They couldn't find anything to indicate foul play, and Lieutenant Eric Douglass said it seemed more likely that she wanted to get away from her husband for a while. "We don't really have anything right now that points to anything else," he said.

But those feelings would change. Investigators learned that none of her belongings were missing. She'd apparently taken nothing with her – not her purse, wedding ring, or clothing. No one had picked her up, and neither car was missing.

Brandy, Kenny, and Brandy's son from her previous relationship.

None of the neighbors reported seeing her getting into a car with anyone. No one had seen her walking through the neighborhood. Her disappearance seemed to be a complete mystery.

Over the weekend after Brandy was last seen, a search began for Brandy in Colfax County. Volunteer firefighters assisted sheriff's deputies by scouring areas in and around Colfax, but no trace of her was found. Friends made missing posters and distributed them all over the area, hoping someone would recognize her picture and call the police.

Detectives interviewed Kenny, but he claimed he could not provide them with any information about where Brandy might be. They also interviewed her friends and co-workers, all of whom insisted she'd never leave on her own. They had no idea what happened to her.

Pam just wanted her daughter to be found. "I don't know if she left because she was so upset or if something terrible happened to her. She's such a sweet person."

After speaking to many of Brandy's friends, Lieutenant Douglass became convinced about a couple of things – one of which was that Brandy would never abandon her sons. "Everything we're getting about her is that this is completely out of character for her. Everyone says there's no way she would just leave her kids," he said.

The other thing he was convinced of was that Kenny knew more than he was telling them. A week after Brandy was reported missing, detectives had only been able to conduct one brief interview with her husband. They had tried repeatedly to schedule another interview but could not reach him. They'd left a dozen messages, but he never called back.

When Brandy vanished, she and Kenny had been married for less than a year, and the marriage was already in trouble. They'd had numerous arguments, some of which she told her friends about, like the one that occurred after she went to work early one day. Kenny accused her of cheating on him and took her car keys from her, refusing to give them back until she admitted it.

A friend that Brandy had lunch with a week before she went missing said that she was nervous and edgy during the meal. This friend was another person Brandy told that if anything happened to her, Kenny probably did it.

Brandy's mom admitted, "I don't know if she was scared about being at home or scared about leaving or what was wrong." Pam didn't want to believe that Kenny was capable of hurting Brandy, but she did have some concerns thanks to his past. In 1988, Kenny had pleaded guilty to robbery charges in Pulaski County. As a result of that plea, murder charges that had been filed against him related to the incident were dropped. He was sentenced to 19 years in prison, though he was paroled after nine.

Pam wanted to know what Kenny knew, but he wasn't talking to her – and he wasn't talking to the police either.

ON JUNE 13, THE SEARCH CONTINUED. Although detectives stated they had no evidence to suggest Brandy was dead, they did attempt to use a helicopter with thermal-imaging equipment to search around Colfax for her body. Unfortunately, the weather didn't cooperate. A thunderstorm grounded the helicopter.

The following day, divers from Carroll and Tippecanoe Counties spent four hours searching a gravel pond outside of Colfax. Sheriff's Detective Rick Morgan told reporters they didn't have any tips directing them to search that area but wanted to eliminate it as a possibility.

Finally, on June 15, detectives managed to track down Kenny and asked him to submit to a polygraph exam about his wife's disappearance. Surprisingly, he agreed and came to the station that same day for the exam. However, investigators refused to discuss the results.

By June 18, Brandy had been missing for two weeks. Her family had started to worry they would never see her alive again. Another search by helicopter was planned, and this time, it went off without a hitch. Hours were spent in the air above Clinton County, but there was no sign of Brandy, alive or dead. As they searched, aerial photographs were taken and later scrutinized for clues, but again nothing was found.

Several dozen tips had come in over those past two weeks, but most were vague and hard to follow up. Most involved seeing her in a passing car or on the back of a motorcycle; none were confirmed.

Brandy should have been celebrating her 25th birthday on July 12, and while Pam prayed she would return home to mark the occasion with her family, the day came and went without any sign of the missing young woman.

Investigators knew things had stalled as the case dragged into its second year. They had no idea what had happened to Brandy. The investigators were, like Brandy's family, hopeful she was alive. They assured everyone they had no evidence to suggest that she wasn't, although they still refused to discuss the results of Kenny's polygraph exam. They wouldn't name Kenny as a suspect, either. While he'd moved out of the house he'd shared with Brandy, he had given the authorities his new contact information before moving to Jasper County, Indiana, to be closer to his parents.

Pam, though, seemed to be more wary of her son-in-law than the police apparently were. She had only seen Kenny once since Brandy vanished, and she had no idea how he was handling the situation. He had always been very low-key, making it hard to tell when he was upset. His parents still cared for Brandy's two children, but Kenny ensured Pam could talk with them on the phone.

On the same week that Brandy would have celebrated her birthday, the sheriff's office received a typewritten letter from someone who claimed to have information about Brandy's whereabouts. They announced that they believed the leads in the letter were legitimate but needed more information from the sender to assemble the pieces. A spokesman declined to discuss the letter's contents but asked the writer to contact the sheriff's office.

But whoever sent the letter was never heard from again.

The case stalled, and more time passed. In December, detectives entered Brandy's DNA and dental records into a national database so they could be compared to any unidentified bodies that were found. However, officials still said they lacked any solid evidence that she was dead.

Pam celebrated Christmas without her daughter and then Mother's Day. A few weeks after that, Brandy had been missing for a year. They still had no answers. Pam told a reporter, "We'd like to know. I would love for her to come home... we'd just like to have some closure."

By then, detectives hadn't received any new leads in months. They'd had to call off the searches because they simply lacked the manpower to carry them out.

They'd also lost track of Kenny. He hadn't stayed in contact with them, and they had no new evidence to justify searching for him. He had custody of his son with Brandy while Pam raised her nine-year-old.

Pam was still unable to get Kenny to return her calls. She hadn't seen her youngest grandson since shortly after Brandy disappeared. Worse, Kenny refused to give her any of her daughter's possessions and feared he'd thrown them out.

Detective Rick Morgan still wouldn't name Kenny as a suspect but did say that Kenny's lack of concern for his wife was a concern for the investigators.

But lack of concern wasn't evidence of murder.

Kenny was still the only person of interest in Brandy's disappearance, even if the police still refused to call him a suspect. By 2015, he was running a dog rescue operation, but he was soon in trouble again. The authorities raided the place after allegations were made about the dogs being neglected. Kenny was charged with 12 counts of abandoning and neglecting the animals found on the property – but there was nothing anyone could do about his missing wife.

No charges were ever filed against him in Brandy's case.

Sadly, Brandy's mother, Pam, died in 2011 without earning what happened to her daughter. Brandy's friends continue to hope that she will be found one day, even if she has been dead for decades. They want her to be given a proper burial and for her children to finally have some answers.

But until then, the fate of Brandy Wilson remains unknown.

2004: "THE FIRST CRIME MYSTERY OF THE SOCIAL MEDIA AGE"

THE DISAPPEARANCE OF MAURA MURRAY

On the Internet, Maura's disappearance is the perfect obsession, a puzzle of clues that offers a tantalizing illusion—if the right armchair detective connects the right dots, maybe the unsolvable can be solved. And so, every day, the case attracts new recruits, analyzing and dissecting and reconstructing the details of her story with a Warren Commission–like fervor.

Bill Jensen

ON FEBRUARY 9, 2004, A YOUNG WOMAN NAMED Maura Murray packed her bags, withdrew most of her money from her bank account, purchased some alcohol, and started driving.

Nearly three hours after she'd left Massachusetts, a call was received by emergency operators about a single-car accident that had occurred near Haverhill, New Hampshire.

It had been Maura who was behind the wheel. While she was still at the scene of the accident when the initial 911 call was made, she was gone by the time the police arrived just minutes later. It was then – and still is now – unclear if she wandered into the woods near where the accident occurred, left willingly, or was picked up by someone in a passing car.

The reason why is because Maura Murray has never been seen again.

MAURA MURRAY WAS BORN ON MAY 4, 1982, IN Hanson, Massachusetts. She was the fourth child of Fred and Laurie Murray

Maura Murray

and had an older brother, Fred; two older sisters, Kathleen and Julie; and a younger half-brother, Kurt. When she was six, her parents divorced, and Maura lived mostly with her mother.

She graduated from Whitman-Hanson Regional High School, where she was a star on the school's track team. She was accepted into the United States Military Academy at West Point, New York, where she studied chemical engineering for three semesters. However, believing West Point wasn't a good fit for her, she transferred to the University of Massachusetts Amherst after her freshman year to study nursing.

But there were some bumpy times ahead for Maura. In November 2003 – three months before she vanished – Maura admitted using a stolen credit card to order food from several restaurants. She was sentenced to probation with the opportunity to have the charges dismissed after three months of good behavior.

Then, on February 5 – four days before she disappeared – Maura was on duty at her campus security job and took a personal call from her sister, Kathleen. Around 10:30 P.M., while still on duty, Maura reportedly broke down in tears. When her supervisor came by her desk, Maura was "just completely zoned out. No reaction at all. She was unresponsive."

The supervisor escorted her back to her dorm room around 1:20 A.M. When asked what was wrong, she only said, "My sister."

The subject of the call would later be revealed by Kathleen, who admitted to her sister that she had alcoholism. She had been discharged from a rehab clinic that evening, but on the way home, her fiancée had inexplicably taken her to a liquor store, and she relapsed. It was upsetting news, but Maura seemed unusually affected by it.

Two days later, on Saturday, February 7, Maura's father, Fred, visited Amherst. He and Maura spent the afternoon car shopping and then went to dinner with a friend. Maura dropped her father off at his hotel after dinner and, borrowing his Toyota Corolla, drove back to campus to attend a dorm party. She stayed at the party until about 2:30 and was on her way back to her dad's hotel when she struck a guardrail on Route 9 in Hadley, badly damaging the front end of the car.

A responding officer wrote an accident report, but there was nothing in the report about Maura being drunk and no documentation of a field sobriety test being conducted. She was driven to her father's hotel and stayed in his room for the remainder of the night.

No one knows what was said between Fred and his daughter on Sunday morning, but he didn't seem upset about the accident. He called his insurance agent and learned that his policy covered the damage. He rented a car, dropped Maura off at school, and left to go home to Connecticut.

Later that night, at about 11:30, he called Maura to remind her to obtain accident forms from the Massachusetts Registry of Motor Vehicles. They made plans to talk on Monday, where they could fill out the forms and make the insurance claim over the phone.

It was after midnight on Monday, February 9, that things really started to get strange. Even after all this time, we have a detailed chronology of what she did next.

Maura used her computer to search the MapQuest website for directions to the Berkshires – the rural area in the mountains of western Massachusetts – and Burlington, Vermont.

And then, nothing happened for almost 12 hours.

Finally, at 1:00 P.M., she emailed her boyfriend, Bill Rausch: "I love you more stud. I got your messages, but honestly, I didn't feel like talking too much to anyone, I promise to call today though. Love you, Maura."

She also called to inquire about renting a place at the same condominium association in Bartlett, New Hampshire, where she'd once vacationed with her parents. The call lasted three minutes, and Maura didn't rent the condo.

At 1:13 P.M., she called a fellow nursing student for reasons unknown.

Just 11 minutes later, Maura emailed a work supervisor on the faculty of the nursing school and told her there had been a death in her family and that she'd be out of town for a week. She promised to get in touch when she returned. I probably don't need to add that it was a lie. No one in Maura's family had died.

Her next call was made at 2:05 P.M. This time, she called a number that provided recorded information about booking hotels around Stowe, Vermont. She listened to the listings for about five minutes.

At 2:18 P.M., she made a less-than-one-minute call to her boyfriend and left a voice message promising they would talk later.

Soon after the call, Maura started packing. She loaded clothing, personal items, college textbooks, and her birth control pills into her 1996 black Saturn sedan. When her room was later searched, campus police discovered that most of her belongings had been packed into boxes, and the art had been removed from the walls. It's not clear if she packed them that day, but on top of the boxes was a printed email written to her boyfriend, Bill. It indicated trouble in their relationship, even though she'd never mentioned any issues in the messages she left for him or the earlier email she'd sent.

Maura left campus around 3:30. The streets were quiet because classes at the university had been canceled that day because of a snowstorm.

Just 10 minutes later, at 3:40 P.M., Maura withdrew $280 from an ATM. It was almost all the money she had in the account. A security camera on the machine showed she was alone at the time.

She was then picked up on security footage at a nearby liquor store. She purchased about $40 worth of alcoholic beverages, including Baileys Irish Cream, Kahlúa, vodka, and a box of wine. The cameras again showed she was alone when she made that purchase.

Maura left Amherst between 4:00 and 5:00 P.M., probably using Interstate 91 North. She called to check her voicemail at 4:37 P.M. This was the last time her cell phone was used.

There is nothing to indicate that Maura told anyone where she was going – and no evidence that she'd even chosen a destination.

THE SUN HAD LONG SET OVER WOODSVILLE, NEW Hampshire, by 7:30 P.M. That was when a resident on the edge of town heard a loud thump outside her house. She got up from the couch where she'd been watching TV and tried to peer out the window into the darkness. Finally, she cupped her hands around her eyes, leaned against the glass to shut off the light behind her, and spotted the source of the noise – it was a car. It was sitting up against a snowbank along Route 112, which locals called Wild Ammonoosuc Road.

The black car was pointed west on the eastbound side of the road. She could see the car's interior light and fog from the tailpipe drifting into the air. It was still running and she couldn't tell if anyone was hurt, but decided she needed to call the Grafton County Sheriff's Office and report the accident – just in case.

She must have been looking out the window when she made the call because, according to the 911 log, the witness said she could see someone smoking inside the car. Later, though, she'd alter that statement and say she saw a red light in the car. She assumed it was the glow of a cigarette but also realized it could have been the light from a cell phone.

Before the police arrived, a passing motorist and a school bus driver who lived nearby stopped at the scene. The bus driver reported seeing a young woman walking around the vehicle, noting that she wasn't bleeding or visibly injured. She just seemed to be cold, he said. He offered to help, and the young woman pleaded with him not to call the police. She assured him she'd already called the American Automobile Association (AAA), although AAA has no record of the call.

The bus driver, knowing there was little cellular reception in the area, continued home and called the police when he arrived there. His call was received by the sheriff's department about 10 minutes after the call made by the first witness.

He could no longer see Maura's car while he was calling, but he did notice several cars pass by on the road before the police arrived. Several others passed after police officers reached the scene. One local resident was driving home from work and reported a police SUV parked nose-to-nose with Maura's car around 7:37 P.M. She pulled over briefly but didn't see anyone in or around either vehicle and decided to continue home. Oddly, this statement contradicts the official police log, which has the Haverhill police arriving nine minutes later at 7:46 P.M.

That official log states that when the police officer arrived at the scene, the woman driver had disappeared. There was no one in the car and no one nearby. The driver's side of the vehicle collided with a tree, damaging the left headlight and pushing the car's radiator into the fan, rendering it inoperable. The windshield was cracked on the driver's side, and both airbags had been deployed.

When the officer approached the car, he discovered all the doors were locked. He also noticed red stains inside and outside the car that looked like red wine. Using a tool from his vehicle, he unlocked the doors and looked through the contents scattered through the interior, noticing a damaged box of Franzia wine on the rear seat, which explained the stains. He also found an empty beer bottle, Maura's AAA card, gloves, compact discs, makeup, jewelry, printed directions to Burlington, Vermont, Maura's favorite stuffed animal, and a book about climbing in the White Mountains called *Not Without Peril*.

What should have been there that wasn't? Maura's debit card, credit cards, and cell phone were never located – or used – after her disappearance. The police later reported that some of the bottles of alcohol that she purchased were also missing.

The sheriff's department traced the vehicle to Maura Murray and initially treated her as a missing person, believing she may have wanted to disappear voluntarily based on her travel plans, which she'd told no one about.

At this point, Maura left her car behind and never returned to it – but this may not have been the last time she was seen.

A short time later, between 8:00 and 8:30 P.M., a contractor returning home from work saw a "young person" moving quickly on foot on Route 112, perhaps four miles east of where Maura's car was found. He described the person – unable to say if it was a man or woman – as wearing jeans, a dark coat, and a light-colored hood. Unfortunately, he didn't report the sighting to the police until three months later when, after reviewing his work records, he realized he'd spotted the person on the same night that Maura disappeared.

Was it Maura? Maybe, although he never saw the person's face. If it was, though, she was never seen again.

BACK AT THE ACCIDENT SITE, THE RESPONDING officer and the bus driver drove up and down area roads looking for Maura but found no sign of her.

Just before 8:00 P.M., an ambulance and fire truck arrived to clear the scene, and within the hour, Maura's car had

Maura's damaged car was abandoned after she disappeared.

been towed to a local garage. The following day, a "be on the lookout" report went out for Maura, but there was little else that could be done besides trying to contact Fred Murray, whose name was also on the car's title.

At 3:20 P.M., a voicemail was left on Fred's home answering machine stating that Maura's car had been found abandoned in New Hampshire. Fred was at work and didn't receive the call, but one of Maura's sisters did around 5:00 P.M. She called Fred to let him know what was happening. Fred then contacted the Haverhill Police Department and was told that the New Hampshire Fish and Game Department would start a search if his daughter were not reported safe by the following morning. It was at that point that Maura was first referred to as "missing" by the authorities.

Fred arrived in Haverhill before dawn on February 11. He met with police officers and joined the search made up of Fish and Game officers, police and sheriff personnel, firefighters, and local volunteers. A tracking dog picked up a scent from one of Maura's gloves about 100 yards east of where her car had been found. The dog lost the trail, but the direction matched the report from the contractor who spotted her on the road east of the accident scene, although no one would know about his sighting for a few months. The dog might have lost the scent because – as the police believed – Maura had left the area in another vehicle.

Around 5:00 P.M. that day. Maura's boyfriend, Bill Rausch, and his parents arrived in Haverhill. They were questioned separately and then together. By now, the police were suggesting that Maura had come to the area to either run away or commit suicide, although everyone who knew her said this was unlikely.

And then things got strange again.

Bill had turned off his cell phone during the flight to Haverhill and remembered to turn it back on at some point. When he did, he discovered he'd received a voicemail when it was off. Nothing was said during the recording, but Bill believed it was the sound of Maura sobbing. The call was traced to a calling card issued to the American Red Cross.

On February 12, Fred and Bill held an evening press conference in Bethlehem, New Hampshire, and the first press coverage of Maura's disappearance appeared in print the next day. It was reported that Maura might be headed to the Kancamagus Highway area, and she was listed as "endangered and possibly suicidal." According to reports, she was reportedly intoxicated at the accident site, although no one actually spoke with her, and the bus driver stated that she did not seem to be impaired.

The search continued for Maura around Haverhill and soon expanded into Vermont, which had not been notified of the disappearance before that time. Just ten days after Maura vanished, the FBI joined the investigation, and soon, the search for the young woman was nationwide.

As the story spread via television, newspapers, and new social media platforms, New Hampshire Fish and Game conducted a second ground and air search using a helicopter with thermal imaging cameras and tracking and cadaver dogs. A ripped pair of white women's underwear were discovered in the snow on a secluded trail near French Pond Road on February 26, but they turned out not to belong to Maura.

By the end of February, Maura's family was exhausted and heartbroken. The police returned the items found in her car to them, and on March 2, they checked out of their hotel and went home. Fred continued to return every weekend to keep searching, but by April, locals had gotten their fill of him. The Haverhill police informed him that there had been numerous complaints about him trespassing on private property and suggested he go home.

The sympathy of the people of Haverhill had finally run out.

THE CASE DRAGGED ON, REFUSING TO TURN COLD. On July 1, the police retrieved the items found in Maura's car from her family to be forensically analyzed.

On July 13, nearly 100 people, including state troopers, rescue personnel, and volunteers, performed a one-mile radius search. It was the fourth search conducted around the accident site, but this was the first search without snow on the ground. The authorities were intent on locating Maura's black backpack, which was not found in her car. They didn't find it. When it was over, the police said the search discovered "nothing conclusive."

While infrequent searches continued, Fred Murray was busy trying to drum up more support and money for the investigation. He petitioned New Hampshire's governor for more help and appeared on several television programs to publicize the case.

He also had a lot of help from social media. Maura vanished soon after a new platform called Facebook was launched, and her story became widely shared across the internet. It has often been called the "first true crime mystery of the social media age." Of course, while this helped spread the word about Maura's disappearance, it also led to the birth of "internet sleuthing," which would turn out to be a double-edged sword. While often a great way of gathering and helping pass on worthwhile information, it can also create false leads and conspiracy theories, which only bog down investigations.

But there was no turning back now, and in the fall after the first anniversary of Maura's disappearance, an internet message board called "Not Without Peril" would play a role in what happened next with the police investigation.

On November 1, 2005, a user named "Tom Davies" logged into the message board, which was dedicated to discussion of Maura's disappearance, and claimed to have seen a black backpack similar to hers behind a restroom at Pemigewasset Overlook, about 30 miles east of Woodville on Route 112. The post got the attention of law enforcement officials, who issued a statement about the backpack – saying they were "aware of it" – but did not disclose whether it had been taken for forensic testing.

As more time passed without a trace of Maura, her friends and family became more discouraged. Searches were launched in 2006, and in 2007, a $75,000 reward was offered for information that could lead to solving the case. It was never claimed.

A photo that Maura took with her father, Fred, who followed every lead and sighting for many years. Another daughter, Julie, now lads the search for Maura.

In July 2008, volunteers led another two-day search through wooded areas in Haverhill. The group consisted of dog teams and licensed private investigators, but they had no more luck than anyone else.

Maura remains missing, but her disappearance would have one positive result. Her case was cited as one of the main reasons for creating a statewide cold case unit in New Hampshire in 2009. Unfortunately, her case would be added to the many unsolved cases in their cold case files later that same year.

In 2014 – 10 years after Maura vanished – the police were forced to admit, "We haven't had any credible sightings of Maura since the night she disappeared." In an interview with Fred Murray that same year, he told reporters that he believed his daughter had been abducted on the night she vanished and was dead. However, he also believed he had information on where she ended up, which would not be searched until 2019.

Back in late 2004, a man had allegedly given Fred a rusty, stained knife that belonged to the man's brother, who had a criminal past and lived less than a mile from where Maura's car was abandoned. The brother and the brother's girlfriend were said to have acted strangely after the disappearance, and the man who gave Fred the knife said he believed it had been used to kill Maura.

Several days after the knife was given to Fred, the man's brother allegedly scrapped his car, which prompted Fred to pass on the story to the police. Detectives investigated but were told by family members of the man who turned in the knife that he'd made up the story to try and get some reward money and had a history of drug addiction. Investigators dismissed the story of the knife.

But then, two years later, in October 2006, another search occurred within a few miles of where Maura's car was found. In an abandoned A-frame-style house that was approximately one mile from the accident site, cadaver dogs allegedly went "bonkers" after identifying the presence of human remains.

The A-frame house that Fred was convinced was connected to Maura's disappearance was finally searched in 2019, but no trace of her was found.

The house had formerly been the residence of the man implicated by his brother, who had given Fred the rusty knife. A sample of the carpet from the house was sent to the New Hampshire State Police, but the test results were never released to the public.

The police eventually forgot about the lead, but Fred Murray never did. During an interview in 2019, he reiterated his belief that Maura was dead but also brought back up his suspicions about the nearby house that the cadaver dogs had responded to. He told a reporter, "That's my daughter."

Fred had been trying to get permission to search the house for years, but the owners had always refused to cooperate. Eventually, the property was sold, and the new owners were happy to help. In April 2019, an excavation was done in the home's basement, but absolutely nothing was found.

Fred was crushed. His hopes of something paying off in that house had been destroyed.

TWO DECADES HAVE NOW PASSED SINCE MAURA was last seen, and even though her case has drawn international scrutiny, there is still no clue about what happened to her back in 2004.

Maura's sister, Julie, is now the spokesperson for the family, and she is, like Fred was for many years, a tireless advocate for

Maura, urging New Hampshire investigators to keep her sister's case alive.

It seems almost impossible to believe that 20 years after she vanished, there is still no more information about what happened to Maura today than there was in February of 2004.

We can only hope the Murray family will finally have the answers they deserve someday.

2004: MISSING IN VERMONT
THE VANISHING OF BRIANNA MAITLAND

VETERAN POLICE OFFICERS DON'T LIKE COINCIDENCES.

In fact, most don't believe in them at all. They don't like the idea of two things happening within a short amount of time and a short distance from one another. That was why so many of them were bothered by what happened in early 2004.

Just over a month after Maura Murray vanished on a snowy highway outside Haverhill, New Hampshire, another young woman named Brianna Maitland disappeared 97 miles away in Montgomery, Vermont.

While the FBI and the state police would later insist that the two cases weren't connected, there's no question that the similarities between them were unnerving, to say the least.

Brianna Maitland was last seen on March 19 while leaving her dishwashing job at the Black Lantern Inn in Montgomery, Vermont. A little before midnight, she left the restaurant to go home. Several co-workers asked her to stay and have dinner with them, but she declined. Brianna was tired and eager to get to the home she shared with her childhood friend, Jillian Stout, in nearby Sheldon. She had a second job as a waitress in St. Albans and had to be up early the next morning for her shift.

With a smile and a wave, she left through the back door – and was never seen again.

BRIANNA MAITLAND WAS BORN ON OCTOBER 8, 1986, in Burlington, Vermont, to parents Bruce and Kellie. She grew up with an older brother on their East Franklin farm near the Canadian border. During her sophomore year, she attended Missisquoi Valley

Union High School before transferring to Enosburg Falls High School in nearby Enosburg Falls.

When Brianna turned 17 in October 2003, she decided to move away from her parents' farm. Her mother stated there were no serious problems at home, but Brianna wanted to be more independent and live closer to friends who attended another high school. She enrolled at the school her friends attended, but her living arrangements were unstable and soon she was moving from place to place, staying with the families of different friends.

Brianna Maitland

Finally, in February 2004, Brianna dropped out of high school and moved in with her childhood friend, Jillian Stout, who lived in Sheldon, about 20 miles west of Montgomery. She'd left school behind but still wanted to complete her education, so she enrolled in a GED program.

Brianna disappeared on March 19, and her mother would later report that something unusual happened that day that she could never explain.

Brianna took and passed her GED exam that morning, so she and her mother went out for lunch to celebrate. Her father, Bruce, was out of town for work. Kellie later recalled her daughter being in good spirits and discussing her college plans.

After lunch, they went shopping, and while they were waiting in the checkout line, Kellie said that something caught Brianna's attention. She told Kellie she needed to leave and would be back shortly. After completing her purchase, she met Brianna in the parking lot and noticed that Brianna seemed shaken and upset. But her daughter didn't want to talk about it. She needed to get home, she said, and get ready for her shift at the Black Lantern Inn that night. Not wanting to pry, Kellie didn't ask any other questions. She dropped Brianna off at home between 3:30 and 4:00 P.M.

This was the last time that Kellie ever saw her daughter.

The abandoned barn where Brianna's 1985 green Oldsmobile was discovered.

BRIANNA WENT MISSING THAT NIGHT BUT unfortunately, no one knew it. On Friday, Brianna left a note for Jillian saying she'd be home that night after her shift, but Jillian went out of town for the weekend. When she returned on Monday, she found the note undisturbed. Assuming her friend was staying with her parents, she didn't call Kellie to ask about Brianna until the next day, March 23.

But Brianna wasn't at the farm – and hadn't been there. That was when everyone finally realized she was missing.

A few days earlier, on March 20 – the day after the last sighting of Brianna and two days before anyone knew she'd vanished – her pale green 1985 Oldsmobile was discovered abandoned off East Berkshire Road and Route 118, about a mile outside of Montgomery.

Oddly, the car had been parked partially inside an unused barn at a place known locally as the "Old Dutchburn Farm." It appeared that the Oldsmobile had been badly backed into the barn, causing some slight damage – although investigators would later believe that the accident was staged.

Searching the car revealed two of Brianna's uncashed paychecks on the front seat. They also found her medication, driver's license, makeup, contact lenses, and what appeared to be most of her clothing. Even stranger was that additional items that belonged to her were found strewn on the ground in front of the car, along with a woman's fleece jacket that didn't belong to Brianna. It was lying in a field a short distance from the barn.

The police assumed a drunk driver had abandoned the car, and it was towed into town. During the search, officers found Brianna's paychecks and assumed she was the car's owner. She wasn't – the car was registered in Kellie's name. If they had contacted her, it would have been realized that Brianna was missing two days earlier. Instead, the police went to where Brianna worked to inform her about the abandoned vehicle. Of course, she wasn't there.

It was now March 23, and Kellie had just learned that Kellie was missing. She began calling Kellie's friends and employers, but none had seen or spoken with her. Failing in her efforts – and still unaware that the car Brianna had been driving had been recovered – she filed a missing person report that same afternoon.

Finally, after three days of delay, someone would be looking for Brianna Maitland.

After word spread about her disappearance, several witnesses reported seeing Brianna's car at the old barn. Some had seen it there the same night she disappeared, including one man who thought he had seen the car's headlights around 12:30 A.M. on March 20. He didn't see anyone in or around the vehicle. Another man who passed by around this same time recalled seeing a turn signal flashing on the car.

A few hours later, around 4:00 A.M., a former boyfriend of Brianna's drove past the barn after a night of partying over the border in Canada. He recalled thinking he recognized her car but didn't see Brianna or anyone else around it.

Strangely, several motorists passed the car later that morning and found the scene so strange that they stopped and took photos of it. One noticed some loose change, a water bottle, and a bracelet or necklace on the ground beside the car.

Once the abandoned car and Brianna's disappearance were linked, the Vermont State Police began an investigation. During the first few days, they were skeptical that foul play was involved, considering the possibility that Brianna was a runaway. The area around the old Dutchburn Farm was searched on foot by police officers and tracking dogs, but nothing was found. On March 30, the car Brianna had been driving, still impounded at the local garage, was processed by the state crime laboratory for evidence. No additional clues were found inside the car, but investigators had the first inkling that the damage that had been done to the Oldsmobile had been staged. Unfortunately, this caused the state police investigators to further suspect Brianna had run away.

But that idea would soon change.

A short time later, the FBI entered the case, trying to discover if there was a link between Brianna and nursing student Maura Murray, who had vanished just a month earlier. Both young women were attractive, had brown hair, and apparently disappeared after car accidents. Personal items were found left behind in both cars. The possibility of a serial killer was raised, but the FBI quickly dismissed them. After further investigation, they concluded that the two cases were not connected.

It was, they assured everyone, just a coincidence.

AFTER THE FBI LEFT THE CASE, VERMONT INVESTIGATORS were back at square one, so they began delving into what was going on in Brianna's life before she disappeared.

Three weeks before she disappeared, Brianna was involved in a physical confrontation at a party. She was attacked by a former friend named Keallie Lacross. While the reason for the altercation was unclear, Brianna's father, Bruce, later stated he believed it was caused by jealousy over Brianna's flirting with a boy at the party. A friend who was there claimed that Brianna – who had, by the way, extensive martial arts training – refused to fight with Keallie, who struck Brianna in the face several times while she was sitting in a truck. She ended up with a broken nose, two black eyes, and a concussion.

Brianna later filed charges against Keallie. At the time she disappeared, the case against Keallie was still pending. The police dropped the charges when Brianna wasn't found, against the objections of Brianna's parents, but Keallie was cleared of any involvement in her disappearance.

About a week after Brianna vanished, the state police received an anonymous tip claiming that she was being held against her will in a rental house in Berkshire, about 10 miles from Montgomery.

The house, then occupied by Ramon L. Ryans and Nathaniel Jackson, two known drug dealers from New York, was raided by police on April 15. They seized substantial amounts of cocaine and marijuana, but there was no sign of Brianna. Later, after interviewing some of Brianna's friends, investigators learned that she had allegedly experimented with drugs in the recent past – specifically crack cocaine – and was acquainted with Ryans and Jackson.

Had Brianna been at the house as the anonymous caller claimed but moved before the police arrived? Maybe. Later that same year, the police received a statement from an anonymous "older female" who implicated Ryans and Jackson in Brianna's disappearance and alleged murder. The signed affidavit contained allegations, written in graphic detail that Brianna had been murdered approximately a week after she vanished.

The witness claimed that Ryan had murdered Brianna during an argument over money she'd loaned him to purchase drugs. Her body was then temporarily stored in the basement of a woman who had recently been incarcerated. Then, it was dismembered and disposed of at a pig farm – where all the evidence was devoured.

It was an interesting story, but it was one that law enforcement could never corroborate.

And those weren't the only wild anonymous stories. Kellie and Butch received many unsubstantiated phone calls from people who claimed Brianna had been "tied to a tree in the woods" or had been disposed of "at the bottom of a lake." There were so many that they eventually changed their number.

As if the couple hadn't suffered enough already, Kellie and Butch separated in the wake of Brianna's disappearance, and Kellie later moved to New York.

SO, WHAT HAPPENED TO BRIANNA?

There are still many who believe that she left on her own. A few of her friends later said that she'd mentioned taking a trip somewhere exciting. It didn't help these rumors that she'd run away before, but eventually, even the police had a hard time believing she'd leave behind her car, her identification, and two uncashed paychecks.

And, of course, some insisted she'd gotten herself into trouble, and her disappearance was drug-related. There had been many serious issues with drugs in the area, thanks to the proximity of the Canadian border. The police had taken those kinds of tips seriously – especially when they involved drug dealers Ryan and Jackson – but Kellie and Butch had insisted that Brianna hadn't been using hard drugs.

There have been few developments in Brianna's story since she vanished. However, in 2006, a woman who resembled her was caught on security footage at a poker table at the Caesars World casino in Atlantic City. Could it have been her? We'll never know. The woman was never identified.

Since that time, her case has gone cold. But if Brianna is still out there somewhere, perhaps there's a chance that she'll be found. She has a family that still misses her and has left behind a mystery that needs to be solved.

2011: BECAUSE OF A LIE
THE DISAPPEARANCE OF ROBERT HOURIHAN

THAT FRIDAY SEEMED LIKE EVERY OTHER FRIDAY. Robert Hourihan finished his coffee, kissed his wife, Tara, and told her to have a good day. He walked out the door at 6:30 A.M. to go to work.

But this Friday, April 8, 2011, would be very different.

His routine continued, though, as the 33-year-old electrician left his home in Fluvanna County, Virginia, and started his 45-minute commute to his job in Richmond. On an ordinary day, he'd take U.S. 15 to Interstate 64, which went directly into the city, but this was not such a day.

This morning, he didn't take his usual route. An acquaintance saw the car he was driving – with a distinctive TARAMAE license plate and Winnie the Pooh sticker – going in the complete opposite direction.

Robert lied to his wife that morning. He wasn't going to work and didn't return home that night. In fact, Robert was never seen again.

WHEN ROBERT DIDN'T COME HOME THAT EVENING, Tara wasn't sure what to think. Her mind raced with terrible possibilities – accidents, injuries, illness, his heart condition that required daily medication – but she never once considered that he'd abandoned her or their six-year-old daughter, Melody. Robert always said they were his reason for getting up in the morning. Tara and everyone who knew Robert never thought he would willingly walk away from his family.

Tara and Robert met when they were kids. They rode the school bus together and went to the same church. Robert had been Tara's first love, but he'd had no idea until one Easter Sunday when the secret got out among the other young people at church. He told her he wished he'd known sooner and promptly asked her for a date. They were together from that day – high school sweethearts and now married for 14 years.

Tara never believed that Robert would lie to her, but apparently, that morning, he did.

Tara tried to call Robert's cell phone several times, but it went straight to voicemail each time she did. She started calling Robert's parents, brother, and friends, but no one had seen him. She also called his work, and that was when she found

Robert and Tara's wedding photograph. Tara had no reason to believe her marriage wasn't happy – until her husband lied to her on the day he disappeared.

out he wasn't scheduled to work that day. He worked as an electrician for the state of Virginia, and when he left the house that morning, he was wearing his work uniform. But he wasn't scheduled – he'd lied, and Tara had no idea why he'd do so. She later told detectives, "I thought he was going to work. He had his uniform on when he walked out the door."

She was aggravated and a little angry with her husband, but those emotions took a backseat to her worry. Robert's heart condition was serious. It required him to take daily medication, and he didn't have his prescription with him when he left. It was still sitting on the kitchen counter.

After waiting a little longer for Robert to come home, she finally called the police.

After speaking with Tara, investigators with the Fluvanna County Sheriff's Office began a search for Robert. Officers followed his usual route to work but found no trace of Robert, or Tara's Chevrolet Cavalier, which he'd been driving that morning. There was no sign of him, and after speaking to his family and friends,

Robert and his daughter, Melody, who was six years old when her father vanished.

a public appeal was made for information, asking anyone who thought they'd seen Robert to contact the sheriff's office.

County Sheriff Lieutenant David Wells told the press that detectives hadn't found any evidence of foul play, but the fact that Robert didn't have his heart medication had them concerned.

One call came from the owners of a deli located at the intersection of Route 53 and U.S. 15. Robert had been in the morning he went missing and had bought a breakfast sandwich. He was a regular customer there, usually stopping in on his way to work.

Another lead came from one of Tara's co-workers who, at the time, hadn't realized she'd seen something important. She said she had been driving on Route 53 on the morning of April 8 and at first thought she was driving behind Tara because she recognized her car. She knew the Cavalier, Tara's personalized plate, and the Pooh sticker on the window. When she got closer, though, she realized it was Robert behind the wheel.

When detectives reported this to Tara, she was confused. Robert had been going in the opposite direction he would take to get to work. But, of course, he wasn't going to work as he'd claimed to be that morning. Where was he going?

A few more days passed, but no further leads came in. On April 15, the local Crime Stoppers announced they were offering a $500 reward for information leading to the location of Robert's vehicle and $5,000 for information leading to Robert's whereabouts.

At some point in the next few days, something changed in the investigation, but the police weren't talking about what it was. All they would say on April 20 was that the authorities now considered Robert's disappearance to be "suspicious" – and that he hadn't willingly left on his own. But again, detectives refused to say why. Lieutenant Wells noted, "We've gotten a lot of information and we're still trying to track it down. I'm hoping when we find the car we might find some answers."

After this announcement, Tara told reporters that she had worried from the start that something terrible had happened to her husband, and the fact that he didn't have his heart medicine with him caused her to fear he was no longer alive. "I have a terrible feeling someone has done something horrible to him because they can't find him and they can't find my car," she said. "It's like he disappeared off the face of the earth."

She added to the reporter, "It's like I've lost my right arm – it's unbearable."

ON MAY 28, THE POLICE HAD THEIR FIRST POTENTIAL break in the case. Tara's Cavalier was discovered in the parking lot of a Target store in La Plata, Maryland – 110 miles from home.

A deputy from the Charles County Sheriff's Office had spotted the car abandoned on the edge of the lot and ran its license plate. It came back belonging to a missing person case and so he immediately identified the authorities in Virginia.

Tara's car – which Robert was driving when he disappeared – was found 110 miles from home. There was no sign of the missing man.

No one could explain what Robert would have been doing in La Plata. He had no connections to the area, and as far as his family and friends knew, he didn't know anyone who lived in the area.

It was unclear how long the car had been in the parking lot. Although there were surveillance cameras that covered the parking area, the footage was only kept for a short time before it was recorded over. Investigators pulled all the available footage, but the car had apparently arrived before the current video footage had started. This meant it had been sitting there for at least a few days before the officer became curious enough to run the license plate.

Detectives hoped to find someone who had seen the car's driver so they could confirm if it were Robert behind the wheel when it had been abandoned there, but a public plea led to no leads.

Investigators found Robert's work uniform shirt and all his tools inside the car. Neither Tara nor the police believed he would have left his expensive work tools behind on purpose. His personal belongings were missing from the vehicle – like his wallet and cell phone – but cell phone records showed he hadn't used his phone since 7:41 A.M. on the day he went missing.

Fluvanna County investigators teamed up with the Maryland and Virginia State Police to see if they could determine how the car ended up in La Plata, but they obtained almost no tips. No one recalled seeing the Cavalier – a common car at the time – even with its personalized plate and sticker. Lieutenant Wells told the press that they still had no concrete evidence as to what happened to Robert but believed that foul play was likely.

After nearly a month had passed, Robert's parents hired a private investigator to back up the police investigation. They also offered their own reward of $5,000, hoping it would help.

But it didn't.

By now, a heartbroken Tara was starting to accept the idea that her husband was dead. He didn't have his medicine for his heart, and his prescription hadn't been refilled anywhere. She knew he couldn't live without his medication – and she wasn't sure she could live without him. But she had to – she had a daughter – and she needed to bring Robert home one way or another.

She told a reporter, "I truly believe in my heart somebody has done something to him and if they had any decency at all they would tell us where they've put him. I would at least like to put him to rest. I don't want him lying out there like he's a piece of trash."

Melody, of course, was too young to understand what was happening fully. She only knew that her daddy wasn't home, and she was devastated by this. Tara said, "I wouldn't wish this on anybody... having to watch my daughter is enough to rip my heart out of my chest. She loves her Daddy so much, and no one will ever be able to fill that void."

More time passed, and Robert's case grew cold. It was too strange and mysterious, and there seemed to be no direction for the search to go.

When the holidays arrived, his family shared their pain with one another. Tara was grateful to have the support of Robert's parents and church members, but she missed her husband and desperately wanted answers. She'd been dismayed to find that Robert had lied to her about going to work on the day he went missing, and although rumors were going around that he was living some sort of double life, she didn't believe it. She knew her husband loved her and insisted Robert would never voluntarily leave her or their daughter.

So, where was he?

AS THE FIRST ANNIVERSARY OF ROBERT'S VANISHING arrived, detectives were forced to admit they knew little more after a year of investigation than they'd known on the day he went missing. The Cavalier had been processed for evidence but failed to offer any clues to Robert's whereabouts or how it ended up 110 miles from any place he knew.

Tara still just wanted answers. "We just want someone to come forward and end this for us. The longer it's drawn out, the harder it is. We just so desperately need to know what happened."

Robert's mother, Melinda, told reporters that she didn't expect to find her son alive, but she wanted to be able to bring him home and give him a proper burial. "Someone out there knows something. We don't care what happened, who did it… we just want to know where he is."

Four more years passed, and in 2015, a single clue was revealed. An acquaintance of Robert's named Daniel Fennel, who lived in Palmyra, Virginia, told detectives that he was supposed to meet Robert on the morning he went missing. He said Robert never showed up and had no idea why he missed the meeting.

I have never found out what that meeting was supposed to be about, but it seems odd that he didn't show. The meeting would have taken him south on Route 53 – the opposite direction he took to work – and he was reported going in that direction by Tara's co-worker. It was also noted by staff at the deli where he bought breakfast that he arrived there at 8:00 A.M. That seems late considering he left home at 6:30 and the deli was on the way to

Interstate 64. That means he backtracked on Route 53, going south, then north, to buy breakfast.

Where had he been for an hour and a half? And why didn't he make the meeting he'd planned?

The last time Robert had used his cell phone was 7:41 A.M., which was between the time his car was spotted and his stop at the deli for breakfast.

Considering these things, it seems easier to understand why this case has been so hard to solve.

Lieutenant Wells believed some people knew exactly what happened that morning, in any case. They were just refusing to come forward and help. He told the press, "I believe there are people locally who know a lot more than they are telling me...their level of involvement, I don't know. I really wish that someone in his group of friends could give me some information."

Wells said that investigators didn't expect to find Robert alive after all this time, but they continued to search for him so that his family could have some closure. "We might never be able to prove what happened or who did it, but at least they wouldn't have to wonder."

In 2021 – 10 years after Robert vanished – interest was revived in the case, and the reward for his whereabouts was increased to $20,000. Detectives still believed he'd met with foul play, although they hadn't had any luck in determining exactly what happened to him. Even after a decade, they hoped the increased reward would jumpstart the stalled and very cold investigation.

Tara, who was interviewed when the investigation was started again, admitted that she'd been forced to adjust to life as a single mother. Even after ten years, she'd never remarried. She was still heartbroken for herself and Melody. "She was so young when he went missing. She doesn't really remember him, and that's what hurts most of all."

Tara remained burdened by her loneliness and sadness, still with no answers about what Robert was doing on the day he went missing. "I wish I knew that was the last time I would see him. I would have held onto him a little longer."

Even now, detectives insist the case is open and ongoing, and they remain tightlipped about what they do and don't know. They'll only say it was foul play that caused the disappearance.

David Wells, who has since been promoted to Major, still oversees the case and continues to say that he believes the case can be solved. "We believe multiple parties were involved and have knowledge of what happened...we're hoping now that so much time has passed, someone will come forward."

Major Wells believes that Robert knew the person or persons responsible for his vanishing, though he has never said how he thinks they were connected.

Tara has stated on many occasions that she doesn't believe her husband was involved with drugs or some other kind of illegal activity – but would she have known?

The fact that Robert lied to her about having to work that day indicates that he'd gotten mixed up in some things he didn't want her to know about. He must have felt she wouldn't approve, whatever it was, so he lied.

Sadly, that lie just might have gotten him killed.

2020: OFF ON THE SIDE OF THE ROAD

THE DISAPPEARANCE OF JASON LANDRY

I WOULDN'T USUALLY INCLUDE A STORY THAT IS THIS recent. I would assume that since it happened less than four years before the writing of this book, there's a very good chance that Jason might be found. He wouldn't need an entry here; it would be pages and ink wasted on a story that's been solved.

Or at least that's what I hope will happen.

When I read about what happened to Jason Landry, it reminded me very much of another story that bothered me so much that I decided to revisit it with new information as the last story in this book.

You'll soon see what I mean.

ON DECEMBER 13, 2020, 21-YEAR-OLD COLLEGE student Jason Landry packed up his things and left his apartment in San Marcos, Texas, around 11:00 P.M. The Texas State University student had finished all his finals and was on his way to his parents' home in Missouri City, Texas, for winter break.

Jason Landry

Everyone who saw him that evening said Jason was in a good mood when he left. And why wouldn't he be? He was a good student; everything he needed to wrap up for the end of the semester was finished, and he was going home to see his family and hang out with friends over the holidays.

He tossed his stuff into his Nissan Altima and got on the road. It was late, but his mom was expecting him. It was 165 miles to Missouri City, so he didn't expect to arrive until 2:00 A.M. but was wide awake and ready to get home.

But Jason never made it home.

His car was found wrecked and abandoned later that night – only 30 miles from his apartment. He wasn't anywhere in or around his car when it was discovered – and he has never been seen since.

Returning home from a call, a volunteer firefighter spotted the Altima on Salt Flat Road near Luling, Texas, that morning. It was a remote dirt road with no houses or structures nearby. Very few people used it, so he was startled to find the wrecked vehicle. It was 12:30 A.M. when he made the call to the police. He reported that the car was off the road and had crashed into a tree.

When a Texas Highway Patrol officer arrived on the scene, he found no sign of Jason. He initially assumed he was dealing with a drunk driver who had crashed his car and fled the scene to avoid getting arrested. He called for a tow truck to pick up the Altima and take it to an impound lot.

A report filed later stated that the headlights on the car were on when it was found. The keys were still in the ignition. All the doors except the front driver's side door were locked. Jason's cell phone and some other personal items were still inside. While searching the area, the officer discovered Jacon's backpack about 900 feet from the car. Inside was a baseball cap, a small bag of toiletries, a plastic container that contacted his beta fish – now dead, Jason's laptop, some gaming equipment, and a small baggie of marijuana.

While waiting for the tow truck, the officer also went through the Altima's glove compartment and found the car's registration. It was registered to Jason's parents, Kent and Lisa Landry, so he called and told them the car had been in an accident.

When they discovered that Jason wasn't at the scene, Kent immediately dressed, got in his car, and went straight to Luling to see what was happening. When he arrived there, he was unimpressed with the way the search was being conducted for Jason. Kent, the senior pastor of a Missouri City church, was desperate to find his son – much too desperate to wait for the Highway Patrol to do something. He returned to his car, determined to conduct his own search of the area.

After arriving at where the Altima was discovered, Kent found several articles of Jason's clothing, including a pair of shorts, a shirt, socks, underwear, shoes, and a wristwatch. Interviews with some of Jason's friends – who saw him when he left school – confirmed that the items Kent found were the clothes he'd been wearing when he left to drive home.

Apparently, Jason had taken off all his clothing after getting out of his wrecked car, even though the temperature was only a few degrees above freezing that morning. Had he changed clothes? Or had he walked away naked?

Investigators could find no evidence that Jason's car had been forced off the road. The only damage they could find was to the vehicle's rear end, where he'd impacted with two trees after sliding off the road. It was suggested that perhaps he'd swerved to avoid a deer and then overcorrected. causing the car to spin around and slam into the trees trunk first. There was no paint, dents, or scratches to suggest another vehicle had been involved.

By that evening, state and local police departments and dozens of volunteers organized a search for Jason. Investigators believed the crash had likely occurred shortly before it was discovered, which meant Jason didn't have much time to get out of the area before the police arrived.

It's unclear why they believed this since Jason left his apartment at 11:00 P.M. and the crash was discovered at 12:30 A.M. – just 30 miles from where his trip started. Even if he stopped for gas and snacks for the road, he still had over an hour to drive 30 miles. The car could have been abandoned on the road for at least 30 minutes before it was seen. No one else came forward claiming to have seen the crash before the firefighter reported it. This wasn't a surprise considering the remoteness of Salt Flat Road.

And they didn't see Jason either. No one reported him on the road or reported picking him up. Investigators didn't know if he'd walked away alone or was in a vehicle.

Texas Department of Public Safety Sergeant Deon Cockrell told the press that a handful of different agencies were assisting in the search. However, by the evening of December 15, they still didn't know what happened to Jason. "We have searched the entire area with DPS helicopters, drones...other agencies have come out, state and local...even the Texas search and rescue team with their canines."

There was no sign of Jason in the area.

Jason's mother, Lisa, was worried that her son had been injured in the crash and was unable to find help. "He's alone, he doesn't have his phone or his wallet, and it's cold outside. Maybe he's hurt." She knew that a few drops of blood had been found on some of his discarded clothing, and while police officers assured her it wasn't enough to suggest he was seriously injured, she was worried anyway.

Although nothing was found that indicated Jason was still in the area, the search continued. Sergeant Cockrell announced, "We're going to keep on searching until we think there's no hope, which could be two days, three days, four days from now. We're going to keep on searching until we either find him or find an answer."

The following day, the search intensified with Texas EquuSearch – a nonprofit organization that provides search and recovery services to families of missing persons – joining the search. Teams combed the remote area northeast of Luling where the car had been found. Felix Cortinas, who owned property in the area, told reporters, "It's a place where someone could easily get lost. A lot of old wells, old wells that were never even capped or cemented, just holes. And a lot of creeks, a lot of steep banks."

Tracking dogs picked up Jason's trail leading away from the car -- which seemed to solve the mystery of whether he walked away -- and kept going toward Luling. They ran for nearly a quarter mile before they lost the scent and stopped. It was possible he got into a car with someone at that point.

The search continued on December 16. Officials decided to search a pond near the accident scene, and search dogs seemed to pick up Jason's scent near the water. The search team brought sonar equipment and found something resembling a person's shape on the bottom. The authorities decided to drain the pond, and as the water lowered, Jason's family tried to prepare themselves for the worst. The pond was emptied, but there was no sign of Jason.

The following day, the Texas Department of Safety and members of Texas EquuSearch went back over several areas near the crash site, looking for anything the earlier searches might have missed. Nothing was found, and even the most optimistic among them were starting to believe that something terrible had happened to the missing young man.

A reporter asked Jason's father, Kent, if he thought Jason might be hiding somewhere, afraid to come home because he had wrecked his car. Kent immediately dismissed this idea, but he directly appealed to his son in case he was watching: "Don't worry... the car is just a stupid car. We love you. Call someone. Call the police. Come home. We just want you home."

ON DECEMBER 20, JASON HAD BEEN MISSING FOR a week, but no progress had been made toward finding him. A prayer vigil was held for him that night, and Kent and Lisa thanked the community for their prayers and support during the search. As Kent said, "We are living the worst dreams of every parent. It feels like a bad dream. A bad dream we've been hoping to wake up from... I pray my son is alive and pray that someone is taking care of him."

With the search for Jason floundering, the Caldwell County Sheriff's Office stepped into the case. They hadn't been called to investigate the disappearance because the Highway Patrol officer who responded to the crash hadn't considered the accident to be unusual. This meant that sheriff's investigators never had the chance to search the car before it was taken to the impound lot. Caldwell County Sergeant William Miller explained, "There were certain things that weren't done in the first hours after the discovery. We weren't conducting a true missing persons investigation."

With the case now being handled by the sheriff's office, they began working quickly to catch up. They started by interviewing Jason's friends and classmates to try to determine where Jason had been in the hours before the crash occurred.

Two days later, on December 22, volunteers with Texas EquuSearch announced they had suspended the search for Jason. They felt the area had been thoroughly searched, and no evidence of Jason had been found. However, they did assure the Landry family that they would launch another search if the sheriff's office found any credible leads about where Jason might be.

Meanwhile, law enforcement officers and volunteers combed through an additional 300 acres of land near Luling but found no sign of Jason. They also used a drone to fly over the area and record video footage, which was painstakingly studied for any potential evidence. As with the other searches, though, nothing was found.

The physical search ended, and Caldwell County Sheriff Daniel Law stated that he was confident that Jason was not anywhere within the 31 square miles that had been searched. "We will not speculate on what may have happened to Jason, but we feel the vast area surrounding the accident scene has been thoroughly searched and Jason still hasn't been found."

Sergeant Miller told reporters that he didn't have enough information to form an opinion about what had happened to Jason, but he was still hoping to find him alive. "We are trying to run down all our leads. It would have been easier if we had started a week ago."

Kent Landry agreed. He and Lisa were very critical of how the Texas Department of Public Safety handled the case at the beginning. They wondered if Jason would have been immediately found if the case had been assigned to the sheriff's department at the start.

Kent made another public appeal, this time to anyone who might have information about Jason's whereabouts. "If someone knows something, might know something, might have seen him -- please tell someone." He explained that he was desperate to have his son home for Christmas.

After interviewing Jason's friends in San Marcos, sheriff's detectives traveled to Missouri City to sit down with Jason's parents, siblings, and friends at home. However, little information could be gained from them.

Jason Landry didn't make it home for Christmas.

ON JANUARY 29, 2021 – A MONTH AND A HALF AFTER the disappearance – they could finally access most of Jason's cell phone and computer data. They learned that he briefly stopped using his GPS to open Snapchat on his photo at 11:24 P.M. on the night he disappeared. This caused him to miss a turn, and he ended up on Salt Flat Road, where his car was found at 12:30 A.M. Although his cell phone stayed on and had a signal, Jason never used it again after 11:24 P.M., and investigators were working to try and determine what happened after that.

There had been rumors that Jason had been traveling to meet someone – or that he had said he was going to meet someone – that night, which was how he ended up near Luling. But it turns out he had ended up on that isolated dirt road by accident because he'd missed a turn when he closed this GPS.

This discovery, which coincided with the sheriff's office and the Texas Rangers working together to submit several of the items found on the road for DNA testing to confirm they belonged to Jason, jolted the investigation back to life again.

On February 26, Texas Search and Rescue began a three-day search for Jason in Caldwell County. They used dog teams, searchers on horseback, volunteers on foot, drones, and helicopters to scour the region. They covered 50 square miles during the search but, again, found no trace of Jason.

Two months later, the Landrys announced a $10,000 reward for information leading to their son's safe return. They also began working with Tuleta Copeland, a retired FBI agent who volunteered to search for missing people. Despite several requests for information from the public, no new leads came in.

By December 2021 – the first anniversary of Jason's interrupted drive home for the holidays – he was still missing. His case was open, but investigators hadn't been able to develop any new leads and had no idea what had happened to him. Additional searches had been conducted during the previous summer and fall, but no clues about his whereabouts were discovered.

More time passed, and the case became cold. By December 2022, Jason had been missing for two years, and no one seemed able to agree about where he was or even how he managed to go missing. Caldwell County detectives now believed that Jason had walked away from the accident and vanished on his own, but his parents and retired FBI agent Copeland were sure that he was the victim of a crime.

Kent believed that the initial officer on the scene dismissed the importance of the accident the moment he opened Jason's backpack and found marijuana. "It just feels like your child is discarded because they treated everything with this investigation with such indifference," he said and pointed out that he was the one who found Jason's clothing on the road – after the car had already been towed.

By 2022, Kent and Lisa had resigned themselves to the fact that Jason was probably dead. They didn't believe he'd leave on his own or purposely cause the pain he knew they would feel by his cruel absence. If he was no longer alive, though, they wanted to know what happened that night and wanted to bring his body home for a proper burial.

Caldwell County Sheriff's Captain Jeff Ferry agreed in 2022 that Jason was likely deceased but didn't believe foul play was involved. The cops were still hung up on that marijuana, and he noted that Jason had messaged his friends about it that night and told them some other, very personal things.

He told a reporter, "When we look at the totality of things, it really paints a picture of almost an internal crisis that Jason is dealing with."

He said he believed that Jason fled on foot after crashing the car and got lost. Unfortunately, they just hadn't been able to find his remains.

But this theory only seems to fit if we leave out the fact that Jason was only on that road because he missed a turn, and it doesn't explain how his car ended up crashing backward into some trees, even though there were no skid marks or tire tracks on the road.

And if he walked away and got lost, why did the search dogs follow his trail for a quarter mile toward town before it suddenly stopped – a widely accepted indication that the person being tracked got into a vehicle?

Jason didn't plan to be on Salt Flat Road that night. And if he got into a car with someone, maybe they didn't plan to be there either. Maybe – even though it was an isolated road – the wrong person came by, and Jason, not knowing any better, accepted a ride with that wrong person.

No one knows.

His parents just want to find him, no matter the reason for his disappearance. Kent still believes that the Highway Patrol seemed to make up their mind right away that Jason was just some college kid on drugs and didn't put much effort into finding him. "They saw his clothes lying in the middle of the road and didn't even bother to pick them up. If you literally think there is some college student naked in 30-degree weather, shouldn't you at least search for him?"

For Jason's family and his friends, he remains more than just another missing college student. They continue to raise awareness about his disappearance and ensure he isn't forgotten.

So, please don't forget. Jason really could be out there somewhere, trying to come home. Who knows who'll be the one to find him?

It might even be you.

WITHOUT A TRACE REVISITED

When I decided to write a sequel to my earlier book about unexplained disappearances, I promised myself that I wouldn't revisit any of the stories from the first book, but I couldn't help it with this one. This story was already strange, but after digging a little deeper into Brandon Swanson's last car ride, I found things were even stranger than I originally thought.

So, don't skip over this and think you already know this story. There's more to this one than any of us originally thought.

2008: THE LAST RIDE HOME
STILL SEARCHING FOR BRANDON SWANSON

SHORTLY AFTER MIDNIGHT ON MAY 14, 2008, a young man named Brandon Swanson drove his car into a ditch on his way home from celebrating the end of the spring semester with fellow students from Minnesota West Community and Technical College.

The crash was minor, and unhurt, Brandon exited the car and called his parents on his cellphone. Unsure of his exact location, he told them he believed he was near Lynd, Minnesota – he could see the lights of town, he told them.

Roused from sleep, his parents dressed and hurried to their car so they could pick him up. They drove for more than a half-hour but were unable to locate him. Brandon remained on the phone with them almost the entire time as he walked toward town.

Then, suddenly, after 45 minutes on the line, he cried out, and the call abruptly ended.

Brandon has not been seen or heard from since.

BRANDON, WHO WAS 19 YEARS OLD IN 2008, GREW UP in Marshall, located in the southwestern corner of Minnesota. He was an avid reader and had worked at the local Hy-Vee grocery store for four years. He graduated from Marshall High School in 2007 and decided to study wind turbines for a year at Minnesota West Community and Technical College in

Brandon Swanson

Canby. After that, he intended to enroll in a four-year college and pursue a career in the sciences.

His whole life was ahead of him, but it would be tragically cut short.

Classes at Minnesota West ended for the year on May 13. Brandon stayed in Canby for the evening to celebrate with friends. He attended two different parties and, according to friends, had a few drinks but not enough alcohol to make him seem visibly intoxicated.

Just before midnight, Brandon left Canby for the 30-mile drive home to his parents' house. He was familiar with the drive from Canby to Marshall since he made it almost daily. And there's really no way to get lost – it's all on one road. The two towns are directly connected by State Highway 68. There's little traffic in the area, and the drive normally takes just over a half-hour.

This time, though, Brandon ran into trouble. It's unknown how or why it happened, but Brandon swerved off the road and ran his Chevrolet Lumina into a ditch. He tried to back out, but it was no use. The car was stuck.

He called his parents after repeated calls to his friends that went unanswered. The phone rang at home at 1:54 A.M. He explained the problem and told them he could not move the car. He wasn't hurt, he assured them, but he needed them to come and pick him up.

Brandon's parents, Brian and Annette, got in their truck and began driving toward where they believed their son had been stranded. He stayed on the phone with them, although the call dropped several times, and they had to keep calling back.

They followed Brandon's directions to where he was waiting with the car. He told them he thought he was midway between the towns of Lynd and Marshall. Based on what he told them, Brian believed he knew exactly where his son was. It should have taken only about 10 minutes to get there.

But the problem is that Lynd is *not* on the road between Canby, where Brandon started his trip, and Marshall, where he was supposed to end up. It's actually a little southwest of Marshall, on Route 23. There's no explanation for why Brandon drove past Marshall toward Lynd or took a side road that put him on the other highway – and no one asked.

In fact, I'm not sure if anyone has ever asked.

When his parents arrived at where he was supposed to be, they didn't see Brandon or his car. Still on the line with him, they told Brandon to keep an eye out for them. After a few minutes, they started honking their horn and flashing the truck's headlights, hoping he'd spot them. They were surprised when Brandon said he couldn't hear the horn and saw no lights on the road. Brian asked if he was certain he'd sent them to the right place, and Brandon said he had.

So, changing tactics, Brandon started flashing the headlights of his stranded car. They could hear the clicking noise it made as he turned the lights on and off through the phone, but they couldn't see flashing headlights anywhere around them – even though wide, open fields surrounded them.

Southwest Minnesota isn't exactly known for its rolling hills, so if Brandon had been anywhere along that dark road, they should have been able to spot him.

By now, Brandon was aggravated. He was sure he had accurately described his location to his parents and couldn't understand why they couldn't follow his directions. They insisted they were exactly where Brandon had told them to go, but he was certain they were the ones who were confused.

Finally, he gave up, decided that things would be quicker if he left the car, and started walking toward the lights he could see up ahead. He believed he was looking at the small town of Lynd and could easily walk there. He told his parents that he'd meet them at the parking lot of a bar in town and for them to wait for him there. Brian agreed, dropped Annette off at home, and drove to Lynd.

Brandon remained on the phone with his father as he walked, updating him on his progress. He said he was walking along a gravel road because he'd taken a shortcut through a field. At one point, he mentioned that he could hear running water nearby but couldn't see it in the darkness. He just kept walking toward what he assumed were the lights of Lynd.

Shortly after 2:30 A.M., Brandon suddenly interrupted his father on the line. "Oh, shit!" he called out. A moment later, the call disconnected.

Concerned, Brian tried to call back but was unable to reach him. He called five or six times, but the calls went straight to Brandon's voicemail. For that to happen, it meant Brandon had turned his phone off, the battery was dead, or something happened to make the phone stop working.

But whatever happened, Brandon Swanson has never been seen or heard from again.

BRIAN WASN'T SURE WHAT TO DO NEXT.

He drove back and forth over the same stretch of road but found no sign of Brandon or his car. Annette and Brian started calling some of Brandon's friends, and they came to help look for him. They searched for Brandon's car, driving side roads and gravel paths throughout the night. But they found nothing.

Finally, everyone met up in Lynd, at the same parking lot where Brandon was supposed to be. There was a chance he'd gotten there, they hoped, but it was dark and empty.

Now, out of ideas, Brian and Annette finally started to panic. They were out of ideas but were certain that something bad had happened to their son. With no other options, they called the police around 6:30 A.M.

Brian and Annette were frantic and worried, but it quickly became clear that the authorities didn't share their concerns. The police in Lynd told them that it was hardly unusual for a young man of Brandon's age to stay out all night after the last day of college classes. Brandon was an adult, and it was, one of the officers told Annette, his right to be missing if he wanted to be.

Annette tried to explain that this wasn't the case of an overprotective parent worrying about a kid who'd stayed out too late. They walked through the situation with the cops again.

Probably slowly and in words of few syllables.

Annette and Brian told them that something happened to Brandon right before his phone went dead, and they were sure it wasn't good. It took more than two hours to convince them, but the Lynd police finally agreed to open a missing persons case.

After a perfunctory search around the town, the local police felt confident that Brandon was not in Lynd. Searching the roads leading into town also failed to turn up anything. As far as they could tell, Brandon wasn't anywhere in their jurisdiction. Basically, after that, they washed their hands of the situation.

Meanwhile, Brian and Annette continued searching for Brandon's car and requested help from Lyon County Sheriff Joel Dahl. He soon had deputies searching the nearby roads. The sheriff's office also managed to obtain Brandon's cell phone records, hoping they would help pinpoint the location of his car.

That's when they made a startling discovery. There was a good reason why Brandon hadn't been found in the search around the town of Lynd – he'd never been close to it at all.

The calls he'd made to his parents the previous night had been made near Taunton, another small town. However, this one is off State Highway 68, which he had driven many times from Canby to Marshall. It is also 25 miles from Lynd, which, as mentioned, was not on the same highway.

Since Taunton was also on the way home, it made sense that Brandon was close to it as he traveled from Canby to Marshall. Less understandable, though, was why he thought he was in Lynd and how he would have gotten there in the first place since it's not on the route home.

There's also one other little issue – why was he in Taunton at 2:00 A.M.? Leaving Canby on Highway 68, it's only 13 miles to Taunton, which should take no more than 15 minutes. Brandon only had another 17 miles from Taunton to reach Marshall. His friends believed he'd left Canby shortly after midnight, meaning it took him nearly two hours to drive only 13 miles.

And for some reason, Brandon believed he was on the other side of Marshall, almost to Lynd, when he drove into the ditch.

Brian's car was found in a ditch – nowhere near where he thought he was on the night he vanished.

By searching near Taunton, county deputies quickly located Brandon's abandoned car in a ditch off a gravel road along the Lincoln County line. It was one mile north of Highway 68.

Brandon's Lumina had gotten hung up on the top of an incline at the road's edge. The car wasn't damaged but tipped so the wheels couldn't touch the ground on one side. This is why Brandon was unable to move it. There was nothing else wrong with the car. The grass and gravel surrounding the vehicle made it impossible to find tracks and determine which direction Brandon might have started walking.

Investigators searched the inside of the car but found nothing to suggest that Brandon had been injured when he slid into the ditch. It was clear that Brandon had accurately described exactly what happened when he called his parents -- the only thing he got wrong was the location. He thought the lights he saw in the distance were from Lynd, but he was nowhere near there.

Again, though, I'm dying for someone to ask *why* he thought he was in Lynd since just a glance at a map shows that it's *not* on the way home.

Officials discovered that Brandon's cell phone calls had been routed through a tower at the intersection of Routes 3 and 10 near Minneota, another small town nearby. The calls had come from within five miles of the tower, which narrowed the search field.

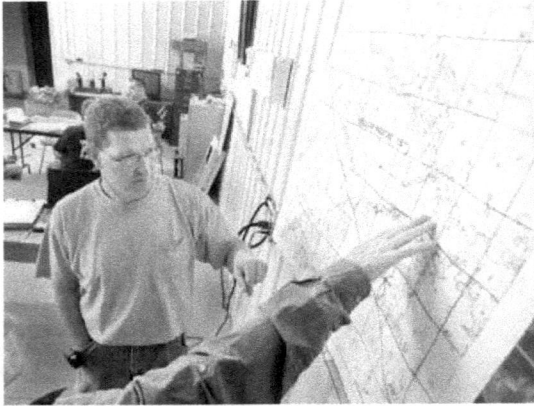

Brandon's father, Brian, during the search for his son in the area around Taunton.

Since part of the search area included Yellow Medicine County on the north, deputies from that sheriff's office also joined the search.

An extensive search was launched using small planes and helicopters to cover the wide-open ground from above. Search dogs were brought in from Minneapolis-St. Paul but a team of bloodhounds from nearby Codington County, South Dakota, first picked up on Brandon's scent.

They followed the trail for nearly three miles as it skirted past fields and headed in a north-northwest direction to an abandoned farm. The dogs continued past the farm and headed along the Yellow Medicine River. When they reached a certain point, the dogs seemed to indicate that Brandon had entered the river at that spot. The river there flowed from knee-deep to about 15 feet, so even if Brandon had entered the water, he likely wouldn't have drowned. It was possible that he made it to the other side, but the dogs couldn't follow the trail any further.

The location seemed to fit Brandon's call to his father. Brian remembered him mentioning fences and hearing water nearby, but he didn't understand why Brandon had left the road in the first place. He said he was following a "shortcut," but how was a three-mile hike through woods and fields any kind of shortcut to town?

Even though it seemed that Brandon likely would have survived falling into the river, boats from the Minnesota Department of Natural Resources were deployed, and deputies walked the riverbanks for miles in every direction. Horses and ATVs covered the surrounding area, but there was no sign of Brandon's body. Investigators believed that if he'd drowned in the river, they would have found him.

The official search for Brandon was suspended after a week, but friends and family continued looking for him independently. On May 24 and June 7, around 100 volunteers joined Brian and Annette as they searched areas to the south and east of where his car was found.

The area along the Yellow Medicine River, where it's believed Brandon's phone stopped working during the call with his father.

There were no signs of Brandon.

Sheriff's deputies were baffled by the case. A few of them even walked the banks of the Yellow Medicine River in their free time, hoping to find one clue that might have been missed.

In the following weeks, Brian and Annette left their porch light on all night, every night, to symbolize their hope that Brandon would eventually return or be found.

To this day, they still do.

THE SEARCH FOR BRANDON RESUMED THAT FALL once all the fields in the area had been harvested and cleared. Dogs were again brought in to assist, and though they seemed to be following a scent trail into an area near the town of Porter, which was northwest of Taunton, they eventually lost the scent. Once again, no trace of Brandon was found.

The search was suspended over the winter, but efforts continued in the spring after the snow had melted and before fields were planted. By this time, 122 square miles had been thoroughly searched, using more than 500 volunteers, 34 dog handlers from nine different states, and countless hours of hard work.

In 2010, two years after Brandon vanished, the Minnesota Bureau of Criminal Apprehension took over as the lead agency on the case. It set up a tip line, which generated more than 90 leads, and they moved the search area towards Mud Creek, a tributary of the Yellow Medicine River directly north of Taunton. They found nothing but have continued to search that area periodically.

But even with the renewed interest in the case, no clues to Brandon's whereabouts were found. Needless to say, this has made it easy to speculate about what happened to him that night on the highway.

Some believe that Brandon intentionally disappeared – that he staged the whole thing. This seems unlikely, though. He was a good student and had just completed a wind energy certification course. He had plenty of friends, no problems at home or school, and plans to transfer to Iowa in a few months to continue his education. He wasn't in any legal trouble and was close to his family.

Besides that, it doesn't seem plausible to get your car stuck on the side of the road, call your parents for help, and then stay on the phone with them for an hour until pretending to experience some kind of shocking event so that you can disappear for no logical reason.

Both Brian and Annette insisted that he wouldn't do that.

Another theory is that Brandon was struck and killed by a car while walking, and the driver panicked and hid his body. This also seems unlikely. Brandon told his father he was cutting through fields, not walking along the road. This was supported by cell phone records and the path followed by the tracking dogs. Both indicate that Brandon was not walking on the highway. Some evidence would have been left at the scene if this had happened. Blood, tire marks, and possibly vehicle pieces would have been found during the extensive searches, but nothing ever was.

If Brandon didn't run away or die by accident, this leaves foul play. Could someone have followed him home from the last party when he left and grabbed him when they had the chance? Did he meet someone after the party and come to harm? Could he have been a victim of chance, running into a killer on the road who saw the opportunity and took it?

These things may not be impossible, but they're unlikely.

The area where Brandon disappeared was sparsely populated. Taunton, for example, had a population of 135 people at the time. Most of the area is farmland, and houses are few and far between. It would have been almost impossible to lie in wait for him because there was no way of knowing ahead of time that he would get his car stuck in a ditch and then continue on foot. The chance that someone spotted him walking in the dark, in the middle of nowhere, and just decided to kill him is also very slim, especially when you consider how few people were around there.

What seems more likely is that Brandon's disappearance was a tragic accident. He was trying to make his way, on foot, along dark fields and side roads in the dark. There were no streetlights to guide him or homes or businesses he could see. He was surrounded by corn and soybean fields that all looked alike in the dark. He mentioned to his father that he heard running water somewhere but didn't seem concerned.

Even so, it's possible that he slipped into the river at some point. This may have been when he cried out while on the phone with his father, and if the phone had gone into the river, it might have stopped working, so Brian couldn't reach him when he had repeatedly called him.

But even if Brian did go into the water, it doesn't mean he drowned. He could've gotten out of the river, disoriented but still alive. He might have even kept walking for a while, but he would have been wet and cold – it was early May in Minnesota, after all – and he could have died from hypothermia.

If he did, his body could have been scattered by animals. There are wild animals in Minnesota – like bears, coyotes, and wildcats – and the body would almost certainly have been eaten if they discovered his remains.

But if that did happen, why weren't Brandon's keys, phone, and glasses found during all those searches? Had they just been missing them, or were they never there at all?

We may never know.

We'll probably never get answers to the questions that I really want answered, like why Brandon thought he was near Lynd that night. And why did it take him nearly two hours to make a 13-mile drive? Where was he during that time?

These questions have never been addressed.

Maybe someday they will be I don't know.

One good thing came out of this. Annette Swanson never forgot the initial response of the police, and she and Brian began pushing for changes in state law that would require an investigation into the case of missing adults under the age of 21.

"Brandon's Law," as it became known, became official later in 2008. Annette knew it wouldn't help her son's case but might save other lives.

And sometimes, that's the best that we can do.

BIBLIOGRAPHY

Ahern, Stephen H. – *A Kitchen Painted in Blood*, Exposit, Jefferson, NC, 2020

Aron, Paul - *Unsolved Mysteries of American History*, John Wiley & Sons, New York, NY, 1997

Bills, E.R. – *Texas Oblivion*, Charleston, SC, History Press, 2021

Canning, John - *Great Unsolved Mysteries,* Chartwell Books, Secaucus, NJ, 1984

Churchill, Alan – *Pictorial History of American Crime*, Bramhall House, New York, NY, 1964
------------------- – *They Never Came Back*, Ace Books, New York, NY, 1960

Colander, Pat – *Thin Air*, Contemporary Books, Chicago, IL, 1982

Crofton, Ian – *The Disappeared,* Quercus Books, London, 2008

Glidewell, Jan – "The Lost Legends of Charlie Hope," *Tampa Bay Times*, April 18, 1992

Greenberg, Eric J. – "Two Teens Hitchhiked to a Concert. 50 Years Later, They Haven't Come Home," *Rolling Stone*, August 2023

Harrison, Michael – *Vanishings*, Trafalgar Square, London, 1981

Hunt, Gerry - *Bizarre America,* Berkley Books, New York, NY, 1988

Landsburg, Alan – *In Search of Missing Persons*, Bantam Books, New York, NY, 1978

Levin, Peter – *Album of Famous Mysteries,* Syndicated Newspaper Column

Martinez, Lionel - *Great Unsolved Mysteries of North America,* Book Sales, New York, NY, 1988

MEDIUM – Publishing Platform, 2012-2024

Miller, Jax – *Hell in the Heartland,* Berkeley Books, New York, NY, 2020

Mokrzycki, Paul – "Lost in the Heartland: Childhood, Region, and Iowa's Missing Paperboys" – *The Annals of Iowa 74*, State Historical Society of Iowa, Winter 2015

Nash, Jay Robert - *Among the Missing*, Simon & Shuster, New York, NY, 1978

---------------------- - *Murder, America*, Simon & Shuster, New York, NY, 1980

Pettem, Silvia – *Cold Case Chronicles*, Lyons Press, Guilford, CT, 2021

Platnick, Kenneth - *Great Mysteries of History*, Stackpole, Pennsylvania, 1971

Pruitt, Sarah – *Vanished!*, Lyon Press, Guilford, CT, 2018

Steiger, Brad - *Strange Disappearances,* Lancer Books, Canada, 1972

Tofel, Richard J. – *Vanishing Point*, Ivan R. Dee, New York, NY, 2004

Wilkins, Harold T. - *Strange Mysteries of Time & Space*, Citadel Press, New York, NY, 1959

Wilson, Colin - *Unsolved Mysteries Past & Present*, Contemporary Books, New York, NY, 1992

Wilson, Colin and Damon Wilson - *Mammoth Encyclopedia of the Unsolved*, Running Press, New York, NY, 2000

Wingate, John – *Lost Boys of Hannibal*, Wisdom Editions, Minneapolis, MN, 2017

Wisner, Bill – *Vanished, Without A Trace*, Berkley, New York, NY, 1977

NEWSPAPERS AND PERIODICALS:

Akron Beacon Journal (OH)
Augusta Free Press (GA)
Augusta Kennebec Journal (ME)
Burlington County Times (NJ)
Camden Courier-Post (NJ)
Cape Cod Times (MA)
Charlotte Observer (NC)
Chicago Tribune (IL)
Columbus Dispatch (OH)

Columbus Republic Archive (IN)
Des Moines Register (IA)
Detroit Free Press (MI)
Franklin News-Herald (PA)
Grand Junction Daily Sentinel (CO)
Hartford Courant (CT)
Hattiesburg American (MS)
Kansas City Star (MO)
Kansas City Times (MO)
Lafayette Journal & Courier (IN)
Muncie Star Press (IN)
Munster Times (IN)
New Castle News (PA)
New York Times (NY)
Philadelphia Daily News (PA)
Pittsburgh Post-Gazette (PA)
Punxsutawney Spirit (PA)
Rock Hill Herald (SC)
South Florida Sun Sentinel (FL)
Tallahassee Democrat (FL)
Tampa Bay Times (FL)
Tampa Tribune (FL)
Waterville Morning Sentinel (ME)
Yankee Magazine (New England)

SPECIAL THANKS TO

April Slaughter: Cover Design
Becky Ray: Editing
Samantha Smith
Athena & the "Aunts" - Sue, Carmen & Rocky
Orrin and Rachel Taylor
Rene Kruse
Rachael Horath
Bethany Horath
Elyse and Thomas Reihner
John Winterbauer
Cody Beck
Trey Schrader

Tom and Michelle Bonadurer
Lydia Rhoades
Cheryl Stamp and Sheryel Williams-Staab
Joelle Leitschuh and Tonya Leitschuh
Scott and Hannah Robl
Nathan, Victoria & Reese Welch
Dave and Donna Nunnally
And the entire crew of American Hauntings

ABOUT THE AUTHOR

Troy Taylor is the author of books on ghosts, hauntings, true crime, the unexplained, and the supernatural in America. He is the founder of American Hauntings Ink, which offers books, ghost tours, events, and the Haunted America Conference, as well as the creator of the American Oddities Museum in Alton, Illinois.

He was born and raised in the Midwest and divides his time between Illinois and wherever the wind decides to take him. See Troy's other titles at: www.americanhauntingsink.